JEAN DE BRÉBEUF

FRANCIS XAVIER TALBOT, S.J.

Author of *Saint among Savages*

Jean de Brébeuf

Saint among the Hurons

IGNATIUS PRESS   SAN FRANCISCO

First Edition *Saint among the Hurons: The Life of Jean de Brébeuf*
© 1949, Harper and Brothers, New York.
New edition reprinted by permission of
HarperCollins Publishers, New York

Imprimi Potest:
David Nugent, S.J.
Provincial, Maryland Province

Nihil Obstat:
John M. A. Fearns, S.T.D.
Censor Librorum

Imprimatur:
+ Francis Cardinal Spellman
Archbishop of New York

Cover art:
Line drawing of Saint Jean de Brébeuf
by John Herreid
and
Map of Huron Country, 1631–1651
Attributed to Saint Jean de Brébeuf
In the Library of Congress, Washington, DC

Cover design by Riz Boncan Marsella

2018 republished by Ignatius Press, San Francisco
All rights reserved
ISBN 978-1-62164-188-9
Library of Congress Control Number 2018931263
Printed in the United States of America ∞

To
Vincent L. Keelan, S.J.,
and
my brothers of the Society of Jesus
in Canada and the United States who
have helped and inspired me in the
preparation of this story about
their martyrs and missioners

CONTENTS

CHAPTER I

From the Old France to the New

One: 1593–1617

JEAN DE BRÉBEUF was a Norman. In the sixteenth century, the Normans occupied that northern Province of France which looked across the Channel to England. The sandy coastline, indented by bays and fortressed by chalk cliffs, extended from the peninsula of Contentan and Cherbourg, along the Bay of the Seine to Dieppe and the Province of Picardy. The jutting peninsula of Brittany formed the eastern border, and an arc of provincial capitals from Rennes to Le Mans to Chartres to Paris closed in the southern boundaries.

The sixteenth-century Norman was a man of violent impulses. He was restless and adventurous, aggressive and fearless in action. He was eruptive and contentious, hasty-tempered and ready-tongued. He could be greedy and rapacious; yet, he could be most generous-hearted and charitable, idealistic and religious-minded, even to fanaticism. He had a deep and abiding love for his home and family, a boisterous pride in his land and his race. He could be subtle and shrewd in diplomatic compromise, if he saw the need for it. He championed liberty and justice for himself and his people. He passionately defended human and civil rights, the due processes of law, the tradition of local government. The sixteenth-century Norman was a composite of soldier, sailor, lawyer, merchant, priest.

The clearly marked characteristics of the Norman derived from an amalgam of ancestry, a fusion of diverse racial stocks and blood. He came of the Celtic tribes who, before history was recorded, roamed the forests and camped along the northern seacoasts. When the Roman legions marched from the south into Caesar's Gaul and established domination over the area they called Lugdunensis Secundus, by the proclamation of law and the process of miscegenation,

9

they refined the civilization of the Celt. Clovis and the Franks, about
A.D. 500, took possession of the old Roman Province and gave the
name of the Kingdom of Neustria to all the country between
the River Loire and the River Seine. The Celtic-Roman people were
consequently compounded with the Franks. During the two and one
half centuries of the reigns of the twenty-two Merovingian kings,
Norsemen from the Norwegian peninsula in sporadic raids drove
their Viking ships into the Bay of the Seine, ravaged the countryside, plundered the towns, raped the women and slaughtered the
men. Charlemagne erected fortifications and equipped fleets to protect the coast against these Viking raids. The Carlovingian kings
petered out in license and luxury; the Vikings increased their forays
of ruin and robbery.

Rollo, a rebellious Norse chieftain, in A.D. 886, swept into the
Seine River with a flotilla of peaked ships loaded with a hardy band
of adventurers. Having captured Rouen, they carved a swathe of
ashes and blood down along the Seine till they reached the gates
of Paris. King Charles the Simple, naturally weak and now paralyzed
with fear, made peace with Rollo and his Norsemen. He gave Rollo
sovereignty over the northern seacoasts, provided Rollo be baptized
and swear an oath of homage to the French Crown. The Duchy of
Normandy was created, Rollo became its first Duke, and the Vikings
intermarried with the racial alloy.

William, the seventh Duke of Normandy, two centuries later
claimed the English Throne, left vacant by the death of Edward the
Confessor. In A.D. 1066 he landed a powerful fleet and an army of
Norman knights and soldiers in England. After defeating Harold, the
Saxon claimant, on the field of Hastings, by armed power and adroit
diplomacy he had himself crowned King of England. Normans settled in England, and Anglo-Saxons formed unions with Normans in
Normandy. For four centuries, the Bay of the Seine and its harbors
were the gateway between English and French in the uneasy periods
of peace and the frequent incursions of war. Normandy was a battlefield until the English were finally defeated in 1430 when they triumphantly and slowly burned Jeanne d'Arc alive in the public square of
Rouen because she was a sorceress and a she-devil.

Thirty years before Jean de Brébeuf was born, the first religious
and civil war flared up in France. The disciples of Jean Calvin, with

the fire of zealots, announced the doctrine of the Reformers. They won numerous converts who formed themselves into a political federation known as Huguenot. Rivalry between the Catholic Guises and the Huguenot Condés for the control of the Throne precipitated eight sanguinary and suicidal wars. Normandy, where the Huguenots were numerous and powerful, again became a battlefield. In 1562, Rouen was besieged, captured and pillaged by the Catholic army. In 1589, the Huguenot Henry of Navarre failed to take Rouen, but held Dieppe and controlled all of Normandy from the River Vire to the River Seine. As in Normandy, so through all of France, Catholic and Huguenot committed brutal atrocities. Towns were burned and ravaged, cities were smashed in sieges. Those defeated were hanged on gallows, decapitated or shot; massacres, such as that of St. Bartholomew, were savagely perpetrated. At the siege of Paris in 1590, famine was so unbearable that the people devoured horses, mules, dogs, and some even ate human corpses. In 1591, the famine in Rouen was only a little less horrible than that of Paris.

An end came to the savagery of the civil wars, but not to the hatred between Huguenot and Catholic, when Henry of Navarre was crowned King Henry IV. By family, he was Huguenot and Calvinist. By descent, he was the rightful heir. By the necessity of bringing peace, he abjured Calvinism and accepted the traditional Catholicism of the Kings of France. Having pronounced his public profession of the Catholic Faith he was crowned King of France on July 25, 1593.

Four months before that, Jean de Brébeuf was born. His parents and his grandparents had lived through all the thirty years of the bloodshed of the eight civil wars and the hatreds of the religious wars. They were defiantly Catholic despite the rampant Calvinism of their part of Normandy. To the baby Jean, they transmitted their Norman racial heritage and their undeviating devotion to their Faith.

The family de Brébeuf belonged to the Norman petty aristocracy. On a tombstone erected near Caen, in 1691, the de Brébeufs were lauded as an "ancient and a noble" family. A contemporary writer attests that "valor was hereditary in this family", and that "during almost seven centuries they furnished loyal and valorous soldiers". Their coat of arms was: "Argent, a bull rampant sable, horned", or, that is, a silver shield, thereon a black bull, with golden horns, standing upon one hind leg, the other three pawing the air. In the Battle

Abbey List of the Normans who invaded England under William the Conqueror in A.D. 1066, there appears the name of Braybuf and other variants in spelling. In the catalogue of knights who accompanied Saint Louis IX in his Crusade of 1248, there is mentioned a Norman de Brébeuf who commanded at the siege of Damiette. Despite such slight indications in preserved records, one may legitimately agree with the tomb and the poet that the de Brébeufs were ancient, noble and valorous.

Jean de Brébeuf was the first of the family to emerge into the clear light of history. Yet, little is known of him till he was twenty-four years old. In an official record, he stated about himself: "*Joannes de Brébeuf, natus Condeai, 25 mars, 1593, in diaec, baioc.* Jean de Brébeuf, born at Condé, March 25, 1593, in the diocese of Bayeux". His birthplace was near the small village of Condé-sur-Vire, seven miles below the city of St. Lô, in eastern Normandy.[1] Until the invasion of Normandy in 1944, on the outskirts of Condé-sur-Vire, stood two stone buildings. One was a small, two-story farmhouse, with narrow windows and doors, and a slanting Norman roof. The other was higher than the dwelling, and for centuries seemed to have been used as a barn. A revived tradition asserted that the larger building had been a chapel, and that the house, or another larger house long since destroyed, was the place of Jean's birth.[2]

Of his father, nothing is known except that his name was probably Jean. Nothing is extant about his mother, not her maiden name, not her family, not the date of her birth or her death, not the manner of woman she was. Likewise, there are no records about brothers or sisters, how many there were, older or younger, except that there was presumably a brother named Pierre. About his own childhood, boyhood, young manhood, he has left no reminiscences, and no one else has written any recollections. A few statements made by him, or contemporary with him, reveal, in addition to the place and date of his birth, that he studied rhetoric for two years, philosophy for two years, and cases, or moral theology, for two more years before he had reached the age of twenty-four. From this data, and his subsequent life, one may legitimately deduce some probabilities.

He was born into a manorial family of landowners and farmers. His parents and relatives were prosperous in their class, and were well respected throughout the countryside. A village tutor or the parish priest of Condé-sur-Vire taught him reading and writing. He was a strong and healthy boy who lived in the out-of-doors, who worked in the orchards and the hedgerows, who fed the horses and other animals, and, in general, when he was not off playing, performed the chores about the house and the estate.

In accordance with the status of his family and because of his own inclinations to become either a lawyer or a priest, he probably sought a higher education than the village tutor of Condé-sur-Vire could impart, by attending an academy in the town of St. Lô. Though no facts can be adduced, it is safe to proffer the assumption that he continued his higher studies at the University of Caen, rather than at the Jesuit College of Rouen. Caen was a short thirty-five miles from his home at Condé-sur-Vire, on the main highway leading to the capital city of Rouen. Founded by Henry VI of England, during the English occupation in 1436, the University of Caen had become the center of Norman culture. By 1600, it consisted of four faculties of higher learning, arts, sciences and philosophy, theology, canon and civil law, and it controlled several junior colleges.

The Society of Jesus secured possession of one of these subsidiary institutions, the Collège du Mont. In that period the Jesuits, spreading their educational system over all France, had been negotiating since 1604 for an establishment in Caen. A third of the population, aggressively Huguenot and bitterly anti-Jesuit, opposed the entry of the Jesuits, and they were strongly abetted by many of the Catholic directors and professors of the University. The legal obstructions were swept away when Henry IV, claiming royal prerogative, in 1609, donated the Collège to the Society of Jesus. But in 1610, when Henry was assassinated and the Jesuits were attacked as regicides, the Society of Jesus was temporarily ousted from the University, maintaining, however, the residence in Caen.

Jean de Brébeuf was sixteen years of age when the Society of Jesus opened its college in Caen, and it may be assumed that he enrolled as one of the first students. When it was forcibly closed in 1610, not unlikely he continued under the spiritual guidance of his former teachers and cultivated their friendship. It is most probable that he finished his courses in the arts, sciences and philosophy at the University of Caen. He seems to have reached the decision, during those years, of becoming a priest and, to that end, took up the study of theology, at least that part known as "cases" or moral theology. It may be presumed that he intended to offer himself as a candidate to the bishop of the diocese of Bayeux; but at the same time it is clear that he was strongly attracted to the Society of Jesus.

Jean had been hearing of la Compagnie de Jésus [the Society of Jesus] from his earliest years. His family was staunchly Catholic and strongly opposed to the Calvinism that had entrenched itself in Normandy. In the bitter dispute about the Jesuits coming to Caen, he and his relatives sided with the Jesuits against the Calvinists. He had heard of the similar conflicts between Jesuits and Huguenots in Rouen and Dieppe, and had undoubtedly listened to the burning oratory of Père Jean Gontery, who had preached in all the Norman Calvinist strongholds. He was witness of the Jesuits' aggressive and uncompromising crusade for the Catholic cause not only in Normandy but in all of France.

The Jesuits were, in his time and in that of his father, the most explosive topic of debate and the source of the most serious conflict. They were hated, feared and attacked by the Huguenots and the disaffected Catholics. They were loved, lauded and patroned by the traditional Catholics, by the zealous bishops, by the Court and the king. In books and pamphlets, in sermons and theological disputes, they pitilessly attacked the Calvinists, and they were, in turn, mercilessly assailed by the ministers and scholars of the new religion. Though they had opposed the Huguenot Henry of Navarre, they became his favorites after he was crowned Henry IV. Despite the opposition of the University of Paris and of the Provincial Parlements, they had introduced their new system of education and established colleges that attracted the sons of the aristocracy. They were suppressed by a royal decree, but after a few years they were recalled and honored by royal favor.

The tumultuous story of the Jesuits in Normandy and in France was well known to Jean de Brébeuf. He must have been debating within himself the question of becoming a priest of the Bayeux diocese or seeking to become a member of la Compagnie de Jésus, when he was forced to discontinue his studies at Caen. According to the scant evidence, he returned to his home at Condé-sur-Vire because of family troubles, perhaps because of the failing health or the death of his father. He was needed to manage the estates and the farms leased out by the family, to take care of the family finances and even of the family itself. He was then about twenty-one years of age, and still determined to complete the studies required for his ordination to the priesthood.

Three years later, in 1617, he had apparently settled the affairs of the family and so untangled himself from his other obligations that he was free to follow his own aspirations and pursue his own course of life. What compulsive ambition for his future led him on is a matter of speculation. The only certainty is the fact that at the age of twenty-four, he applied for admission into the Society of Jesus.

Two: 1617–1625

Jean de Brébeuf rode into Rouen in early November, 1617. He picked his way through the narrow, cobbled streets till he came to the heart of the city, in the neighborhood of the Hôtel de Ville and the Church of St. Vivien. He drew up before a lofty door, set in a small granite house that broke the length of a high stone wall. After he had rapped with the brass knocker on the heavy oak door, he was admitted into the dark, musty hallway of the Novitiate of Rouen.[3]

In a short time, le Père Maître des Novices, while welcoming him, appraised him most keenly. He had received the contents of the official reports of the four examiners of M. Jean. All were favorable in regard to his spiritual solidity and aspirations, his health and character, his aptitudes and his adaptability for the form of life practiced in the Society of Jesus. Now, the Master of Novices was making his own evaluation of Jean. He was twenty-four years of age, a bit old; he was exceptionally tall, more than a head higher than the average Norman; he was somewhat lean, but broad-shouldered and well built; his head was oblong, rather tapering at the top; the features were pronouncedly Norman, with prominent nose, generous lips, high cheekbones, and good eyes that looked steadily and unafraid; his bearing, it seemed to the Master of Novices, was that of an old-time Norman knight.

Jean felt strange as he was courteously ushered through the long, gloomy corridor of the Novitiate and given a small room. Soon, a

young, soutaned novice came to him and explained that he would
be his guide and companion while he was a postulant. In the dead
quiet behind the Novitiate walls, Jean de Brébeuf was contented; he
retained no reservations; he felt God had called him to the Society of
Jesus. He had willingly left all that he had and had known at Condé-
sur-Vire; he was eagerly resolved to devote himself to God in this
new kind of life in religion.

On November 8, 1617, he was formally accepted as a novice of
the Society of Jesus and, without ceremony, was clothed in the black
soutane. He entered upon the novitiate schedule that morning, with
Mass at daybreak. Jean had been well instructed that this routine was
rigid in its external activities, but that it was designed to mold his
character and to help form the life of the soul. During the day, he
met the other novices, fifty or sixty of them, all of them younger than
himself and all of them shorter, many of them looking like schoolboys. They were vivacious and high-spirited, in the recreation period
in which they were permitted to talk, and relieved him somewhat of
the strangeness he felt in his new surroundings. They derived mostly
from Normandy and the surrounding Provinces and were young
gentlemen of the better families of their district. Among these, and
with these, Jean was to spend his next two years.[4]

For his proper orientation in the spiritual life, Frère Jean was
required to pass thirty days of prayer and meditation in accordance
with the Spiritual Exercises of Saint Ignatius. Four or five hours a
day, he spent in solitary meditation. During other hours he listened
to conferences and read pious books; and when he was not otherwise occupied, he prayed in private. He was not permitted to speak
to anyone, except his spiritual director, certainly not to his fellow
novices, except on the three or four days that broke the thirty-day
continuity. He was told that some corporeal chastisement would be
good for him, such as lashing himself with a small whip, or binding
on his arm or leg a sharp-pointed chain, or abstaining, in measure,
from food.[5]

Under the direction of the Master of Novices, he was guided
through the Spiritual Exercises. He thought deeply on why he was
created, why other things were created, what was sin and what were
its consequences. He had opened to him the meaning of Christ's
redemption of mankind, the lessons that Christ taught in His birth

and childhood, and the ideals that Christ proclaimed in His manhood. He was challenged by Christ's appeal for volunteers who would go forth and spread His Gospel to all the world. He had explained to him how Christ suffered on the cross and why, how he himself must suffer for Christ and why. He was given a glimpse of the Resurrected Christ and the all-enveloping love of God for His creatures, and for his part, of the aspiring love he should have for God.

There followed long months in which he faithfully observed the rigid regime of the novitiate. While emotionally, intellectually and spiritually aroused by this defy of God to make himself a saint, and while answering with a total immolation of himself to God, he did not find it too easy to have his day broken up into half hours at the sound of an insistent bell, nor to beat down his irritation at the grinding routine, nor to be caged up behind high walls in the heart of Rouen. He was twenty-four years old, he had been free to follow his own ways in the open country, to arrange his own mode of life, and to make decisions for himself and his family. But the spirit prevailed. He had shed his past and his freedom. All of the future demanded that he will to become a worthy member of the Society of Jesus.

In a single regard he had a doubt. He came to the conclusion that he should relinquish his ambition of being ordained a priest and seek to spend his life as a Jesuit brother. It has been assumed that his motivating reason was that of excessive humility, of a sense of his utter unworthiness; but just as likely, his motive might have been a realistic survey of himself. He might have judged that he could not pursue the exacting and long years of study which his younger brethren in the novitiate regarded so lightly. Then, it may be he was too conscious of his bulk and strength, for he punned about being *vrai bœuf*, a real ox. He may have concluded that he could use his great body for greater advantage to the glory of God by being a brother than he could exercise his dull wits as a priest. Whatever his desires or doubts, they were judiciously and emphatically snuffed out by the Master of Novices.

On November 8, 1619, in the domestic chapel of the Novitiate of Rouen, before the Blessed Sacrament, in the hush of the early morning and the dusk of candlelight, Frère Jean de Brébeuf pronounced his first vows in the Society of Jesus. These vows were binding for life: he must obey his Superior in everything, sin excepted; he must preserve a virginal chastity of mind as of body; he must practice poverty, in fact and in spirit; all of this, in accord with the Rules and the Constitutions of the Society of Jesus.

Since he had already completed his study of the classics and philosophy, he was not sent to le Collège de la Flèche with the other younger Jesuits of his class. He was given the assignment of teacher in the Sixth Form, the lowest elementary class in the College of Rouen.[6] The College was around the corner from the Novitiate, a few minutes' walk. While the Novitiate was a sombre, straight-walled building, relieved only by the dormer windows of the peaked roof, the College was in the flamboyant Norman style, with arched windows, jutting pillars and stone decorations. He had, as students of the Sixth Form, lads about twelve years old, with all the normal propensities that wear out patience. He taught them in all of their subjects, and supervised them in their play. What happened in his first year as teacher is not recorded. In 1620 he advanced with his Rouen garçons to the Fifth Form. In the course of the year he fell sick and was forced to discontinue teaching.

The nature of his illness has not been disclosed. It would appear, however, that he contracted heavy colds, perhaps some form of pneumonia or influenza. His lungs being weakened, tuberculosis developed. Perhaps the change from his out-of-door life and his muscular activity to the confining indoors of the Novitiate and the College had affected him. For most of the year, he was unable to teach. In the annual catalogue of official appointments for 1621–1622, there appeared the statement "*Frater de Brébeuf, ob infirmam valetudinem non occupatus.* Frère de Brébeuf, because of ill health, not employed." Jean, who had been so healthy and strong, was an invalid and his huge frame was shrinking to that of a skeleton. He was gripped with periodic fever, he was racked by coughs, his cheeks were hollowed, his legs were shaky, and his spirits depressed. During his novitiate, he had had such great hopes of laboring for God and helping others. Now, a year or two later, he had become a burden without much life left before death.

During his sickness his intellect was clear. Since he had studied moral theology before he entered the Society, and since, within a year or two, he would have been a candidate for Holy Orders, one of the professors of the College was deputed to teach him whatever theology, Sacred Scriptures and canon law would be required for his ordination. The Père Rector and the Père Provincial deemed it advisable that he should be consecrated a priest before he died. Jean de Brébeuf breathed new life into himself and rose out of his weakness into an ecstasy of hopefulness.[7]

In September, he was judged strong enough to journey in a lumbering carriage over the sixty or more miles from Rouen to Lisieux, where the bishop was conferring the subdiaconate on the Saturday of the Ember Days. There in the ancient Cathedral of St. Pierre in Lisieux, on September 18, 1621, kneeling before the bishop, he grasped the chalice and paten and missal, and heard the words ordaining him a sub-deacon. Gaunt and weak, he was carried back to Rouen and his sick room.

In December, he was bundled against the winds that swept between the sea and the hills of Normandy, and was brought to Bayeux, some 125 miles east of Rouen. In the massive Cathedral of Notre Dame, on December 18, he bowed his head as the bishop imposed his hands on him and pronounced the words raising him to the order of deacon. He returned safely to Rouen and devoted himself to the remaining studies required for the priesthood.

The day of ordination was set for the Saturday of the Ember Days following Ash Wednesday, 1622. The place was Pontoise, about fifteen miles north of Paris. He must attempt another long journey of about a hundred miles along the winding roads of the valley of the Seine. He lodged at the residence of Pontoise, where the Jesuit professors conducted a select seminary for the diocesan clergy. Père Provincial Ignace Armand, Père Pierre Coton, the renowned confessor to the King, and other priests might have attended the ordination, since the case of Jean de Brébeuf was notable. On February 19, 1622, spectral looking in his white alb, wearing the stole over his left shoulder, Jean de Brébeuf was presented to the bishop as a candidate for the holy priesthood. The bishop, by the power of Jesus Christ handed down from the apostles, imposing his hands over Jean and pronouncing the solemn prayer, ordained him a priest forever.

His first Mass was delayed till the Feast of the Annunciation, his twenty-ninth birthday. In 1622, however, March 25 was Good Friday; the feast was, accordingly, transferred to April 4. Clothed in the white vestments of Our Lady, he ascended to the high altar of the College Church of Rouen and with profound reverence celebrated Mass for his first time.

Nowhere has it been asserted or claimed in the contemporary records that his cure was miraculous. But because of his prayers, and those of others, he seemed to improve miraculously after his ordination. He began to feel that his lingering would not be for an early death, but would be, at least, for a tenuous life. During the worst days of his sickness, he had been able to study. Now in his rapid recuperation, he was eager to perform some work that would not tax his strength. He had had some experience in the administration of the holdings of his family, in business and financial affairs. Since the Père Rector judged that he was a man of meticulous care in details, of balanced judgment, of a Norman shrewdness for values and prices, he appointed Père de Brébeuf as the assistant treasurer.

The following year, 1623, he became treasurer or, as it was called, procurator of the College of Rouen. This was neither an easy charge nor a light responsibility. Before opening a college in any city, the Society of Jesus demanded that the funds be supplied in advance not only for the erection of the buildings but for the support of the institution. These funds were in the nature of an endowment, contributed it might be by a wealthy benefactor, by civic grants, or by public donations. They were in the form of income from properties, from investments, from ecclesiastical benefices, and the payments were in annual revenues.

In addition to these higher financial transactions of computing and gathering these revenues, which at Rouen happened to be particularly complicated, Père de Brébeuf had to keep the accounts for the expenditures connected with the administration of a college of more than six hundred students. He interviewed farmers for food, merchants for goods, workmen for repairs, bankers for investments and lawyers for disputes. Necessarily, he became not only cognizant of, but involved in, the whole business and financial life of the city. Thus, he gained a maturer insight into the cold war that continued to exist in Rouen between the Catholics and the Calvinist Huguenots, who were mostly merchants, financiers and lawyers.

During 1623, the Palais de Justice was in a perpetual state of turmoil about the trading companies of New France. The Parlement had on its calendar suits and countersuits that were an inextricable maze. Some of these had been on the books for twenty-five years, ever since the first monopoly was given for the fishing and fur trade in New France. Rouen was the legal and financial center for this trade, as it was the selling center for all France. Père de Brébeuf, being interested for his own reasons in New France, sought to learn as much as he could about the latest dispute between the Corporation of Merchants of Rouen, whose monopoly was dissolved four years before it expired, and the newly formed Société de Montmorency, organized by the Viceroy of New France and given the monopoly formerly held by the Rouen Corporation. The contentions in the law courts and in the exchequer were the daily topic of talk in all Rouen and were dripping with bitterness.

Appointed once more in the summer of 1624 to the office of procurator, Père Jean was able not only to labor without any recurrence of his deadly illness of two years before, but was called upon for extraordinary activities. At Dieppe, the seaport of Rouen some fifty miles up the Seine, the Jesuits occupied a small residence at which were stationed Père Stephen Chapuis, Père Ambroise Guyot and Frère Benoit. In the course of his spiritual ministrations, Père Guyot, an overzealous, simple-minded priest, sharply reprimanded the Curé d'Estran, François Martel, for his scandalous life. Martel bitterly resented Guyot's castigations, though shortly afterwards he was arrested and condemned to be burned alive, while his valet, Galeran, was sentenced to death by hanging, so loathsome were their crimes.

In prison, Martel bethought himself of a way to avert his sentence. He alleged that Guyot had conspired with four Spanish sailors to assassinate King Louis XIII. The Huguenot Governor of Dieppe eagerly forwarded this charge against Guyot to the Chief Judge of the Parlement of Rouen, Fauçon de Ris, one of the most bitter haters of the Jesuits in all Normandy. De Ris immediately ordered the three Jesuits of Dieppe to be arrested and brought to Rouen for trial on the charge of plotting regicide.

Just a week before, Père Honoré Nicquet had been appointed Rector of Rouen College. In this critical situation, he turned to Père de Brébeuf for advice and action. First, they secured the release of Père Chapuis and Frère Benoit from the Rouen prison. Then, de Brébeuf hurried up to Dieppe to investigate the charges against Guyot. Not only was the story a complete fabrication, he learned, but the action of the Dieppe governor was totally illegal. Meanwhile, Martel failed to secure the reprieve of his sentence. The date was set for him to be burned alive. He repented his perjury and, in the presence of a dozen witnesses, withdrew his false charges against Père Guyot.

The retraction, having been fully attested, was forwarded to de Ris at Rouen. Nevertheless, de Ris persisted in the procedure of the trial of Guyot. He saw an opportunity to make this a *cause célèbre* by reviving the slander that the Jesuits not only taught that it was justifiable to assassinate a king but that they had actually been party to the murder of Henry IV and now plotted to kill Louis XIII. Being influential in Rouen and Normandy, he roused a fury of attack against the Jesuits. Since he was, likewise, well known in court circles in Paris, he counted on the support of powerful Huguenot personages.

Pères Nicquet and de Brébeuf realized that this charge against poor Guyot was rapidly becoming an attack against the Jesuits, not only in Normandy but in all of France. They knew how venomously de Ris hated the Jesuits. Now de Brébeuf uncovered evidence of how unscrupulous he was. Upon further investigations in Dieppe, de Brébeuf discovered that de Ris was suborning witnesses and instructing them as to the nature of the perjured testimony he wished them to bring at the Guyot trial. The Rector deemed it obligatory to refer this nasty situation to the Père Provincial in Paris. He chose Père Jean as his messenger, since he was cognizant of the filth and the malice involved; besides, he was the best horseman in the community. In the dawn of a mid-January day, when the cold was damp and penetrating, he took horse for Paris and lashed the 120 miles through wooded roads and wayside towns.

After three days of hard driving, he reached Paris about noon and drew up before the residence of the Provincial. He met the community as they were leaving the dining room, after having feasted in celebration of the appointment of a new Père Provincial, Pierre Coton. He received Père Jean immediately and listened with intense concentration to the story about Guyot. As confessor and court preacher to King Henry IV, and also when he held the same offices under Louis XIII, he not only was acquainted with Fauçon de Ris but had often been in conflict with him. He realized that de Ris would stop at no perjury and no crime that would tend to ruin the Jesuits and to lead to their expulsion from France. This case of de Ris and Guyot was dangerously explosive.

Père Coton doubted whether he should appeal immediately and directly to the King and Council of State for an order restraining de Ris, or should first make appeal to de Ris and the Rouen Parlement. The latter procedure seeming to be more prudent, he commissioned the former Rector of Rouen, Père Jean Phillippeau, who also had experience of the anti-Jesuit bigotry of de Ris, to hurry back to Rouen with de Brébeuf.

Toward the end of January, when they reached Rouen, they called immediately on Fauçon de Ris. He was holding a reception, and pretended not to see the two Jesuits when they walked into the room. Père Phillippeau, undeterred by the studied insult, strode up to de Ris and told him very plainly and bluntly that Guyot was innocent, that de Ris knew he was innocent. De Ris insolently challenged Père Phillippeau to repeat the statement before his guests.

"I am prepared to assert in the presence of the King himself what I have come to say to you in private," declared Phillippeau. "I take these gentlemen as witnesses of what I have to say: 'You have solicited certain persons to bear false witness against Père Ambroise Guyot. I have these letters signed by yourself to prove my assertion.'"

The friends of de Ris tried to dissuade him from further action against Guyot. He could not be persuaded until he received an order from the King, dated February 21, to the effect that the case of Père Guyot be referred to the Council of the King and taken out of the jurisdiction of the Rouen courts, since it was a matter involving a plot against the King's person. Père Guyot was transferred under guard to Paris and Fauçon de Ris was temporarily foiled. But he succeeded in fomenting such a rabidly anti-Jesuit crusade that the case of Guyot and the alleged theory and practice of Jesuit regicide was debated through many acrimonious sessions of the King's Council.

Three: 1625

The few days at Paris on the Guyot case were providential for Jean de Brébeuf, since he learned more about the persistent rumors that the Jesuits were opening a mission in New France. Last October, in Rouen, he had met two Récollet missioners just returned from the New World. One of these, Père Irénée Piat, had spent two years in

Quebec. The other, Frère Gabriel Sagard-Théodat, had lived through the winter with some savages called the Hurons, whose country was a thousand miles inland from the French settlement. In his garrulous flow of talk, Sagard let it be known that the Récollet Pères of Quebec were desperate, that they could not alone carry on the labor of converting the savages and of battling against the mercenary trading companies, that they were inviting the Society of Jesus to join them in the mission. Père Irénée, he indicated, was carrying a secret report to the Récollet Provincial in Paris.[8]

Sagard's talk was true, de Brébeuf learned at Paris. In November, the Récollet Definitory of Paris approved the resolutions of their brethren in Quebec to invite the Society of Jesus to share the labors of the Mission of New France. In December, Père Piat had approached the former Jesuit Provincial, Père Ignace Armand, who immediately sought the approval of the General of the Society of Jesus, Pater Mutius Vitelleschi. He also sounded the views of influential persons in Paris. He was informed that, while Sieur Samuel de Champlain, Lieutenant Governor of New France, would be most desirous of having the Jesuits come to his colony on the St. Lawrence, the Montmorency Company, which held the trade monopoly and was predominantly Huguenot, would violently oppose the Jesuit entry into New France.

That January, a totally unexpected event lightened the negotiations. Le Duc de Ventadour, a nobleman of great wealth, who had retired from the Court and become a priest, bought out all the rights of his uncle, le Duc de Montmorency, to the Montmorency Company, and was being named Viceroy of New France. His professed reason for becoming Viceroy was his zeal for the conversion of the savages. His inspiration came from his Jesuit confessor, Père Philibert Noyrot, an ebullient, stuttering little priest whose life ambition was to live and die as a missioner in New France.

Being in complete agreement, the Récollets and the Jesuits presented their joint petition to le Duc de Ventadour. Heretofore, the Récollet Order held a singular power whereby they alone had the exclusive right to send their missioners to New France and to forbid all other religious Orders from living or laboring there. Now, they felt God's glory would be better served if members of the Society of Jesus would assist them in New France. Though de Ventadour

was enthusiastically favorable, he, the Récollets and the Jesuits agreed
to hold their resolution secret until full approval had been given to
the project by the General of the Society of Jesus and by a decree
of the King. Otherwise, they feared it would be obstructed by the
court influence and the devious machinations of the directors of
the Montmorency Company who would prefer the devil to the Jesuit
in New France.

After hearing and pondering all of these unexpected develop-
ments, Jean de Brébeuf buckled up his courage. In one of his inter-
views with Père Coton he naïvely volunteered to go as a missioner
to New France. The Père Provincial, very kindly and graciously,
informed Jean that dozens of others had made the same request, that
his problem was not in finding candidates, but in choosing the two or
three best fitted for the missionary apostolate. He gave no hope but,
just for the record, asked Père Jean to write him a letter.

His ambition to live, labor and die as a missonary priest among the
savages of the New World was no impulsive idea but had persisted
through many years. As a boy in Normandy, he had been enthralled
by the sagas of the Norman fishermen who, having sailed the heav-
ing ocean from spring to autumn, would bring back their cargoes of
codfish and wild-animal skins. As a religious novice, with the fervor
of complete self-immolation, he prayed to be chosen to serve God
in some dangerous mission in some part of the world. His Norman
blood impelled him toward New France, and his Jesuit zeal was par-
ticularized after he had read the *Relation of New France, of Its Lands,
Nature of the Country and the Inhabitants, Also of the Voyage of the Jesuit
Priests to Said Country and of Their Work There to the Time of Their Capture by the English*. The author of the narrative was Père Pierre Biard,
of the Society of Jesus. It was published in 1616, just a year before
Jean entered the novitiate.

What Biard related was well known to Jean de Brébeuf by hearsay
and by the violent arguments he had listened to or been involved
in as a young man in Caen and St. Lô. The French colony of Port
Royal in Acadia was governed by Sieur de Poutrincourt, who also
held the trading rights, and was financed mostly by Huguenot bankers. In 1608, the two Jesuits, Pierre Biard and Ennemond Massé,
secured royal authority to be chaplains at Port Royal and to evangelize the savages. Poutrincourt and his backers wanted no Jesuit

mischief-makers in the colony, and through three successive years devised devious means of sailing without the priests. In 1611, a pious and influential lady of court, Marquise de Guercheville, bought out the Huguenot interests controlling Port Royal and shipped the two Jesuits to the Acadian settlement. For two years, Port Royal was a habitat of strife and discontent, with Poutrincourt treating the Jesuits outrageously and the Jesuits contentiously opposing his tyranny. The dissension was carried to France and further kindled the Huguenot fury against the Jesuits.

The Marquise de Guercheville, being determined in her ambition to convert the savages through the ministrations of the Jesuits, secured full title to all Acadia which, according to the original grant, extended from Florida to the St. Lawrence River with the exception of Port Royal. She and her friends financed a new settlement to be known as Saint-Sauveur and dedicated it exclusively to the purpose of evangelizing the natives. In 1613, she sent out to Acadia Père Jacques Quentin, Frère Jacques du Thet and thirty colonists under the command of Sieur la Saussaye. After picking up Biard and Massé at Port Royal, they sailed across the bay and landed on Mount Desert Island. Scarcely had they put up their tents and huts than they were attacked by an English buccaneer named Argyll from Virginia. Frère du Thet was killed. Massé and fourteen sailors were loaded in a small boat and told to find their way back to France. Biard, Quentin and the remaining colonists were taken aboard the English ship, carried down to Jamestown, back to Port Royal, which was destroyed, then to the Azores and finally to England. Thus, Biard, having been in the hands of the English for nearly ten months, reached France in August, 1614.

De Brébeuf remembered the passionate accusations and the violent denunciations hurled at Pierre Biard. He was condemned for plotting to ruin Port Royal and was branded as a traitor in that, according to Poutrincourt and his supporters, he piloted the English Argyll to the settlement, thus causing it to be destroyed entirely. The charges against Biard were widened to include all the Jesuits who were execrated as being treacherous and treasonous. Nearly everybody connected with the trade and colonization of New France swore that the Jesuits never more must be permitted to live there. Even Samuel de Champlain, who founded Quebec in 1608 and had been begging

Père Coton to send missioners, deemed it wiser to keep the Jesuits out of his colony.

Champlain then invited the Récollets, a reformed group of Friars Minor or Franciscans, to found a convent in Quebec in order to minister to the French and labor among the natives. Gladly they accepted the opportunity, and they were granted by royal and papal decrees the sole and exclusive right to appoint missioners to New France. By contract, they were to be supported by the Montmorency Company, since theirs was a rigidly medicant Order. In 1615, Père Joseph Le Caron and three brethren landed at Quebec. From the beginning, they found conditions unbearable. They were at the mercy of the greedy trading corporation for their scant subsistence. They were under the domination of the Huguenot agents, and were obstructed in their efforts to convert the savages. Their complaints were the same that Champlain had been voicing against the trading corporations since he established Quebec. For ten years, the Récollets as well as Champlain had been sending to the directors of the company and the personages governing the affairs of New France their charges and their petitions for the redress of their grievances. Since they themselves were unable to correct the abuses, they decided to invite the powerful Society of Jesus to become their spiritual allies and co-laborers along the St. Lawrence.

The Jesuits accepted this invitation of the Récollets as a clear answer to prayer. Ever since their expulsion from Acadia, they burned with an ardent desire to return to New France. Père Massé talked incessantly to the young philosophy students at La Flèche College about his experiences and his prayer to go back, while Père Jean de Bretesche at Clermont College inspired the students of theology with an ardent ambition to labor in New France. These had bound themselves in a League of Prayer, in which many cloistered communities of women joined, for the purpose of petitioning God once more to open the door of New France to the Society of Jesus.

To these other ardent petitioners Jean de Brébeuf united himself, not only for the general intention, but for his private entreaty. All his soul had for years cried up to God that he might be chosen to spend his strength and to give his life for the salvation of the souls of the savages. Now that the Jesuits were gaining entry once more into Canada, his prayers were suffused with more intense fervor. But he fooled himself with no illusions. He was a Jesuit only seven years, and a priest only three, and that by accident. Except for the novitiate, he had undergone none of the regular training of younger religious in the Society. Four years ago, he was slowly wasting away to death, and though he had regained his vigor, he might quickly relapse and be invalided. A missioner must be in perfect health in New France, with its arctic winters, with the food of the savages, with the exhausting fatigues. More than that, he had not completed the tertianship, that third year of novitiate that was so essential, and he had not pronounced his final vows. He wrote again to Père Provincial, not daring to hope he would be sent to Quebec that year but that his plea might be remembered some five or six years hence.

The proclamation of the Viceroy, with full royal assent, was published in March, 1625. The Society of Jesus was empowered by decree to establish a residence in Quebec and other parts of New France, and to associate its members with the Pères Récollets in the conversion of the savages. This was a sweet victory, long delayed, for Pierre Coton. He it was who had sent Massé and Biard to Acadia, who had persuaded the Marquise de Guercheville to finance the Mount Desert Colony, and who had refused to associate the Jesuits with Champlain. Having made a woeful mistake fifteen years before, now he could rectify his series of bad judgments and again could appoint priests and brothers to labor in New France.

The directors, managers and owners of the Montmorency Company, in Paris and Rouen, fumed. They denounced the Jesuits, the Récollets, the Viceroy. They determined to fight this decision even up to the Council of State and the King. They refused to accept Jesuits in Quebec and they swore they would find ways of excluding these Jesuits. Since they had influence in the financial circles and among the nobility, de Brébeuf was worried about their shrewd strategies, lest they possibly make good their threats against the Jesuits.

Jean de Brébeuf was the most astounded man in all Normandy. He was handed a sealed letter by the Rector, Père Nicquet. He read with incredulous eyes that he had been selected to go to New France, that he must be prepared to leave with the ships sailing from Dieppe within the next month. He looked at Père Nicquet for confirmation of what he read. Never, in his wildest longings, had he expected this appointment, this spring. He felt limp and dazed, then, exhilarated.

Despite all the good reasons against his selection this year, despite all the dozens of others who had volunteered, he was chosen by Père Provincial Coton.

Four others were going. The Superior was Père Charles Lalemant, then director of students at Clermont College, Paris; he was thirty-eight years old and formerly was a professor of logic and science. The second was fifty-year-old Père Ennemond Massé, then the assistant to the Rector of La Flèche College; he had been ousted from Acadia by the English twelve years before, and since then had only one ambition in life, a return to New France. Two lay brothers were to be of the party: Frère François Charton, a robust, industrious and exemplary religious of thirty-two, and Frère Gilbert Burel, a man of forty and a Jesuit for fourteen years.

It was late March when Père de Brébeuf received his orders. The fleet was being readied in Dieppe and would be sailing about the middle of April. Relatives had to be notified, the treasurer's books had to be balanced and a successor be instructed, personal necessities had to be bought and packed. De Brébeuf and his comrades had only three or four weeks to gather all they needed for a full year in Quebec. Food had to be taken, for Quebec produced scarcely any. Clothes had to be purchased and made, since the Quebec winters were far more severe than those of France. Blankets, mattresses, kettles, cutlery and all household utensils had to be secured. Tools were needed for building a house and cultivating a farm. Medicines, books, and such miscellaneous items for themselves, beads, trinkets, iron goods and the like for the savages, had to be thought of. The sacred vessels, bags of wheat and kegs of wine, vestments and all the chapel goods had to be procured and packed. They drew up their lists and scoured the stores. What they failed to bring with them, they must do without until the ships arrived the next summer.

They trundled all their baggage into Dieppe by the middle of April. They crowded into the little residence on the heights, from which one could look out to the sea on one side, and down to the quays on the other. They smiled, for the street was called rue de Bœuf. Père Lalemant came up from Paris, where he had been detained by endless conferences. At the Récollet convent was Père Joseph de la Roche Daillon, who was also going out to join his brethren in Quebec. He had with him a copper-skinned young man, Peter Anthony, who was returning to Canada after five years in France, where he had learned the language and French manners. The Récollets had trained him to become a great apostle among his people.

Samuel de Champlain arrived in Dieppe for the embarkation. He was remaining in France for the coming year, since he would be needed for the reorganization of the affairs of the company under de Ventadour. To the Jesuits, Champlain now expressed his gratification that they were going to New France. Previously, during the negotiations, he had to speak and act most discreetly, lest the Huguenot bankers and fur merchants turn their ire and wrath on him as the one responsible for bringing the Jesuits to New France.

One man and his many agents made no secret of their hostility. Guillaume de Caen was the executive director of the Montmorency Company, the commander of the fleet and the manager of the fur trade. He and his nephew, Emery de Caen, then in Quebec, had organized the Montmorency Company, and almost completely controlled it. He and his principal agents were staunch Huguenots. He foresaw endless trouble and danger from the Jesuits, for they would intensify the accusations made against him by Champlain and the Récollets. He loudly asserted that he was taking them on his ships only because of the imperative orders of the new Viceroy.

A few days before the sailing, a messenger rode posthaste into Dieppe. He carried orders from the Viceroy and the Montmorency directors that none of the support accorded to the Récollets be diverted to the Jesuits. Père Lalemant and the Jesuits were puzzled. They did not want and they did not need subsidies from the trading corporation, since Ventadour himself and other wealthy benefactors paid all their expenses. Later, they learned that the Paris Récollets suspected that the Jesuits had come to a secret understanding with the Montmorency directors and had appealed to Ventadour. This was another malicious trick, Lalemant, Brébeuf and Massé concluded, to alienate Ventadour and the Récollets from them.

By the third week of April, the large vessel and the two smaller boats were calked, rigged and pronounced seaworthy. The baggage was securely balanced in the hold. The three ships were towed out of the inner basin of Dieppe, past the jetties and breakwaters to the roadstead. On Wednesday, April 23, de Caen sent out the call that all should board the ships. Before they climbed into the shallops that would ferry them out to the vessels, the Jesuits, Récollets and other Catholics clustered on the quays and recited the *Itinerarium* and other prayers, while a short distance removed, the band of Huguenots with full lungs chanted their own hymns in reverberating tones.

That night, aboard the ship swaying from side to side, Père de Brébeuf enjoyed a peace such as he had not known, except at his entrance into the Society, except at his ordination to the priesthood. When he surrendered all to God, it seemed to him that God gave all to him. He was leaving France, he was leaving all he loved, but he was not moved by that. What moved him to the depths of his soul was the thought that God gave him more than he left.

The boats rocked in the roadstead, waiting for tide and wind. On Thursday, April 24, Commander de Caen shouted his order and ran up the signal streamers to the two other ships. On the topmost mast floated the white flag with the fleur-de-lis of France. Jean de Brébeuf looked back on the humped hill of Dieppe, on the deep strip of grayish sands and the sparkling cliffs. He tried to discern the jutting peninsula of Contentan behind, where lay St. Lô and the hedgerows of Condé-sur-Vire. Soon, he was beyond all land. He swayed with the little boat that was lifted upward on glassy swells to the crests of the waves and dropped precipitately into the valleys surrounded by the foamy walls of the ocean.

CHAPTER II

With Montagnais in the Mountains

One: 1625

T HEY CAME UP OUT OF THE SEA about the first week of June and
sailed through the southern passage of the Gulf of St. Lawrence.
Schools of oily black porpoises lunged up and down, white sea gulls
floated about the masts and sails, and far off at one time was the
dark line of Cap Gaspé on the left, and the Isle Percée, at another
time, to the right. Only three hundred more miles of gulf and river
stretched before them. For seven weeks they had been cooped
up in the little ship. Though impatient, they were more relaxed as
they watched the shores of the great river close in nearer to them,
scented the perfume of the pines and the forests, and spotted the
canoes of the natives here and there along the shore. A cry from the
lookout told them they were nearing Tadoussac, the first trading
place on the river. De Brébeuf saw a low gleam of sand in the deep
green waters, and on the right, a beak-shaped promontory curving
hundreds of feet down to the water edge, then another and another
promontory black with trees and scarred by gray rock.

About June 16, the ships rested in the roadstead of Moulin Baude.
Anchors were dropped, sails were lowered, all waited till tide and
current were favorable for the short final passage into the cove of
Tadoussac. Fires gleamed along the shores and amid the trees. Small
shells of canoes darted dexterously about the ships, while the naked
red-skinned paddlers chanted a song and beat the rhythm against
the edge of their bark boats. The evening fragrance of the earth
and the glory of the resplendent heavens filled the soul of Jean de
Brébeuf with joy as he lifted his eyes to the Maker of it all in thanksgiving and in love. The next day, since conditions were favorable,
Commander de Caen guided his ships from the outer roadstead,

doubled the spreading shoals of the Pointe de tous les Diables, kept this side of the tapering sand ridge of the Pointe aux Allouettes, and floated into the rounded, calm harbor of Tadoussac. Smooth gray slabs of rock were on the left, mounting hills to the right, and at the far end of the arc of the cove gleamed a wide beach of sand, with green banks and trees above, and hills beyond.

The rocks, the sand, the rim of grass were crowded with native men, women and children. Their bodies were practically naked; the men wore nothing but a bit of leather or a loin cloth tied to the waist; the women were clothed in a loose sack hanging from the shoulders or the waist; the children were as they were. Their skin was dark, a brownish copper with a reddish hue. Their features were uniformly alike, beady black eyes peering out of nearly closed eyelids, broad-spread noses, bulbous lips, cheekbones rounded and high near the eyes, white teeth gleaming from loose mouths. Their hair was jet black, almost as rough as horsehair, shiny with grease and close-packed to the head. In height, the men were about the same as Normans, though some were taller. Their shoulders were broad, their arms and legs strongly muscled though not so shapely as the French. They were bony men, with few fat men among them, and in their movements they were as lithe as animals.

The strand was a babble of voices, those of the men being deep-throated and guttural, as if they were emitted from the pit of the belly. The sounds were harsh gurgles, like the croak of a crow or a frog, loud, raucous and resonant. Some of the men, their faces and bodies hideously streaked with patterns of red, blue, black and white grease, their heads decorated with tight-fitting bands of moose hair and eagle feathers, weaved their way through the crowd to an open space where they followed one another in a long serpentine line, chanting a savage, guttural song, digging their heels into the turf with each step, waving their arms and bodies in symbolic gesticulations, while some old men seated nearby shook in rhythm their rattling tortoise shells and pounded drumlike upon sheets of bark. This was the welcome dance for the Ouemichtigouchiou, as they called the French, "the man who is in a boat of wood".[1]

While Père de Brébeuf and his Jesuit companions were observing the natives with rapt fascination, the redskins were eyeing this new kind of Frenchmen with astonishment. They were accustomed to the

Récollets, in their gray robes, white cinctures and flapping sandals, for they had been seeing them for ten years now at Quebec. But they were confounded with awe at the sight of these five, clothed in black gowns from neck to foot, with broad-rimmed black hats on their heads, with iron chains and black beads hanging from their belts, with heavy black boots on their feet, with black hair hiding their mouths and chins. These five were sights their eyes had never witnessed before. One especially surpassed all they knew existed, a black-robed man as tall as a young tree, whose shoulders were broader than its branches. Though he went among them with wide-open eyes and a friendly smile, they could scarce believe that he was just a man. They suspected that he must be a demon.

The ocean-going ships remained at Tadoussac all summer. Barques and shallops carried the freight and the passengers up the St. Lawrence River to Quebec. Guillaume de Caen, after opening the trade with the natives, left in a swift shallop for Quebec. De Brébeuf and the others followed in slow-moving barques that sailed with the incoming tide and the wind, and anchored in a bay when both were against it.

De Brébeuf was hypnotized as he gazed up at the stupendous promontories that loomed up from the stones of the river bank. Tree covered, they stood massive and impenetrable, wild, barbaric and inscrutable. As far as the eye could see up the river, they rose black against the sky, one after another, and still another, in serried order, interminably. At night, they slept on the open deck, drugged by the damp odor of the woods and the profound blackness and a stillness intensified by the hum of millions of night insects. With the morning came the ringing clamor of the songs of countless birds and the sun spreading its golden glow across the river. Everywhere was a vastness, an immensity, a beauty that evoked in Jean the thought of the infinity and the omnipotence and the glory of God.

After four or five days stumbling up the narrowing river, they reached the rocky, tree-laden shore of the Isle d'Orléans. They gaped in wonderment at the massive headland of the south shore, then, as they passed the rocky tongue of the island, the promontory on their left retreated and they were confronted by the soaring, perpendicular Rock. "Quebec! Quebec!" Their cries resounded and re-echoed. The barques reefed toward the point of the shore beneath the wall of Rock. It was Sunday morning, June 15, the fifty-second day since they had sailed from Dieppe.

Emery de Caen, the nephew of Guillaume, and acting Commandant of Quebec, climbed aboard the barque. He welcomed the Récollet, Père de la Roche Daillon, and authorized him and the other passengers to disembark. Then he stood stockily before the five Jesuits. He asked to see their letters of introduction and the documents giving them permission to land at Quebec.

Père Lalemant and the others stared at him stupefied. They did not have any such letters or documents. Suavely, he told them that, under orders, he could permit no one to settle at Quebec without letters patent from France. Lalemant assured him that they were authorized to come to Quebec by the Viceroy, the Duc de Ventadour, by Sieur de Champlain, by the directors of the Montmorency Company. Guillaume de Caen, his uncle, could testify to this; no one had offered written documents to them, and they had never thought such documents were required in Quebec. Emery de Caen expressed his regrets. He was obliged by duty to refuse permission to land to anyone not carrying the proper credentials. Politely, he advised that they return to Tadoussac by the same barque, and there await the return of the ships to France. He climbed down the ladder and returned to Quebec.

The five Jesuits, standing on the deck, looked with dismay at one another, then looked at Quebec, a hundred yards away. They were being refused entry; they were ordered back to France. They were dumbfounded, then they became aroused. They had the right to land in New France, despite the de Caens, they hotly told one another. Meanwhile, the Récollet Superior, Père Joseph Le Caron, rowed out to the barque and greeted them cordially, for he it was who had first broached the request for their coming. When they informed him that Emery barred them from going ashore, he was infuriated and hurried back to Quebec.

He assailed Emery for his illegal actions and his insults. Emery was adamant in his refusal to receive the Jesuits into Quebec. Guillaume listened indifferently; he had fulfilled his orders to transport them; he had no more concern for their well-being. Père Le Caron, seeking support, consulted with Louis Herbert, who had lived in Acadia when the Jesuits came to Port Royal. But he, with other of the habitants

and nearly all the Huguenot agents, fearing the Jesuits would cause
dissension, approved Emery's technical reason for excluding them.

Père Le Caron, nevertheless, demanded that the five Jesuits be
allowed to leave the barque and stay in Quebec until the legal documents be secured. Emery de Caen said there was no room for them
in the fort or the habitation. Le Caron answered that he would make
room for them in the small Récollet convent, and assume full responsibility for their landing. Emery and Guillaume were indifferent. They
had gained their point. They had observed their instructions about
credentials, they had made it clear that the Montmorency Company
had no obligation to support the Jesuits, and they had given evidence
that they intended, in all possible ways, to obstruct the Jesuits.

Père Joseph released the five Jesuits from the barque and, without touching at the point on which the few houses of Quebec were
planted, cut across the Bay of St. Charles, turned into the little St.
Charles River, guided the boat around a wide loop to the left, then
a sharp curve to the right, and landed them before the clearing of
the Récollet convent. The house was small, too small even for the
four or five Récollet priests and brothers. Yet with true Franciscan
simplicity and charity, he offered to the five Jesuits all, and the best,
he had in his poverty. This was to be their common home until the
Jesuits could build their own quarters. The two communities, it was
agreed, would preserve their own identities and live according to
their own Rules and Institute. Both were free to carry on their own
missionary activities and enterprises, but in close union and accord.[2]

Père Le Caron, smarting under the latest insolence of the de Caens,
told the full story of his tragic experiences with the Huguenots and
the Montmorency Company. When he came out as a pioneer with
Champlain in 1615, he had expected that the dissolved Rouen Corporation, and later the Montmorency Company, would send out a
steady stream of colonists, artisans and laborers to Quebec, would
support these colonists and help them clear the ground for farms
and homes, would erect a fort and provide an ample supply of guards,
muskets and munitions for the protection of the colony. All of these
things and more were in the contract granting them a monopoly
of the fur trade.

They did none of these things to which they had obligated themselves. They bought furs and skins from the natives for a few trinkets,

and sold them at exorbitant prices in France. They kept the profits and spent as little as possible on the upbuilding of the colony. In fact, they did not want a colony at Quebec, since they could gain their profits through summer trading stations managed by their agents. Greed, avarice, and knavery characterized their activities for the past ten years, Le Caron asserted. Even now, in 1625, he exclaimed, seventeen years after Champlain founded the colony as the beginning of a great French empire in the New World, there were only fifty-one French hivernants, or winter residents, in all of New France. There were only six families, numbering eighteen men, women and children. The other thirty-three were Montmorency Company agents, many of whom lived with the savages most of the time. As for buildings, there were only a few wretched shacks, outside of the house of Champlain and the warehouse.

The Rouen Corporation first, and the Montmorency Company later, had throttled the hope of a French empire in America. They were powerful enough to beat down every complaint and charge against them made by de Champlain and the Récollets. That was one reason, Père Le Caron said significantly, why Champlain and the Récollets had invited the Jesuits. With their aggressiveness, their fearlessness, their power at court, the Jesuits could either force the Montmorency Company to honor its obligations or ruin it.

Another reason for inviting the Jesuits, Le Caron revealed, was the despair of the Récollets, by themselves, to evangelize the natives. They lived on alms, hence could not expect much support from France. The Jesuits had wealthy friends and benefactors. The French Récollets were few in number; hence they could not send out many missioners. The Jesuits were numerous and growing rapidly; they could spare many for the Mission of New France. The Récollets were hampered in every way by the Huguenot directors in France and the company agents in New France, practically all Huguenots or bad Catholics. Père Le Caron, with a smile, assumed that the Jesuits would be able to correct this state of affairs.

He confessed that the efforts of the Récollets to bring the savages to God had been futile, even at Quebec. They had found few willing to listen to them, fewer they could safely baptize, and scarcely any who remained constant to their baptismal vows. The Algonquins and Montagnais who came to Quebec, he explained, were nomads and gypsies, who might be here today, then away for months in their fishing and hunting haunts. How instruct them? How, even, learn their language? Especially when the company agents, who spoke an Algonquin patois, refused to teach the missioners.

But, Le Caron said decisively, there was one nation of the far west that could be brought to Christ. The French nicknamed these natives the Hurons, because the men fashioned their hair like the headtufts of a wild boar. He had gonè up to their country in 1615, shortly after his first arrival in New France. That same summer, Champlain had brought soldiers up to the Hurons and had helped them in their war against their enemy, the Iroquois. He regretted that he had no missioners to send to the Hurons until 1623, when he, Père Nicolas Viel and Frère Gabriel Sagard-Théodat again wintered among them. In 1624, he and Frère Gabriel returned to Quebec, leaving Père Nicolas alone in Huronia.

The Hurons were a totally distinct racial stock from the Algonquins, he explained. They were sedentary, cultivated corn, and lived in permanent houses in palisaded towns. They were more intelligent than the Algonquins, and far more advanced in their culture. They were eager for the French trade and for a strong French military co-operation against their traditional enemy, the Iroquois. From the very beginning, Champlain had welcomed their trade and their friendship. He visioned a French outpost among the Hurons, and the domination of all the country between them and Quebec, of all the unknown country beyond, thus truly creating a French empire in North America. Le Caron had the same vision as Champlain. In this outpost, missioners could easily bring these Huron souls to Christ. From it, missioners could spread the tiding of the Gospel among all the surrounding tribes and nations.

They were all persuaded by Père Le Caron's declarations and arguments in favor of sending more missioners to the Hurons. Père Le Caron appointed Père de la Roche Daillon to go up to assist Père Viel. Père Charles Lalemant, as the Jesuit Superior, gave the order to Père Jean de Brébeuf. Understanding that he had been a religious for such a comparatively short time, and that the dangers to the soul were even greater than those to the body, one of his Superiors commented: "For so high an enterprise was required an accomplished man, and especially one of eminent holiness. This is what he did not see in himself, but what all those who have known him have always admired in him—a virtue in which nothing was wanting and which seemed to be natural to him; however, that which appeared without was nothing in comparison with the treasures of grace wherewith God continued to enrich him, from day to day, and with the favors which He showed him."

Two: 1625

Two weeks after they had landed in Quebec, Jean de Brébeuf and Joseph de la Roche Daillon were on their way up the St. Lawrence. Under the experienced direction of Père Le Caron, they had packaged in bags and boxes what they needed for the winter: peas and hardtack, blankets, cloaks and heavy clothes, breviaries, a few books, what was needed for Mass, and, of course, hatchets, knives, kettles, porcelain beads and the like for barter with, or presents to, the Hurons. Most valuable of all their possessions was a copy of the list of Huron words and phrases collected by Le Caron and Sagard-Théodat.

During their few days with Père Le Caron, they had been vividly informed of the dangers and the fatigues of the long canoe journey of thirty or more days, through fearsome northern jungles, in the company and at the mercy of excitable savages, some of whom were vicious and murderous. De Brébeuf and de la Roche were not daunted by these frightening dangers. Rather, they had waited impatiently until they could board the barques bringing them to the Huron trading place up the river. With gaiety, they had said their good-byes to the other priests and brothers, and had turned their faces away from Quebec, up the river, toward the horizon of shrouded headlands.

The river and the banks were more mellow above Quebec. Some eight or ten miles beyond, the pilot pointed out Cap Rouge, where Jacques Cartier had wintered almost a century before, in 1536, and where beneath the Cap, de Roberville had attempted to found a colony made up of convicts and alley women from Normandy and Brittany. Beyond, the banks for the most part rose from green swamplands and tree-covered meadows to the hills, soft against the sky. No longer was there the frightening, awesome procession of promontories of the lower river.

After three or four days, the barque rounded the headland of Cap de la Magdelaine and anchored near the place the French called Trois Rivières. Here the natives of many nations were wont to gather for council. Here, likewise, the French established a most favorable trading post. The Metaberoutin River, that there emptied into the St. Lawrence, flowed from the mountains far to the north, and was the waterway by which the numerous Algonquin nations brought down their furs and skins for the French trade. There, also, the nations from the south transported their peltries, by rivers and lakes, from the opposite shore of the St. Lawrence.

After a few days at Three Rivers, the de Caen traders, taking with them de Brébeuf and de la Roche, sailed up the St. Lawrence to meet the Hurons at their trading place which the French named Cap de la Victoire, in memory of Champlain's victory over the Iroquois. They had not long to wait. De Brébeuf watched the flotilla of Huron canoes advance in serried order across the St. Lawrence, and dexterously land on the sandy shore. The savages haunched on their buttocks in council, then leaped up to celebrate their safe arrival and their welcome to the French in a chant and dance as barbaric as ever de Brébeuf could have imagined.

Some wore their hair sticking up in a tuft from the crown of the head, the rest of the skull being closely shaved. Some cropped the hair on one half the head, while the hair on the other half was either greased and twined with splinters to stand upright, or was flattened out against the ears and neck. Many had ridges of hair, two or three fingers in breadth, alternating with clipped furrows, from the forehead to the nape of the neck.

Their faces were masked with paint. One wore a broad black band from ear to ear, with nose red like a beak, and circles of white about the cheeks and mouth. Another had white circles about the eyes, with daubs of red, purple and blue about the mouth and chin. Another had crisscross lines of yellow, black and blue that quite obliterated his features. Each had followed his fancy in multicolored, multiformed designs and patterns. Their chests and bellies, backs and arms, likewise, glistened with the greasy paint. From their shoulders hung necklaces of wampum and porcelain beads; from their ears swung strings of wampum beads and pendants; about their arms were bracelets of beads; from their thighs dangled strings of wampum. They were in holiday dress, for the purpose of impressing the French with their magnificence and wealth.

The Hurons, de Brébeuf observed, were stalwart men, big-chested and broadbacked, their arms bulging with muscle, their legs sturdy and supple. They appeared to be and had the reputation of being arrogant and proud men, quick to take offense and ruthless in vengeance. De Brébeuf yearned to tame these wild sons of the forests and the elements and lead them upward out of their savagery and barbarism to the light of the Gospel and the teachings of the gentle Master.

Père de Brébeuf was aware that the Hurons were filling their eyes with him. They measured his height and his breadth. They wondered at his blackness, from his hat to his beard, from his robe to his boots. They stared at him as if he were some grotesque oddity. They would have stories to tell of this odd French paleface when they reached their country. They made him repeat his name, Jean de Brébeuf, again and again. Since they did not close their lips in speaking, they could not say Brébeuf. Jean, however, they could say. They dubbed him Echon.[3]

The Hurons and the French held a peace council, renewing their pledges of friendship and exchanging presents. The rest of the first day was given to feasting and ceremonial dances. For three more days they traded and bartered. The French hawked with shouts and vivacious gestures their metal pots, iron knives, javelins, iron arrowpoints, axes and hatchets, their blankets and woven cloth, their porcelain beads and trinkets. The Hurons with grave, immobile faces bargained quietly as they offered their bundles of beaver skins, the furs of other small animals, their soft brown and black bear skins, their stiff moose skins, their cakes of black tobacco. Their faces were masks, and their manner was devious, for they were shrewd traders.

Père Nicolas Viel, the Récollet, was reported as coming down with the Hurons after his two winters among them. He was bringing with him an Indian lad, named Ahuntsic, whom he had baptized. He and the boy were in a canoe with three Huron men. These three arrived at Cap de la Victoire without Père Viel and Ahuntsic. They revealed that Viel and Ahuntsic had been drowned when the canoe upset in the last rapids. They gave the French what had been saved:

the box with the chalice and Mass goods, some clothes, a packet of
sheets on which Viel had written his diary and his Huron word list.

A subtle change permeated the Hurons and was shared by the
French. Both were uneasy and uncertain. These three Hurons were
known to be evil-tempered and, though they concealed their feelings, disliked the French and hated the Grayrobe, whom they suspected of being a sorcerer. The Huron chiefs and the French had the
same suspicion, namely, that these three Hurons murdered Père Viel
by hurling him from the canoe into the whirling cascade. The suspicion formed into a conviction.

Yet, the Huron chiefs must accept the word of their kinsmen.
They made presents to the French and expressed sorrow that their
brother Viel had died. They could not admit the fact that he had been
murdered, since Viel was under the guardianship of their nation. If
they admitted the murder, the French would demand vengeance
which might disrupt the friendship and lead to war. The French, on
their side, had to admit the story of accidental drowning, since they
could never prove that Père Viel had been murdered.

De Brébeuf and de la Roche had previously made friends with
some chiefs and had had assurance that they would be taken up to
the Huron country. Now the chiefs were evasive; they could not find
room in their canoes; they advised that the robed Frenchmen wait
another summer. The Frenchmen, interpreters and agents, who had
been persuading the Hurons to embark the missioners, now judged
it would be better not to trust them to the Hurons. There was dissension among the chiefs about the death of Père Viel. Some Hurons
were thinking evil, and could not be controlled from some treacherous act. De Brébeuf and de la Roche protested that they were not
afraid, and that they were determined to go with any Hurons who
could find a place in the canoes for them.

De Caen and his agents had no power to restrain the two priests.
But they declared that Champlain, if he were present, would forbid
their taking passage. First, a faction among the Hurons would treat
them abominably. Then, some irresponsible Huron braves might
split their skulls or otherwise do away with them. Bad-feeling would
inevitably come between the French and the Hurons. The death of
Père Viel had to be settled before it was safe for any missioner to ven-
ture among the Hurons. Reluctantly, dejected and heartbroken, de

Brébeuf and de la Roche submitted. They were not afraid of death, but they did not want to be responsible for bringing enmity between the Hurons and the French. This summer, they agreed to wait. Next summer, they would take canoes for the Huron land.[4]

When, in mid-July, de Brébeuf returned to Quebec after his abortive effort to go to the Huron country, he found the two communities living amicably in the small Récollet convent. The building was only thirty-four feet in length and twenty-two in breadth. The lower floor was divided into two rooms, a small chapel and a larger room used as a kitchen and as sleeping quarters for the workmen. The second floor was divided into one larger room and three compartments. Four Récollets and five Jesuit priests and brothers lodged in these constricted quarters. As Père Le Caron had promised, half the house, half the food, half the garden was given to the Jesuit community.

The priests had been holding conferences and had arrived at definite resolutions. Père Le Caron was returning to France. He believed that this coming winter was the propitious time for correcting all the abuses against which he had been protesting for the past ten years. He would have Champlain as his ally; he would have the power of the Jesuits to back him; he was assured that the Viceroy, le Duc de Ventadour, would favor his recommendations and would curb the mercenary greed of the Montmorency Company.

Le Caron drew up his demands, with which Père Lalemant and the Jesuits agreed. He was prepared to denounce the Montmorency Company as being a wolfish, heartless and miserly corporation that violated all its pledges and contractual promises, that prevented Quebec from becoming a colony and kept it only as a summer trading post, that positively impeded missionary work among the natives. Aware of the purposes of Père Le Caron, both the de Caens, Guillaume and Emery, also decided to go back to France to defend themselves against the charges of the Récollets and Champlain, now aided by the Jesuits. This could easily be a most critical and dangerous year in France for the Montmorency Company, not only for its management but even for its existence. They left as Commandant of Quebec the veteran pioneer François du Pontgravé.

That August, the Jesuits chose the site of their own residence. They had rejected the idea of settling close to the habitation along the rocky shore below the mountain cliffs. They wanted an easy landing place for their boats and canoes, space for their own dwelling and another large house for the many workmen they planned to bring over next year, and spacious farmland. They chose a level, forested space along the St. Charles River, halfway between the Récollet convent and the bay, where the little Lairet River flowed into the St. Charles, above the spot in which Champlain had discovered the hulk of a half-buried ship abandoned by Jacques Cartier in 1536. From the habitation and the Rock, it was about two miles by boat, and by foot along the shore about fifteen hundred paces. Thus, it was near enough to the settlement, but yet far enough away. It offered room for expansion, even for the erection of an Algonquin village.[5]

They staked their claim to this unassigned land, and sent their petition to the Viceroy through the good offices of Père Le Caron. On September 1, 1625, Père Charles Lalemant formally blessed the site in the presence of the Récollets, Sieur Pontgravé, the hivernants and company agents, and dedicated it Notre Dame des Anges. After the ceremonies they all joined in a noonday dinner and, with great joviality and good will, spent the afternoon felling the first trees.

In September, great crowds of Montagnais and other Algonquins invaded the environs of Quebec for the eel season, a time of plenteous food and feasting. They pitched their cone-shaped tents of bark all along the shores of the St. Charles Bay and the St. Lawrence. The men spent the night fishing, sometimes spearing or netting hundreds of eels. They ate as many as they could hold. The squaws sliced the rest down the back, cleaned and smoked them over the sooty fire, then rolled them in bundles they would later carry off to their winter hunts.

This concourse of the Montagnais offered a splendid opportunity for de Brébeuf to learn their language. He could walk into their cabins, which, by custom, were open to all who cared to enter. He could listen to any group of them that were talking, and no one could object. Having a quick ear and a retentive memory for languages, he soon learned their exclamations, their names for things, the intonations of their sounds.

It seemed to him that the best way to master the language would be to attach himself to some family and, like the interpreters, accompany them in their nomadic wanderings during the winter. Living with them as they lived, he would gain a clearer insight into their minds, he would learn better their customs and habits, and would, possibly, win their closer friendship. Most of the families and clans would be leaving about the middle of October, when the eel season finished. De Brébeuf found a chief who accepted his presents and adopted him as a member of his party. Thereafter, Jean was a son or nephew to the older people, a brother or a cousin to those his own age, an uncle to the children. He had a right to their fire, their kettles and their cabin.

He realized fully the dangers that would hover about him, from the savages and their rages, from the wild animals they might encounter, from the cold of the winter high in the mountains. He heard many stories of those who were abandoned because of sickness or accident, who lost their way and starved to death. But he feared such hazards less than those of the soul. He would be living in the midst of women and men who made a virtue of sexual promiscuity. He would be deprived of the consolation of confession for months to come. He could neither celebrate Mass nor receive Communion. He would be alone, with himself and with God.

Three: 1625–1626

On a Friday morning, October 20, Jean de Brébeuf fastened his bags and blankets on his shoulders, and tied his smaller pouches to his belt. He knelt for the blessing of Père Lalemant and the other priests, then with a quick jaunty step joined his Montagnais family. They were of all ages from tottering old people to suckling babes. The men, robed in cloaks of beaver and bear, carried nothing but their snowshoes, bows and arrows, javelins, knives and clubs. The squaws and girls were loaded like beasts of burden. A broad, leather band on their foreheads supported the packs on their shoulders, the blankets, winter clothing, rolls of barks for the tents, bundles of dried eels. From another leather band about their waists dangled their kettles, knives and sundries.

The chief of the clan shrilled the signal and padded off along the trail in a brisk trot. The hunters and boys, chanting a weird song that echoed through the woods, followed him in single file. De Brébeuf, with his black gown tucked up, trotted with them along the trail.

The women and girls, jogging on as best they could under their burdens, brought up the rear. A pack of whitish dogs, with pointed ears and with wolflike snouts, bayed and bounded along through the underbrush. The rests through the day depended on the whim of the chief. Those who could hold the pace kept in line, while those who could not followed later at their own risk.

Until they caught some game, their food was smoked eels warmed in tepid water. Each one dipped his hand into the greasy pot for his portion, and wiped his hands on his hair or on the dogs. De Brébeuf followed their example. At night, when the weather was not too cold, each piled a layer of leaves and pine needles on the ground about the fire, or wherever one chose to sleep. All night, insects buzzed like a great orchestra, while persistent flies sucked blood. For the morning meal, the squaws put more eel into the unwashed kettles, and each one dug down into the slimy pots for his food.

By November, they were in the lofty foothills above the St. Lawrence, in vast forests, thickset with huge trees, moldering logs, earth shrubbery and tangling vines. The air was dank with moist odors of decaying wood, sharp with the perfume of autumn and the pines and firs. The trees on the hills far off were a tapestry of flaming crimson, russet and yellow. Always upward they climbed. Though the trail looped down into valleys, it rose to higher ridges and plateaus.

In the early days, de Brébeuf's limbs and back ached with the plodding and trotting from one stopping place to the next night's camp. The body pains passed, but in his soul was a pain of aloneness amid the savages and in the vast, fearsome forests. For the most part he lived undisturbed, thinking his own thoughts, reading his breviary, kneeling to pray. Only in the evenings, when the men returned from their hunting and the women ended their chores, could he listen with attention to the sounds of their guttural talk, dare to ask them for names of more things, and repeat to their amusement the words he had learned. Fierce and savage-looking though they were, rough-tongued and impatient as they showed themselves, the Montagnais families treated Jean as one of their own. They might shout at him raucously and threaten him viciously if he did something contrary to their wishes or their customs. But such was their manner toward one another and the dogs. They soon lost their first fear of this giant Blackrobe and almost concluded he was not a monster sorcerer who would bring them bad luck and disaster.

Here and there along the way, they camped at fishing haunts near the countless lakes and streams, and if the catch were good, they gorged themselves at fish feasts. The hunters brought back bristling porcupines about the size of suckling pigs. After plucking out the quills, which they valued, they roasted and ate porcupine until they belched. They ranged the forests in search of other small game, such as squirrels, rabbits, martens, whistlers. They filled their greasy pots with them and devoured them ravenously. But always, they were searching along the streams for the beaver dams. De Brébeuf followed with them in these hunts, for he marveled at the instinct of the beaver, in felling logs to build their dams, in constructing lodges with hard rounded tops and doors above and below the water. Likewise, with admiration he watched the dexterity and the stratagems of the savages in trapping and otherwise outwitting the beaver. When they were lucky and caught beaver, they were supremely happy for the skins were prized and the flesh was succulent.

Through November and December they wandered restlessly through the gleaming, soft snow and the leafless, black trees from one camping place to another, halting sometimes by a lakeside, sometimes in the shelter of a hill, sometimes in a mountain glen near a soggy little stream. Whenever their dreams or their manitous revealed to them an area where the beavers were waiting to be captured, the women built the tents. They slashed down saplings, ten to twelve feet high, and planted them in a wide circle on an angle so that their tapering ends could intertwine above. They tied their robes and skins over the upper skeleton of poles, and formed the lower walls with rolls of supple bark. In the center they banked a fire with stones. In this protected cabin, the whole family slept in their furs, packed close to one another for warmth, with the dogs finding any open space among them. De Brébeuf was suffocated by the stench of furs, bodies and smoke, and maddened by the body insects that infested him.

In the warmth of the cabins, the men reverted to their summer attire, with or without a loin cloth, while the women threw off all but their sacklike skirts. Outside, when the cold nipped their skins, men and women alike wore four articles of tanned moosehide. Two sleeves extended up from the wrists and were loosely tied about the chest and back. Two leggings, tight at the ankle and wide about the hips, were bound together by thongs around the waist. Their moccasins, also of moosehide, were formed of one piece, laced from the toes to the ankle, large enough to be stuffed with rabbit skin, and cloth of moosehair. Over their shoulders, when not in action, they threw robes, some of beaver skins stitched together, some of whole bear skins, some of supple moosehide. Their closely matted, rough hair served as their hat.

High up in the mountains the December wind blew bitterly through the naked trees. Even in a shelter, the intense, steady cold bit into the marrow of the bones. De Brébeuf suffered from the freezing air that watered and glazed his eyes, blistered his lips, potted his skin with chilblains, chapped and cracked his hands and knuckles, stiffened his beard with ice, bit his nose and numbed his fingers and toes. Within the cabin the sickening stench of dirty bodies, stale food, excrement, freshly skinned furs, dogs and, most of all, the smoke from the fire of wet wood, were more nauseating than the fresh air was cruel.

Then came hunger. They had passed out of the region of the small game on which they had feasted gluttonously. It was only a chance they might find a bear, and it was too early for the deep ice-crusted snows in which they could easily catch the deer and the moose. Nothing was left but the shrinking store of smoked eels. More than any other evil the Montagnais feared hunger. There came times when they had nothing to eat for days, even for weeks, except acorns or roots or the shreds of skinned trees. Piteously, they invoked their manitous and demons to save them. In despair, they broke camp frequently, seeking hunting grounds in other valleys and beyond other mountain ridges.

Concealing his weakness and the gnawing of his insides, Père Jean roved with them over the trails slippery with snow and ice, through the notches of the mountains and along the rims of precipices, across bleak, white valleys shut in between grim mountain peaks and hazy ridges. While they wandered and camped, blinding blizzards of snow laid new layers on the deepening blankets that whitened the earth. The Montagnais rejoiced, for now they could slaughter the deer and the moose, whose thin legs sunk into the snow while they themselves coursed swiftly on its surface with their snowshoes.

With the snow everywhere waist deep and crusted with ice, de Brébeuf learned how they built their winter cabins. The chief of the band drew a rough oval on a drift of snow in some sheltered spot. With pieces of bark, they shoveled out a hole in the snow and packed it tight along the rims, thus forming walls the height of a man. In these walls, they implanted sapling and tree branches extending toward the center of the cleared space, and over the framework of the roof they slung their rolls of bark and their mooseskins. Over the wet ground, they scattered a thick layer of cedar, fir and pine twigs, and in the center and along the snow walls they built up fires. About these they slept, huddled close to one another and glad of the warmth of the dogs that stretched over them and between them. Père Jean had equal rights with anyone to a place near the fire and among the medley of savages. But if he wanted warmth, he must endure the blinding smoke from the fires, the sickening, nauseating odors of the bodies and the furs, the breathing and snoring of the closely huddled savages. If he tried to sleep outside of the pack of the Montagnais men, women and children, he exposed himself to the almost unbearable cold and listened to the whine and the roar of the wind about the flapping roof, and at times heard the trees crack like muskets or cannon from the cold and the wind.

A day of rejoicing it was when the hunters stalked proudly into the snow camp and announced they had killed a bear. The squaws, squealing with joy, raced off to locate and carry the bear back to camp. Hunger was gone, for now they would feast on the fat bear meat. They stroked its brown fur lovingly, for that would be fashioned into a robe, and they gloated over its red flesh. Kettles were sunk into the fires. Messengers were dispatched and signals were lighted to invite all the clans in the region to come to the feast of bear. During and after elaborate ceremonials, hunters and squaws feasted voraciously, pulling out slices and joints from the tepid pots, gulping them down in loud swallows, skimming the grease from the surface, eating ravenously till they were almost insensible. There might be days of hunger again but they were not provident for the future. When they had food, they were gluttons; when they hungered, they were patient and hopeful.

He was confused by their sexual habits. There were no concealments or reticences in regard to the body or its functions. Men and squaws presumably bound themselves together in a family union for the rearing of children. But, outside of blood relationships, which were strictly observed, males and females of all ages were as promiscuous as the dogs. This was all too evident when other wandering bands joined with his party for feasting or hunting or at the camps along the way. Père de Brébeuf, knowing that some of the French agents, interpreters and sailors had adopted the free Algonquin custom, had difficulty explaining that he did not wish to accept their habitual hospitality. From their looks and the tones of their voices, they made it clear that they rather despised him, and judged him to be a strange creature, neither French nor Montagnais.

Here in the forests and mountains, when they had food, they were far different from what they showed themselves in Quebec. No longer did their faces wear the air of taciturn stolidity and inscrutable mystery. They were a happy people, talking volubly in loud shouts, laughing in shrill cackles or sputtering grunts. They were flattered when, at their ease, he asked them the meaning of the sounds they made, and they made great sport of him when he tried to talk to them. He studied them minutely. In speaking they did not use the lips or mouth, but emitted their words from their palates and throats in such a manner that the sounds seemed to originate in their lungs or in their stomachs. Their words were formed mostly of the hard-sounding consonants. Their intonations and cadences seemed to have distinctive meanings. He was increasing his vocabulary daily, and was learning so much, that he began to speak with confidence.

He was gaining, likewise, an insight into their superstitions and rites. Dreams ruled their lives. Their personal manitous, also, were their guide. He watched the savages consult their demons living in a pebble or a tooth or a bone or a strand of moose hair, which were carried sacredly in a pouch on their person. He observed them tossing a porcupine bone into the fire and watching it color, or throwing a branch of pine into the cinders and muttering some incantation, or pouring grease over the faggots with accompanying words, or slitting the throat of a small bird and examining it closely. An infinite number of superstitions governed their every action. With the beaver, no blood must touch the earth, and the bones must be burned, but dogs might eat the entrails. With the bear, girls and unmarried women were excluded from the feast; neither the entrails nor the bones could be given to the dogs, but all must be destroyed by fire. He sought from the Montagnais the reasons for these things, but they were not communicative.

Ever since he had taken the trail with them, he was aware of the power of the sorcerers who abounded in each clan. In times of peace and plenty, they performed their rites of dance and chant with light solemnity. When hunger or sickness depressed them, their rituals grew wild and fantastic. The sorcerer, painted or masked to look ferocious, raised his voice in chant and kept rhythm with his tortoise-shell rattle, while the old men struck the beat on bark drums. Naked or draped in grotesque trappings, he whirled about the fire dizzily, twisted himself into horrible contortions, screeched in ear-splitting cries, howled like wolves and beasts of the night, recklessly hurled about burning faggots and coals, while the onlookers joined in a fren-zied crescendo that was not human but sounded like the fury of the souls damned.

De Brébeuf abhorred these repulsive orgies that seemed like hor-rifying pictures of hell itself, and that were intended, he suspected, as incantations to the devils who possessed the souls of these bar-barians. Cooped up in the cabins with them, he felt the living, fetid presence of Satan in their midst. Often, he crawled out into the snow and ice of the night, in horror, even in terror, and prayed God to save him from the evil spirit and to lift these people from their deg-radation and the power of hell. He witnessed other scenes in which the sorcerer entered a small tent prepared by his command and there invoked the demons, who responded with answers that roused the savages to unutterable deliriums of mad hysteria. He could only conclude that Satan bewitched and possessed these souls created by God.

Whether or not they believed in any deity supreme above their so-called demons, de Brébeuf with his slight grasp of the language could not then discover. From what he could see and hear, their divinities were vague beings residing in the forests, the mountains, the air, the sun, the moon, the waters, in all material things. These unseen spirits brought luck or caused mischief. One was more powerful than the other, but no one of them was all-powerful. De Brébeuf discerned very clearly that they believed in a life after death, and that in the future life they would eat, hunt and marry as in this life on earth.

When the snows were deep in January and February, the hunters were scouring the hills for moose. When, skimming swiftly on snow-shoes, they tracked down a moose floundering in the snow, they slaughtered it by their javelin thrusts in its throat. Back to camp, the squaws brought their prize on snow sledges. They deftly skinned off the whole hide, and in their ravenous gluttony ate the bloody raw meat. Though the beaver and the bear were more delicious delicacies, the deer and the moose were more valuable prizes. From its hide they got their clothes and leather for all purposes; from the tendons, nerves and muscles they made their thread; from the bones and antlers they devised useful tools and ornaments. But most of all, they had venison to devour as much as they could, through the day and through the night, vomiting at their feasts so they could eat more.

Then, too, they had food that would ward off death by hunger till the summer, for they smoked the venison as they did the eels. The squaws laid large slabs of the bloody meat on flat rocks or firm ground. Barefooted, they trampled on the flesh with all their leg power and body weight, to flatten it and press out the blood and juice. They pounded it with clubs and stones, the more to desiccate it. Then they slashed it with knives, this way and that, and hung the slabs over slow, smoky fires to cure it completely. When the meat was black as soot and hard as dried wood, they tied it in layers. These they would carry with them in their wanderings till they went back to the great river for the spring and summer fishing.

During this season of their winter relaxation, de Brébeuf learned more and more of their customs and habits, their sorceries and divinations. Truly, they were a degraded and barbaric race. They were wanderers on the face of the earth, living between the hazardous extremes of starvation and plenty, with little forethought for the future, wild and untamed as animals, ferocious at times as beasts, without law or authority or any restraint. Could these men and women, truly as savage as any on earth, be brought to any level of culture or civilization? Could they be taught the doctrine of Christianity and be persuaded to live a Christian life? The task, de Brébeuf concluded, was not for men. Only God could grant them the grace of redemption through his own poor ministrations.

In the early part of March the hunting season in the mountains was at an end, and the Montagnais felt the urge to wander down along the trails leading to the lakes and waterways. The downward climb over slippery, slushy trails was even more difficult for de Brébeuf than the ascent. There was joy in his heart, however, as he neared the foothills of the mountains and breathed the air of a milder spring. He had made friends, he knew, with his Montagnais families. He comprehended their manners and customs, and he had penetrated into some of their secrets. He could now converse with them in their own language, with a fair degree of fluency. He had written a dictionary of their words and phrases and had even made some progress on a grammar.

On Friday, March 27, 1626, two days after his thirty-third birthday, Père Jean swung open the gate of the Récollet garden and was welcomed by his brethren. They appraised him, they embraced him, and they joined him in the chapel where he and they offered their prayer of thanksgiving for his safe home-coming. More than five months had passed since his last visit to the Blessed Sacrament, since his last confession, since his last celebration of Holy Mass. Now, in the strangeness of the chapel, he felt within himself the peace and sweetness of God's love, and the stronger determination to do all for God, to give all to God.[6]

CHAPTER III

Herald of Faith to the Hurons

One: 1626

AFTER HIS WINTER among the Montagnais, Jean de Brébeuf was hungry for company and news. The brethren told him their little items: Jesuits and Récollets had lived in union and peace, despite their cramped quarters; the French at the habitation were fervent and friendly; the ill-feeling against the Jesuits was replaced by kindness; the winter had been mild; Lalemant had gone off with some Montagnais but returned after a week because his people found no game; Massé and the two brothers, assisted by some carpenters lent by Pontgravé, were progressing with the building of the Jesuit residence.

They, in turn, were eager to hear of his experiences. He entertained them with some stories and horrified them with others. He had learned much about the language, new words, new phrases, the manner of inflecting the voice, the speaking tones and the like. He illustrated his theories about using the gorge of the throat and flapping the lips. He confessed, however, that he despaired of ever discovering the root words, or the declensions and conjugations, but he felt sure that the Montagnais tongue was well developed.

In their conversations, they discussed the paramount problem of all, how the natives could be taught the Christian creed and could be persuaded to accept the Christian code of morals. In instructing the Montagnais, they could find no means of communicating spiritual or abstract ideas, since the savages had words only for material and specialized objects. It would be necessary to create an entirely new vocabulary before the savages could be made to understand about God and the supernatural world.

Even though the natives finally grasped the eternal verities, how could they be brought to the point of abandoning their diabolic practices and accepting the Christian Commandments? De Brébeuf and the others lamented that the savages were deeply mired in their belief in dreams, in their faith in their manitous and demons, in their sorcerers and medicine men, in their whole complex system of apparently satanic superstitions that held them in fear and terror. Their whole mode of life was that of a human animal following its most depraved instincts. Even the best were inconstant and treacherous, arrogant and defiant, ruthless and vengeful. It would be folly to think of baptizing any of them for years to come.

Toward the end of June, to the hilarious joy of all, five ships arrived at Tadoussac. Samuel de Champlain proudly took possession of Quebec on July 5, not only having been reappointed Lieutenant Governor but given additional authority in all civil and military affairs. His victory over the de Caens was sweeping and decisive. With him came Père Le Caron, who was voluble about the winter of controversy in France and the decisions given by Ventadour, favoring the Récollets and Jesuits, all condemnatory of the de Caens and the Montmorency Company. Guillaume de Caen was ousted as commander of the fleet, and refused permission even to sail to New France, while Emery, though permitted to superintend the trading in the summer, was forbidden to remain in Quebec.

On July 14, three Jesuits landed at Quebec. Père Philibert Noyrot had won his heart's desire of becoming a missioner among the natives, after spending the year in combat with the Montmorency directors, and after collecting a large sum of money for the Jesuit Mission. With him was Père Anne de Noüe, a quiet, poised man of thirty-nine, who had been a page and officer at Court. The third was a stocky, strong brother, Frère Jean Gaufestre. During the month, the twenty workmen whom Noyrot hired to labor for the Jesuits at Notre Dame des Anges reached Quebec and, with difficulty, were lodged. They were under contract to work for a limited time and then make their choice, either to settle in the colony or to sail back to France.

Noyrot, who had achieved wonders in France, was violent in his denunciations of the de Caens, the Montmorency Company, and all Huguenots. When he, his workmen, his baggage were ready to leave Dieppe with the fleet, the de Caens informed him there was no room on their ships for him and his people. He fumed, but they refused to take him. Though Noyrot had forced them to accept the Viceroy's terms during the winter, he was now at their mercy since they were the owners and masters of the four ships. He was finally able to lease another ship from the de Caens, the eighty-ton *l'Allouette*, but at an exorbitant price. His joy in being at Quebec was short-lived. He was ordered by Père Lalemant to go back on his ship and to continue his campaign against the Montmorency Company, the while he collected more funds for the support of his workmen. He begged and pleaded, but had to obey.

The Récollet, Père de la Roche, and the two Jesuits, Jean de Brébeuf and Anne de Noüe, were granted their desires to attempt a second time the thousand-mile journey up to the Huron country. Delayed until mid-July, they sailed up the St. Lawrence and reached Cap de la Victoire only a day or two prior to the departure of the Hurons. They were almost too late; the first councils had already been held; the bartering was finished; and only the final councils, in which peace and friendship would be renewed, detained the Hurons from their homeward journey.[1]

Père de la Roche was assured of a canoe place by a group of Hurons who had wintered near the Récollet convent in Quebec. But de Brébeuf had the problem of winning sponsors and guardians for himself and de Noüe. He had little success, and the company agents scarcely any more, in bargaining with the Huron canoe men. The Hurons knew the French, whom they called Agnonha, "the men clothed in iron", reminiscent of their first meeting with Champlain; and they were now used to the Chitagone, "the men who go bare-footed", as they called the grayrobed Récollets. But they were rather suspicious of these different paleface Frenchmen who were garbed in black from head to foot, and they were as fearful as they had been last year of Echon, the giant Blackrobe. They observed that the other Frenchmen respected and liked him, that he himself smiled nicely at them and was agreeable, that he was so eager to live in their country that he offered them valuable presents. Nevertheless, none of them wanted to accept his gifts.

On July 24, the eve of the day set for their departure, a French agent persuaded one of the chiefs to take the Blackrobes in his party, but only after piling up extraordinary presents. Early the next morning, the Hurons stowed their French goods into their canoes and

were ready to push away from the strand. De Brébeuf and de Noüe
stood waiting near their hosts. These measured Echon with their eyes
and pounded his shoulders and thighs. They seemed hesitant; yet
they held the canoe while he climbed into it, knelt on the crossboard
and eased himself down on his heels. They kept shouting at him in
a testy, irascible tone. Two paddlers took their position, stroked the
canoe out from the shore, then turned back and motioned Echon to
get out.

With the help of an interpreter, de Brébeuf learned what they
were trying to tell him by gestures. He was too big; their canoe
was too small; they could not take him. Echon and the interpreter
argued with them and offered more presents, but they protested that
it would be dangerous to take such a heavy giant in such a light
canoe. They were persuaded to try again, but when Echon placed
himself in the middle of the canoe, it dipped dangerously near the
water level. They maneuvered in the shallow water near the shore.
The paddler in the stern complained that he could not see ahead of
him because of Echon's shoulders. They brought him back to the
beach and unloaded him and the presents he had given them, thereby
releasing themselves of their promise to take him.

Left on the shore, de Brébeuf was perplexed and utterly disheartened. Most of the Hurons had gone. He was being left behind this
second year. Then, as if it were a direct answer to his prayer, another
Huron chief, looking down at the valuable presents at Echon's feet,
told the interpreter that he had a large canoe, big enough for seven
men, and could take Echon. Eagerly, they offered him the presents
returned by the former hosts. He demurred somewhat, and indicated
to the interpreter that the gifts must equal the height and the weight
of the Blackrobe. De Brébeuf was willing to pay any price, so after
some further bargaining, the chief and his band motioned Echon to
get into the canoe. Almost before he realized what had happened, he
felt the canoe slide out into the morning mist over the river.

As one petrified, he haunched on his buttocks in the canoe. He
had been told that the Hurons were fretful and petulant on a journey,
that he must not irritate them in any way, that he must be dead baggage, not change his position, not put his weight on one side or the
other. He felt the jerk and the slack of the canoe beneath his knees,
saw the lithe backs of the Huron paddlers as they dug their blades in

the waves and lugged back powerfully. He dared not speak since, for less than no provocation, they might abandon him along the shore. That morning he had been elated; then despairing; then surprised when this new band agreed to carry him. Everything happened so quickly and so unexpectedly that he felt dazed. De la Roche was far ahead with his Hurons and, he hoped, Anne de Noüe was with some other band.

The canoe trembled with the pull of the paddles and bounced with the waves, the July sun beat down on him, the glare of the ripples blinded him and, after a few hours kneeling in the canoe, his bones ached agonizingly. Hours passed while his back was cramped and his legs were numbed. Except for the grunts of the savages, he was in a silent world of water and far-off forests. Not until the sun was sinking below the fringe of treetops did the Hurons with a twist of their paddles send the canoe toward a strip of sand along the shore. De Brébeuf lumbered out of the bark into the shallow water and walked on unsteady legs to the green hillock where they would camp that night. Soon they assembled around a little fire, over which they slung a kettle filled with corn mush flavored with fish. Before the dusk had spread beneath the trees, they were asleep, oblivious to the swarms of mosquitoes and the night bugs buzzing about them. De Brébeuf found the earth soft and soothing after the long day cramped in the little canoe.

With the dawn, the Hurons cooked their pot of mush and were again in the canoes. From his experience wintering with the Montagnais, de Brébeuf knew he must be as inconspicuous as if he were not with them, since the slightest mistake would drive them into a rage. This second day, they turned into the fast-flowing waters of the outlet of the Rivière des Prairies. After an hour or two in the swirling stream, bounded by boulders and arched with overhanging branches, the Hurons drew into a cove and motioned Echon to disembark. The sonorous roar above, he judged, was the first of the cascades. The Hurons, attaching heavy thongs to the canoes, dragged them past the billows foaming against the rocks. Into this cauldron, he remembered, Père Viel had been cast last summer.

They took to the canoe above the Sault, and battled against the heavy current until they came to another thundering rapids and, later in the afternoon, to a third waterfall. Out of the defile of the Rivière

des Prairies, they sped across the smooth waters of the Lake of the
Two Mountains. Their camp was anywhere on the shore, their food
was half-warm corn mush, their bed was under a tree on the sod.
After a few days, they made the great hulk of Echon use the paddle
with them.[2]

In the muddy waters of the Ottawa River, they began the long
fight against the down-rushing flood. In the overpowering rapids,
cascades and waterfalls, sometimes they could haul the canoe along
the splashing, foam-crested ripples of the banks, sometimes they
were forced to carry their baggage and the canoe up the rocks and
along slippery dirt trails till they came to clear water again, sometimes they had to portage through the forests for a few miles. The
Hurons, though grim and tense in these back-breaking operations,
were pleased with Echon because he carried not only his own but
their loads on his broad shoulders.

Through days lengthening into weeks, they struggled against the
dangerous, treacherous enemy river. At times it would broaden out
into a placid lake; then it would narrow into a gorge that seethed
with tortured waters; again it would come dashing down over shelves
and points of rock. Other rivers and streams poured into the Ottawa;
on the right, a river tumbled down over a debouchure of flat stone; on
the left, another river arched forty or fifty feet high in a broad silver
sheet more than a thousand feet wide that majestically curved down
into a bursting cloud of spray; beyond, there was a cascade in which
the water was whipped into roaring foam as it swept down fifty feet
over tiers of stone and humps of massive boulders.

They paused at the place called Asticou, "the cauldron", where
the fall of water had hollowed out in the ledge of rock a wide, deep
basin in which the water whirled about and fumed in a vortex. The
Hurons made offerings of tobacco to the powerful demon who
lived in the depths of the cauldron. Proceeding, they climbed up
the mossy rocks and slimy ledges that fringed the cascades, labori-
ously carrying with them their goods and canoes. After a stretch of
paddling in still water, they would again beach the boats for more
portaging. Having wrestled their way up the Ottawa River against
the buffeting, staggering current, they finally reached the Islands
that were the home of the Algonquin nation known to the French
as the Allumette or Island savages. Since they were an ill-tempered,

treacherous tribe that demanded tribute from the Hurons for passage through their country, and exacted heavier payments because they resented the friendship and trading of the Hurons with the French, the Hurons did not delay among them.

Beyond the Islands, there was another long stretch of cascades and rapids foaming through gorges cut out during countless ages by the spring tides. At last they reached the higher plateau and turned from the Ottawa into a series of small streams that led to the lake called after another Algonquin nation, the Nipissings. Since these were friendly people, with whom the Hurons preserved a lasting peace, they rested a day or two. During three weeks, now, they had battled up against the down-flowing floods. For de Brébeuf, it had been a barbaric journey through weird miracles of nature. He was exhausted by the all-day pulls of the paddle, the long portages, the scant bits of food at dawn and at dusk, the stings of the hordes of mosquitoes, flies and gnats that devoured him at night and during the portages. He had been nauseated by the filthy habits of the savages and near to anger at their arrogance and threats. He had curbed his temper, however, and had kept his health; for these blessings he thanked God.

From Lake Nipissing, the route fell downwards along the French River in another succession of rapids. The region was gloomy and depressing, the water black from the drainage of the swamps, the rocks bleak and ragged. Through three or four days, they carefully guided the tossing canoes through treacherous channels until, with joy and exultation, with shouts and halloos, they came out into the ocean-like expanse that Champlain had called *la Mer Douce*, that the French referred to as the Lake of the Hurons, and that the Hurons named Karegnondi. Only ninety miles remained of easy paddling in the level, sparkling lake. They kept close to the shore and wound their way among the thousands of pine-clad islands that clustered closely in amazing beauty and peace. One of the paddlers burst out in a guttural grunt, the others took up the chant. They pointed out to Echon a purplish line above the water. Beyond this mound was their homeland. The Hurons swished their paddles with gusto and strained the muscles of their naked backs.

Soon, they were abreast of the mountainous island of Ondichaouan bulging up from the Lake of Ahoendoe, and other beetling, green-clad islands. They pointed the canoe across the choppy waters of the mouth of a far-stretching bay, and toward forested headlands. With quickening stroke they skirted the rocks and the beaches, until they rounded a point and swung into a bay nestled beneath the high encircling hills. At its far end, de Brébeuf saw the gleam of a sandy beach from which a wall of green trees rose up to the sky.

Two: 1626–1627

Jean de Brébeuf stretched himself out of the canoe into the tepid waters of the beach. Sinking to his knees on the soft sand, he bowed his head to the earth and lifted his face to heaven, in a most fervent prayer of thanksgiving to the good God who had led him through so many obstructions and along such tortuous routes to this Huron land of promise. He was oblivious of the shouting, shrieking women, of the stampeding children, of the naked, copper-skinned men who stood grimly about him. Having finished his thanks to the Almighty through whose Providence he had safely arrived, he stood erect and greeted the savages whose souls he had come to save.

Evidently, the men of his party gave a good report of him; he caused no trouble, he was not sick, he did not anger them, he paddled, he carried bundles over the portages. Only one thing worried them about Echon. Along the way, morning and night, he knelt as he had done on the beach, speaking to someone they could not see, lifting and lowering his head, and also talking to a little book on which he kept his eyes fixed. It might be sorcery, they concluded, but it brought no bad luck on them.

All mobbed about him, gaping at him and yelling remarks to one another. Last year, the traders had told them of this strange creature, taller and broader than any Huron, shrouded so completely in black that one could see only his white hands and his white face, which also was clothed in a black beard. Now they beheld this monstrosity with their own eyes, here in their own country. It was said he was a demon, but no one knew yet whether for good or evil. Whatever else he was, he was a being of mystery whom they must watch closely.

De Brébeuf loaded his bags on his shoulders and struggled after the chiefs up a steep hillside path till they came to the summit and a level trail through the forest. About a mile on, he and the howling mob

of savages gyrating about him reached a stump-covered field, beyond
which rose the gray, spear-pointed walls of the stockade. Following
his hosts through the narrow gateway, he strode between the bark-
covered longhouses and entered the low door of one of the houses.
He and the leader of his canoe haunched about the fire and stared
silently into its embers until the squaws handed them bark platters of
corn mush, wild pumpkins and fish. Only after one had eaten, was it
proper for one to talk.

That night, the cabin was in turmoil, with the villagers and those
of other villages from miles about pushing in and milling around to
see the giant Blackrobe Echon. Their eyes were burning with curiosity, and the hearts of some were quivering with fear of this unbe-
lievable black prodigy. In the dim flicker of the fires, they judged that
his were the eyes of peace and friendliness; that his speech was gentle
and sincere in tone; that his manner of acting was courteous and
agreeable. What helped most in their welcome was the good report
of his canoe men and the display of rich presents they had received
for carrying Echon with them.

The village to which de Brébeuf was brought was named Toanché.[3]
He was told that the Chitagon, de la Roche, had already arrived in
another village and, not much later, Père de Noüe was conducted,
amid great excitement, to de Brébeuf's cabin. He, too, was an endless source of wonderment but, it would appear, he was not in very
good favor for his Hurons complained of him. De Brébeuf could
see the reason. Père Anne, fresh from France and the hardships of
the ocean, totally unused to the savages, looked drawn and tense.
He had suffered from hunger and retchings, from the long exertions
in the canoe and at the portages, from the humid heat of the day and
the damp coolness of the night, from the growling and blows of the
Hurons for his mistakes, and above all from the terrifying loneliness
in this eerie, sombre, perilous wilderness. He felt all was well, however, now that he was under the protective care of Père Jean.

Toanché, situated high above the lake on a knoll of the northern
headlands of the Huron country, consisted of a cluster of some fifteen longhouses. These houses, unlike the cone-shaped, temporary
cabins of the Montagnais, were rectangular and built for permanent
habitation. They varied, de Brébeuf noted, from twenty feet in
length to sixty or eighty feet. Most were about twenty or more feet

wide, with the roof curving about fourteen feet high. The walls were shingled with large patches of gray or blackish bark of cedar and other trees. The roof, likewise of bark, was rounded and ridged at the center. The only apertures were the low, narrow doors in the end walls. From the outside, they looked like long, shaggy barns.

Within, the longhouse appeared to de Brébeuf to be an extended dark tunnel. There were no windows or other openings except that which extended the length of the cabin along the roof ridge. Down the center of the house, from door to door, stretched an open space, ten to twelve feet wide, along which small fires gleamed every six or eight feet. This central aisle was bordered by lines of sturdy sapling poles, thus cutting the house into three lengthwise sections. The central posts were bound to the heavier posts supporting the outside walls by crosspoles and an intricate maze of branches. The sustaining, outside poles were arched to form the roof and were tightly lashed together at the central ridge.

No partitions closed out the view from one end of the house to the other. From the central aisle to the side walls was a platform, or shelf, about four feet high and six or more feet deep. This shelf was used for sleeping or storage, as was the bunk beneath it. The upper part of the longhouse was crisscrossed with beams which more firmly bound the walls and roof together and served as racks on which could be hung the robes and skins, the smoked meat and dried fish, the hunting and war weapons, and all their possessions.

Groups of families, united by blood, marriage or friendship, lived together in these longhouses. Each family had for its own use the six or eight feet of space that extended from the central posts to the bark walls. It shared the fire in the central passageway with the family lodged opposite to it. Thus, in each longhouse, according to its length, there might be dwelling as few as six or as many as twenty families, consisting of parents and children, old people and other dependents. There was no privacy anywhere for anyone in any part of the house. The affairs of all the members of the families were as open as the longhouse, and the affairs of all the families were matters of common interest.

It was not long before de Brébeuf and de Noué had full experience of the discomforts of their lives in the Huron household. The cabin was smoke-soaked, while the fresh smoke from the numerous fires along the center, having no outlet save the slit in the roof and the

two small doors, floated in clouds. Apart from the smoke, the air was
fetid with the stale fetor of decaying food and urine, was nauseating
with the putrid odors of grease and human bodies, was reeking with
the variegated smells from drying fish, uncured furs and other garments dangling from the roof poles. Mice and rats overran the dirt
floors, while lice, fleas and crawling things infested the clothes and
the bunks. Everywhere was filth and dirt and grease, thick and sticky.

The Huron men, as a whole, were taller than the French or
Montagnais, de Brébeuf judged, and were well shaped and sturdily
built. Their faces, longer and more sharply featured than those of the
Algonquins, had protruding, hooked noses, high cheekbones, white
teeth gleaming between thick lips, and beady, furtive eyes. The skin
of the children was reddish-brown, but that of the adults was a blackish copper. They were hairless on chin and body, but their head
hair was abundant, straight as a wire and jet black. During the warm
weather and in the cabins, the men and boys went naked, except for
a breech cloth or a dangling pad of decorated leather.

The older women were broad-backed, heavy-footed, and dour-
faced, but Champlain noted that "there is a moderate number of
pleasing and pretty girls, in respect to figure, color and expression,
all being in harmony." Their hair was greased flat to the crown of
their heads, and hung in a braid down their shoulders. More matured
women might clothe themselves in a shift of skin or cloth that hung
loosely from the shoulders to the knees, but most of the younger people wore only a short skirt about the hips and upper legs. As for the
children, girls and boys, they were concealed by no sort of garment.

With these people and in such surroundings, de Brébeuf was overjoyed to begin his apostolate, while de Noüe was determined to conquer his more delicate sensibilities. The friendliness and hospitality of
the savages heartened de Brébeuf. "They never close their door to a
stranger," he wrote, "and having once received him in their houses,
they share with him the best of what they have and never send him
away. When he leaves of his own accord, he acquits his debt with a
simple 'thank you.'" Thus it was that he and de Noüe could live in
any cabin they chose, eat from any pot, and remain as long as they
wished. Among themselves the Hurons were happy and carefree,
laughing and garrulous, jovial and hearty, seeking companionship so
much, he remarked, that they were in their neighbors' cabins more

than they were in their own. All day and through much of the night, Toanché was a place of contented noise and turmoil.

Père de la Roche was living in the village of Quieunonascaran, further west along the same headlands. De Brébeuf and de Noüe found him in the old lodge built for Père Le Caron in 1615, and used by the Récollets and the Frenchmen employed by the trading company as agents among the Hurons. Though built of posts and covered with bark in the native manner, the interior of the cabin was divided into three rooms. De la Roche offered hospitality to his Jesuit brothers, but de Brébeuf thought it more advantageous to endure the horrors of the Huron cabin, in order the better to learn the language and observe the customs.

The region in which the three missioners settled belonged to the Bear nation. It was required by traditional diplomacy that they should present themselves to the elders and chiefs of the Bear nation in their capital village of Quieuindohan. This village, de Brébeuf observed, was fortified by a triple row of palisades, with posts planted closely and knit firmly, rising to a height, perhaps, of twenty feet. Within the enclosure, he counted as many as fifty longhouses, and was told that there were more than five hundred family groups. It was one of the most populous of all Huron villages, and its leaders were among the most powerful of the Huron peoples.

Echon and his companions were welcomed with hearty hospitality. In the council that was convoked, he declared through an interpreter that he and his comrades came as friends, in the same manner that the Hurons visited the French, that their purpose in living in the villages was to reveal to the people great truths heretofore unknown, and that to certify the sincerity of his words, he offered gifts of great value. The auditors applauded with vigorous belly grunts, "*Haau! Haau! Haau!*" and pounded their fists on the earth in approval. In a subsequent council, the Bear spokesman returned the answer of his nation: the presents of the French were accepted, the pledges of friendship and peace were renewed between the two peoples, and the Blackrobes and Grayrobe would be guarded as brothers.

These savages whom the French nicknamed the Hurons, de Brébeuf learned, called themselves the Ouendat, or People-of-one-land-apart. This appellation was shared by three principal nations and some smaller clans, racially related; though leagued together in a federation, each remained a unity in itself. The most northern nation was that of the Bears, the Attignawantan, among whom de Brébeuf lived; to the south and east dwelt the Cord nation, the Attigneenong-nahac; and to the center and south, the Rock nation, the Arendarho-nons; the smaller clans were scattered here and there in the country. All belonging to this federation occupied the peninsula that jutted up from the south into the western sweep of Lake Huron. It was a small, constricted area, not more than forty miles from north to south and, in its widest part, about the same from east to west. The French agents computed there were about twenty-five settlements, large and small, with a population of about thirty thousand.

The Ouendats were a totally different race from the Algonquins, but were of the same stock as other neighboring nations, such as, to the west, the Khionontateronons, whom the French called the Petun or Tobacco nation, and to the south, the Attiwandarons, referred to as the Neutral nation because it preserved peace both with the Hurons to its north and the Iroquois federation to its east. Of the same blood and stock as the Hurons were their most violent enemies, the five nations of the Iroquois confederacy. All of these people spoke dialects of the same tongue and generations ago had formed one people.

These nations, Jean de Brébeuf vowed, would be his apostolate for life. His first and most important step in their evangelization was that of mastering the Ouendat language. To begin with, he had the list of Huron words compiled by the Récollets and the help of the French agents who used some sort of a jargon. But he knew that he himself had the task of discovering for himself the vocabulary and the construction of this tongue, and that without teachers. Secondly, he must familiarize himself with the customs of the savages, must learn their beliefs, and understand their myriad forms of superstition. These two preliminary aims he could attain best by ingratiating himself with the Hurons and winning their affection and confidence. Thus, that autumn, he mapped out his strategy for his first year.

Père de la Roche planned differently. He proposed to visit the Petuns to the west, and winter among the Neutrals to the south. He was following not only his own inclinations toward new adventures, but was acting on the advice of his Superior, Père Le Caron, in opening new mission fields, and of Champlain, in seeking alliances and attracting these nations to the French trade. On October 26, de la Roche, accompanied by two agents, started on his tour, not without misgivings on the part of the friendly Hurons, and not without deep suspicions of his purposes on the part of those who were hostile.

Through the winter that followed, de Brébeuf learned how to live as a Huron and also learned how the Hurons lived. The food was corn, and, in season, fish, beaver, bear and moose meat. The corn was eaten in all forms, but preferably as meal, boiled or baked into biscuits. Delicacies, for example, were unripe corn mashed with grease and fish, or little cakes made of green kernels masticated into a pulp by the squaws; but the most tasty of all were ears that had been buried in stagnant swamps until they were putrified. De Brébeuf agreed with Sagard in saying that these ears smelled like a sewer and that the odor remained in the cabin for days. Fish, the other staple, was sometimes pounded into a fine flour, or else smoked, or hung up in the cabin to dry and slowly rot.

The Huron men were councilors, warriors, fishers, hunters, traders, sorcerers and cabin builders; they did no other work. When they were not engaged in these manly occupations, they feasted, played games and lolled about in interminable ease. The squaws performed all the duties about the cabin, cared for the cornfields and chopped the firewood, tanned the furs and skins, and carried the baggage during the journeys. Woman was a drudge from her infancy. In most ways, they were more untamed than the men, quicker to anger, more snarling in their insults, more savage in vengeance, more frenzied in times of trial. Though not devoid of a maternal tenderness, they had none of the gentleness and sentimentality of the French female.

The women and the men satisfied their sex instincts as openly as they glutted their hunger. No law or custom, no public feeling condemned such relationships; rather, they were encouraged. Champlain related that, when night came, young men and women ran from cabin to cabin, and husbands and wives went with whom they wished. Sagard declared that "males had the liberty of giving themselves to evil from their earliest years, while females prostituted themselves as early as they could," adding that "fathers and mothers are panderers for their own daughters." He related that, on the arrival of the Récollets, "one of our greatest and most troublesome embarrassments was their continual pursuit of us, begging to marry us or make a family alliance.... In these importunities, the women and girls were more insistent and plagued us more than the men themselves who came to petition in behalf of the women."

Some of the French agents living among the Hurons, such as Étienne Brûlé, were as degraded as the savages and, according to Sagard, "were scandalous, brutal, godless, sensual, brutes, atheists, carnal, so that they prevented the conversion of the Hurons". Their conduct made it all the harder for de Brébeuf and de Noüe to resist the advances of the women and to explain to the men why they did not follow the customs of the country. Seeing all this, de Brébeuf understood the magnitude of the task of leading these animalized savages up to the Christian code.

The first process was personal; he must teach chastity by practicing it. In this sewer of sexual filth, he realized he must keep himself immaculately pure in soul and body, and to that end must build, with God's help, an impregnable defense about himself. What was attested about him at a later date was undeniably true in his first dealings with the savages in the Huron villages. His confessor stated: "His chastity was proof; and in that matter his eyes were so faithful to his heart that they had no sight for the objects which might have soiled purity. His body was not rebellious to the spirit; and in the midst of impurity itself—which reigns, it seems, in this country—he lived in an innocence as great as if he had sojourned in the midst of a desert inaccessible to that sin. A woman presented herself one day to him, in a place somewhat isolated, uttering to him unseemly language, and breathing a fire which could come only from a firebrand of hell. The Père seeing himself thus attacked, made upon himself the Sign of the Cross, without answering any word; and this spectre, disguised beneath a woman's dress, disappeared at the same moment."

All through the winter, too, he was witness of the superstitions that ruled every moment of their lives, of their so-called feasts, of the debauches and orgies that were enacted in frenzied tumult night after night, of the power of the sorcerers, enchanters and medicine men, of the inhuman barbarism and the other influences of the devil. All of these inborn and traditional customs, someday, he must condemn, and he must bring these savages to renounce them. In their stead, he must substitute the teachings of Jesus Christ and must introduce the practice of Christian virtues and ceremonies. He despaired of victory through his own efforts, but through the power of God he believed that this Ouendat people could be redeemed and saved.

In the late winter, rumors became more insistent that Père de la Roche was being badly treated by the Neutrals, and reports were frequent that he had been murdered. De Brébeuf was worried, for the death of de la Roche would entail most serious consequences. He persuaded one of the French agents to travel the six-day journey down to the Neutral country and bring de la Roche back, if he still lived. Toward the end of March he returned, safe and far from dead. For three months, he said, he had been hospitably entertained by the Neutrals; but then, Huron mischief-makers spread calumnies against him. "They told the Neutrals," he fumed, "that I was a powerful magician, that I tainted the air in the Huron country, that I had already poisoned many Huron people, that I was going to be killed soon to prevent me from setting fire to the village and burning all the children to death." As for the Neutrals, de la Roche believed that they could be converted more easily than the Hurons, and could be persuaded to form alliances for peace and trade with the French.

Père de Brébeuf had been striking at the hearts of the French agents against whose immorality Sagard had raged. De la Roche wrote: "What consoled me on my return from the Neutrals was to see that our fellow countrymen had made their peace with Our Lord, for they confessed and received Communion at Easter. They have put away their women, and since then have been more restrained." Their good conduct, the three missioners believed, was not only salutary for themselves, but removed obstructions from the way of converting the savages. Père de Noüe, with his kindly manner, had contributed much to the reform of the agents. But he himself was almost totally discouraged. He could not learn the Huron tongue, nor could he win the affection of the people. De Brébeuf thought it better that Père Anne should return to Quebec with the Huron traders in June.

Since the old Récollet cabin in Quieunonascaran was by now uninhabitable, de Brébeuf and de la Roche were desirous of having a new cabin for themselves and the Frenchmen near Toanché. The elders and chiefs were flattered by the wish of the Chitagon and Echon to dwell in their village, but offered many reasons why they should not live by themselves in their own longhouse. The missioners, however, insisted so strongly in their demand that the chiefs finally yielded and ordered the men of the village to build a house for the Longrobes and the French. In short time, the skeleton of posts and poles was bound together and the slabs of bark were fastened along the walls and on the roof. Instead of the effigies and totems that decorated the cabins of the Hurons, the priests hung a large cross above the door and painted it a crimson red. De Brébeuf was glad to be settled in a place where he could pray without being suspected of witchery, where he and those who would come in later years could celebrate Mass, where he would be free of the filth, the promiscuous sexuality and the frenetic orgies of the sorcerers in the Huron cabins.

Jean de Brébeuf bade farewell to his Jesuit comrade, Anne de Noüe, in June, when hundreds of the Hurons and the French agents departed for the trade at Cap de Victoire. He and Père de la Roche passed a summer of peace in their new cabin at Toanché. Most of the people had deserted their longhouses, some to camp in the fishing haunts among the islands and up the lake, some to live in the woods near the cornfields, some to wander about the country or to the neighboring nations for visits of friendship. The two missioners, likewise, tramped the trails to the other villages of the west and south, the better to acquaint themselves with the people and their settlements.

Three: 1627–1628

In September, the French agents reported dismal news and carried disturbing letters from Quebec. The fleet brought less food than usual, with the prospect that Quebec would be hungry next winter. Père Noyrot left Honfleur with provisions for the Jesuits and their workmen, but his ship was thought to be lost at sea. Charles Lalemant was forced to send the Jesuit workmen back to France, since he could not support them through the winter at Quebec. He himself was deputed by Champlain and the Récollets to return to France and to carry on the attack against the de Caens and the Montmorency Company who were failing worse than before in their pledges to support New France. For de Brébeuf, the saddest of all the news was that no Jesuit was coming to companion him among the Hurons.

The Hurons were on the warpath against their traditional enemies, the Iroquois. Chiefs and braves, hideously streaked with crimson and black paint, roused themselves to fury by blood-curdling cries and serpentine dances about the red war post, and whirled off to their man hunt. Some stole back wailing and told of the death of their comrades. Others triumphantly led back their captives and boasted of the scalps dangling from their belts. In regard to the treatment of the prisoners, de Brébeuf was to write later:

> When they capture some of their enemies, they treat them with all the cruelty they can devise. Five or six days will sometimes pass in assuaging their fury, and in burning them at slow fires. Not satisfied with roasting their skin, they slash the legs, the thighs, the arms and the fleshiest parts, and thrust glowing brands or red-hot hatchets against them.... After having finally killed the victims, they tear out their hearts if they were brave men, roast them on the embers and distribute pieces of them to the young people. They consider that this will make them brave. Others make incisions in the upper part of the throats of their own young men, and cause some of the dead man's blood to run into it; they say that since the blood of the enemy has been mingled with theirs, they will never be surprised by him and will be enabled to know of his approach, however secret it may be.... The victims are put into the cauldron piece by piece; although at other feasts, the head, whether of a dog, bear, deer or big fish, is the portion of the chief, in this case the head is given to the lowest person. Some taste this dish and the rest of the body only with much horror. But there are some who eat it with pleasure. I have observed savages speaking with gusto of the flesh of an Iroquois, and praising its goodness in the same terms they use for the flesh of a deer or moose.... This is being cruel; but we hope, with the help of heaven, that the knowledge of the true God will entirely banish such barbarity from this country.[4]

More clearly than in his first year, de Brébeuf began to comprehend their incredible superstitions. Dreams ruled and tyrannized their whole existence. At a later date, he recorded: "The dream is the oracle that all these poor people consult and obey, the prophet that predicts future events to them, the Cassandra which warns them of misfortunes threatening them, the doctor in their illness. It is the most absolute master they have. If a chief argues one way, and the dream speaks another, the dream will be obeyed. The dream presides in their councils; trading, fishing and hunting are usually undertaken by its permission, and almost as if to satisfy it.... A dream prescribes the feasts, the dances, the songs, the games; in a word, the dream does everything here, and in truth, is to be regarded as the chief god of the Hurons."

Supreme and infallible credence was likewise put in their personal charms, called Oqui. "Nothing is more commonly seen here," he wrote, "than charms. Children inherit them from their fathers, if they have been found to be good." These charms, foolish things like a beaver's tooth, a small fish bone, a splinter of wood, a queer-shaped pebble, and ashes of a bird, were consulted on all occasions because in the charms were demons who had power to help or destroy, and who must forever be obeyed no matter what they directed.

Swaying the lives of the Hurons were the sorcerers. "Among this people," he explained and argued,

> there are men who claim to command the rain and the winds; others to predict future events; others to find lost objects; others, lastly, to restore health to the sick, and this with remedies that have not the slightest relation to the illness. Nobody will dare to say that they have these gifts from God. That all their doings are trickery and imagination scarcely accords with the reputation they have acquired and the length of time they have made these claims. How is it that their impostures have not been exposed during so many years, and that their craft has acquired so high a standing and has been so well rewarded, if they have succeeded by pure imagination alone? No one dares to contradict them. There is some evidence that the devil sometimes guides their hands and reveals himself to them for some temporal benefit and for their eternal damnation.

"The most famous of these sorcerers are the Arendiowane," he continued, "who, after a feast or a sweat, undertake to tell a sick man the origin and nature of his illness. Some order the person to make a dog feast, another to play games of crosse or dish, another to sleep on a certain skin, and other foolish and diabolical extravagances." These medicine men assumed that all diseases, no matter what their nature, were caused by little demons that somehow had crawled into the body of the sick person. Their problem was to frighten the demon so that he would escape from the sick person. They sought solutions in dreams, oquis and incantations. Whatever they commanded was regarded as an inviolable law, no matter how impossible it was, no matter how absurd or how obscene.

When a person was sick, the Arendiowane, streaked in fierce patterns of paint or wearing a grotesque mask, danced, leaped, tumbled, shrieked, growled about the patient in their efforts to dislodge the demon. Often, they ordered all in the cabin to join with them in howling, stamping and pounding on bark drums. In quieter moods, they would demand presents be given the sick person. In more difficult cases, they would declare that a cure could be effected only by elaborate ceremonials and rites, for example, the festival of the madmen, the fire dance, the nude dance, or by ritual feasts such as the eat-all or the vomit feasts. "In my opinion," de Brébeuf wrote, "these people are true sorcerers who have access to the devil. Some only interpret the illness, by pyromancy, hydromancy, necromancy, by feasts, by dances, by songs. Others seek to cure the illness by blowing, potions and other ridiculous burlesques, which have not the least natural virtue or efficacy."

Through the russet autumn and the bleak, white winter, Père Jean observed and pondered over the reign of Satan among the Huron people. Not alone at Toanché, but in the neighboring towns and in the distant villages which he visited, he found it everywhere the same, the people living in dreadful bondage and being dragged out of this life into hell itself. "This people is not so stupefied," he said by way of conjecture, "that it does not seek and acknowledge something more lofty than the senses. Since their licentious life and their lewdness prevent them from finding God, it is very easy for the devil to insinuate himself and to offer them his services in the urgent need in which he sees them." He prayed for the courage and the guidance that would one day lead him to drive out Satan and salvage the Hurons for God. "May He who has saved us by the blood of the Immaculate Lamb," he prayed then, as he related in the future, "consent to remedy these [superstitions and possessions by the devil] as soon as possible, accepting for this purpose, if need be our souls and our lives, which we most freely offer to Him for the salvation of these peoples and the remission of our sins."

And yet, despite their evidences of savage degradation, and his admission that they were "lazy, liars and thieves", that they were proud, arrogant, treacherous, cruel and vindictive, de Brébeuf discovered in them natural virtues that increased his hopes for their eventual conversion. They were lovable and amiable to one they liked, were generous and kindly in their rough way, were charitable and patient in adversity. "They endure hunger better than we do," he attested, "so much so that after fasting two or three whole days you will see them still paddling, portaging, singing, laughing, teasing, as if they had dined well.... One observes a great love and companionship which they are careful to develop by their marriages, gifts, feasts and frequent visits.... Hospitality toward every kind of stranger is remarkable here.... This makes me hope that if it once pleases God to enlighten them, they will respond perfectly to the graces and inspirations of His son.... What shall I say of their strange patience in poverty, famine and sickness? ... It is on such dispositions that we hope with the grace of God to build the edifice of the Christian religion among this people."

With persistent, inexorable enthusiasm, he labored through this second winter to master the language. Because he had such an amazing gift for tongues, a stupendous memory for words and intonations of speech, he progressed more rapidly than any other Frenchman before him. He was not satisfied with the ability to understand and be understood, but sought to discover the mechanism of the Huron language so that he could more clearly teach the other missioners who would come in later years.

He noted, among other things, that

they have one letter different from any of ours, which we express by Khi; its use is common to the Montagnais and Algonquins. They do not have the letters B, F, L, M, P, X, Z; and I, E, U are never consonants with them. The greater part of their words is composed of vowels. They lack all the labial letters. This is probably why they always have their mouths open so ungracefully, and why they can scarcely be heard when they whisper or speak low.... Compound words are those most generally in use, and these have the same force as the adjective and substantive joined together. Like us they have a diversity of genders and of numbers, like the Greek. They have, besides, a certain relative declension which always includes in itself the possessive pronoun. As to cases, they have them all, or supply them by means of very appropriate particles. The remarkable thing is that all their words are universally conjugated.

In his studies, he was puzzled as to how he could express abstract and spiritual concepts. Their vocabulary was limited to specialized, concrete, material things that they knew through their senses. They had no word for a supreme being, God, and could not comprehend the idea except through a circumlocution such as He-who-made-all, or He-who-knows-all. The formula of the Sign of the Cross could not be translated into Huron. De Brébeuf explained: "A relative noun with them always includes the meaning of one of the three persons of the possessive pronoun, so that they cannot say simply 'father, son, master, servant' but are obliged to say 'my father, your father, his father.' On this account, it is impossible to say in their language: 'In the name of the Father and of the Son and of the Holy Spirit.' Would you consider it fitting, while awaiting something better, to substitute instead: 'In the name of our Father, and of his Son, and of their Holy Spirit'?"

Père de la Roche, likewise, struggled with the intricacies of Huron as he strove to fathom the depths of the Huron degradation. Though he did not attempt a second tour among the Neutrals, he and de Brébeuf frequently journeyed through the land of the Hurons along the trails, leaf-covered in autumn, ice-caked in the long winter, muddy and slippery in the spring. The country was a beautiful panorama of wide-sweeping valleys and smooth-sloping ridges of hills, cut by meandering small rivers and dotted by pools. It had none of the terrifying promontories and towering mountains of the lower St. Lawrence and Quebec. It was a rolling, soothing country fringed on all sides by sandy beaches and surrounded almost entirely by the bays of Lake Huron.

In the spring, Père de la Roche judged it better that he return to Quebec. Living by themselves in their own cabin, the priests were obliged to seek their own food through bartering. For this, they needed French artifacts from Quebec, and French clothes, since their garments were already in tatters. De la Roche, feeling the strain of this existence which was almost as savage as that of the Huron life, needed rest and change. But most of all, he wished to represent to Père Le Caron, to Champlain and the company directors the advantages of cultivating the Neutrals in addition to, and independently of, the Hurons.

Toward the end of June, the large flotilla of Huron canoes, loaded with furs, assembled from all the villages and started on the

journey down the Ottawa to Cap de la Victoire. With them went
the French agents who were carrying down with them the stores of
peltries they had stocked during the year. Père Joseph de la Roche
found a place in a friendly canoe. Affectionately, Jean de Brébeuf
bade farewell to his Récollet comrade, with an almost certain assurance that other Récollet and Jesuit brethren would be sent to join
him in the autumn.

Four: 1628–1629

Beginning his third year at Toanché, Jean de Brébeuf was the only
priest among the Hurons. He had little companionship but many
contentions with Brûlé and the French agents who used his cabin
as their headquarters. His consolation, however, was with the savages. He had progressed so far in the language that he could converse
with them, and he intended, during the coming year, to press forward more vigorously in instructing them. No longer was he feared
as a black monster, but was welcomed in the cabins, and accepted,
according to their mode of speaking, as a good nephew to the old
people, a faithful brother or cousin to those of his own age, and a
tolerated uncle by the otherwise impudent and mischievous children.
Though suspicions of him as a sorcerer lingered in their minds, and
though antagonism to him as a foreigner provoked malicious acts,
he had won the affection and the confidence of the villagers. As yet,
however, even after two years, he failed to win a single savage for
baptism and for God.

During the summer, Toanché and the whole northern region
suffered from drought. Since the corn was rotting and there would
be famine in the winter, the women were growing hysterical. They
invoked the help of a powerful sorcerer, Tehorenhaegnon, to make
rain. Failing several times in his incantations, he announced that his
demon had revealed the cause of his failure: the Thunder Bird would
not bring clouds because it feared the red cross on Echon's house. An
old chief addressed Echon: "My nephew, here is what is said. What
do you answer? The corn will not ripen and we are ruined. You do
not wish to be the cause of our deaths. We believe that you should
take down that red cross and hide it in your cabin or in the lake, so

that the clouds may not see it. Then, when the rain comes and the harvest is gathered, you may put it up again."

Echon answered: "My uncle, I shall never take down or hide the cross on which He-who-brings-blessings died. I cannot prevent you from removing it, but be on your guard against making the Master-of-All angry." He pointed out to them how foolish was the sorcerer's remedy, and urged that they remove the figures and paintings on their own cabins. Since the clouds were afraid of the red color, according to the sorcerer, he stated his willingness to paint the cross white. "The cross was painted white, the drought continued," says de Brébeuf, "and the wrath of the crazed people turned on the sorcerer."

They begged Echon to make rain. After telling him of what the cross meant to Christians, he invited all the people to venerate it, and suggested that each person should bring a dish of corn as an offering to the One-who-governs-all, the corn later to be distributed among the needy. He again painted the cross red and on it hung a small crucifix. The next day the villagers gathered before his cabin; he recited some prayers, then he and the Hurons in turn kissed the crucifix. He related that "they did so well that, on the very same day, God gave them rain, and in the end a plentiful harvest, as well as a profound admiration for the Divine Power."

The Huron traders were angry at the French when they returned that autumn. They had carried their canoeloads of peltries down to Cap de la Victoire, but no French came to trade, despite their invitations. They carried back their own furs instead of the French goods which they desired and needed. Some of them thought of uniting with the Algonquins who were holding council about warring on the palefaces because one of their people was imprisoned by Champlain. The reason for this de Brébeuf learned from the company agents. Quebec had been hungering all winter and that spring was starving because the de Caens and the company had not, last summer, sent enough food. Not enough articles for the Huron trade, likewise, had been brought over in last year's ships. This summer, the French fleet had not come, and there were probabilities that it would never arrive, for it was rumored that English ships were anchored down at Tadoussac.

This was shocking, even tragic news for de Brébeuf. His Jesuit brethren at Quebec had found no way of sending him the food, clothing, beads and French artifacts that he so direly needed for the coming year. Even more depressing and disheartening to him was the fact that no priest would be with him all through the months to come. He was alone among the Hurons, with no companionship except the vulgar and loose agents, with no spiritual help by way of confession and mutual encouragement, with nothing human but only God to aid him.

That God did not fail may be deduced from his attestation. "As for the dangers of the soul, to speak frankly, there is none for him who brings the fear and love of God to the Huron country. On the contrary, I find unparalleled advantages for acquiring perfection." In another place, he declared: "One thing here, it seems to me, might give some apprehension to a son of the Society, to see himself in the midst of a brutal and sensual people, whose example might tarnish the lustre of the most, as it is also the least, delicate of all virtues for him who does not take special care of it—I mean chastity. Dare I say that if there is any place in the world where this so precious virtue is safe, for anyone who is ready to be on his guard, it is here. Do you remember that plant, named 'the fear of God,' with which it was said in the beginning of our Society that our Fathers charmed away the spirit of impurity? It does not grow in the land of the Hurons, but it falls abundantly from Heaven, if one takes the slightest trouble to cultivate the chastity one has brought here."

With no trepidation, though alone, de Brébeuf faced the third winter of his novitiate among the Hurons. His greatest disappointment was that no priest had come to learn the language and the customs of the savages with him, and his gravest fear was that he might be recalled. With fresh exuberant energy, then, he renewed his efforts to master the language perfectly and to delve deeply into the traditions, the beliefs and the mores of this primitive people. All that he could now learn would be for the advantage of the apostles who certainly would cultivate this field in later years.

In his explorations, he learned that the so-called feasts of ritual were almost entirely held for the cure of the sick, since illness was considered almost a greater evil than death. Of these, he attested: "As regards the feasts, they form an endless subject. The devil holds the people so strongly attached to them that they could not possibly be more so, knowing well that it is the way to render them ever more brutal and less susceptible to supernatural truths." After describing an eat-all feast, held for the cure of the sick, in which the guests must continue eating sometimes for several days until the cauldrons are empty, he exclaimed: "Is it not true, on hearing this and other examples of gluttony which I forbear to describe, to say that, if the kingdom of God is not in eating and drinking, it certainly is the one that the devil has usurped over these blind people. May it please Our Lord to have pity on them and to deliver them from this tyranny."

In certain kinds of feasts, he recalled, "in the midst of the songs and dances, some take the opportunity of knocking down their enemies as if in play. Their most usual cries are *hen, hen,* or *heeeee* or *wiiiiiii.*" Another feast was the Aoutaerohi, "which was a remedy for the sickness called by the same name, from the little demon as big as a fist, that was supposed to be in the sick person." The ceremonies connected with this were barbaric, and sometimes lunatic and lubricious. "Here is enough cause for tears at the feet of the altar. Apart from those [feasts] I have described, I could still count as many different kinds of feasts as there are extravagances in their dreams; for, as I have said, it is usually the dreams which order the feasts. From them come those vomiting feasts which horrify most of them, but which they must attend if they are invited, for otherwise the feast would be spoiled."

"There are up to twelve kinds of dances," he stated, "which are as many sovereign remedies for illness. Now, to know whether this or that is appropriate for such and such an illness, only a dream or an Arendiowane can determine. Of three kinds of games especially in use among these peoples, namely, la crosse, dish and straw, the first two, they say, are absolutely certain to bring health. Amid all these puerilities, I dare not relate the infamies and obscenities which the devil insinuates into them, causing them to see in their dreams that they can be cured only by wallowing in all sorts of filth."

Though the Hurons believed in a world of unseen spirits, they were unaware of the concept of an infinite God. "They have neither sought nor acknowledged God," he reasoned, "except in direct connection with those things from which they hope for happiness or dread misfortune. They turn to the earth, to the rivers, to the lakes, to dangerous rocks, but above all to the sky, believing that all these things are animate and that some powerful demon resides in them. They are not satisfied with making vows, but often accompany them with a sort of sacrifice. They have recourse to the sky in almost all their needs, revering the sun, moon and stars above all created things, and they observe in the sky something divine."

"There are some indications," de Brébeuf thought, "that they formerly had some more than natural knowledge of the true God, as may be seen in some details of their fables. But, not being willing to revere God in their manners and actions, they have lost the thought of Him and have become worse than beasts in His sight and in the respect that they have for Him." One of their most repeated fables traced the origin of their nation to a woman called Aataentsic who fell from heaven. "They do not agree," he commented, "as to the manner in which this so fortunate descent took place." At any rate, when she fell the whole earth was covered with water; but land formed around her, and she gave birth to twin sons who, when they grew up, quarreled. One of these named Iouskeha, brought forth men; as to the manner by which he created them, there were many versions. What happened later, in the story of the beginnings of the Hurons and in other fables, de Brébeuf could not learn. When he asked, he was told: "So it is said. We do not know, since our fathers did not teach us further."

They believed that they had, not one soul, but many, and to these various souls they gave distinctive names. But the principal soul, according to de Brébeuf, they conceive as being material and divisible. After death, they contended that the soul separated from the body but in such a way that it did not entirely abandon it. By night, they believed, it came from the cemetery, walked about the village and into the huts where it ate what was left in the cauldrons. "The stronger and more robust souls," de Brébeuf quotes them as saying, "have their final meeting place toward the west, where each nation has its own village. The souls of those who died in war form a band apart, as do the souls of those who kill themselves. According to them, the village of souls is in no way unlike the village of the living. They go hunting, fishing and to the woods. In a word, everything there is the same, but with this difference, that they do nothing day and night but groan and complain." Countless were the fables about souls who revealed what happened in the other life.

During this year, de Brébeuf understood better their mode of government, and was impressed by it. He had long recognized their power of logical reasoning, their shrewdness in material things, their wisdom in their orations. He had also experienced the ill effects of an anarchy in which each person had liberty to act as he wished. The government, he observed, was effective not through force but through persuasion and was binding only through democratic consent. There were two kinds of chiefs, the one group settling the problems of war, the other group dealing with the civic and social affairs of the people; there were as many civil chiefs as there were kinds of affairs. They were chosen by popular acclaim, because of their intelligence, popularity, wealth or power of oratorical persuasion, so that those with the ablest minds became the greatest chiefs.

The chiefs were solely the executives of the resolutions passed by the councils, though they were also the promoters of the decisions, since they were the councilors. Greatest in influence were the older chiefs who had given up their active duties. The local councils governed the affairs of each village, the national assemblies those of the nation. In the general council of the nation, the deputies from each village, locality or clan seated themselves together, so that they might easily consult on the questions proposed. After the matter to be discussed had been clearly delineated by the presiding chief, the various groups discussed what their reply should be. Each spokesman was heard in order and concluded his speech with the words, "Such is my mind," to which the presiding chief answered, "It is well." They settled the question by a plurality of opinions.

In these councils, as in the feasts of pure hospitality, de Brébeuf was now competent enough to teach the Christian beliefs in the Huron tongue, and at the same time could refute the absurdities of their fables and condemn their superstitious rites. One elder exclaimed: "Echon, the people of your village are worthless and have no sense. They are wicked. They do not reveal what you tell them. What you have told us is so important that we should talk of it at a council of the whole land." Not by hearing alone were the Hurons to be brought to God, de Brébeuf knew; but, through hearing now, they would be conditioned for future acceptance of God. Remembering the discussions at Quebec about the folly of baptizing any of the savages until they had been long tested, Père Jean held back from administering the Sacrament to any Huron, except in the imminence of certain death.

While he wandered among them, day by day, seeking to be their
friend and aiding them when he could, he kept his ears open in order
to absorb their speech. During this third year, he solved many of the
mysteries and intricacies of their language. He kept compiling page
after page of his dictionary, spent long hours analyzing these words
and reducing them to rules for his grammar, and struggled to find
equivalents in Huron for the abstractions of the French and for the
spiritual concepts of the Catholic belief. His most arduous labor was
that of translating from Latin into Huron the elementary catechism of
Ledesma, an admirable pamphlet of four short chapters. This would
be the handbook for future missioners to memorize and teach to the
future Huron catechumens.[5]

Toward the end of May, a French agent who lived among the
Algonquins appeared at de Brébeuf's cabin. He was sent by Champlain and carried a letter from Père Massé. Despondently, he informed
de Brébeuf that the French at Quebec were starving; last summer an
English fleet had threatened Quebec and had captured the French
fleet. Champlain feared that the English or the French Huguenots
would again blockade the St. Lawrence this summer and possibly
attack Quebec. The agent was intructed by Champlain to tell Père
de Brébeuf and the Frenchmen among the Hurons to carry down to
Quebec as much corn as they could gather from the Hurons.

Père Jean read Massé's letter. Curtly, it ordered him, under holy
obedience, to find means of returning to Quebec at the earliest possible moment. His dreams were tattered. Instead of new missioners
coming he must abandon his Hurons just at the time when he was
prepared to bring them to God. He had no alternative but to obey,
and that promptly and in good spirits. He and the agents persuaded
the masters of twelve canoes to load their boats with corn and hurry
down to Quebec, the while they secured promises from other chiefs
to follow with more canoeloads.

Throughout the country the word passed that Echon the Blackrobe was leaving them. One old man reproached him: "Listen to me,
my nephew. You have told us that you have a father in heaven who
made all. You warned us that anyone who did not obey him would
be cast into the flames. We have asked you to teach us more. What
shall we do when you go away?" Another addressed him: "Echon,
I am not baptized and you are leaving us. My soul will be lost, but

what can I do about it? You say you will come back. That is good. Go then, and be brave, but return before I die." One of his last acts was that of baptizing a baby boy at the request of a friendly man named Houtaya, who remembered that Echon said he could give happiness after death.[6]

The twelve canoes of Jean de Brébeuf's party, together with eight canoes of agents and other Hurons, struck out of the cove below Toanché about the middle of June. They knew it would be a hazardous journey, for the Ottawa would be swollen by the spring thaws, and the forty and more cascades would be frothing cataracts. Greater dangers lay along the downward route than the upward, for the current more easily could swing the canoes into the swirl of the rapids. They labored with muscles taut and eyes acutely watching every moment. Along the way, La Marche, an agent, failed to come out of the woods after a long portage. The Hurons, following the law of the forest, were unwilling to wait for him, but de Brébeuf led a searching party and found him three miles back, dazed and helpless. They dropped safely through the gorges of the Ottawa, through the defile of the Rivière des Prairies, and out into the broad St. Lawrence.

Stretching the day's paddling from dawn to dusk, they drove their canoes feverishly along the remaining 180 miles to Quebec. After four grueling days of paddling, at last they came abreast of the bristling wall of the Rock, and triumphantly swung into the landing place before the habitation on Tuesday evening, July 17. The Frenchmen greeted them briefly, then hungrily unloaded the bark casks of corn. Champlain came rushing down from the Fort to welcome them, but questioned them as to how much corn they had brought. Père Massé hurried over from Notre Dame des Anges, with Père de Noüe and the three brothers. All of them, staring at Père Jean as they would at a ghost, kept repeating again and again: "Thank God, thank God, you have come in time."

CHAPTER IV

Exiled in the Homeland

One: 1629

T HAT NIGHT, JEAN DE BRÉBEUF learned the reason for his recall. Grimly, he listened to Père Massé and Père de Noüe, as they sat about the flickering lamp in the community room of Notre Dame des Anges. An English fleet was known to be somewhere down the St. Lawrence and, it was expected, would soon attack Quebec. The English, last year, had threatened Quebec and had later captured the French fleet in the Gulf of St. Lawrence. As a result, no provisions and no supplies had reached Quebec. The sixty Frenchmen living at Quebec had been hungry all through the winter; by the spring, they had consumed practically all their food; about May, they were forced to live on acorns and edible roots; in June, they had exhausted the supply of these in the vicinity of Quebec and had to search for even these far in the forests. Now, in July, all in Quebec were starving and there was little prospect for a sufficient harvest to support them in the coming winter.[1]

Sieur de Champlain, likewise, was depressed, even to despair, when de Brébeuf called on him the next morning in Fort St. Louis. Despite all his efforts to obtain food from the natives, he could not find enough to keep his people alive. He had given Desdames his only shallop to search for food around Tadoussac, and had patched up his only barque to send Boulle with twenty-nine women and children to the Gulf, in the hope they might find support among the Algonquins in that region and, eventually, that they might be taken aboard some fishing boats bound for France. Not even an Algonquin rumor had come back to him. The silence along the lower St. Lawrence was baffling and ominous.

He hurled himself out of his despair into anger and rage at the Montmorency Company, which controlled the trade and had failed not only to build Quebec into a citadel but even to support it as a habitation. He railed against the Huguenot bankers who squeezed out the profits, and against the governing authorities of France who, by their stupidity and intrigues, had doomed this colony which he had founded twenty years before. All that he had predicted, year after year, was being finally consummated. There remained no hope for Quebec and the French empire in the New World save by the miraculous and immediate arrival of a French battle fleet.

Last summer, he told de Brébeuf, he had bluffed the English when they demanded the surrender of Quebec. He could not have resisted them if they had attacked him. The English fleet was back again this summer, and the English commander would be delivering to him another ultimatum. He could not play them off with bold words, and he could not fight them. He had fewer than forty men; he had powder and balls for only a few volleys of his cannon; he did not have more than eight hundred rounds for the muskets. If the English came, he must surrender Quebec. If they did not come, he and those still at Quebec were in danger of death by starvation. He could do nothing more. He must await the end in anguish of soul.

All the habitants with whom de Brébeuf talked suffered the same pangs of hunger and the same dread that bowed down the proud head of Champlain. He made his way slowly and sadly back to Notre Dame des Anges. He bore the added sorrow that he could not return to Toanché and the Hurons. On Thursday morning, July 19, while he was admiring the progress Père Massé had made in building the Jesuit residence and the house for the workmen and in cultivating the small farm, the Montagnais called La Nasse burst through the gate and breathlessly shouted that three ships were passing behind the Isle d'Orléans. After hurriedly informing Massé and de Nouë, de Brébeuf hastened over to the Fort.

Almost at the same time that he reached Champlain, a servant came running in with the news that the vessels were spotted across the river, behind Point Lévis. Champlain dashed out to the edge of the Rock. They must be English if they hid behind the Point; the French would have sent a shallop in advance. He summoned the habitants and company agents, the Récollets and Jesuits. With cold

calmness he declared that resistance was useless, that he must surrender and seek the best terms he could obtain. He ordered that the
women and children, together with the religious men, should take
shelter in the Fort. He assigned the fighting men to their posts.

Gathered again on the edge of the Rock, Champlain, de Brébeuf,
de la Roche and the others looked down on the three ships as they
slowly turned Point Lévis. A shallop, bearing a white flag, detached
itself and waited. Champlain raised an answering white flag and
descended the curving road to the landing dock. An English officer
climbed out of the shallop and after decorous greetings presented a
letter to Champlain. The document, signed by Louis and Thomas
Kirk in the name of their brother General David Kirk, courteously
demanded the immediate surrender of Quebec and gave assurance of
honorable terms of settlement.

Champlain, observing the proprieties, informed the English officer that he would return his answer later in the day, but warned
him, meanwhile, to keep the ships outside the cannon range of the
Fort. Champlain and his advisers drew up the terms under which
they would peacefully surrender. These demanded that General
Kirk show clear proof that France and England were at war, and,
furthermore, that General Kirk present the credentials authorizing
him to attack New France. The terms included the following: that
a special vessel be assigned to carry all the French and their possessions back to France; that this vessel be prepared to sail three days
after the arrival of the French in Tadoussac; that provisions for the
voyage be given in exchange for the peltries stored in the warehouse; that no violence whatsoever should be used toward anyone
during the occupation.

Père de la Roche delivered Champlain's answer aboard the flagship of Louis Kirk. He and his consultors returned the answer that
they could produce evidence that they were commissioned to wage
war in New France and at Quebec, and that they accepted the terms
for surrender with the exception of those demanding a special vessel for the French. They pledged themselves, however, to give safe
passage to all who wished to return to France. Champlain, through
de la Roche, advised Louis Kirk that he would sign the articles of
surrender the following morning.

During these negotiations, Père de la Roche had held friendly
conversations with the two Kirk brothers. He warned de Brébeuf

and the Jesuits to be on their guard against the Kirks who were half French and Huguenots, and who had expressed the greatest aversion to the Jesuits. Their hatred was intensified, de la Roche revealed, by two French agents whom they had captured down the St. Lawrence. They were told by these two, Le Baillif and Raye, who turned traitor to Champlain, that the Jesuit house in Quebec was filled with beaver, bear and moose skins. Louis Kirk confided to de la Roche that if he had been forced to attack Quebec, he would have delivered the first assault against the Jesuit house.

In view of the warning, Massé, de Brébeuf and the other four Jesuits worked feverishly in putting their affairs in order, since they feared Kirk and the English would evict them on the morrow. According to the articles of capitulation, the Jesuits and Récollets were forbidden to carry anything away with them except their books and clothes. The vestments, they judged, were clothes, but what about the sacred vessels? Would they be permitted to take these with them? Père Massé resolved to hold them in his possession until they were taken away by force. De Brébeuf, with a sad heart, carefully covered with leather his Huron dictionary, phrase book and grammar, his Huron translation of Ledesma's catechism, and his Montagnais dictionary. Running through his mind was the thought of begging Père Massé to allow him to return to the Hurons. The Récollets had talked about slipping away and wintering with the Montagnais since they were convinced that France would recapture Quebec next summer. But he did not make his request to Père Massé, who was moaning and weeping with indignation and grief because the English had driven him out of Acadia in 1613 and now for the second time the English were expelling him from Quebec.

The next morning, Friday, July 20, Champlain went aboard the English flagship and signed the documents surrendering Quebec. He sought and was given assurance that soldiers would be assigned to guard the premises of the Jesuits and the Récollets, since they were about two miles from the habitation. Champlain came ashore and climbed the hill to Fort St. Louis. Then Kirk, accompanied by 150 English soldiers, landed and paced up to where the French were gathered. With dignity, he received the keys to the warehouse from the chief agent of the Montmorency Company. He and his men marched up to the Fort, demanded the formal surrender by Champlain, and took possession in the name of the King of England.

There was no violence and no disturbance. Louis Kirk treated the
Héberts, the Couillards, the other habitants and the company agents
with bonhomie, and tried to persuade them to remain in Quebec.
But in his inspection of the Jesuit premises, he was unfriendly, harsh
and imperious. He searched for the beaver and other skins about
which he had been told, and not finding them showed further dis-
pleasure and irritation. He took some pictures that appealed to him,
and the Lutheran chaplain, who accompanied him, asked for some of
the books. He next visited the Récollet convent. With the friars he
was most affable and considerate. He assured them that he, himself,
would most willingly allow them to remain in Quebec, if he were
not ordered to deport all priests.

In his diary, Champlain recorded: "From the time the English
took possession of Quebec, the days seemed to me like months."
He requested that he be shipped down to Tadoussac, there to await
the departure for France. Four days after his surrender, on July 24, he
sailed down to Quebec. The Jesuits were just as eager as Champlain to
get away from Notre Dame des Anges, and the Kirks were even more
desirous to banish the Jesuits out of their sight. All of them had to content themselves until boats could be provided. Meanwhile, the English
soldiers appointed to guard the Jesuit premises looted the houses,
searched everywhere for the furs alleged to be hidden away, and bul-
lied and berated the priests and brothers as if they were criminals.

In the days of waiting, de Brébeuf spent most of his time with the
Hurons who had paddled him to Quebec. They were mystified by
the war between the English and French. No one fought, no one
was killed, all talked like friends, English took village of Quebec,
French sailed away on English boats; yet they were enemies at war.
They were sorry that Echon refused to go back again with them for,
they said, now that he could talk with them in their own language,
he could explain the things of great importance that had first brought
him to their villages. De Brébeuf's heart was breaking that he must
abandon them now and that he knew not when he might return
to them.

On July 28, four days after Champlain had sailed, the Jesuits were
ordered to embark for Tadoussac. Louis Kirk supervised their depor-
tation and closely scrutinized their bundles. He demanded that the
small box containing the chalice and paten carried by Père Massé be

opened for inspection. Kirk grabbed at the chalice, but Massé holding it out of reach, exclaimed: "Monsieur, this is a sacred object, so please do not profane it." With an oath, Kirk shouted out: "We put no faith in your superstitions." He seized the chalice, waved it in defiance and ridicule of the Jesuits, and tossed it back at Massé. He and his men made it clear that the expulsion of the Jesuits was good riddance for them.

With filmy eyes, de Brébeuf, Massé and the others looked across the bay toward Notre Dame des Anges and watched the Rock of Quebec hide behind Point Lévis as the barque sailed by the Isle d'Orléans. God alone knew if ever again they would have their hearts' desire of living in New France. Slow days passed as they gazed on the endless parade of the dormant, gigantic headlands, fringed with pines and stolid with mystery. At last, in the first days of August, they were landed on the beach in the cove of Tadoussac. The commander, David Kirk, greeted the Jesuits with even greater malevolence than his two brothers at Quebec had shown them on their departure.

Champlain welcomed them heartily and seemed in fine spirits. To their surprise, Emery de Caen was at Tadoussac and told them a startling story. Peace had been concluded between France and England in April; therefore, the seizure of Quebec by the Kirks was illegal. Furthermore, he asserted that, before he sailed from France, a large fleet of merchant ships was being readied and Cardinal Richelieu had ordered Admiral de Razilly to convoy the merchantmen with battleships. Champlain, de Caen, de Brébeuf and all the French were buoyed up with hope that the battle fleet of de Razilly might arrive in time to drive the English out of the St. Lawrence.

Tadoussac was a scene of turmoil and confusion. Hundreds of copper-skinned Algonquins with their women and children, congregated for the trade and to watch the war between the palefaces, swarmed everywhere. Loud-mouthed, hard-featured English and French Huguenot soldiers and sailors swaggered about the rim of rocks and the landing beach. The six Jesuits, in their long, black soutanes, were in violent contrast to the English and French who went about almost as naked as the savages in the sweltering heat. Through the weeks of August, the Jesuits and the refugees from Quebec slept where they could find a place in the wooded hills. Rations of rough food were given to them, and no restraint was placed over them.

De Brébeuf and his brethren escaped as much as they could in the mounds and hills along the Saguenay River and consorted mostly with the Montagnais in their cone-shaped cabins.

They found more friendliness among the savages than among the white men. The English looked on the Jesuits with suspicious curiosity; in their country, they boasted, Jesuits were hanged and quartered if they were found. The French Huguenots, who served under the Kirks, bore hate and detestation and a desire for revenge on the Jesuits. Whenever they met the priests they abused them and uttered blustering threats against them. David Kirk was as violent as his men. He forbade all Catholic services at Tadoussac and expressed indignation that his brother Louis had permitted the sacrilegious Mass at Quebec.

De Brébeuf used the days of waiting to study further the Algonquin language and to compare it with the Huron. He likewise took every opportunity to teach the savages about God and the Catholic belief. But he was horrified at the increasing debasement of the natives under the English influence. They traded brandy and wine for peltries. The savages, children and women as well as men, became roaring maniacs under the influence of the fire water. Though the Algonquins had a code of promiscuity rooted in the instincts of hospitality, the Englishmen turned the women into pigs or tigresses. Many of the more responsible Algonquin chiefs lamented to de Brébeuf that their people were being ruined by the new palefaces. Many of them withdrew their clans and families from Tadoussac, while others advised raising the war hatchet against these new invaders.

By September, the Kirks had completed the investiture of Quebec and had transported to Tadoussac all the agents and habitants who elected to return to France. About September 12, the four Récollets joined the Jesuits. They related that they enjoyed peace with the English during the past seven weeks. Le Caron and de la Roche were so well satisfied that they wanted to live in Quebec during the winter in order to minister to the thirty Frenchmen who decided to remain there. They were so convinced that the French would recapture Quebec the next summer that they had packed their chalices and chapel utensils in a heavy leather sack and buried it secretly in a thicket of the woods.

When the English ships, in the words of Champlain, were "careened slightly, cleaned, tarred and tallowed", and almost ready to sail, there occurred the strange death of Jacques Michel, first officer of the fleet. He was a Huguenot from Dieppe, formerly employed as a pilot by the Montmorency Company but now serving under the Kirks. He was a violent-tempered man who reviled and raged against the French and the English, the Kirks and the de Caens, as the mood seized him. His *bête noire* was Jean de Brébeuf, whom he may have met in Dieppe during the Guyot incident. De Brébeuf had restrained himself under the continued vituperation of Michel, but his calmness and imperturbability infuriated the man the more.

On the last occasion of their meeting, David Kirk and Michel were baiting de Brébeuf and the Jesuits. "Gentlemen, you have had pretty much your own way in Canada," said Kirk pompously. "You derive profit from the trade that belonged to Sieur de Caen, whom you have dispossessed." De Brébeuf answered: "Pardon me, Sir, nothing has brought us to Canada, here to brave all the dangers and perils, except a pure desire to promote the glory of God and to effect the conversion of the savages."

Jacques Michel snarled: "*Oui, Oui,* to convert the savages! Say rather, to convert the beavers!" Stung by the taunt, de Brébeuf answered quickly: "*Cela est faux.* It does not follow!" Michel raised his hand as if to reach up and strike de Brébeuf. He restrained himself, however, and exclaimed with bravado: "It is only out of respect for the General that I don't slap your face for giving me the lie." More mildly, de Brébeuf apologized: "I did not mean to give you the lie. I should be very sorry to do so. The term I employed is one that we use in our studies when a false statement is advanced. I beg that you will pardon me, therefore, and will believe that I did not speak with the intention of offending you." Michel continued to mouth his oaths and blasphemies and later swore: "May I be hanged if I don't give a couple of blows before we sail to that Jean de Brébeuf."

Shortly afterwards, Jacques Michel was stricken with apoplexy, and died without having gained consciousness, under mysterious circumstances. Disputes immediately flared up. The Catholics interpreted his death as an act of God for threatening to strike Jean de Brébeuf, while the Huguenots proclaimed that his death was an act of God because he failed to trounce de Brébeuf. Champlain recorded in his diary: "There was good reason why his soul was tormented and why he died of mortification; that was the real cause of his death and not what Kirk and the others alleged: namely, that it was because he had *not* given a blow to the Jesuit Père, a man who was the embodiment of wisdom and virtue, as the journeys made by him into the interior of the country have abundantly proved." They buried Jacques Michel at Tadoussac, and paid him the most elaborate military honors at his interment.

Champlain, the Jesuits, Récollets and people from Quebec still hoped from day to day that the French war fleet, about which Emery de Caen had informed them, might arrive before the English ships sailed. Their expectations were intensified when some Algonquins told about seeing ten large vessels in the vicinity of Gaspé, at the mouth of the Gulf. While the French increased their petitions to God that these relief ships might arrive in time to rescue Quebec and save New France, the English became apprehensive and hurried their final preparations to sail. Champlain was taken aboard the flagship of David Kirk, the Récollets and Quebec people were distributed on other ships, and the Jesuits were given bunks on the vessel commanded by Captain Breton, an Englishman who received them in a gentlemanly and courteous manner.

On Friday, September 14, Commander Kirk raised the signal and headed down the St. Lawrence. Jean de Brébeuf was as disconsolate, watching Tadoussac recede, as he had been exhilarated four years before when he discerned Tadoussac emerging from the river. Champlain kept exact tally of events. In his autobiography, he recorded: "We then weighed anchor and set sail, not without considerable apprehension of meeting the Sieur de Razilly, because some savages had assured us that they had seen ten well-armed vessels at Gaspé, which were awaiting us at that place. For this reason, we passed very close to Anticosti, fourteen leagues from Gaspé, so as not to be noticed. Kirk at the same time said he was not afraid of them in the least. We were kept back by very bad weather, accompanied by fogs, till we reached the Great Bank. On the sixteenth of the month of October we came into soundings, and on the eighteenth we came in sight of the Scilly Islands."

Two: 1629–1632

The five ships of the English fleet, after rolling from port to starboard, after being lifted with the waves and bouncing down in the troughs, rode safely into the battlemented port of Plymouth on October 20. General David Kirk strutted down the plankway with prideful importance. Samuel de Champlain landed as soon as possible, for he wished to verify the reports of peace given him at Tadoussac by Emery de Caen. All the other French, including the Récollets, went ashore in holiday mood, overjoyed to be able to plant their feet on solid ground. The Jesuits stayed on board, and had to be content to look at Plymouth, its docks and harbors, the houses and castles on the hill, from the ship rail. They were forbidden by the penal laws from making entry into England, and were liable to be apprehended, imprisoned and executed if they were found in Plymouth.

David Kirk returned to his ship a much worried man. He had expected meritorious decorations as well as profits for capturing Quebec. But he learned that he might be indicted for piracy; at the least, he might probably be involved in countless lawsuits and would possibly be obliged to make restitution, with consequent ruin for himself and the bankers who financed him. What de Caen told him at Tadoussac was true; England and France had signed a treaty of peace at Suza on April 24, nearly three months before he had seized Quebec. He was guilty of an act of war during the time of peace. Champlain chuckled as he wrote in his diary: "We ran into Plymouth, where we got news of the peace, which greatly angered the aforesaid Kirk."

After five days in Plymouth, Kirk sailed one of his vessels along the southern coast of England to Dover. There he secured passage across the Channel to France for the Quebec returnees, the Récollets and the Jesuits, while he with Champlain proceeded to London for discussion of the entanglements resulting from the unwarranted occupation of Quebec. Père de Brébeuf with his Jesuit companions landed probably at Calais at the end of October and proceeded to Paris. He gave written and verbal reports of New France to Père Provincial, and was called into conferences about the capitulation of Quebec by the directors of the Company of One Hundred Associates. He was gaped at as a specimen as strange, he felt, as he had appeared to the Hurons, and was, in addition, exhibited and honored as some sort of a hero. Everybody in Paris, it seemed to him, was curious to learn about his experiences with the savages.

But he was even more eager to learn about the mysteries of how France had failed to support and defend Canada. His keen Norman mind pieced together the story of the past three years. In 1626, when he went up to the Hurons, Père Noyrot was sent back to France to present the accumulating accusations against the de Caens and the Montmorency Company. Noyrot, a crusading propagandist, poured out to the Viceroy and other personages his charges that the de Caens, by their niggardly policy and their violation of their pledges, were weakening New France and would eventually bring about its complete ruination. Noyrot reached even Cardinal Richelieu, who listened to him with rapt attention.

In the summer of 1627, Noyrot was unable to send out his supplies, and the de Caens forwarded only a starvation allowance to Quebec. In the autumn, Père Lalemant came back to France with the Jesuit workmen from Quebec, since he could not support them through the winter. Lalemant joined Noyrot in his campaign against the Montmorency Company and the de Caen management. They were determined either to force the company to fulfill its pledges to support, develop and defend Quebec, or to bring about the dissolution of the company.

Cardinal Richelieu, in 1627, decided to use all his resources in building a colonial empire in North America. He took over from le Duc de Ventadour the office of Viceroy and dissolved the Montmorency Company. In 1628, he secured the royal signature on the articles creating a new company, that of the One Hundred Associates. This company would be controlled by himself and would be managed by reputable and philanthropic directors. The profits on peltries and other exports from the colony were to be used to people Quebec with hundreds of colonists each year, and to support them until they were settled on their farms. Subsidies were granted for missionaries and their churches, and full quotas of soldiers and ample munitions were guaranteed for the defense of the St. Lawrence against foreign invaders and the savages.

Thus, de Brébeuf learned, the summer of 1628 was to inaugurate a new and prosperous era for New France. The Company of One Hundred Associates equipped four large vessels, loaded them with food, clothing, utensils and munitions, and filled them with two hundred colonists, many of whom brought their wives and children. The fleet sailed on May 3, 1628, under the command of Claude de Roquemont. Two Jesuits, Charles Lalemant and François Ragueneau, accompanied de Roquemont, while Père Noyrot chartered his own ship, packed it with the supplies he had been collecting for two years, and brought with him thirty workmen for the Jesuit missions.

Earlier that same summer of 1628, the English fleet under David Kirk, taking advantage of the Huguenot war in France and the uncertain relations between England and France, invaded the St. Lawrence and captured the French fleet under de Roquemont. Noyrot's vessel escaped during the battle and returned to France. As a result of this disastrous defeat, no ships and no supplies reached Quebec. There followed the winter of starvation about which de Brébeuf had heard when he returned from the Hurons.

But why, he asked impatiently, had not the French sent aid to Quebec this present summer of 1629? The answer was another story of tragic frustration. France concluded peace with England on April 24. The Company of One Hundred Associates equipped another merchant fleet, and Cardinal Richelieu, determined to assert French supremacy in the New World, ordered Admiral Isaac de Razilly to convoy the merchantmen with his war ships. On April 22, the four company vessels, under the command of Captain Charles Daniel, proceeded from Dieppe to La Rochelle, and waited for the battle fleet of de Razilly. On board Daniel's vessel were Père Barthélemy Vimont. On the ship again chartered by Père Noyrot were Père Charles Lalemant, Père Alexandre de Vieuxpont, Frère Louis Malot and twenty-four workmen in the employ of the Jesuits.

Through May and the greater part of June, the five ships lay idly at La Rochelle. Finally, Captain Daniel was informed that the warships of de Razilly were ordered elsewhere, since there was no danger of an English attack. Being instructed to sail for Quebec without the convoy, his five ships got under way on June 26. It seemed incredible to de Brébeuf that no one in France suspected that David Kirk and his ships left England in March, three months earlier, for the express purpose of capturing Quebec. It was most mysterious, likewise, that the French fleet under Daniel had neither reached the St. Lawrence before the middle of September nor returned to France before November, five months after it had sailed from La Rochelle.

After his stay in Paris, Père Jean was assigned to the College of Rouen and there, late in November, he gathered the story of the French fleet. A tempestuous windstorm struck the five ships and scattered them in all directions. Three were blown back to France. Noyrot's vessel was dashed against the rocks of Canso on Cape Breton

Island on August 24. Père Noyrot and Frère Malot were swept out
to sea. Lalemant and Vieuxpont were washed safely to shore. Subsequently, Lalemant was taken aboard a Basque fishing vessel, which
was wrecked near San Sebastian in Spain; but he saved himself and
finally reached France.

Not until December did Captain Daniel ride into the port of
Dieppe. Having been blown toward Acadia, he discovered an English
settlement established on French territory. He attacked and destroyed
it, and then set his crew and colonists to the building of a French fort
near the Grand Cibou River. He left forty of his men to pass the
winter at this new settlement. With them remained Père Vimont and
Père Vieuxpont, who had joined Daniel's company after his escape
from Noyrot's shipwreck.

Champlain arrived in Rouen about December 8. He told de
Brébeuf that he had been in London urging the French Ambassador to advise Cardinal Richelieu to make a formal demand that
England restore Quebec and New France. He had also drawn up
claims against the Kirks in the name of the Company of One Hundred Associates. "Having heard my story," Champlain stated to de
Brébeuf, "the Ambassador decided to mention the matter to the King
of England, who gave him good reason to hope that the place would
be restored to us, together with all the furs and goods, which Kirk
had caused to be seized." For nearly five weeks, Champlain complained to de Brébeuf; he awaited official letters and action from
the French Crown. Then he thought he could bring quicker action
by returning to Paris. "The Ambassador," said Champlain, "assured
me that the King of England and his Council had promised him to
restore the place to the [French] King."

Père de Brébeuf, after Champlain's visit, had little doubt but that
Quebec would be restored to the French. In the coming spring of
1630, the Company of One Hundred Associates would again be
sending out their vessels, Champlain would again be the Governor,
Quebec would once more be French, and the Jesuits and Récollets
would be living once more in their residences along the St. Charles
and sending missioners up to the Hurons.

The query in his mind was whether or not he would be sent back
with the fleet that coming spring. Normally, he should be assigned to
the Novitiate at Rouen, where he had entered twelve years before as

a novice, and should receive further spiritual training in a third year of noviceship, called the tertianship. Here he would be cloistered from the world and worldly things, would spend the days in prayer, in spiritual reading, in listening to ascetical conferences, in studying the Institute of the Society of Jesus more thoroughly. More important than all else, he would engage himself for thirty consecutive days in the Spiritual Exercises of Saint Ignatius. Though there is no record that he went through the required routine of the tertianship, it is more than likely that he spent some weeks at the Novitiate under the Instructor of Tertians, Père Louis Lalemant, who bore the reputation of being an exalted saint. With gentleness and intuition, he could solve whatever scruples Père Jean had accumulated during his years in New France and could calm whatever tumults and agonies of soul he was experiencing in retrospect.

Père Lalemant, in his private spiritual direction and in his vibrant conferences, was not content with a high spiritual level. He communicated to all who were capable of following him a supreme love for God and raised them to spiritual heights where they were absorbed by God. Père Jean had experienced strange, even unfathomable movements of soul while dwelling among the sin-corrupted savagery of the Hurons. He had felt the living presence of God, somehow, somewhere in and about him. He had sometimes been frightened by these blinding illuminations and visions. From Père Lalemant he could learn not only the correct discernment of spirits but much more, what God demanded of certain souls and what love He revealed to them.

Since there was a probability that he might sail in 1630, he devoted himself to the Spiritual Exercises during early January in preparation for his final vows as a Jesuit. He welcomed this opportunity of reviewing his past and preparing for the dangerous years of the future. He hungered for a clearer understanding of God, His graces, His will. He wanted to know Christ more intimately so that he could imitate Him more minutely.

Some of his spiritual notes reveal the interior motions of his soul.[2]

In January, 1630, I felt within myself an overpowering desire of suffering something for Christ. And I feared for my reprobation from the fact that thus far He had dealt too kindly with me, especially since

I might have offended His Divine Majesty so grievously. Only then, happily, shall I hope for my salvation when occasions of suffering shall present themselves.

On the eleventh day. I have reviewed my sins; on the one hand, I found that they were grave and innumerable; on the other, I seemed to see the Divine Mercy extending His arms to me to embrace me sweetly and, furthermore, condoning for me all my past sins through an amnesty, bringing to life again my good works, performed in charity but killed through sin, and moreover calling me to Himself in sublime friendship, and saying to me as was said to Paul: "A vessel of election he will be to Me, so that he may carry my name among the nations." Accordingly, I gave thanks and offered myself to Him and I said: "Do with me harshly, Lord, according to Thy heart. Teach me what You wish me to do. Nothing in the future will separate me from Thy charity, not nakedness, not the sword, not death, etc. So far has it been forgotten by me that I am the son of the most holy Society; that I might be the future apostle of Canada if I should respond to You; that, though I have not been endowed with the gift of tongues, I have been granted a great facility in them. Oh, the wickedness, the foulness, the deformity of my life!"

Following this entry of self-abasement, he recorded a contradictory confession on the very same day. "I have never perceived in myself any disposition toward venial sin, in such manner that I would take delight in committing any venial sin." In another spiritual mood, the same day, he divulged: "Lest God cut me down as an unfruitful tree, I have prayed to Him that He should still pass me by this year so that I might bring forth better fruit." With a sense of surprise, he wrote: "9th of February. It seemed to me that, being totally enraptured, I was torn away from all my senses and united to God. However, this happened with some commotion of the body, and this ravishment was only momentary."

During January, there was more talk of the resumption of the French rule over Quebec. In order to be prepared for the eventualities, Père Jean was notified that he would be granted the final vows of a Formed Spiritual Coadjutor in the Society of Jesus. Since he had not completed the required studies nor taken the comprehensive examination in philosophy and theology, he was not eligible to pronounce the Solemn Vows of the Professed. He drew up his final will and testament divesting himself of present and future possessions, wrote out in his own hand the formula of the vows, and pronounced them before the Blessed Sacrament, binding himself again to poverty, chastity and obedience according to the Constitutions and Institute of the Society of Jesus. He recorded the fact briefly in his spiritual diary: "On the 20th of January in the year 1630, I pronounced the vows of a Formed Coadjutor in the chapel of the College of Rouen, at the hands of R. P. Jacques Bertrix, Rector."

During May, his spiritual notes testify that he again cloistered himself in spiritual retreat. A memorandum in his notebook reveals: "Beginning the Exercises in 1630, May 12. Lord Jesus Christ, my Redeemer, You have redeemed me by your blood and most precious death; therefore, likewise, I promise that I will serve You through all my life in the Society of Jesus, and that I will serve no one else, unless for You and because of You. This I have subscribed with my own blood and my own hand, being ready to pour out my whole life as freely as I pour this drop of blood."

Estimating himself one day in his meditation, he came to the following conclusion: "I recognize no talent in myself, only that I am disposed to obey. It seems to me that I am fit only to be the porter at the door, or to prepare the refectory, or to assist the cook. I shall conduct myself in the Society as if I were a beggar, admitted only by favor, and I shall think that all is done for me out of charity alone." In another note he stated his resolve: "May I be rent, rather than I shall voluntarily violate any rule." And again he affirmed: "The conversation of my soul shall be with God: there must not be traffic with creatures in my heart." With fervor, he exclaimed: "Never shall I take my rest; never shall I say *satis.*"

Through these months of spiritual concentration, Père de Brébeuf would at times forget Rouen and the College and find himself dreaming of the broad St. Lawrence, the shaggy Rock, the far purple mountains, the canoe beating against the rapids, the thunder of cascades, the crinkled surface of the Great Lake, the tree-crested islands, the voices floating through the forests, the rough bark of the cabins, fires, odors, naked backs, wrinkled old men haunching, mischievous olive-skinned children, sorcerers, dances, feasts, orgies, captives tortured—dreaming till he again woke up in his walled room in the College of Rouen.

Once more, he assumed his old duties as treasurer of the College of Rouen. During March and April, 1630, he learned that Cardinal Richelieu had ordered six large ships outfitted for war and that four smaller ships were being careened and tarred in preparation for the voyage to New France. Admiral de Razilly was given orders to convoy the merchant fleet. The One Hundred Associates were piling supplies and gathering colonists. France would again take over Quebec. Then he learned that the English were protesting against the arming of a French fleet to capture Quebec, since they had promised to restore it peaceably. All the orders for the fleet were countermanded because Richelieu wished to avoid ill-feelings with England. Just then, he was concentrating his power on the war with Spain which he was waging in Savoy over the Mantuan succession.

During the early months of 1631, there was even less hope that France would reoccupy New France than there was in 1630. Richelieu was still in Italy, fighting the Spaniards. He would not hazard an English war at the same time, but he kept the negotiations alive. Encouraged by Richelieu's preoccupation and delay, the English began placing conditions in regard to the restitution of New France. Being the possessors of Quebec, they were in no hurry to reach a settlement.

By the end of 1631, Richelieu drove the Spaniards out of Mantua and Savoy. He then looked at England. By his orders, the French and English commissioners presented, on March 5, 1632, the draft of proposals conceding New France to Louis XIII. On March 25, he ordered Admiral de Razilly to equip ten fighting ships for service in New France, merely as a precaution. On March 29, the treaty between France and England was signed at Saint-Germain-en-Laye. By Article One, the King of England agreed to restore to the King of France all places occupied by the subjects of his Majesty of Great Britain in New France.

Cardinal Richelieu decreed that Quebec be reoccupied that summer of 1632. Since the Company of One Hundred Associates was not prepared, after its losses of 1628 and 1629, to bear the expenses of an expedition, the much-abused yet indispensable de Caens were authorized to take over all the properties seized by the Kirks. In the absence of Sieur de Champlain, who was to remain that year in France, Guillaume Duplessis-Bochart was appointed Lieutenant Governor and was commissioned to assume possession of Quebec and New France in the name of King Louis XIII.

Three: 1632–1633

While they rejoiced over the glorious reconquest of New France, the Jesuits were profoundly disturbed. They, as well as the Récollets, were being excluded by order of Cardinal Richelieu, who decreed that only one religious order, the Capuchin Friars, would be permitted to send missioners to Quebec. The Jesuits and the Récollets joined in protests and remonstrances, and united in pleas and arguments that they be permitted to resume their missionary labors. But since the will of Cardinal Richelieu was law, they were advised to submit quietly, for the present; in a few years, the Cardinal might allow other religious to share the missions with the Capuchins.

On their side, the Capuchin Friars were as surprised as the Jesuits and Récollets by Richelieu's decision. They were, likewise, embarrassed because the other two religious orders held a prior claim to this missionary field and, normally, should have the right to take up anew their apostolate. Besides, they did not have enough priests to supply the needs of New France and did not have any means of support except the amount doled out to them by the Company of One Hundred Associates. Through their Capuchin brother, Père Joseph, the Cardinal's only confidant, they begged to be relieved of the honor and the obligation of sending missioners to New France.

Cardinal Richelieu accepted their petition to be excused, but he held to his determination that only one religious order be allowed to establish itself in New France. He chose the Society of Jesus in preference to the Récollets. They were dismayed when they found themselves banned from Quebec, and the Jesuits, whom they had invited as their helpers, being granted the missionary monopoly they had held. To all their protests and petitions, the answer was again given that they should bide their time, since it was very likely that, in a few years, when the colony was firmly established, they would be admitted to New France.

With no loss of time, Père Barthelemy Jacquinot, the Jesuit Provincial, announced his appointments of the Jesuits to New France.

Père Paul Le Jeune, Superior of the residence at Dieppe, was named Superior of the New France Mission. Père Anne de Noüe and Frère Gilbert Burel were assigned with him to Quebec, while Père Antoine Daniel and Père Ambroise Davost were stationed at the settlement begun by Captain Daniel on Cape Breton Island in Acadia. With keen disappointment, Jean de Brébeuf accepted the will of his Superior. He had been sedulously studying his Huron and Algonquin, and praying that he might be chosen. Even greater was the sorrow of Père Charles Lalemant, then Rector of the College of Eu, and greater still was that of Père Massé, who was confident he would be appointed this year.

Père Jean applauded the choice of Paul Le Jeune as Superior. They had become close friends during the past two years and had talked on every opportunity about Canada and the missions. Le Jeune was forty-one, two years the senior of de Brébeuf. Born of Huguenot parents, he was converted to Catholicism as a young man and entered the Society of Jesus. He was tall and strong, brilliant in mind and firm in will, yet kindly and calm-mannered despite his naturally exuberant disposition. He and his comrades were informed by the Provincial that they must reach Havre de Grace within ten days, since the fleet was nearly ready to sail.

De Brébeuf undoubtedly superintended the hurried efforts to gather food, clothes and the other necessities for a winter in New France, and accompanied the five missioners to Havre de Grace. About one hundred agents and colonists assembled for embarkation. Emery and Guillaume de Caen, back in command, expeditiously loaded their ships with the baggage provided by the Company of One Hundred Associates. They sailed the first Sunday after Easter, April 18, 1632, with those on the ships and those on the quays shouting their farewells jubilantly because once more the fleur-de-lis would be raised over Fort St. Louis on the Rock of Quebec.

Père de Brébeuf was sent for the ensuing year to Eu, a seaport town some twenty miles beyond Dieppe. He was again entrusted with the office of treasurer in the small Jesuit college, and was engaged in preaching throughout this strongly Calvinistic section of western Normandy. He was buoyed up with enthusiasm, for the Père Provincial gave him assurance that he would be sent as a missioner to New France in the coming spring of 1633. He was informed that

Père Massé was also going back with him. Charles Lalemant, who had been transferred from Eu and appointed Rector of the College of Rouen, had been denied his wish, and expressed his feelings in a letter: "Why should I not be able to accompany P. Massé and P. de Brébeuf next year? *Aussi bien*, I do nothing here but languish, and three years have passed since I have been Rector, both at Eu and here at Rouen."

That autumn of 1632, Père Jean received a copy of Le Jeune's long letter about New France. It was a packet of about eighty pages, dated "from the midst of a forest more than 800 leagues in extent, at Kebec, this 28th of August, 1632". De Brébeuf, fascinated, read about the ocean voyage, about Tadoussac and the painted savages, the torture of three Iroquois captives, and then a paragraph about the Hurons. To convert them, asserted Le Jeune, "it is only necessary to know the language. If Père de Brébeuf had not been forced by the English to go back from there, they having taken possession of the French Fort, he would already have greatly advanced the glory of God in that country [of the Hurons]."

Brushing aside the tears of remembrance, de Brébeuf read Le Jeune's description of how, on July 6, Duplessis-Bochart and the de Caens took possession of Quebec. When the English were dislodged, Le Jeune wrote, "We again entered our little house. The only furniture we found were two wooden tables. The doors, windows, sashes were all broken and torn away, and everything was going to ruin." The Récollet convent was in even worse state. De Brébeuf recognized the truth of Le Jeune's description of the Montagnais under the influence of the brandy given them by the English, and by some of the French. "Since I have been here, I have seen only drunken savages. They are heard shouting and raving day and night. They fight and wound each other. The women get drunk and shriek like furies." Then, de Brébeuf recalled old Jacques Michel, who had been stricken so strangely, when he read: "I have learned here that the savages exhumed his [Michel's] body, and showed it every imaginable indignity, tore it to pieces and gave it to their dogs. Such are the wages of traitors."

De Brébeuf was pleased when he learned that "several savages ask us news of Père Lalemant and Père Massé and Père Brébeuf, whom they call quite well by their proper names, and inquire if they will return next year." And then, at the very end of the letter, tears must have welled up in his eyes. Le Jeune wrote: "I saw the Hurons arrive. There were more than fifty canoes of them; they made a very fine sight upon the river. They are large, well-made men. They are worthy of all compassion since they do not know the Author of the life they enjoy and have never heard of Him who gave His life and shed His blood for them." He added: "Louis, formerly Aman-tacha, came to see us and promised that he would come back next year, to return with Père Brébeuf to his [Huron] country." Greater yearning than ever seized Père Jean as he finished the absorbing *Relation* by Paul Le Jeune. The winter at Eu would be long, but then would come the break of spring, and in the summer, please God, he would again sail up the St. Lawrence to Quebec, and take canoe to begin a new winter among the Hurons.

Père de Brébeuf's duties as treasurer at the College of Eu were so light that he was free to leave for preaching and business trips to Dieppe and Rouen. Thus he was able to keep himself informed about the affairs of New France. The Company of One Hundred Associates, he gleaned, was financially weakened by the loss of two fleets, and it was wavering in its enthusiasm about the colony. To save the company, the directors organized a subsidiary corporation of merchants, bankers and lawyers that was granted the monopoly in furs and other exports for five years. This group, however, was pledged to carry out the articles of the company, whereby colonists would be attracted and supported, provisions and munitions would be liberally supplied, and subsidies be granted to the missions among the savages. De Brébeuf feared that this new trading corporation would become as grasping, miserly and unscrupulous as the other corporations, until he learned that the president of the One Hundred Associates, Jean de Lauzon, was the supreme executive by direct appointment of Cardinal Richelieu, and that Champlain was granted almost plenipotentiary powers as Governor of New France.

For Champlain, this appointment and the reorganization of the trading companies was one of the great victories of his life. He was then sixty-three years of age, with health unsteady. Since 1608, when he first raised the French flag over Quebec, he had crossed the ocean twenty-one times, and he confided to de Brébeuf that this could well be his final passage. He had finished his autobiography, he had drawn up his last will and testament, and he was bidding farewell, perhaps forever, to his thirty-two-year-old wife, Hélène Boullé. Happily, now, he was returning to the only place he loved, Quebec.

Jean de Brébeuf and Ennemond Massé, in early March, met in Dieppe, then becoming the packed and excited seaport preparing for the sailing of the Canada fleet. Three vessels were being heavily freighted with abundant supplies, and nearly two hundred agents and colonists, some with wives and children, were daily arriving, in high hopes of creating a new home on the shores of the St. Lawrence. De Brébeuf and Massé were given quarters on the 250-ton le Saint-Pierre, the flagship of Governor Champlain. They sailed from Dieppe on Wednesday of Holy Week, March 23, 1633.

After a month of tolerably favorable weather, they encountered the fog and rain of the Great Banks, and were tossed about in mountainous waves. On Ascension Thursday, May 5, they anchored before Daniel's Fort on Cape Breton Island. There they found Antoine Daniel and Ambroise Davost, who had passed a wretched winter and discovered few natives to convert. Massé ordered the two Jesuits to proceed to Quebec. In the Gulf of St. Lawrence, Champlain sighted two vessels as large as his own, undoubtedly English, poaching on the French trade. He raged and itched to attack them, but his prudence prevailed, remembering he had noncombatants aboard and that then his sole objective was Quebec.

All the way up the river, Champlain unfolded to de Brébeuf his exact mariner's familiarity with the shoreline, the tides, the wind, the distances. The good Saint-Pierre was far too slow for their impatience. Finally, on May 17, they anchored at Moulin Baude, and with the tide crept into the cove of Tadoussac. Champlain and de Brébeuf transferred to the smaller ship, le Saint-Jean, and pointed up the river. At nightfall on Trinity Sunday, May 22, they reached Cap de Tourments, but they dared not risk sailing in the darkness past the Isle d'Orléans.

The black night ebbed away before the filmiest gray of dawn. Captain de Nesle shouted his orders, and le Saint-Jean shook into motion before the light was more than a haze on the river. Passing by the Isle d'Orléans, and around Point Levis, they anchored in the roadstead of Quebec before the sun had touched the top of the Rock. Champlain barked an order, and a great cannon shattered the silence of the dead morning. Another cannon belched a white cloud and echoed back from the hills. A third salute burst with a deafening roar.

Jean de Brébeuf slipped down the ladder into the first canoe that reached the ship. At the strand he learned that Père de Noüe, having rushed over to Quebec after the cannon shots, was returning by the shore trail to give Père Le Jeune the news. De Brébeuf, in a Montagnais canoe, cut across the bay and up the loop of the St. Charles. He leaped out on the soft loam and ran up the embankment and across the field. No one was about. As he flung open the door, he heard the chant of the *Te Deum*. De Noüe had returned with the good news that the cannon shots were fired by a French ship. Père Jean joined in a new and triumphant *Te Deum*; Le Jeune recorded: "God knows that we received and embraced him with glad hearts."

For them at Notre Dame des Anges, it had been a morning of consternation. Knowing that English ships had been to Tadoussac and might be coming to attack Quebec, Duplessis-Bochart, at the public Mass the day before, had warned that all should immediately hurry to the Fort at the signal of two cannon shots. That morning, said Le Jeune, they were startled by the first cannon; at the second boom, they seized what they needed. A third cannon thundered, and de Noüe raced across to Quebec. Then, to their utter amazement, they had heard Père de Brébeuf himself pounding into the house.

They shortened their talk that morning in order to hurry over to the habitation. At noon, the ship's cannon thundered again. A shallop pushed out from the vessel and drew up at the landing place. Sieur de Champlain alighted in gleaming helmet, burnished breast plate, and dangling sword. Armored soldiers, with muskets and long pikes, formed into ranks. To the tapping of the drummers, they marched up the winding steep hill to the Fort. Standing at attention were Emery de Caen, Guillaume Duplessis-Bochart, the habitants and agents, the Jesuits, and mobs of bare-skinned, painted Montagnais.

An officer proclaimed the Commission, signed by King Louis XIII, dated March 1, 1633, creating Sieur Samuel de Champlain Lieutenant Viceroy and Governor of New France. He read another document signed by the Prince Cardinal de Richelieu appointing Sieur Guillaume Duplessis-Bochart Admiral of the Fleet and Administrator of the Company of One Hundred Associates in New France. Governor Champlain called upon Emery de Caen to surrender the keys of the Fort and the habitation to Duplessis-Bochart, whom he appointed the Acting Commandant until he, himself, took formal possession the following day.

Jean de Brébeuf, like a soul arrived in paradise, returned to the haven of the house that they had patched together some two hundred paces back from the little River St. Charles. Until he left for the Hurons, this would be his home under the patronage of Notre Dame des Anges.

Four: 1633

A few Hurons arrived about July 1, among them Louis Amantacha, whom the Récollets had sent to France in 1626. He sought out the Blackrobes, and confided to Echon that, though the Hurons wished to barter a great store of peltries for French goods, they were afraid to meet Champlain and the French. This past spring, he revealed, some Hurons had split the head of Étienne Brûlé and eaten his flesh. De Brébeuf was stricken with horror. He had lived with Brûlé for three years, and knew him to be one of the most vile and vicious of all the French agents. After turning traitor to Champlain in 1629, he had gone back to savagery among the Hurons and been killed in all his sins. Knowing the Huron code, de Brébeuf realized that Brûlé's crime must be heinous in the eyes of the Hurons if they boiled and ate his body.

De Brébeuf and Louis hurried over to Champlain, who immediately called a council of all the Hurons. He assured them that he would not demand the murderers of Brûlé, nor would he require presents of reparation. He explained that Brûlé had treacherously joined the English in 1629 and was no longer a Frenchman under his protection. Furthermore, he declared that he himself would have punished Brûlé severely if the man had come to Quebec. He loaded the Hurons with presents and, through them, invited their countrymen to come to the trade without any fear.

The next day, July 2, while visiting the Huron tents on the plateau, de Brébeuf was startled by loud shouts and people rushing to the edge of the Rock. A Frenchman, with his skull split in two, lay crumpled in a little stream. Champlain, aroused to a fever of anger, ordered a search for the assailant. If one Frenchman were killed by the natives, and if his murder went unavenged, no Frenchman anywhere would be safe. It happened that just then savages of various Algonquin nations were camping about Quebec. Champlain interrogated them, but neither he nor his men could find the slightest clue as to the identity of the murderer. Finally, an interpreter elicited the name of an Algonquin who belonged to the so-called Petite nation which lived along the Ottawa River.[3]

Champlain apprehended the Algonquin and locked him in the prison room of the Fort. The man did not deny the murder. He justified himself by stating that a sorcerer in his own country urged him to kill another certain Algonquin; not being able to accomplish this, he struck down the Frenchman in place of the Algonquin. The friends of the man testified that he was drunk, and hence, it was brandy that killed the Frenchman. According to their custom, they offered presents to dry the tears of Champlain and the French. Champlain, observing the French code, refused the presents and proclaimed that he would hold the murderer in the dungeon and might probably hang him. The Algonquins held council; some spoke in favor of raising the war hatchet against the French; others, more prudently, urged that they should bide their time and use other means to secure the release of their kinsman.

The French were warned not to leave their houses after nightfall, lest some of the savages commit another crime. During this tense period, the trusted La Nasse one evening pounded on the door and begged Père Paul to baptize a baby that was dying. Despite the prohibition, Le Jeune resolved to go with La Nasse. But de Brébeuf persuaded him to remain at home, since he was running a fever, and volunteered to take his place, with Père de Noüe as companion. They were guided by La Nasse along the dark paths to a cabin some two miles away, under the cliff of the Rock. The relatives of the baby refused to show it to the Blackrobes, lest they cast a spell over it and cause it to die. De Noüe, frightened by the baleful looks of the savages in the cabin, slipped out to bring the interpreter, Olivier Le Tardif, to protect de Brébeuf. Together, they persuaded the mother that her baby would be happy if it were baptized. She finally agreed if the father, who was drunk in another cabin, would also consent. He was awakened and sent back word: "Although I am drunk, I understand what you say. Tell the Blackrobes I know they will do my son no harm if they baptize him." Père Jean poured the waters and named the child Francis Xavier. They returned to Notre Dame des Anges about ten o'clock. Le Jeune said to de Brébeuf kindly: "Mon père, are you not very happy that you ended the day so well?" "Helas!" exclaimed de Brébeuf. "For this one single occasion I would travel all the way from France, I would cross the great ocean to win one little soul for Our Lord."

Echon waited for the Hurons. Would they believe Champlain's assurance? Would they be disturbed by Champlain's action in imprisoning the Algonquin murderer? In mid-July, a flotilla of eight Huron canoes slid quietly into Quebec. They had met Amantacha, who gave them Champlain's pledges. They were glad to welcome Echon, but they were subdued and silent. A week later came a band of twelve more canoes. They greeted Echon cordially but spoke cautiously. When de Brébeuf asked them for passage back in their canoes for himself and two other Blackrobes, Antoine Daniel and Ambroise Davost, they were evasive, declaring they must await the arrival of their great chiefs who were detained by the Island Algonquins along the Ottawa River.

At last, on July 27, Louis Amantacha came, announcing that the main body of the Hurons would arrive in a day or two. The Algonquins of the Island and the people of the Petite nation had warned them that Champlain was angry about the murder of Brûlé and that he would seize some of them and kill them. They described how Champlain had imprisoned one of their kinsmen for killing a Frenchman. Some of the Hurons, Amantacha reported, lacked courage and went home, while others lost their peltries gambling with the Algonquins. The great number of those who dared to come to Quebec, said Amantacha, gave extraordinary presents to the Island Algonquins for permission to pass down their river.

The next afternoon a magnificent echelon of canoes floated out from behind Point Diamond. One hundred and forty of them spread out in orderly parade, six or seven hundred paddlers, chanting and gesturing and pounding their blades on their gunwales. Like a flock of birds, the canoes deployed into the shore, and in a moment, the savages leaped out on the strand, their faces masked in varicolored paint, their bodies naked save for their wampum decorations and their leather pendants, their hair stiffly standing up in tufts and ruffles. They were frightening and ferocious as they swung into their ceremonial dance, one paddling after the other in a serpentine curve.

The Hurons were still apprehensive lest Champlain take vengeance on them for the murder of Brûlé. However, they made great show of affection for Echon, since to know him among the French was much in their favor. They expressed surprise that he could still talk to them in their own language. Echon questioned them about the death of Brûlé. No one knew anything about who killed him or why. But, de Brébeuf learned, after his death they had abandoned the village of Toanché, where he was killed, and the families divided themselves in new hamlets. Such dissension was a further proof that Brûlé's death was premeditated and was an act of vengeance for some crime of sorcery or treachery against the nation.

On July 29, the Hurons held council with the French on the plaza opposite Fort St. Louis. After they had all sat in long, meditative silence, a Huron orator, in tremolo council tones, enumerated the names of the chiefs and elders of each village and nation who were present. This proved that they had authority from the Ouendat people. A chief, rising with dignity, addressed Champlain. He declared that the Hurons were cold during his absence. Now they were warm before his fires. They had brought fuel to keep the fires burning. He hung three packages of beavers on the post. All grunted "*Haau! Haau! Haau!*" in approval. The Hurons wanted peace with the French, he said, and offered the bonds that made all brothers. He hung more beaver packages. Another orator strode forward. "When the French left," he related, "the earth was no longer the earth, the river no longer the river, the sky no longer the sky. Now that Champlain and the French are back, the earth is the earth, the river is the river, the sky is once more the sky." Another orator spoke: "We of my nation are timid. We are easily frightened. But we are courageous when Champlain and the French are our allies."

Champlain accepted their presents, and assured them that he loved the Ouendat people. He warned them against other nations who tried to prevent them from coming to visit the French. As a mark of his love and of his desire that the Ouendats and French would be one people, he had resolved to send Echon and two other Blackrobes to live with them. Pointing to de Brébeuf and the other two, he declared: "Behold, these are our teachers. We love them more than we love our children, more than we love ourselves. . . . It is not hunger or need that brings them to this country. They do not seek after your possessions or your furs. They have left their relatives, their friends, their country in order to tell you things about which you do not know, and especially, to teach your children things that are wonderful and necessary. If you love the French as you say you do, then love these Blackrobe fathers. Honor them and listen to them when they teach you the way to heaven. Here is Amantacha, a youth of your nation. He has been in France. He will tell you that I speak the truth."

Young men did not speak in Huron councils. However, Amantacha was listened to because Champlain had asked his testimony. He confirmed Champlain's praise of the Blackrobe fathers, but complained: "The Blackrobes are too few. They are only three for so many thousands of Ouendats." Echon, addressing the Hurons in their language, professed that he and his brothers loved the Ouendats, that he was happy to go again to be warmed at the fires of the Bear nation, which had adopted him, that he was bringing two brothers with him, and when they learned the language, they would live in other villages and among the other nations. He assured them: "We will teach you how to be happy forever."

De Brébeuf was projecting the very important question of which Hurons would take the missioners and where they would live. After the council, a chief of the abandoned Toanché took Echon aside. "Open your heart to us. Conceal nothing. Where do you wish to live when you come to our country?" He expressed the wish to return to the people he knew at Toanché. "Do you wish to live in our longhouses or in your own house, apart from us?" "I wish to have a French house apart," he answered.

"That is well," agreed the chief. "All of us will build our houses around your house. We broke up our village after the death of the Frenchman. We separated; everyone went away, some here, some there. When you choose the place, we will all return to be with you. You will protect us. Without you, we do not know what to do."

Very secretly, later, the chief of Quieuindohan, the capital town of the Bear nation, approached Echon. Recalling the fact that the

Grayrobes had once lived in his town, he urged Echon: "Come with me. You will be safe with my people. No one will steal from you. I hold the whole country on my shoulders. I will protect you. You will want for nothing. Our country is the best among the Ouendats. We all love you."

When Echon paused before answering, the chief continued: "I see clearly that you have fear of offending those of the village where you formerly lived, and who wish to have you among them. You are master of your own actions. Tell them that you wish to come with us. They will have nothing more to say about it." Such rivalry was as unexpected as it was mystifying. Champlain and Le Jeune advised de Brébeuf to accept the offer of the great chief of the Bear nation and settle at Quieuindohan.

At the final council, Champlain announced that he was entrusting three Blackrobes and three young Frenchmen to the care and protection of the great chief of Quieuindohan, since he desired the French to live together in that village. All the chiefs, except those of the Toanché area, applauded. Champlain offered his presents in return for theirs, to bind the Ouendats and French into one nation. Then arose a chief, who indicated that he was troubled and sad. A young man of a nation allied to the Hurons had foolishly struck down a Frenchman; the relatives had offered presents, but the French had refused these amends. The relatives were much grieved that the young man was kept locked in a room. He and the Ouendats were adding other presents to those of their Algonquin brothers, to bring about the release of the foolish young man.

The French had feared this crisis. Champlain believed that he could not condone the murder of a Frenchman through the native code of gift-giving. He explained that the French did not accept presents when one of them was struck down, but required that the murderer be punished and even put to death. The Hurons were offended that Champlain rejected their appeal. However, the council concluded with expressions of universal good will.

After much troublesome negotiations, de Brébeuf won the definite promise of some canoe leaders to adopt him, Daniel, Davost and three other Frenchmen for the journey. On Thursday afternoon, he, Daniel and Davost carried their bundles of clothes and bags of supplies to the cabins of their Huron hosts. That night, they proposed to sleep in the warehouse nearby so that they might be ready to join the Hurons who were leaving at daybreak the next morning, August 5. Le Jeune and de Noüe joined them in the warehouse so as to be able to bid them farewell.

About eleven o'clock, de Brébeuf was awakened by a strident crier in the Huron camp nearby. An Algonquin, speaking Huron, was proclaiming: "Be on your guard! Be warned not to take any Frenchmen in your canoes! The relatives of the man held prisoner by the French are watching along the rivers. They have resolved to kill any Frenchmen that try to pass along their rivers! Do not take any Frenchmen in your canoes!"

De Brébeuf waited outside the warehouse, while Le Jeune and de Noüe clambered up the hill to Champlain. He summoned the interpreter, Olivier Le Tardif, and instructed him to go immediately to announce to the Hurons that he wished to hold council with them before they left. Le Tardif found the Huron chiefs seated about the fire in council with the Algonquin chiefs. He delivered Champlain's message. All listened in silence, but no one answered. De Brébeuf kept vigil near the Huron camp, for he feared the Hurons might reject Champlain's invitation to hold council and might slip away during the night. About the time of aurora, he heard a Huron proclaiming: "Let no one leave today! Let the young men keep the peace! Let those who have not finished their trading, sell their furs and tobacco! Let no one go off in his canoe today."

About eight in the morning, the council was held between the French, the Hurons and the several Algonquin nations. Champlain inquired why the Algonquins had advised the Hurons against taking any Frenchmen in their canoes. An Algonquin chief very suavely responded: "The whole country is in a state of alarm. The relatives of the prisoner are waiting along the banks of the rivers. They are determined to kill any paleface Frenchmen who pass through their country. That would be hurtful to all. Some young men might raise the war hatchet." Turning to Champlain he cried out: "I have acted as a friend. I wished to warn publicly the Hurons and the French of the wicked designs of the kinsmen of the prisoner." In a smooth tone, he concluded: "If the prisoner be released by the French, the troubles will be ended. The rivers and the whole country will be free. All will be at peace."

Champlain asked the Hurons if they would still take the Blackrobes with them. A chief adroitly answered: "The river does not
belong to us, but to the Algonquins. One must have regard for their
rights and wishes, if one tries to pass through their country safely.
As for us, we would wish to take the French with us." Another
Huron addressed the Algonquins: "Open your ears and listen. When
you return to your councils, say to your countrymen that we have
pleaded in behalf of the prisoner. Champlain has given good reasons why he will not set free your countryman. The French are our
friends and your friends. If the decision rested with us, we would
embark the Frenchmen in our canoes."

Champlain decided that soft words would not answer the menace
of the Algonquins nor the wavering of the Hurons. He again quoted
the French code about punishing a murderer, and flatly declared
he would not release the prisoner. He threatened the Algonquins
with more severe punishment if any one of them injured a Frenchman. If necessary, he would wage war against them. An Algonquin
responded soothingly: "My people do not seek war. We desire peace.
But we have no power to hold back the arms of our young men. To
preserve the peace, we have warned you in advance. We give you
peaceful advice: 'Let the French wait till next summer.' By then, our
young braves will have taken the warpath against the Iroquois. The
river will be free."

By pre-arrangement with Champlain, Le Jeune addressed the
council. Seeking to win the good will of the Algonquins and the
Hurons for the Blackrobes, he asked Sieur de Champlain to pardon the murderer and to release him to his kinsmen. Champlain
asserted that he must close his ear even to the words of the Blackrobes whom he loved. What answer could he make to the great
King of the French across the ocean, who ordered that a murderer
be punished and executed? Le Jeune then requested Champlain not
to kill the prisoner until he should receive an answer from the King
of France next summer. Champlain assented and the savages grunted
their approval.

Turning to the Hurons, Le Jeune told them how deeply Echon
and the Blackrobes loved them. Addressing the Algonquins, he assured them that the Blackrobes had always been their friends, and asked
their chief: "If the relatives of the prisoner knew that we Blackrobes

were pleading for the life of their kinsmen, would they not allow the Blackrobes to pass through their country on their way to the Huron land?" The Algonquin responded dourly: "What answer do you wish me to give? All I know is that the relatives and nation of this prisoner are furious. If he is not set free, there is no safety and security. His kinsmen will spare no one."

The interpreter, Le Tardif, swelling with anger, hurled back the challenge: "If they act like devils, we shall also be devils." Champlain rose in choler, and thundered defiance at the Algonquins: "Guard yourselves well! If you are seen with arms, I will tell my men to fire upon you and kill you. Some of you have threatened me, and have had evil intentions on me because I have gone about alone. Hereafter, I shall not go about like a child, but I shall be armed like a soldier." To the Hurons, their faces like carved stone, he spoke gently: "I am a friend of all. You are my friends. I love you. I have risked my life for you, I will risk it again. I will protect you. But I am the enemy of those who do evil."

At this deadlock, the French, Hurons and Algonquins consulted among themselves. More than ever, Champlain and his counselors rejected any compromise about the murderer. It was even thought that it might be well to execute him. To release him would be a sign of French weakness and cowardice, and the savages would kill more Frenchmen, on any whim. All realized that if the upper Algonquins along the Ottawa might retaliate on the French and Blackrobes passing through their country, there would be war with all the Algonquins. Champlain concluded that the risk was too great, and that de Brébeuf, Daniel and Davost must not attempt to pass through the Algonquin territory. In vain did de Brébeuf protest that he was not afraid of being killed. Père Le Jeune finally persuaded him, and later attested: "Père de Brébeuf saw that it would be foolhardy to undertake the journey—but not through fear of death, because I never saw them more resolute—both he and his two companions, Père Daniel and Père Davost, than when they were told they might lose their lives on the road which they were about to take for the glory of God."

When the council convened and after Champlain announced the decision about the Blackrobes, Echon addressed the Hurons: "You are our brothers. We wish to go to your country, to live and die with you. Since the river is closed, we shall wait for the next year when all will be peaceable. It is you who will bear the greater loss. Now I am beginning to talk to you without an interpreter. I wish to teach you the way to heaven, and to reveal to you the great riches of the future life. This misfortune deprives you of all these blessings."

The Hurons responded that they, also, were very sorry. But, said they, "a year would very soon pass away." After the council, de Brébeuf went to the Huron cabins to collect the bundles and bags. They gathered about Echon sadly and again gave voice to their regrets. The chief of Quieuindohan offered Echon and the Black-robes passage in his canoes, despite the Algonquins. But Echon reluctantly had to refuse.

That night Louis Amantacha slept in the Jesuit house, and before dawn attended Mass and received Communion. At daybreak, on Saturday, he, de Brébeuf and the others hurried over to the camp. The Hurons were swarming everywhere, dismantling their bark cabins, carrying their French goods to the shore, and packing them in the canoes. De Brébeuf watched them gloomily. Suddenly, as if by magic, the seven hundred men were in the canoes, and the 140 canoes skimmed away in the hazy river. Jean de Brébeuf, standing at the river edge, lifted his hand over them in a final blessing. For him the dawn of this August day was hollow.

CHAPTER V

The Far Journey to Huronia

One: 1633–1634

A YEAR WOULD VERY SOON PASS AWAY, the Hurons had said. For de Brébeuf, this year at Quebec would seem as long as the past three years at Rouen and Eu. He had this consolation, however, that he was back in New France and, God willing, that he would go to the Hurons next year. He had proved to himself and to them that he could speak their language. His task for the coming year was that of teaching Daniel and Davost so thoroughly that they, too, would talk in Huron before they left Quebec with him next year.

With de Brébeuf, Le Jeune analyzed the debacle of the attempt to reach the Huron country. Two reasons "stronger than two great locks seem to have closed the door to the Hurons for us". The first reason was the obstacle placed by the Algonquin nations occupying the Ottawa River. They wanted a monopoly of the trade with the French and wished to exclude the Hurons. Their difficulty in enforcing a blockade or demanding payments was increased when the Hurons carried French passengers in their canoes. The second reason alleged by Le Jeune was the fear of the Hurons. "They understand that the French will not accept presents in condonation for the murder of a Frenchman. They fear that their young men may commit some reckless deed. In that case, they would have to give up, alive or dead, anyone who might commit the murder, or else would have to break friendly relations with the French. This makes them nervous in having Frenchmen living among them."

Quebec was quiet after the Hurons left. It settled down into utter solitude a week later when the sailors and traders sailed down to join

the fleet at Tadoussac. Not many more than two hundred Frenchmen were left for the winter. Champlain kept his men on the alert,
for many of the upper Algonquins still lingered about and were smoldering with anger because the prisoner was kept locked up in the
Fort. Such punishment, in their minds, was more insulting than that
of execution.

At Notre Dame des Anges, the seven Jesuits and their five or six
workmen lived in crowded quarters. There were only four small bed-
rooms above the kitchen, which also served as dining room, common room and sleeping room for the lay helpers. The chapel was so
tiny that they could scarcely fit into it. That summer, they all labored
to enlarge the house and to build a barn. They were engaged, too, in
clearing more land for their vegetable gardens, and in chopping down
some twelve hundred saplings for a stockade they proposed to erect
around their grounds as a protection from prowling savages.

Père Jean was seeking something more than the peace, comfort
and security he would enjoy living among the French. He aspired
to the dangerous life in the service of God, such as he would experience among the Huron savages. When they refused to take him to
their barbarous country, apparently he felt frustrated. The following
notation is recorded of him: "About the year 1634, in the memoirs
that he wrote, making the review of his conscience from month to
month—here follows what he says of himself: 'I feel in me a great
desire to die, in order to enjoy God; I feel a great aversion for all
created things, which it will be necessary for me to leave at death. It
is in God alone that my heart rests; and outside of Him, all is naught
to me except for Him.'"

In September, flocks of Montagnais and other Algonquins set up
their cabins along the bay and the river. They awaited the eels that
would be swarming down all the waterways into the St. Lawrence.
They were in festive mood, for now they would eat till their bellies
were full and have smoked eels to carry off on their winter journeys.
De Brébeuf mingled with them both to learn their language the better and to teach them the truths of salvation. He progressed better in
learning the language than in teaching them the truth.

"Your God has not come to our country," one of them remarked.
"That is why we do not believe in him. Make me see the One-who-
made-all and I will believe in him." De Brébeuf explained that we

have eyes of the body and eyes of the soul. The Montagnais had an answer: "I see with the eyes of my body. I do not see with the eyes of the soul except when I am asleep. But you tell us that we must not believe in the dreams we see with the eyes of the soul."

In October, the nomads were wandering off to the forests. Père Le Jeune, exasperated by the difficulty of learning Algonquin, decided to follow the example of de Brébeuf and spend the winter with some families. He persuaded Peter Pastedechouan to form a party. Though educated in France by the Récollets, he had degenerated and became as treacherous and immoral as any of the savages. Peter and his brother Mestigoit, a man as powerful as he was amiable, agreed to take Le Jeune with them. They left on October 18 under the leadership of Mestigoit, who assured de Brébeuf and Champlain that he would protect the Blackrobe. "If he dies," swore Mestigoit, "I shall die with him and you will never see me in this land again."

Before leaving, Père Le Jeune appointed Père de Brébeuf the Acting Superior of Notre Dame des Anges. The little community was deeply spiritual and exact in the religious observances, and labored incessantly in the tasks of building the home and clearing the ground. De Brébeuf was an inspiration to them by his prudence and zeal and by his fervid love of God. He had no need to urge Daniel and Davost to study Huron, for they were avidly eager to learn. Through the winter, there was peace and union under God in the Jesuit house on the St. Charles.[1]

Quite frequently, de Brébeuf visited Champlain and the other French living in the habitation and on the heights. His friendship with Champlain deepened as they talked of their visions of a greater New France and a stronger outpost among the Hurons. Both were convinced that the Hurons could be easily converted to God, and that through their conversion not only the Algonquins but the Neutrals and Petuns and other western nations could be brought to baptism and the Faith.

In January, de Brébeuf learned that a Montagnais named Sasousmat was very sick. He was the younger brother of Peter and Mestigoit with whom Le Jeune was wintering. The man was in a death coma, and Père Jean related, "We made a resolution, the other priests and I, to offer to God the Sacrifice of the Mass the next day in honor of the glorious Saint Joseph, patron of New France, for the salvation and conversion of this poor savage." Early the next morning, at Mass time, Sasousmat became conscious. He continued to live and as often as Père Jean visited him begged to be instructed so that he could be baptized. On January 26, he fell into a stupor, and de Brébeuf, fearing that he would die, conferred the Sacrament on him and gave him the name of Francis Xavier. Sasousmat regained consciousness and was overjoyed when he learned he had been made a Christian. He lingered for two days praying continually, and he died on January 28.

That same evening, de Nouë and some workmen chatting in the common room were startled by a great light flashing on the frosted windows. They leaped up in surprise; the light flashed a second time, and then a third time; they rushed outside, for they thought there was a fire in the nearby building. Outdoors, all was quiet, cold and dark. They were mystified and believed, as de Brébeuf wrote, "that God was declaring through this phenomenon the light that was being enjoyed by the soul that had just left us". The relatives wished to carry the body of Sasousmat off to the woods and there bury it with their own ceremonies. De Brébeuf, however, was determined to give Francis Xavier a Christian burial. After a Requiem Mass for him in their chapel, they buried him with all solemnity in the consecrated plot near the Jesuit residence. All the Montagnais camping about Quebec gathered for the funeral and were deeply impressed by the French obsequies. Sasousmat was the first adult Montagnais to become a Christian since the Jesuits returned to Canada.

On Shrove Tuesday, February 28, about daybreak, when Père de Brébeuf was preparing to say Mass, there sounded a pounding on the door. They opened it to Sieur de Champlain, who wished to assist at Mass. He had walked the two miles across the frozen trails from the Fort, bareheaded and barefooted, "in reparation for the licentiousness which is carried on in other lands during the carnival time", he confided to de Brébeuf.

Their old friend Manitougache, whom they called La Nasse, was brought to the Jesuit house by his wife and daughter. He was sick and wanted to be treated as was Sasousmat. De Brébeuf brought him in when he found that the man was apparently near death. They began a novena of prayers to Saint Joseph for his conversion. Manitougache had often listened to the teachings of de Brébeuf and the others, but never expressed any desire for baptism. As the novena advanced, he seemed to have a spiritual quickening. After a month of instructions, Père de Brébeuf believed that Manitougache was ready for baptism. He performed the ceremony on April 3 and gave him the name of Joseph. Manitougache was thus the second Montagnais adult to become of his own free will a Christian. He lingered on, though desperately ill. One thing he desired before he died, to see his old friend Père Le Jeune.

On April 9, Palm Sunday morning, about three o'clock, de Brébeuf was wakened by resounding thumps on the door and by shouts of Le Jeune. They opened to him, Peter and Mestigoit, all three caked with ice from cap to boots and shaking with the cold. De Brébeuf and the others warmed them, fed them, and made them sleep. Later, Le Jeune told them the harrowing story. Since Wednesday, he and his two Montagnais had been struggling to cross the ice-packed St. Lawrence. Saturday evening they attempted to land in St. Charles Bay, but all the shore was piled high with slabs of ice. So they searched for a landing place near the point of Quebec.

Mestigoit guided the canoe with his superhuman strength amid waves great enough to swallow a ship, between blocks of ice that threatened to crush them, against a furious northeast wind. Finally, he leaped upon a mound of ice so high, declared Le Jeune, that one could scarcely touch the top. Then Mestigoit lowered his foot till Le Jeune could grasp it. Holding tight, Le Jeune was able to climb up the slippery ice pack. Standing there in the cold night, continued Le Jeune, "we looked at each other. Mestigoit took a deep, long breath and said: 'My friend, a little bit more and we were dead men.'"

For weeks, Père Le Jeune lay in a state of complete exhaustion. Since the end of January he felt so sick that he expected to die in the mountains, he told de Brébeuf, who could well understand, having gone through the same experiences. In their conversation, de Brébeuf mentioned the strange lights on the night of Sasousmat's death. Startled, Le Jeune consulted the diary he had kept. They compared the date, January 28, and the time. Le Jeune calculated he was about 120 miles from Quebec. His guide, Mestigoit, the brother of Sasousmat, saw the light burst and fade three times. He was horrified and called the others to witness. It was not lightning, for it lingered; besides it was too cold for lightning. "It is a bad omen," averred Mestigoit. "It is a sign of death."

On Easter Saturday, Joseph Manitougache, the second adult Christian, died piously in the Jesuit residence. He had resisted the pleas of his family and the threats of the sorcerer. They buried him with Mass and solemn ceremonials in the little plot next to Sasousmat. The Montagnais, who gathered in great numbers, were so impressed that many begged for baptism, which would insure them a like Christian burial.

In June, the ships from France arrived, bringing with them a heartening number of colonists and six more Jesuits, among them Père Charles Lalemant. Champlain could well be satisfied that Cardinal Richelieu and the Company of One Hundred Associates were grandly fulfilling their promises to people New France with distinguished families, with sturdy artisans and farmers, and that they were liberally supplying all that was needed for the upbuilding of a strong colony. Champlain was most gratified that there arrived that summer Sieur la Violette and a company of men commissioned to build a French stronghold and a permanent habitation at Three Rivers.

During June, Jean de Brébeuf and his fellow missioners, Daniel and Davost, waited impatiently for the time when the Hurons would be arriving. Four workmen, Baron, Petit-Pré, Le Coq and Dominique, were hired to accompany them and to assist them in their labors among the Hurons. Two lads, Pierre and Martin, were added to the party so that they might learn the language and later serve as interpreters. Meanwhile, la Violette and his men were busy assembling their provisions, tools and munitions for the erection of the fort and cabins at Three Rivers. The Jesuits and their workmen, la Violette and his company, bade their farewells to Quebec toward the end of the month and proceeded upriver on their lumbering, heavily laden barques.

On July 4, they drew into the cove near the mouth of the Metaberoutin River. La Violette and de Brébeuf, with their people following, marched up the hill to the top of the mound. Père de Brébeuf blessed the plot in the name of God, and la Violette planted on it the white flag of France, while his men fired the salute. Laying aside their firearms, they took up their axes and hacked at the primeval trees that crowned the level hilltop on which would be built the town of Three Rivers.

Two: 1634

That same evening, July 4, a few Huron canoes slipped quietly into Three Rivers. The paddlers were close-mouthed and taciturn. They answered nothing to de Brébeuf's question as to whether other canoes were coming. Four days later, eleven more canoes arrived. De Brébeuf was determined to force passage, if any way could be found. To the assembled Hurons, he proposed that they take into their canoes himself, the two Blackrobes and the four Frenchmen. For this purpose, he offered fine presents of good will. The Hurons were evasive and reluctant to accept the gifts, though a few promised, more or less, that they might take a few Frenchmen up to their country.

When the Algonquins from the Upper Ottawa heard this, they gathered late at night in a secret council with the Hurons. In the morning, the Hurons called Echon. With soft words, they returned his gifts, and expressed regret that they could take no Frenchmen with them. They were too few, they alleged, and the waters were too dangerous. De Brébeuf argued, pleaded and scolded them for violating their promises, but they remained obdurate. Later he learned the reason. The Nipissing chief, called La Perdrix by the French, had warned the Hurons that the Blackrobes were demons bringing disease and death. Furthermore, he said the Algonquins would make it difficult along the river, if Hurons carried any French in their canoes.

After the joint refusal of the Hurons, a chief of the Cord nation whispered to Echon: "Arrange for me to trade my tobacco for beads. If my canoe is thus unloaded, I can take a Frenchman." De Brébeuf, though suspicious, agreed to help him make a good sale if he would take five Frenchmen in his five canoes. The chief bartered; he could arrange for three. De Brébeuf firmly said five. Though the conversation ended there, de Brébeuf thought it was a good sign.

That same morning, a swift shallop carrying Duplessis-Bochart, director of the trade, drove into Three Rivers. When he heard how the Algonquins were terrifying the Hurons, he sent criers through the cabins and woods calling the Algonquins and Hurons to a council. Duplessis-Bochart, after some words of love and amity for his brothers, the Hurons and the Algonquins, said he was troubled. Last year the Hurons had promised to take Echon and the Blackrobes with them. This year they refused. He, somehow, had heard that La Perdrix had overturned the minds of the Hurons.

With poise and suavity, La Perdrix swore that he loved the French and the Blackrobes so much that he was fearful for the Frenchmen making the journey to the Hurons. The road was not yet leveled, the rapids were very violent, the young men could not be controlled. Duplessis-Bochart answered his reasons. La Perdrix then replied that he feared the French would not be safe in the Huron country, even though they reached there. Duplessis-Bochart blurted out violently that this was no concern of the Algonquins. If a Frenchman died among the Hurons, that was a question between the French and the Hurons, not the Algonquins. La Perdrix professed complete agreement. He would send word to the chiefs and braves along the river to permit the Blackrobes and other French to pass through.

The Hurons held council among themselves. They knew La Perdrix was speaking treacherously. They noted how cleverly he had drawn Duplessis-Bochart into his trap about the murder of a Frenchman in the Huron country. They decided not to take the risk. Their spokesman answered that, while the Hurons were eager to have their French brothers living with them, their canoes this year were very small, and the French had many bundles; they were only a few men, and the French were very many; moreover, many of their canoemen were sick. De Brébeuf and Duplessis-Bochart promised that the French would paddle, and would carry their own baggage over the portages, but the Hurons refused by remaining silent.

De Brébeuf was losing hope. He wrote to Le Jeune: "Out of respect for one another, they agreed not to embark any Frenchmen. No arguments, for the time being, move them. And so, our enterprise seems again to be cut off with a stroke." But he still plotted to persuade the Hurons. His strategy, now, was to break the council solidarity. He told Duplessis-Bochart of the offer of the chief of the Cord nation; in the barter that day, the agents gave preferred treatment to the Cord Hurons. Some men of the easternmost Rock nation became suspicious that the Cords had made a secret agreement with the French. That evening, the chief of the Rock nation happened to tell Echon that his six canoes would be leaving the next morning, and he implied that he might find place for some Frenchmen. After much diplomatic indirections of talk, he assured Echon he would carry one Frenchman in each of his six canoes if Echon would guarantee presents of French goods. Straightway, Echon concluded his deal with the Rock Hurons. Six of his people were thus provided for. Discreetly, he sought out the chief of the Cords and accepted his proposition of taking three Frenchmen.

Lest they again change their minds, de Brébeuf told his people to carry their bags and bundles to the Huron cabins along the shore. He instructed Daniel, Davost, Petit-Pré, Baron, Dominique, Le Coq, young Pierre and little Martin as to which canoes they were to attach themselves. That evening, Duplessis-Bochart gave a large feast of three kettles to the Hurons. He promised them rich gifts in the morning before they left, for the purpose of showing his gratitude for taking the French and the Blackrobes. Even at this apparently favorable solution, de Brébeuf still felt uneasy. Some of the Hurons were undoubtedly infected with the strange sickness of fever, skin rashes, watering eyes and loose bowels that raged among the St. Lawrence Algonquins.

With the first light of Friday morning, July 7, Père Jean and his people gathered at the cove. Duplessis-Bochart, Couillard and other French agents were also there to supervise the embarkation. Strangely, the Hurons delayed their appearance and, when they did come, some announced that they would not leave that day and others decided that they were too sick to take any Frenchmen with them. Then they changed their minds, and said they would all go and would take the French. The leaders of the three canoes carrying Père Daniel, Baron and Petit-Pré decided on leaving immediately. De Brébeuf and Duplessis-Bochart begged them to tarry a bit until the other canoes were ready. Some other parties wanted to slip away without any Frenchmen, complaining about their sickness and their inability to load so much baggage into their little boats. De Brébeuf, Duplessis-Bochart, Couillard went from group to group, trying to hold them to their pledges, while the Hurons wavered in their plans and shifted their answers. Everybody, French and Hurons alike, became totally confused.

The Hurons asked for more gifts, and Duplessis-Bochart satisfied their demands. They declared they would accept only the French who could paddle and who carried muskets. The leader of Echon's canoe said his men were sick and had decided not to go off. Those carrying Daniel, Baron and Petit-Pré were intent on leaving at once, without the Frenchmen. The wrangling grew louder and the disorder more bewildering. De Brébeuf feared that all the Hurons would suddenly leap into their canoes and desert him and the French. Duplessis-Bochart bargained with them and increased the amount of his gifts. Some accepted the presents, some rejected them, and then reversed their decisions. De Brébeuf by this time was reduced to utter despair. He turned away from the hubbub and the turmoil, and lifted his eyes and his voice to heaven. Rapidly, piteously, he prayed to Saint Joseph as the patron of New France and the Huron Mission and pronounced a vow to offer Mass twenty times in honor of Saint Joseph as soon as he reached the Huron country.

As he walked back toward the canoes, the clamor seemed to have quieted. Duplessis-Bochart had finally persuaded the Hurons to take Daniel, Baron and Petit-Pré. Since de Brébeuf's men had definitely postponed their departure, Duplessis-Bochart suggested that Echon be given Petit-Pré's place. They refused, declaring Echon was too big for their small canoe and wished to bring too much baggage. Echon assured them that he would paddle and portage, and that he would carry only a few bundles. When Duplessis-Bochart added more gifts, Petit-Pré slipped out of the canoe and de Brébeuf quickly climbed into it. The question of his baggage now arose, and remembering his vow of Masses, he chose to carry the chapel box with him. They objected, saying that because it was so large and heavy it would punch holes in the canoe. They were persuaded by additional gifts to ship the box. As a final offering, Duplessis-Bochart presented a blanket to each man in Echon's canoe. Those in Daniel's canoe also demanded blankets for themselves. The three canoes slid out into the river, amid hurried shouts of farewells and a volley of musketry.

Despite the presents, the Hurons were in ill humor. In their fretfulness, de Brébeuf feared they might reconsider the wisdom of taking him. They might return him to Three Rivers, or they might even put him ashore at some point where another canoe could pick him up. The day passed without any unpleasant incident and, toward evening, they were well up Lake St. Peter. De Brébeuf, Daniel and Baron helped to build the fire and to prepare the supper of corn meal. Despite the hordes of insects, sleep was a balm.

The next morning, the Hurons ordered Echon, Antwen, as they called Daniel, and Baron to take paddles. The Hurons were pleased, but the three Frenchmen ached that night. After a few days, the Hurons were not so cranky. Their only irritation was the large box of chapel goods which, they were afraid, might capsize the canoe or make it unwieldy in the rough water. They tried to force Echon to cache it, and let one of the larger canoes in the rear pick it up. But this he refused to do.

De Brébeuf had promised to write Le Jeune a narrative of their experiences. This he could do only early in the morning or in the evening after a long pull. Concerning the departure from Three Rivers he stated: "Never have I seen an embarkation about which there was so much nonsense and so much opposition due to the strategies, I believe, of the common enemy of man's salvation. It was only by a stroke from heaven that we have been taken, and in particular, through the power of the glorious Saint Joseph, to whom God inspired me, in my despair of all solutions, to promise twenty Masses in his honor. I beg your Reverence to thank Sieur du Plessis in the warmest fashion, for it is to him, after God, that we are indebted in the largest degree for our embarkation." He added his regrets that poor Père Davost was left behind, and added a hope that he and the other Frenchmen had found canoes.

When he found an opportunity, he continued his epistle: "We are going by short stages. We are quite well ourselves, but our savages are all sick. We paddle all the time and do it the more since our men are ill. For God, and for the souls redeemed by the blood of the Son of God, what ought one not to do? All our savages are well pleased with us, and glad they embarked us rather than the others. They speak most highly of us to those whom they meet. May your Reverence pardon this writing, the order and all. We start so early in the morning and lie down so late, that we hardly have time enough to devote to our prayers. As a matter of fact, I have been obliged to finish this by the light of the fire." He signed the letter "at the Long Sault, some eighty leagues beyond Quebec", and gave it to some Hurons bound for Three Rivers.

They approached the country of the Island Algonquins with some trepidation, for they remembered the threats against the French last year and this. But the Island people were magnanimously hospitable. The chief begged Echon to remain with him and to teach his people the great truths of the French. The Hurons, he said confidentially, were liars and evil-minded men; they might split his skull and devour him, as they did Brûlé; they had almost abandoned him during the journey, and they might yet leave him in a deserted place along the route; his people, on the contrary, would treat Echon well and would protect him. De Brébeuf, aware of the cunning behind these fair words, replied that Champlain loved the Island Algonquins and that next year the Blackrobes would accept their invitation to stay with them. This year, Champlain ordered him and his brothers to live with the Hurons. If he were killed, Champlain would make inquiries among the Hurons.

Echon's Hurons were uneasy, and remained but one night with the Island Algonquins. They looked closely at Echon when he took his place in the canoe, for they sensed the meaning of the private conversations. Echon was free to live with the Algonquins, as far as they were concerned; but if he remained, they would brand him as a traitor to the Hurons. They were happy that he continued with them on their journey.

For more than three weeks, they had steadily paddled and portaged in the gorge of the Ottawa. Finally, they came to the Lake of the Nipissings, again with anxiety, because of the threats of vengeance expressed by La Perdrix at Three Rivers. But the Nipissings were so friendly that the exhausted Hurons rested a full day with them. The sickness, de Brébeuf saw, had reached these northern Algonquins, but had not yet ravaged them as it did the peoples along the St. Lawrence. He wrote to Le Jeune: "I also know that not one who returned by canoe from the trade but was afflicted by this contagion. It has been so universal among the savages with whom we have acquaintance that I do not know of any who have escaped its attacks."

At Nipissing, he described for Le Jeune the impetuous cataracts and thundering waterfalls, the labor of the portages and other experiences: "I kept count of the number of portages, and found that we carried the canoes thirty-five times and dragged them at least fifty. I sometimes took a hand in helping my savages; but the bottom of the river is full of stones so sharp that I could not walk for any length of time barefoot.... As to the food, it is only a little Indian corn coarsely crushed between two stones, and often taken whole with plain water.... One sleeps on the bare earth, or a hard rock and one must endure continually the stench of tired-out savages. One must walk in water, in mud, in the darkness and the entanglements of the forest, where the stings of an infinite number of mosquitoes and gnats are a serious annoyance. I say nothing of the long wearisome silence to which one is reduced."

They paddled across Lake Nipissing and turned into the French River, which poured down in another succession of hazardous cascades to Lake Huron. On one occasion, the canoe was caught in a roll of water swelling toward a waterfall. Frantically, the Hurons and de Brébeuf tried to point the prow toward shore. Failing, the Hurons slipped over the sides and, floundering in the swift current, they shoved and dragged the canoe out of the surge. From the eddies, where they finally rested, de Brébeuf could see the churning, frothy waterfall over which he, alone in the canoe, had almost been dashed.

Through sedgy, marshy channels they floated out into the open sweep of the Lake of the Hurons. Normally, the Hurons would be less taut and would pull a more leisurely stroke, now that they were on their home stretch. But being feverish and fatigued, they urged one another to have courage and to hurry to their cabins. On the thirtieth day of the journey, August 5, de Brébeuf saw the purple mounds of islands that marked the north headlands of the Huron homeland. It was midafternoon when they fared across the mouth of the bay that separated the Huron peninsula from the mainland.

De Brébeuf wondered why the Hurons swerved the canoe into the bay rather than cut straight ahead along shore beneath the headland. He was more puzzled when they swung around a bulging curve into a narrower land-locked bay, then doubled a smaller point to their right, and floated into a sandy beach. Without words, the Hurons motioned him out of the canoe and helped him carry his chapel box and his other few things to the strand. The paddlers were righting their baggage in the canoe as if they were departing. Echon, suspecting their intention, exclaimed: "You are not abandoning me here, are you?" They said they were sick; they had a long journey to make to their village of Teanaustayé; they wished to be home before night.

"This shore is deserted!" he objected. "I do not know the way to the village! Five years have passed since I was here. Toanché has changed its site." They assured him the village was not far away, that someone would find him.

"But delay a few minutes! Show me the trail! Help me carry the big box," he pleaded. Becoming more curt and surly, they growled out that someone would come along. "Wait here a bit, till I find the trail and the new cabins. If you are sick, remain the night here." They gazed silently in the water. He begged them in the name of all the presents, of all the favors he had done them in their sickness on the journey, of all their pledges. One answered that they had kept their word and brought him to the country of the Hurons. The leader grunted, they dug in their paddles and the canoe spurted out into the bay.[2]

Three: 1634

"They went away," De Brébeuf wrote to Le Jeune. "At once, I prostrated myself upon my knees to thank God, Our Lady and Saint Joseph for the favors and mercies I had received during the journey. I saluted the Guardian Angel of the country. I offered myself, with all my feeble labors, to Our Lord, for the salvation of these poor peoples. Since Our Lord had preserved me and guided me with so much goodness, I took hope that He would not abandon me here."

He looked about; it seemed to him that he remembered this little cove as one of the landing places of Toanché. But five years had passed, and Toanché had moved. The cove, almost enclosed, was on the side of a small bay; few canoes would pass by. The bushes and weeds were shoulder high; no one, apparently, would chance to come down from the hills. The spot was deserted, the sun was low, the silence was a void. He had eaten nothing save a little gruel at daybreak. He cached his box and small bag, and picked his way through the tangled vines and low-lying branches up the bank.

Reaching the hilltop, he wandered about through the pale-green hue of the forest. He halloed, but his voice sounded hollow in the silence. He blundered on what seemed to be an overgrown trail, and following the slightly indented path, he prayed that it was leading him in the right direction. With a quickening of the pulse, he seemed to recognize signs of the Toanché trail. He hurried on and, of a sudden, came to a clearing, and there, before him, were the ruins of his old cabin of 1629. He related: "I looked with tenderness and emotion on the place where we had lived, and where we had celebrated the Holy Sacrifice of the Mass through three years."

Beyond the cabin was a sight of death. The houses of the Toanché he had lived in were mounds of black ashes beaten by the storms. Toanché had been burned to the ground because of the murder of Brûlé, with all his sins upon his soul. De Brébeuf recorded: "I saw the place where poor Étienne Brûlé had been barbarously and treacherously murdered. This made me think that some day they might well treat us in the same manner, and it caused me to hope that it would happen while we were earnestly seeking the glory of God."

He was now sure of the trail to the new village; but how would he be received? He pulsed up his courage and, like a Huron returning home, strode toward the longhouses. Someone screamed: "Look, Echon! He has come back!" They mobbed about him, shouting their welcome: "*Quoy!*" "*Haau!*" De Brébeuf did not return their greetings, but walking straight toward the largest cabin, he sat like a stone on a mat before the fire. When they put in his hands a bowl of sagamite, he ate it gravely, while all the villagers pushed and gabbled about him. When he had finished, he grunted the Huron way of thanks: "*Haau! Outoechti!*"

At his request some young braves volunteered to go back with him in the twilight to the landing place, about three-quarters of a league distant, to fetch his box and bag. "That evening and the next day," de Brébeuf wrote, "passed in a show of affection, visits, greetings and cheering words from the whole village. On the following day, several whom I knew from other villages, came to see me. And all took away with them, in exchange for their visit, some trifling present."

"*Quoy*, Echon," they said. "And so you have come back! It is time! We were wishing and earnestly asking for you. We were heartily glad when they told us you were at Quebec and intended to come up here." In their welcomes, they added reasons for their gratification. Some regarded him as a good sorcerer who made rain for their crops. "We are glad you have come. The crops will no longer fail. During your absence we have had nothing but famine."

The most important reason of their pleasure was connected with Brûlé. "If you had not returned to our village," they explained, "the trade with the French was lost for us. The Algonquins and even the Hurons of the other villages warned us that we should be killed if we went for the trade, because of the murder of Brûlé. But now, we shall go to trade without fear." His host, Aouandoïe, told him that they still feared Champlain's vengeance, despite his reassurance given last year. Their suspicions were increased when they heard Champlain ordered the Blackrobes to live, not with them, but with the people of Quieuindohan. They were completely reassured since Echon, who lived with Brûlé for three years, should so trust them that he returned to their cabins.

After Brûlé's murder, the families of Toanché broke away from the village and built new hamlets. The one de Brébeuf had chanced upon was called Teandeouiata. He had chosen the longhouse of Aouandoïe with forethought, as he explained in his letter to Le Jeune: "You can lodge where you please; for this nation, above all others, is exceedingly hospitable toward all sorts of persons, even strangers. You may remain as long as you please, being always well treated according to the fashion of the country.... I lodged with a man named Aouandoïe, who is, or at least was, one of the richest of the Hurons. I did this on purpose, because another with lesser means might have been inconvenienced with the large number of Frenchmen whom I was expecting and who had to be provided with food and shelter until we had all gathered together and our cabin was ready."

Père Daniel reached the capital Bear village of Quieuindohan, called La Rochelle by the French, about four days after de Brébeuf arrived. He had had a dangerous journey with his sick savages, but was finally rescued by a Bear chief. Simon Baron, de Brébeuf learned, was abandoned by his men on the shore some miles away. He had had narrow escapes in the rapids and suspected the Hurons were trying to get rid of him. He was carrying most of the baggage, and his savages when leaving him tried to steal much of it till he threatened to shoot them. Then came Petit-Pré, about August 19, and after him the youth named Pierre. Following them arrived the workmen, Dominique and Le Coq, who had left Three Rivers two weeks after de Brébeuf and had had an easy journey. They reported that Père Davost was being treated frightfully by his sick Hurons.

Davost, dazed and despairing, was landed about August 24. He had been sick from the time he left Three Rivers; because he could not paddle, he was beaten by the Hurons; all his baggage was thrown away; they abandoned him when they reached the Island Algonquins; he thought he would die until some Hurons rescued him. De Brébeuf, when he noted how physically fatigued and mentally dejected Davost was, feared that he would never recover.

All had now reached Huronia except the lad Martin who was being cared for by the Nipissing Algonquins. De Brébeuf related: "I was busy for some two weeks in visiting the villages and bringing together all the party who landed here and there. Since they did not know the language, they could have only found us out after much toil.... All the French suffered great hardships, experienced great losses, considering the few possessions they had, and faced extraordinary dangers.... He who comes here has need of much strength and patience. Anyone who decides to come here for any other reason than God, will have made a sad mistake."

Having collected his eight Frenchmen, de Brébeuf had to provide for them, and to build his own house. The choice of location was a delicate decision. Prudence dictated that he remain with the Bear nation. There were two preferences. The first was that of erecting his cabin at Quieuindohan, the largest Bear town. This place was the choice of Champlain, Le Jeune, and himself, but it was an old village, and next spring it would be moved to a new site. The second preference was to raise his cabin near a very small hamlet called Ihonatiria, midway between his present village, Teandeouiata, and nearby Oënrio. All of the families of these two settlements had once been united at Toanché. Since these people had listened to his instructions during his first sojourn, they should be more easily converted. He reflected, also, that a small place would be better than a large place while his Frenchmen were learning the language and absorbing the Huron customs.[3]

Having made his decision, Echon proclaimed to the chiefs and elders that he had the mind to live with them. "*Haau! Haau! Haau!*" they uttered in gratification and pounded their fists on the earth. In testimony of his words, he presented them with gifts and declared that he desired to have his own longhouse. They demurred at this, and argued that he and his French should live in their cabins for the winter. He demanded insistently that they build a separate cabin for the Frenchmen. They explained that houses were never built in September, when the bark of the trees was dry; it would be better to await the spring. He insisted that he wished his house to be finished before snows covered the earth.

Fearing lest Echon might settle in some other locality, they voted to erect a house for him. They cleared the space he selected, chopped down saplings and branches for the posts and the rafters, and sliced off slabs of bark for the walls and roof. Their first enthusiasm waned, but Echon scolded and pleaded with them in Huron fashion. By October, they completed the French longhouse, which was about thirty feet in length, eighteen feet wide, and fourteen feet from the ground to the ridgepole. The French workmen fashioned the interior according to their own plan. They threw a wall of sticks across one end, thus forming an antechamber and a storage place for provisions. They closed off the other end of the house with a little room for the chapel and a closet for tools and muskets. The center portion, about eighteen feet long, was in the Huron fashion, with a wide aisle down the center, and the shelf along both sides. The savages marveled at the strange ideas of the French in blocking off their house instead of leaving it open from door to door.

Père de Brébeuf was now quite well grounded among the Hurons, with his own home, with two priests to help him, and six good Frenchmen as his aides. He found opportunity for much charity, since the scourge of sickness was prevalent. Carried from the St. Lawrence by all the natives who had gone to trade, the influenza epidemic spread the full length of the Ottawa and now raged in Huronia. Describing it to Le Jeune, he wrote: "This sickness begins with violent fever, which is followed by a sort of measles or smallpox, different, however, from that common in France, accompanied in several cases by blindness for some days, or by dimness of sight, and terminated at length by diarrhea which has carried off many and is still bringing some to the grave."

With the sickness came the sorcerers and medicine men, and all the humbuggery, incantations and orgies that he had so often witnessed. He was now better equipped to oppose the Oquis and to expose their absurd claims and hysterical remedies. He, with Daniel or Davost, visited all the nearby cabins day by day, and observed carefully those whom he might salvage before death. His first baptism was a five-month-old girl baby, in the cabin of Houtaya, a friendly and influential old man. She died on September 6 and went to heaven with the name of Josepha. The next day, he won the consent of a chief to baptize his two-year-old daughter; she was named Maria and died four days later. Her grandmother, Oquiaendis, aged and sick, wanted to share in the promises Echon made about the baby. De Brébeuf instructed her and, thinking she would soon die, baptized her on September 26, giving her also the name of Maria. To his concern and her joy, she was cured immediately, and exultantly told her son, the chief, and all her people how Echon brought her back from the dead by pouring water on her head.

On October 20, de Brébeuf went on a visit to the Petuns, a people of the same stock as the Hurons, but a distinct nation. His journey was some fifty miles along the trails to the south and west, around the curve of the lake. Primarily, he wished to renew acquaintance with them, to establish pledges of friendship, and to prepare the way for missioners. He was cordially received in their principal villages, and had the consolation of baptizing three children before death took them. By November 20, he was back in Ihonatiria.

During his absence, Père Daniel had baptized two of his old friends, both in danger of death. One named Joseph had died, but the other, Houtaya, also called Joseph, recovered and like old Maria attributed his cure to the baptism. Added to these was Tsindacaiendoua, a man of eighty, whom de Brébeuf described as "one of the best-natured Hurons I have ever known". He lingered in his last illness and professed belief in all that Echon taught him. At his request, de Brébeuf baptized him with the name of Joachim and persuaded him to promise that he would tell his relatives he wished to be buried in the French way. Remembering the deep effect of a Christian burial on the Montagnais, de Brébeuf hoped now to impress the Hurons. When Joachim died, his body was carried to Echon's cabin. Père Jean, in sacred vestments, intoned the prayers and preached, with Père Daniel and Père Davost assisting in surplices and the workmen bearing the cross and lighted candles. Chanting the *Benedictus*, they carried Joachim to the little plot of consecrated ground and there interred him with all the rites of the Church. The Huron onlookers were so impressed, wrote de Brébeuf, that "several desired us to honor their burial in the same way."

So favorable was the mood of the villagers, that de Brébeuf was able to convoke councils of the elders in his cabin. With a white surplice over his black gown and a biretta on his head, he orated, in the tremolo council tone, on the theme that their souls were immortal, that after death their souls would go either to paradise or to hell, that they must choose one place or another during life. An old man expressed the general sentiment: "Let any one who wishes, go to the fires of hell. I intend to go to heaven." The men enjoyed listening to the truths Echon told them, but they were argumentative, and delivered speeches on what their ancestors had taught them. Meanwhile, Père Daniel was attracting the children to the cabin. He taught them to chant the prayers in Huron and to answer the questions in the Ledesma catechism that de Brébeuf had translated. That winter, the people about Ihonatiria seemed eager to become Christians.

In January, de Brébeuf traveled the snow-covered trail of twenty miles to Teanaustayé, the capital town of the Cord nation. For immediate objectives, he had the purpose of thanking the Hurons who had brought him up to Huronia last summer. More important, he wished to visit Louis Amantacha, who had recently escaped from the Iroquois. Through the help of Louis and his family, de Brébeuf hoped to establish the Faith among the Cord people. With intent, perhaps, de Brébeuf arrived in Teanaustayé when the chiefs of all the Huron Federation were consulting about peace with the Seneca Iroquois. It was proposed to send Huron deputies to conclude the peace, and the chiefs, wishing to strengthen their embassy, invited Echon to go as a representative. Aware that it would be imprudent to involve the French and that, if there were any treachery on either side, he would be blamed for it, he refused their invitation. If he went to the Senecas, he reported to Le Jeune, he would go only as a preacher of Jesus Christ.

On his return to Ihonatiria, he was overjoyed with the increasing prospects of a Huron church. A sickly young man, Oatii, who had been well tended by the French, sought baptism. De Brébeuf christened him with all solemnity in the chapel. The Hurons again gasped in admiration at the French ways, and many sought to be treated like Joseph Oatii. On April 14, for the first time in the Huron land,

Père de Brébeuf administered Extreme Unction to Joseph and, on his death, conducted the full Catholic ritual in his burial.

In the spring of 1635, de Brébeuf concluded his first annual report to Le Jeune. He had learned a great deal about Huron beliefs in his winter councils. "The Hurons cannot entirely fail to recognize that there is a divinity," he wrote, "but their souls are very much obscured by their long ignorance, their vices and sins.... They believe in the immortality of the soul, which they assume to be corporeal.... Their superstitions are infinite.... Through them, the devil misleads this poor people.... We hope, by the grace of God, to change these superstitions into the true religion.... There are a large number of medicine men called Arendiowane. These persons, in my opinion, are true sorcerers who have access to the devil."

Laboring through many days and writing many pages, de Brébeuf pictured for Le Jeune and the readers in France the customs of the Hurons, analyzed their virtues and their vices, and evaluated the hopes for their acceptance of the teachings of Jesus Christ. "We have won souls for Our Lord to the number of thirteen," he stated. "May it please Our Lord to accept these first few fruits, and give us strength and opportunity to gather more."

He concluded the report of his year among the Hurons with the poignant thoughts:

> Our hope is in God and in Our Lord Jesus Christ who shed His blood for the salvation of the Hurons as well as for the rest of the world. It is through His support, and not our own efforts, that we hope one day to see here a flourishing Christianity.... All we have to fear is our own sins and imperfections, and I more than all. Indeed, I judge myself most unworthy of this employment. Send to us those who are saintly, or pray God that we may be such as he desires. A thousand entreaties for the Holy Sacrifices of your Reverence and of all our fathers and brothers. Your Reverence's
>
> > Very humble and obedient servant in Our Lord,
> > Jean de Brébeuf, S.J.

> From our little house of St. Joseph in the village of Ihonatiria in the Huron country, this 27th of May, 1635, the day on which the Holy Spirit descended visibly upon the Apostles.

Four: 1635

Early in April, the squaws of the Ihonatiria region planted their corn seeds in the little mounds of the clearances. Strangely, no rain fell in April; the drought continued in May. Without rain, the corn would not sprout; if it did not grow, they and their families would starve next winter. In fear and despair the squaws consulted their dreams, their oquis, their special demons. Piteously, they appealed to their Arendiowane who frantically prescribed special feasts, dances and games, and other rites that would please the cloud gods and draw them over Ihonatiria. But the heavens beamed blue and cloudless. The sorcerers not only failed to bring rain clouds but they could not discover the sorcery that held off the rain.

Tehorenhaegnon, the great Arendiowane of nearby Andiatae, having failed to produce showers, finally learned from his special demon that Echon and the Blackrobes were the witches causing the drought. He proclaimed that Echon concealed a most powerful demon in the cross above his cabin. Unless the cross were taken down and destroyed, the corn would be ruined and the people would starve. His prophecy was repeated from village to village, so that a great rout of savages from all the region swept into Ihonatiria and invaded the French cabin. Echon faced them calmly. They yelled the words of the sorcerer at him, shrieked their abuse, demanded he take down the cross, threatened to tear it off, shot arrows against it, and warned him they would burn down his longhouse.

De Brébeuf recalled that he had quieted the villagers years ago in a like exigency. Now, however, the mob was more frenzied and the purpose of the sorcerer more malicious, since he sought to brand Echon as an evil-minded witch seeking to kill people by famine. But he resolutely refused to remove the cross. He invited them to attend a council to be called by the chiefs of Ihonatiria. As the council convened, Echon grieved that the corn was withering and rotting. He denied that either a Huron sorcerer or a French Blackrobe could bring rain when they needed it. He-who-made-all, and He alone, was the master of the clouds and rain. He advised them to pray to this Master. As for the cross, that had been erected ten months before; it could not be the reason since there had been rain and snow all winter. The real cause, he told them, was to be found in themselves.

They had listened to the sorcerers who had consulted with wicked spirits. Thus, they had angered God, the Master of all things.

Echon urged them to promise to serve God and to hate sin. When they promised, he prescribed that they join him in a procession every day for nine days. That night, de Brébeuf, Daniel and Davost each vowed to offer a novena of Masses in honor of Saint Joseph. The first of these was on June 5. That day, de Brébeuf, the priests and the six Frenchmen, followed by the copper-skinned savages, marched solemnly about the village. Through eight days, the sun shone brightly and none but the fleeciest clouds hovered in the sky. On June 13, the last of the nine days, de Brébeuf and the French, though they still trusted the powerful Saint Joseph, were in agony.

When they and the savages gathered for the procession, the sky was clear. As they walked about the village and chanted their prayers, clouds gathered. Before they returned to the French cabin they were drenched by a torrent of rain. De Brébeuf was no less grateful than the Hurons. He wrote: "These rains stifled the false opinions and notions conceived against God, the cross and ourselves. The savages that knew declared that in the future they would serve God. They uttered a thousand abusive words against their Arendiowane. To God be forever the glory of the whole. He permits the dryness of the soil in order to bedew all hearts with His blessings."

Another drought endangered the corn crop in late July. While sorcerers again invoked their demons all through the Bear land, the people about Ihonatiria once more appealed to Echon to save them. He and the priests vowed to celebrate a novena of Masses in honor of Saint Ignatius, whose feast was approaching. He gathered the pagans in procession and chanted his prayers through the village and along the trails. On the second day of the novena, July 23, the heavens were shrouded in black clouds and the rain plenteously watered the parched cornfields. The savages throughout the Bear nation and in distant villages all conceded that Echon was the most powerful sorcerer in all the land.

About the same time, and later through the summer, the people were panic-stricken by war alarms. While the Seneca Iroquois were observing the semitruce that had been negotiated, the four other Iroquois nations were on the warpath. They made frequent raids in the southern and eastern country, and were often rumored as being along the northern headlands. Time and again, breathless runners burst from the trails shouting, "The Enemy! The Hotinonsionni!" Grabbing their bark pouches of corn and their robes, the squaws and children fled away from the village in order to secrete themselves in coverts and thickets in the deep forests. Only the sick and the decrepit lingered despairingly in the cabins, resigned to be killed. De Brébeuf and the French resisted the hysteria and remained in the village, though prepared to take flight also. The alarms proved to be false and the villagers crept back to their homes, ready, however, to scamper away at the next warning.

During the summer's heat, the missioners devoted themselves to two occupations. The first of these was the study of the Huron tongue. While teaching his comrades, Père Jean struggled to solve further the intricacies and complexities of the language. He no longer had difficulty in speaking fluently, but he labored to assemble a dictionary and to compose a grammar in order the easier to teach the future missioners. He was revising his manuscripts almost daily, so many discoveries was he making in the declensions and conjugations, in the manner of compounding words, in the spelling and the pronunciation. His very advanced quest was the mastery of their double talk. He stated: "Metaphors are used to the greatest extent. If you are not used to these, you will understand nothing in their councils where they speak almost entirely in metaphor." He confessed: "It is, indeed, an exceedingly difficult task to understand in all points a language that is as different from our European languages as is heaven from earth, and this without a master and without books."

Their other pursuit was that of employing themselves for eight or ten days in the practice of the Spiritual Exercises of Saint Ignatius. Père Jean commented: "For these Spiritual Exercises we have so much the more need, since the sublimity of our labors requires so much the more a union with God, and since we are forced to live in continual turmoil. This makes us frequently realize that those who come here must bring a rich fund of virtue with them, if they wish here to gather the fruits thereof."

A fellow priest who, at a subsequent date, lived and labored with him, recalled: "By day, his neighbor's needs not allowing him to occupy himself in solitude with God according to the extent of his heart's desires, he anticipated the usual hour, rising very early.

Nevertheless, for the same reason, he urged every day far into the night, until nature was powerless to go further. Sleep constraining him to succumb, he lay upon the ground, fully dressed as he was, and a piece of wood serving him as a pillow. He gave to the body only what he could not, in conscience, have denied it."

The same friend attested his own and others' admiration and astonishment, when he declared about Jean:

> It is very true that his humility caused him to embrace with more love, more joy, and, I may say, with more natural inclination, the humblest and most painful duties. If he were on a journey, he bore the heaviest burdens; if it were necessary to go through channels, he rowed from morning till evening; it was he who first sped to the water, and left it the very last, notwithstanding the rigors of the cold and ice when his bare legs were all red therefrom and his body all chilled. He was the first to rise, to make the fire and to cook, and the last of all in bed, finishing by night his prayers and his devotions. And however harassed he was, whatever fatigues he endured over roads which cause horror and in which the most vigorous bodies lose courage, after all the labors of the day and sometimes thirty days in succession without rest, without refreshments, without relaxation, often even not having the means to take a single meal with leisure, he nevertheless found time to acquit himself of all which our rules would require from a man who was not so urgently employed, omitting none of his usual devotions, whatever occupation might come unexpectedly upon him. Accordingly, he sometimes said that God gave us the day for dealing with our neighbor, and the night for conversing with Him. And what was most remarkable in those fatigues which he took upon himself is that he did this so quietly and so cleverly that one might have supposed, to see him, that his nature had found its motive therein. "I am an ox," he said, alluding to his name, "and am fit only to bear burdens."

As he tried to divert attention from himself in the sacrifices he endured in helping others, so likewise he concealed as best he could the penances he performed in private for his own sanctification. According to his spiritual director: "To the continual sufferings which are inseparable from the duties which he had in the Missions, on the journeys, in whatever place he was; and to those which charity caused him to embrace, often above his strength, although below his courage, he added many voluntary mortifications: disciplines every day, and often twice each day; very frequent fasts; haircloths and belts with iron points; vigils which advanced far into the night. And after all these, his heart could not be satiated with sufferings, and he believed that he had never endured aught."

Rumors had been reaching de Brébeuf, from Algonquin sources, that the French at Three Rivers and Quebec were dead of the plague. With greater joy, then, did he welcome Père François Le Mercier on August 13 and Père Pierre Pijart four days later. They not only denied the reports but amused de Brébeuf by the rumors at Quebec, to the effect that the Hurons had abandoned him and the other Frenchmen during the upward journey last autumn. De Brébeuf embraced his two new helpers with an exuberant joy. Le Mercier was a well set-up, hardy and wiry man of thirty-one. He was a Parisian, scholarly and accomplished, but wanted the hard life of the Hurons; Pijart, likewise a Parisian, was only twenty-seven years of age. Strangely, he was a Jesuit only six years and was excused from finishing the usual course of studies. Though not tall, he was powerfully built and seemed capable of enduring great hardships.

All the Huron traders returned well pleased with their visit to Three Rivers that summer. They were given great feasts and fine presents, had held council with Champlain, and again pledged peace and brotherhood with the French. They handed Echon a folded packet of paper. It was a letter in which Champlain repeated what he had spoken to the Hurons at the council. De Brébeuf read it aloud. Champlain had told them, at the council, that they must love the Blackrobes and other Frenchmen who lived in their country, that they must believe in the God who made all things if they wished to preserve and strengthen their friendship with the French, that they must listen to what Echon and the Blackrobes commanded and give no heed to what the sorcerers proclaimed.

The Hurons were astonished, for Champlain had said these very things to them. They could not comprehend how Echon could hear with his eyes. They were more completely astounded when Echon continued to repeat Champlain's exact words: "The French will go in goodly numbers to your country. They will marry your daughters when they are baptized Christians. They will teach you to make hatchets and knives." They wondered how Echon could hear these things at a place thirty-days' journey away. De Brébeuf continued reading what Champlain had spoken: "Next year, you must bring some of your boys down to Quebec and leave them there for the winter. This will bind the Hurons and the French more closely together. Then, up in your own country, you must hold a great council of all the chiefs of the Ouendats to consult on these matters. You must invite Echon to speak at that council." All agreed that these were the exact words Champlain had spoken. But how had Echon known that? They concluded that there must be a demon in that piece of paper who had listened to Champlain and who was repeating it all to Echon.

In the autumn and winter Echon gathered the older men in his cabin. His most cogent point of contact with their minds was the fact of death and a future life, of happiness in heaven or of eternal torments in death. He convinced their intellects that there must be one God and drew his illustrations from the laws of nature. "The Hurons are astonished," he wrote. "They have no answer. They confess that we speak the truth and that there is a God. They say they desire to know Him and to serve Him. They ask with insistence that we teach them every day." He advanced to the teaching of how they must live if they believed in God and wished to go to paradise. He explained the practices required by the Ten Commandments. He related that his Hurons "judged the Commandments of God to be very just and very reasonable.... They thought these were matters of great importance, worthy of being discussed at the councils." Their acceptance was only of the brain. "They know the beauty of the truth," he stated sadly; "they approve of it, but they do not embrace it.... They condemn their wicked customs, but when will they abandon them?" They resisted the step from belief to practice.

Antwen, as they called Daniel, devoted himself to the children. Though they were lawless and bad-tempered, since Huron parents never trained or corrected them, Daniel had become a favorite with them. He succeeded sometimes in attracting them to the cabin for prayers and lessons. This year he had a further device of encouraging them, as in a game, to make the Sign of the Cross and to chant their prayers in their longhouses. Through the children, the older people began to learn the prayers, with the result that the Christian invocations became the most popular Huron songs. "What a consolation it is," remarked de Brébeuf, "to hear these countries resound with the name of Jesus, here where the devil has been, so to speak, adored and recognized as God during so many ages."

Three little girls showed such aptitude and enthusiasm, and gave such promise of fidelity, that Daniel and de Brébeuf judged them ready for baptism. They planned to perform the ceremony in the French longhouse, with all possible solemnity, on the Feast of the Immaculate Conception, December 8. They made public proclamations inviting all to attend. The villagers crowded the cabin and watched with awe and curiosity as the three little girls, fully clothed in arm and leg sleeves of new mooseskin and ornamented with strings of wampum and porcelain beads, were anointed and baptized.

That same morning, Père de Brébeuf and his community dedicated themselves and their Huron Mission solemnly to the Immaculate Conception of Our Lady. They vowed to offer twelve Masses in the next twelve months for the intention that a permanent church with the title of the Immaculate Conception be erected in the Huron land. De Brébeuf recorded: "We believe that the Blessed Virgin has accepted our humble devotions. Before the end of December, we baptized twenty-eight." The seeds were being planted in good soil; soon would grow the harvest of souls.

CHAPTER VI

The Wail and Portent of Death

One: 1636

IHONATIRIA WAS IN A STATE of frenzied alarm. It might be at night before the dawn, it might be at twilight before the night, that excited couriers sped into the village shouting that the Iroquois were near. Reports of attacks to the south and the east came to the northland. Hurons were slaughtered and carried off as prisoners; Iroquois were massacred and tortured. Being a small hamlet, Ihonatiria had few fighting men and no palisades. Those who had relatives in the stronger Bear villages escaped. The braves slept with their bows, arrows, knives, hatchets and clubs at hand. The squaws packed their sacks of corn near the door. There was safety only in flight through the snow to hiding places along the shore or in forest hollows.

These winter rumors seemed more certain than those of the last summer. De Brébeuf planned, in case of an attack, to bury the chapel goods and other valuables in a pit, as much against the Iroquois as the Huron thieves. He and four Frenchmen with good arquebuses would go to the aid of the first village attacked, while the other four priests and workmen would join the Huron refugees in the thickets. In regard to those warnings de Brébeuf commented: "These frights have not been useless. Besides the prayers and vows we made to turn aside the scourge, the pains each one took to prepare himself for death or slavery, the opportunity we seized to impress upon the savages the help they might expect from God, we were able to make ourselves liked and worthy of respect, as well as useful to all the country."

In the midst of the Iroquois scare, a medicine man named Ihongouha dreamed that, in order to become an Arendiowane, he must fast for thirty days in a hut that the people must prepare for him in a deserted place. His dream being sacred, all were eager to help him.

His fast was interrupted a few days later, however, when a sick person dreamed that Ihongouha must come to cure him, since he was a leader of the feast of Aoutaerohi. This dream, too, had to be obeyed. Ihongouha chanted and feasted so mightily that he became mad and rushed stark naked out into the snow and woods, singing and howling all the night and all the next day.

The whole country sought remedies for Ihongouha. Then, his demon revealed the cure to him. The villagers must give him a canoe, eight beavers, two ray fish, six score gull's eggs and a turtle; furthermore, he must be adopted as a son by a chief. Since these gifts did not cure his madness, he dreamed that a dance of the masks would make him sane. The elders ordered the dance, and, according to de Brébeuf: "You would have seen some with a sack over their heads, pierced only for the eyes. Others were stuffed with straw around the middle to imitate pregnant women. Several were naked as the hand, their whole bodies whitened, their faces black as devils, with feathers or horns on their heads. Others were smeared with red and black and white. In short, each adorned himself as extravagantly as he could, to dance this ballet and contribute something to the health of the sick man."

When the ailment increased, the sorcerers blamed Echon for the man's insanity, since Echon had condemned the Aoutaerohi feast and the dance of the masks. Others argued that Echon was not to blame, but that Echon's God was angry because Ihongouha had mocked and derided Him. The madman haunted the French cabin, and Echon gave him raisins, which, he said, did not break his fast. Ihongouha next dreamed he should be given a poison feast, the Akhrendoiaen. Though this was not practiced in the Bear nation, no one dared to question a dream. Couriers were sent to all the villages. After a fortnight, a band of eighty persons, including six women, all members of the Brotherhood of Madmen, arrived at Ihonatiria. After chanting and dancing wildly, they concluded that the only cure was the dance called Otakrendoiae.

De Brébeuf excused himself from describing it in detail: "Let it suffice to say, in general, that never did frenzied Bacchantes of bygone times do anything wilder in their orgies. Here it was a matter of killing one another, they say, by charms which they throw at one another. These charms consist of bears' claws, wolves' teeth, eagles' talons, certain kinds of stones, dogs' sinews and so forth. When they have fallen under the charm and been wounded, blood should pour from the mouth and the nostrils. This is simulated by a red powder they take by stealth. There are ten thousand other absurdities that I pass over.... Certainly, here are many silly things: and I am afraid things darker and more occult."

He was inclined to believe in satanic possession and diabolism among the Hurons. "Since their lewdness and licentiousness hinder them from finding God," he argues, "it is very easy for the devil to insinuate himself and to offer them his services." Again, he observes: "There is, therefore, some foundation for the belief that the devil sometimes guides their hands, and reveals himself to them for some temporal profit and for their eternal damnation.... Amid all these fooleries, I dare not relate the infamies and the uncleanness which the devil suggests to them, causing them to see in their dreams that they can be cured only by wallowing in all sorts of filth."

In the midst of his reflections, he prays: "May He Who has saved us by the blood of the Immaculate Lamb, grant a remedy to all of this as soon as possible, accepting if need be, for this purpose, our souls and our lives which we most freely offer to Him for the salvation of these peoples and the remission of our own sins."

François Marguerie, an Algonquin interpreter, arrived unexpectedly on March 28. He was in company with the chief of the Island Algonquins, Le Borgne, and three other envoys. They proposed to the Hurons a joint expedition against the Iroquois. When the Hurons refused to accept their presents for this purpose, Le Borgne was bitterly angry and threatened the Hurons that next year he would permit none of them to pass through his country for the French trade. He sought hospitality with de Brébeuf, who knew how treacherous he was. Confidentially, he advised Echon to escape from the Hurons, since they were a wicked people, and recalled that they had murdered Brûlé and drowned the Grayrobe. He accused the Hurons of being liars, thieves and murderers, so that no Frenchman was safe among them. He invited Echon and the French to live with his people where they would be safe and well-treated.

Echon did not permit himself to become involved in these forest politics and enmities. Even Le Borgne's visit to him would arouse Huron suspicions of treachery. Yet, he needed the friendship of the

Island Algonquins for the safe passage up the Ottawa for the mission-ers. Promising that soon Blackrobes would live with the Algonquins, and giving him a canoe, de Brébeuf was glad to see Le Borgne and his comrades start homeward, and recorded: "They uttered a thou-sand thanks and promised to treat our priests well when they passed through their territory. We endeavor to gain for ourselves the friend-ship of all these peoples, in order to conquer them for God."

In the dissensions among the Hurons themselves, de Brébeuf had to move warily. Aënons, chief of Oënrio, was seeking to persuade the family groups of the five small villages of the region to unite in one large town, such as Toanché had been. He had been one of the great Bear chiefs and had held the most exalted honor, that of Master of the Feast of the Dead. His reputation, however, was nearly ruined because he was believed to have caused the murder and eating of Brûlé. Aënons realized that he needed Echon and the French, if he were to build up a large and powerful village. If the French erected their house in this projected village, he and his clan would gain great prestige in the Bear nation, would profit in the French trade, and would forever be rid of the stigma of the Brûlé murder. Ever since the autumn, Aënons had been begging Echon to promise to live in the new village. That spring he was most insistent, and on one occasion spoke with such persuasiveness and force that de Brébeuf wrote out his discourse in full, and added a note: "This is the harangue of this chief. In my opinion and in the judgment of many, it would pass for one of Livy's if he had dealt with the subject."

De Brébeuf had been thinking deeply about his own plans. The house at Ihonatiria, having been built at the wrong season and hast-ily, was falling to pieces. He would have to get another house built. Would it be better to remain with Aënon's people in the extreme northeast of the Huron country, or to move toward the south? The new capital village of the Bear nation, Ossossané, called La Rochelle by the French, had offered to build him a cabin near theirs. An added complication arose from the fact that Aënons and his group were in almost open rebellion against the leading Bear chiefs of Ossossané. This split had been increasing during the year, and grudges on both sides were multiplying. It would not be prudent, he judged, to insult the chiefs and elders of the Ihonatiria and Oënrio region by moving over to Ossossané.[1]

De Brébeuf gave his answer to Aënons. He and the French would remain, provided the chiefs of the five settlements would join in the plan for one village, would listen to and follow the things he taught them, and would build him a new cabin. At a council held subsequently, the leaders of the clan, agreeing unanimously to Echon's proposals, declared: "Echon will teach us and we shall do all that he desires." However, they later decided to postpone the building of the new village for a year. That spring they were too involved with their strife against the Ossossané chiefs, particularly about the Feast of the Dead, which would be held in May. To test their good intentions, de Brébeuf asked them to repair and enlarge his cabin since he expected more Frenchmen to come. They responded enthusiastically, for now they were assured that he would not move to another part of the country. "The pledges of good will," he stated, "were not merely words; they were followed by good results. They set to work so diligently and worked so zealously, that they erected a new cabin for us in three days. No one spared himself. The old men were foremost in the work. Some, forgetting their age, climbed to the top of the cabin. Others went to see and prepare plenty of bark to cover it, or worked at setting up the frame thereof."

During the last autumn and winter, the great chiefs of the Bear nation held many councils. The time was coming when they would hold the Feast of the Dead, or more properly, the Feast of the Souls. It was the ceremonial in which they honored their dead and bound the living into an unbreakable people, and professed their supreme belief in a future world. So hallowed was this festival that they did not pronounce the real name of it even in their councils. When speaking of it, they used euphemisms and metaphors. To refer to the dead as dead either was an insult or the cause for new mourning. De Brébeuf explained: "They hardly ever speak of the Feast of the Dead, even in their most solemn councils, except under the name of *The Kettle*. They appropriate to it all the terms of cookery. In speaking of hastening or postponing the Feast of the Dead, they will speak of stirring up or scattering the embers beneath the Kettle. He who would say, 'The Kettle is overturned,' would mean, 'There will be no Feast of the Dead.' "

After one of the general councils of the nation, Aënons announced to de Brébeuf that he had been deputed by the chiefs to confer with him. Twelve years had elapsed since the last Feast, he stated, and they proposed to stir up the embers under the Kettle. Since they counted the French as their brothers, they invited Echon and his people to participate in the ceremony. They wished to know if Echon would "raise" the bodies of Guillaume Chaudron, who was buried near Ossossané, and of Étienne Brûlé, and inter their bones in the common grave with the bones of the Ouendats.

De Brébeuf recognized immediately the importance of the dilemma. If he refused, he would insult them; if he agreed, he would violate the Catholic principle of burying the baptized with the unbaptized. In the Huron manner, he pondered his answer, in silence, without moving. Finally, he commissioned Aënons to declare to the chiefs this decision: first, since Chaudron and Brûlé were buried in the woods and not in a real burial field, he would consent to exhume them; second, they must be reinterred in a pit, near to but separated from that of the Hurons; third, with them must be buried the bones of all the Ouendats who had died after having been baptized. Aënons himself assented to Echon's conditions, and later informed him that the chiefs had accepted his proposals.

In his report, de Brébeuf explains the significance of his answer:

Four principal reasons led us to make this reply. (1) As it is the greatest pledge of friendship and alliance that they have in this country, we were conceding to them in advance this point which they sought; and we were making it appear that we desired to love them as brothers, to live and die with them. (2) We hoped that God would be thereby glorified, mainly in this, that in separating the bodies of the Christians from the Unbelievers, with the consent of the whole country, we would not find it difficult afterwards to obtain permission from individuals to have their Christian relatives interred in a separate cemetery which we would consecrate. (3) We were intending to inter them with all the ceremonies of the Church. (4) The elders, of their own accord, wished us to erect a magnificent beautiful Cross, as they stated afterwards in private. Thus, the Cross would be authorized by the whole country and honored in the midst of this barbarism. They would, thereafter, not impute to it, as they have done in the past, the misfortunes that might overtake them.

All went well for a time. Then, the rivalry between Aënons' chiefs and the Ossossané chiefs widened into an almost complete break. A new council was convened in April to heal the schism and to unite the Kettle. Being now committed to rebury the French dead in conjunction with the Huron Feast of the Dead, Echon was invited to participate. All the notables of the whole country being assembled, they asked Echon if he were of the same mind as previously. He repeated to them his proposition, that the French and the baptized Hurons be interred together in a pit apart from the unbaptized. They were satisfied with this answer, but questioned him further. If there were two Kettles, meaning two ceremonies of the Feast of the Dead, that of Ossossané and that of Aënons' villages, with which did he wish to join? Fearful of offending either faction he answered that since they were friendly and wise, he would defer to their decision. The Ossossané chief, condescendingly, declared that he sought nothing: the chief of Oënrio might have the bodies of the two Frenchmen. Aënons answered that he laid no claim to Chaudron, who was buried at Ossossané, but Brûlé belonged to him, since he had brought him up to their country. In a loud undertone that all could hear, someone remarked that it was reasonable for Aënons to honor the bones of Brûlé, since he and his people had killed him.

In the public council, despite the animosity, no angry words were spoken by the orators. As de Brébeuf testified: "The matter passed off with all the gentleness and peace imaginable. At every turn, the Master of the Feast of the Dead, who had assembled the council, exhorted all to be courteous, since this was a council of peace.... It was a matter of great astonishment to see such moderation of words in these embittered hearts." After the council, however, Aënons and the Ossossané chief exchanged fiery epithets. But Aënons ceased to lay any claim to the body of Brûlé, and the Ossossané elders lost interest in Chaudron. De Brébeuf was greatly relieved; all the time he had been worried about burying the sinner Brûlé in consecrated ground.

During this council, de Brébeuf found the opportunity that he had been seeking since the preceding summer. In the presence of the assembled chiefs of the Bear nation, and of envoys from other Huron nations, he repeated what Champlain had said at the council at Three Rivers. He urged a closer alliance with the French, first through inviting more Frenchmen to come to their country, and second, through sending Huron boys to live with the Blackrobes at Quebec. This would make them happy in this world; then, if they followed what he and the Blackrobes taught them, they would be assured of happiness in the world after death; otherwise, they would be condemned to suffer and be tormented forever in the fiery furnace of hell.

The chiefs listened intently, with all the polite deportment customary in their councils. Echon displayed before them a beautiful collar made of twelve hundred porcelain beads. This collar, he said, was a pledge of the truth of his words and would level the road to heaven. The chiefs, in answer, protested that they dreaded these fires of hell and wished to take the road to heaven; therefore, they accepted his present. One dissident voice was heard. Whether seriously or sarcastically, someone shouted out that it was very fine that all the chiefs and elders were so eager to go to heaven and be happy; as for himself, it would not matter much if he were burned in hell.

Two: 1636

Twelve years had elapsed since the last Kettle of the Bear nation. Even in anticipation, the people throbbed with the most profound emotion. From time beyond remembering, their forefathers had reverenced the bones of their forefathers. The bones were so sacred that they were called Atisken, meaning the soul. Two souls were contained in the body at the time of death, they believed. One of these was released, yet remained about the cemetery until the bones were finally deposited in the common pit at the Festival of Souls. The other remained in the bones even after the final burial. The ceremony attending their final entombment was so hallowed that, if any traditional detail were omitted, doom would fall upon the entire nation. Each family had its own solemn duty of observing the ritual in regard to its own dead. Each village or clan was obligated to choose a chief, called Aiheonde, whose office it was to direct the traditional rites. The supreme council of chiefs and elders elected the Master of the Festival of Souls, and on him conferred the title of Anenkhiondic.[2]

During the first week of May, 1636, the villages and clans stirred with the first preparations for the momentous ceremony. On a clear dawn, the Aiheonde led his people in solemn, silent procession to the cemetery where the bodies of the dead rested on their scaffoldings.

He and his assistants tore off the bark coverings and lowered the decaying bodies to the earth. While the men haunched in silent repose, the squaws and girls raised shrill lamentations as they looked upon their loved ones, seated before them as at death, with knees drawn up to the chin. Wailingly, they called again and again the names of their dead, wept over them and stroked them lovingly as if they were alive. Deeply moved by this spectacle, de Brébeuf observed: "The flesh of some was quite gone, and there was only a parchment over their bones. Some bodies looked as if they had been dried and smoked, and showed scarcely any signs of putrefaction. Others were all swarming over with worms."

After contemplating the bodies for some time, the women stripped off the skin and flesh, which they burned in a fire kindled from the bark and robes of the first sepulture, and cleansed the bones. These they wrapped in furs and carried back to their longhouses, where they hung them upon the posts or propped them up on the earth. The bodies of those who had died within a year or two were borne intact, even though corrupting, to the cabins and covered with clean robes. That night, in the presence of the Atisken, the souls of their dead, they ate their funeral feasts. Echon, when he visited the longhouses, was suffocated by the unbearable stench, but the savages seemed not to smell the stink of the bones and the rotting flesh.

The local leader, the Aiheonde, proclaimed the holding of the village festival of souls in the largest longhouse. Each family brought its Atisken and corpses to the general assembly and ranged them along the edge of the central aisle. When all were in place, the Master announced what viands were in the pots and invited all to eat. He and other chiefs meanwhile discoursed on the virtues of the deceased and the greatness of the heroes of the past. When they had eaten, at a signal, they leaped from their mats, hurriedly seized their bones and rushed out of the cabin shrilling the cry of the souls, "*H-a-e-e! H-a-e-e!*"

While these regional rites were being transacted, de Brébeuf had been receiving urgent messages from the Supreme Master, the Anenkhiondic, inviting him to attend the Kettle at Ossossané. "You would have thought that the Feast of the Dead would not be successful without us," he remarked. Knowing that the chiefs were perturbed lest he absent himself because of the controversy about splitting the Kettle and the burial of the Frenchmen, he sent Père Daniel to Ossossané to announce that he would arrive in good time with his villagers.

On the appointed day, the local Aiheonde led his people in procession to the Kettle at Ossossané. The men, their faces and naked bodies smeared with paint, their shoulders and arms decked with beads and ornaments, wearing their most precious robes, walked slowly and meditatively in advance. The squaws followed in file, holding their pouch of souls on their shoulders by means of a thong attached to their foreheads. They clothed themselves and their precious burdens with their most prized cloaks of fur. Other women and girls bore bags of food, enough to last their families for a full week. As they paced slowly along the trail, they complained that the souls were heavy and they paused for frequent rests. Along the way, like the call of a flock of birds, they squeaked the cry of the souls, "*H-a-e-e! H-a-e-e!*" They camped at each settlement along the route, and were joined by new groups and clans in their pilgrimage. Though the distance to Ossossané was only twelve miles, they crept along so slowly that they passed three days in their journey.

When they had come to the plateau of Ossossané, they were greeted by the villagers and the visitors, those on the one side piercing the air with their cries, and those arriving whining more vehemently the wail of the souls. On their arrival, each family was assigned a longhouse in which to lodge. Though the place was densely overcrowded, there was no confusion. Echon and the French were given a fireplace and bunks in a longhouse in the old village of Quieuindohan, about a mile distant. Twenty other families, each with its pouches of bones, shared the bark house with the French. De Brébeuf related: "They hung and fastened upon poles fully a hundred souls. Some of these smelled a little stronger than musk."

The burial pit, as described by de Brébeuf, was located about a quarter of a mile from Ossossané, in a level and extensive field. Dug in the middle of the clearing, it was about twenty-five feet in diameter and ten feet deep. Surrounding the cavity was a circular scaffolding about ten feet high and twelve feet wide. Poles extended from the top of the scaffolding out toward the center of the pit; on these arms would be suspended the bags of souls. Back from the scaffolding, posts were erected in a circle about three thousand feet in circumference. On these, each family group would display the presents it was wealthy enough to distribute.[3]

During the day, the young people engaged in sports of strength and agility, while the older people gambled in their games of dish or stick. In the evening, everyone feasted, chanted and danced, and late through the night they held councils at which the orators recalled the prowess of their ancestors and the old legends handed down through the generations. Echon, as the envoy of their French brothers, was treated with the greatest courtesy as were the official guests from about twenty other nations.

The burial was to take place on May 10. The evening before was threatening with clouds and rain. Since this was a bad omen, the ceremony was postponed till the morrow, but that day, too, was cloudy. On the third day, about noon, when the Master of the Feast proclaimed that the ritual would begin, the women took down and opened their pouches of bones, and paid their last farewells, with weeping and lamentation, stroking the bones fondly. At a signal, they bundled again their precious souls and suspended them from their foreheads. The whole corpses they carried on litters. Having formed in solemn order, they marched in procession to the burial place, where each family deposited its bones and corpses on the ground. They then hung upon the outer poles surrounding the scaffolding the robes and valuables they intended to bury with their dead or to offer as gifts. Later in the afternoon, at the proclamation of the Master of the Feast, the corpses were moved to the edge of the pit. At the next command, appointed bearers of the pouches of bones breathlessly raced to the scaffolding, scurried up the ladders, and fastened the pouches to the poles reaching out over the pit.

The official chiefs then announced the gifts that were to be made. The crowd jostled from pole to pole to note how rich and worthy were these gifts, as the Master cried out the names of the donors and the recipients. Meanwhile, de Brébeuf observed, they were spreading out beaver robes along the bottom and sides of the pit. He calculated there were about forty-eight such robes, each of ten or more skins. As the dusk thickened, the Master proclaimed that the whole corpses were being lowered into the pit. All the thousands of Hurons crowded in to witness the ceremony, which de Brébeuf described: "We had the greatest difficulty getting near. Never have I been better able to imagine the confusion that reigns among the damned. You saw them on all sides letting down the half-rotted bodies. On all sides was to be heard a horrible din of confused voices of people who spoke and did not listen. Ten or twelve men were in the pit, arranging the bodies next to one another all around the sides. They put in the very middle of the pit three large kettles; these could only be of use for souls; one had a hole through it, another had no handle, and the third was in scarcely better condition."

That same night, Monday, May 12, the Hurons camped in the field about the mortuary pit. Each group of families had its own fires, each village had its own area, near to where their corpses rested on soft beaver skins in the pit, and their pouches of souls hung above on the poles. This night was their vigil of souls. The field sparkled with hundreds of copper fires, the air was tangy with the smoke of green wood, when de Brébeuf set out for the old longhouse. He proposed to return before daybreak for the final ceremony of burial of the Atisken.

About dawn, when he was starting along the trail to the burial field, he was startled by piercing shrieks and screams. He ran along the slippery path as fast as his lengthy legs could carry him. At the field, the shouting and wailing savages were rushing here and there in excited mobs. "We saw a true picture of hell as we drew near," he related. "The air resounded with the confused voices of these barbarians." Naked men on the scaffolding hurled the bones out of the pouches toward the center of the pit. Down in the hole, a dozen men with poles were spreading out and leveling the skulls and other bones that came hurtling from the top of the scaffold.

The fright and wild consternation were caused, he learned, by an accident of evil omen. One of the bags holding the bones had fallen from the pole and dropped the twenty feet to the bottom of the pit with such a crash that it wakened those sleeping near. Thereupon, all the custodians of the bones leaped upon the scaffold and wildly emptied the pouches, without waiting for the signal of the Master. They and their people would be doomed forever if the bones were not buried all together at the same time.

When the skulls and bones were all in the burial pit, and the trepidation had subsided, the Anenkhiondic raised his voice in the Chant of the Souls. The thousands of mourners, sitting haunched and motionless, joined their voices in chorus. According to de Brébeuf, "they began to sing, but in a tone so lamentable and so lugubrious that it represented to us the horrible sadness and the abyss of despair into which these unhappy souls are forever plunged." While the mourners chanted, the bones were leveled at about two feet from the top of the pit. Those in charge covered them with robes, mats and large pieces of bark, and filled the pit with sandy soil over which they threw logs and poles.

The rest of the morning was spent in distributing the presents and gifts with harangues and ostentation. The Head Chief of the Bears presented to Echon a beautiful robe of ten new beaver skins, both as a testimonial of their gratitude for his participating at the Kettle and in return for the collar of twelve hundred porcelain beads he had given them to show them the way to heaven. Echon did not accept the robe, diplomatically alleging that he had presented the collar for the single purpose of persuading the Ouendats to become Believers. "You cannot thank us," he said, "in any better way than by listening to us willingly and believing in the One-who-created-all." About the burial, he reflected: "We have fifteen or twenty Christians buried with these unbelievers. We said a *De Profundis* for the repose of their souls. We had a firm hope that, if the Divine Goodness continues the flow of His blessings on these peoples, this Feast will never more be held; or if it is, it will be held only for Christians, and then, with ceremonies as sacred as theirs are foolish and useless."

In his harangue at the council before the Feast, Echon spoke plainly and strongly about the Hurons sending their young sons down to Quebec, where they would be cared for by the French and the Blackrobes. Since he was given general approbation by the chiefs, he and Daniel went about seeking for parents who might consent to let their boys travel down with the Huron flotilla that spring. Both de Brébeuf and Daniel were fully persuaded that if these Huron lads were removed for a time from their savage environment and were taught the Christian truths, they could be formed into a corps of apostolic workers on their return to their people. After the Festival, during the latter half of May and June, de Brébeuf and Daniel visited the villages in which they hoped to find their young recruits.

De Brébeuf had been ordered by his Superior, Père Le Jeune, to write a *Relation*, or a "Narrative", of the experiences of himself and his companions among the Hurons. In the past summer of 1635, he had sent down a fairly lengthy account of the happenings of 1634–1635. Le Jeune, though delighted with it, was not completely satisfied. He demanded that Père Jean not only include the events of the year but that he give a comprehensive survey of all that he had learned about the Hurons. Le Jeune pointed out that Champlain, after a short visit, had described the savages at some length; that Sagard-Théodat, the Récollet brother, had written a volume on them, after one winter; that he, after five years, knew the language and the Hurons better than any other white man and was most competent to draw up an authentic document for publication.

De Brébeuf realized the value of such a *Relation*. He remembered how he had devoured Le Jeune's *Relation* of 1633–1634. He had heard how Le Jeune's succeeding *Relations* had become the most popular books in France. They aroused enthusiasm for New France and its missions, they begot prayers and aspirants for the missions, they were the source for gifts and donations to support the missionary labors. Though possessed of a good style and flow of language, de Brébeuf was less eager to write about the Hurons than to labor actively among them. However, being under obedience, he set himself down to his task.[4]

In his introduction he stated his belief that, if God continues to bless the missioners and Hurons as He has done hitherto, there was hope of an abundant harvest of souls, "despite the many errors, superstitions, vices and very evil customs that must be uprooted." Concluding his preface, he averred: "Enough, however, of generalities. There is need to go into details. This I will do willingly and completely, assuring you that I shall set down nothing that I have not witnessed myself or that I have not learned from persons worthy of belief." He divided the work into two parts: the first dealing with the events of 1635–1636 and matters that affected the implanting of Christianity among the Hurons; the second concerning itself with the Hurons themselves, their beliefs, their customs, their mode of life.

The first part began with a chapter on "The Conversion, Baptism and Happy Death of some Hurons, and the Condition of Christianity amid This Barbarism". He described his second chapter as "Containing in the Order of Time the Other Remarkable Things that Occurred during the Year". In his third chapter, he gave expression to thoughts that had been burning in him during ten years, ever since he first came to the Hurons. Letting his quill flow freely, he offered "Important Advice for Those Whom It Shall Please God to Call to New France, and Especially to the Country of the Hurons".

On the last page, he wrote: "I finish this discourse and this chapter with this sentence: 'At the sight of the difficulties and the crosses that are here prepared for us, if someone feels so strengthened from above that he can say, It is too little, or, like Saint Francis Xavier, *Amplius, Amplius*, More, More,—I hope that, amidst the consolation granted him, Our Lord will draw from his lips this other confession, that the consolation is too much for him, that he cannot endure more, *Satis est, Domine, satis est!*'" He concluded the first part with a chapter entitled "Concerning the Language of the Hurons".

The second part was entitled "Concerning the Belief, Manners and Customs of the Hurons". In the first chapter he discoursed "What the Hurons Think of Their Origins". He proceeded in his second chapter to discuss "The Ideas of the Hurons Concerning the Nature and Condition of the Soul, both in This Life and after Death". His third chapter was devoted to the theme "That the Hurons Recognize Some Divinity; Concerning Their Superstitions and Their Faith in Dreams". He continued the topic in his fourth chapter: "Concerning the Feasts and Dances, the Games of Dish and Crosse, What They Call Ononharoia". The fifth chapter discussed his perplexities about diabolism in certain rites and is entitled "Whether There Are Sorcerers among the Hurons". He explained in chapter six: "The Polity of the Hurons and Their Government". He continued this dissertation in chapter seven: "Concerning the Order the Hurons Observe in Their Councils". Chapter eight covered "The Ceremonies They Observe in Their Burials and Mournings". He devoted chapter nine to "The Solemn Feast of the Dead".

"Shall I finish the present *Relation* with this funereal ceremony?" he asked. "Yes, since it is a very clear token of a future life that nature herself seems to furnish us in the minds of these peoples, as a most fitting means to persuade them to enjoy the promises of Jesus Christ." He exulted, in one way, on his most fervid hopes for their speedy conversion, and in another way he lamented, with the most dismal realization on the obstacles of the flesh that prevented them from accepting the Christian code.

He dated his *Relation* "July 16, 1636, at the residence of Saint Joseph among the Hurons, at the village called Ihonatiria". He added another document of a more private nature, which he entitled "Directions for the Priests of Our Society Who Shall Be Sent to the Hurons". Minutely, he told them how they should act with the savages, how they must show affection for them, never keep them waiting, keep a tinderbox to light the fires, eat their food though it be disgusting, eat only with them morning and night, not bring sand into the canoes, be silent and do not ask questions, carry something at the portages, wear a nightcap not a wide-brimmed hat, never be irritable, show a cheerful face, etc. "Jesus Christ is our true greatness," he concluded. "It is He alone and His cross you should seek in following after these people. If you strive for anything else, you will find nothing but bodily and spiritual affliction. Having found Jesus Christ and His cross, you will have found the rose in the thorns, the sweetness in the bitterness, all things in nothing."

Among the other letters he had to write that early summer was his official report, as Superior, to the Reverend General of the Society of Jesus, Mutius Vitelleschi. In his conclusions, he stated his conviction: "Among the other qualities with which the laborer in this Mission ought to shine, gentleness and patience hold first place. This field will never bear fruit except with amiability and patience. One should never hope to force it by violence or severity. All who are here are zealously striving for perfection. It seems to me that I alone am weak, to my own great disadvantage."

Three: 1636

Champlain's appeal, that the Hurons entrust some of their boys to the care of the French at Quebec, and de Brébeuf's oration at the Feast of the Dead won an unexpectedly favorable response. Twelve Huron lads were willing and were being permitted by their parents to pass the winter with the Blackrobes at Notre Dame des Anges. These boys, it was hoped, would later return to their people as Catholic apostles. Père Daniel was appointed to care for and to instruct these first Huron schoolboys, and Père Davost was chosen as his assistant. Three of the lads departed with Antwen and a party of ten

canoes on July 22. Teouatiron, about eighteen years old, was the
nephew of one of the most famous war chiefs. Satouta, about fifteen,
was the grandson of another renowned chief. The youngest, Tsiko,
son of a council chief renowned for his oratory, had inherited his
father's gift of eloquence. These three youths, in the estimation of
de Brébeuf and Daniel, had minds capable of grasping Christian doctrine, had sufficient strength of will to observe the moral code, and
seemed disposed to absorb something of the French culture.[5]

With the departure of the canoes and with the families scattered
in their summer haunts, Ihonatiria was deserted. The French house
seemed lonely without Daniel, Davost and the workmen who had
gone to fetch supplies for the coming year. De Brébeuf, Le Mercier
and Pijart found the time conducive to a more intense study of the
language. They were surprised by a visit from the father of Louis
Amantacha on August 8. He was just returned from Quebec and
brought to Echon a packet of letters. They rejoiced in the receipt of
news from France and Quebec, "sweeter since it came so early and
unexpectedly", they exclaimed.

With hungry eyes they read the long letter from Le Jeune. He was
enthusiastic about the arrival of eight ships, the largest French fleet
ever to sail up the St. Lawrence. It carried hundreds of colonists and
an abundance of French goods. They were more cheered when they
read that six priests and two brothers had arrived at Quebec, and
burst out in exclamations of thanksgiving to God when they were
assured by Le Jeune that three new missioners were being assigned to
labor with them among the Hurons.

There was sad news, however, especially for Père Jean. His friend
Samuel de Champlain was dead. He had suspected this, for all through
the winter rumors were current that a great white chief had died
at Quebec. Champlain had a stroke in October and lingered until
December 25. De Brébeuf looked back sorrowfully through the years
and remembered how Champlain had suffered agonies of soul and
body through twenty-eight years in order to build Quebec and New
France into a strong and self-supporting colony. And now, when his
dreams and his hopes were being realized, God took him from life.
Père Jean appreciated Le Jeune's tribute: "Truly, he led a life of great
justice, equity and perfect loyalty to his King and towards the Gentlemen of the Company. But at his death, he crowned his virtues with

sentiments of piety so lofty that he astonished us all. They deputed me to preach the funeral oration and I did not lack material for it. Those whom he has left behind here have reason to be proud of him. Even though he died far away from France, his name will not be any less glorious to posterity."

Toward evening of August 12, de Brébeuf was told that a Black-robe landed at the cove beneath Ihonatiria. Though this seemed incredible, since the flotilla would not be returning for another month, he rushed down the trail and found Père Pierre Chastellain, who had been brought by Aënons. The following day, Père Charles Garnier arrived in the canoe of Kionché. Hearty was the welcome given them by de Brébeuf, Pijart and Le Mercier, who wrote: "The joy which is experienced in these reunions seems to be some foretaste of the happiness of the blessed upon their arrival in Heaven, so full is it of sweetness."

Chastellain and Garnier were the same age, about thirty. They had entered the Society of Jesus together, had been friends through all their period of studies, and now, together, had gained their life's ambition of laboring among the Hurons. Chastellain was rugged and heavy set, while Garnier was delicate looking, with shapely features and a fair skin, without the trace of a beard. Even at a glance, de Brébeuf could see that they both had mettle and spirit and a great zeal to suffer and spend themselves for God. They were bursting with talk about how Chastellain, who was named Arioo, was offered passage by Aënons in return for the gift of a canoe, how Père Le Jeune gave the canoe, how Kionché then agreed to take Garnier, whom they called Ouracha. But their greatest news concerned the arrival of a governor to succeed Champlain. He was Charles Huault de Montmagny, Chevalier of the Order of St. John of Jerusalem, a nobleman of distinction and a most exemplary Catholic. They had crossed the ocean on his vessel and were loud in their praise of him.

In early September, seven Iroquois prisoners were triumphantly escorted into the Huron land. One was apportioned to the chief of Onnentisati who, in turn, presented him to the chief of Arontaen because his nephew had recently been killed by the Iroquois. De Brébeuf, with Le Mercier and Garnier, hurried over the five-mile trail to Arontaen. The Iroquois had already been tortured; some of his fingers were torn or chewed off; other parts of his body were gashed and blistered. De Brébeuf managed to get close enough to speak to the captive. The Iroquois raised his eyes and stared at Echon with suspicion and defiance. But gradually as he listened to and watched him, he judged Echon had good intentions.

The Hurons, while waiting for the decision of the chief of Arontaen as to the fate of the captive, treated him with friendliness and cordiality. They cleansed his putrefied fingers and picked from them the maggots. They prepared a feast of dog for him, and chatted amiably as if he were a friend come to visit them. Echon sat beside the captive and assured him that he felt pity for him and wished to ensure him happiness after death. The Iroquois, who belonged to the Seneca nation, grunted approval when, with the help of a Huron translator, he understood Echon saying: "You will suffer during the short bit of life left to you; but if you listen to me and believe what I tell you, you will have eternal happiness in heaven after you die." Echon, aided by the pagan Hurons, instructed him about God, heaven and hell, baptism and salvation. As the conversation continued, Le Mercier and Garnier prayed, and vowed they would say four Masses in honor of the Blessed Virgin, if she would win him the grace of baptism.

That night, the prisoner was led to the longhouse where they lodged and de Brébeuf found further opportunity of conversing with him. The Hurons crowded about the Seneca and the Blackrobe, and were strangely quiet while Echon discoursed on the theme: "There is a God who made all things. This God loves all men, the world over. He loves the Iroquois as well as the Hurons. He loves the captive as well as the free. He loves the poor and the miserable as well as the rich. To win His love, one must believe in Him and obey His Commandments." Not only the captive but the elders and chiefs seemed fascinated by the idea of this God of love. Echon asked the prisoner if he would believe in the One-who-made-all and if he wished to be happy with Him in the place where souls go. The Seneca uttered a vigorous grunt of assent. Le Mercier put a bark cup of water in the hands of Père Jean, who, while the Hurons watched, baptized the captive and gave him the name of Joseph.

Again the next night, they feasted Joseph the Iroquois, since the chief had not yet decided whether to adopt or to kill him. The elders and chiefs not only permitted but urged Echon to tell more about his God. Seated before the flickering fire, Echon explained the meaning of the Commandments of God. They interrupted him frequently to ask him questions and to offer their own comments. Most particularly, they inquired how it was possible for men and women to live alone and not enjoy one another. When Echon told them about himself and the Blackrobes and thousands of other men and women who, of their own free will, vowed to preserve perpetual chastity, they were utterly astounded. Several hours passed in such discussion, to the delight of the Huron auditors.

After treating the Iroquois like a son for two days, the chief decreed that he must be burned and tortured. Echon clung closely as he could to Joseph and taught him to repeat, even in his sufferings, the invocation: "*Jesus taiteur!* Jesus, have pity on me." On September 4, about noon, he held his farewell feast, the Atsataion, and as host offered them the viands that had been given him. While the Hurons ate, he kept proclaiming: "My brothers, I am about to die. Amuse yourselves boldly about me. I fear neither your tortures nor death." He chanted his songs of defiance and pounded out a dance up and down the cabin as if he were in a festive mood. The Hurons encouraged and applauded him, and at times joined him in his dance and chant.

After sundown, eleven fires were lighted in the longhouse of the war chief. While the older men and women packed themselves on the platform along the walls, the young braves crowded the central passageway and roused themselves to fury. As soon as the prisoner was thrown into the cabin, they battered him with flaming torches and pursued him as he ran from one end to the other. "He shrieked like a lost soul," Le Mercier related, "and the whole crowd imitated his shrieks, or rather smothered them with horrible shouts. The whole cabin appeared as if on fire, and athwart the flames and the dense smoke these barbarians seemed like so many demons who would give no respite to this poor wretch. They often stopped him to break the bones of his hands with sheer force; others pierced his ears with sticks; others bound his wrists with cords, the ends of which they pulled with all their might."

On the seventh round of the cabin his strength failed and the elders stopped the tortures lest he should die that night. Later, they revived him, and again began to burn him about the legs, which were then in shreds. They tied slow-burning withes about his waist, and forced him to stand on red-hot axes. "You could hear the flesh hiss," reported Le Mercier, "and could see the smoke rise even to the roof of the cabin." All the while they were taunting him with merry remarks and enraging him with their mockeries.

Occasionally, they would quit, to give him water and roasted corn. During these intervals, de Brébeuf was able to get near to console the victim. The Hurons also rested and listened to Echon, as he offered to Joseph all the joys of paradise. They could not understand why Echon was so fond of this Iroquois. "Do you think that because of what you say and do now to this Iroquois, the Iroquois will treat you better if some time they come to ravage our country?" one asked him. Echon answered: "That is not what concerns me. All I think of now is to do what I ought. We have come here only to teach you the way to heaven. In regard to ourselves, we leave that entirely to the providence of God." Another snorted: "Why are you sorry that we torment him?" To this, Echon responded: "I am not opposed to your killing him, but to your torturing him this way."

At dawn, Joseph the Iroquois still lived. Outside the village, they tied him to a post on a scaffolding some six feet high. There they seared him more cruelly than ever, thrusting firebrands down his throat and forcing them into his fundament. They burned his eyes and hung red-hot hatchets about his shoulders, till he fainted away. Since they feared he might die of fire, one cut off a foot, another a hand, and a third finally severed the head from the shoulders.

The head was presented to Chief Ondesson, so that he might make a feast of it. The trunk was dismembered and put into the kettles, and the people of Arontaen ate the meat of the Iroquois. After the slaughter that morning, de Brébeuf, Le Mercier and Garnier returned the five miles to their cabin at Ihonatiria, with the shrieks still ringing in their ears and the ghastly cruelty in their eyes. They said their Masses for the repose of the soul of Joseph, the first Seneca that died a Christian.[6]

There seemed, now that it was September and most of the Hurons had returned from the St. Lawrence, no hope that the other missioner who had been promised would make his way up. With surprise, then, on September 11, de Brébeuf learned that a Blackrobe and a boy were at Ossossané. He hurried over the headland trail, and there found Père Isaac Jogues, whom he had known as a young teacher in Rouen, and a frail-looking lad named Jean Amyot. Jubilantly, he led them back to Ihonatiria, where there was a new reunion, for Jogues was a student at Clermont College with Garnier and Chastellain.

Jogues reported that Daniel and his three little Hurons had arrived at Three Rivers on August 19. That same day, the Hurons held council with Duplessis-Bochart and the French. They said nothing about bringing the Blackrobes to their country, and nothing about leaving their boys at Quebec. Only one boy, Satouta, was willing to remain at Quebec and Jogues despaired of finding passage to the Huron land. Duplessis-Bochart convened another council with the traders, who then were eager to start their journey home. After the usual formalities, Duplessis-Bochart argued: "Why do you not show the friendship you profess for the French? You give beaver robes to the French, and the French give you hatchets. This is trade. It is not an evidence of real love. We show love by sending the Blackrobes to live with you and to teach you. Not one of you will live among the French. Why do you not trust us? Why is there only one village of Hurons which shows its love for the French?"

The Huron spokesman responded that this matter of leaving their children with the French was so important that it must be discussed with their chiefs in their own country. Daniel answered that Echon had been given the approval of the chiefs at the council that spring, and that his presents had been accepted. The spokesmen alleged there was danger from Iroquois along the road. Duplessis-Bochart asked if there were greater danger for the Hurons than for the French? The speaker told how dearly Huron mothers loved their sons. Duplessis-Bochart responded that French mothers also loved their children, yet they allowed them to live among the Hurons.

An old chief then spoke mild words. He praised Satouta for his spirit and courage in wishing to live with the Blackrobes. If Satouta were treated well by the French, he promised, then they would bring down many more Huron boys to Quebec. That night, a few chiefs sought out Daniel. They had Tsiko and another younger boy with them. They wished to show their love for the French and would leave the two boys as comrades of Satouta. Later, a few other canoes arrived with three more boys brave enough to spend the winter at Quebec. Thus, Daniel had six Huron schoolboys.

During all this time, Jogues related, he was waiting in hope that the Hurons would adopt him. After the final feast, an Ossossané chief asked Daniel: "Have the French less love for Ossossané than for other Ouendat towns?" Daniel saw that the remark of Duplessis-Bochart had nettled the man. He answered that the French loved all the Huron villages. "Then why do you not give us some French for Ossossané?" the chief demanded. Daniel and Le Jeune offered them the Blackrobe Isaac Jogues and the boy Jean Amyot. "They adopted me," said Jogues, "and gave me the name of Ondessonk."

Père Jean found much to thank God for that September. Six priests would be living at Ihonatiria and, when all returned, at least five lay helpers. This coming year he planned to extend the missionary labors to other villages throughout the country. He was satisfied that the savages were beginning to understand Catholic truths and was convinced that they could be taught to follow the Commandments.

Four: 1636

The influenza epidemic of last year and the year before was again raging all along the St. Lawrence, all the way up the Ottawa, and was prevalent in the Huron villages. The French had escaped its ravages during the past two years, but Père de Brébeuf feared for the coming year. Little Jean Amyot had been quite sick during his journey up, and was feverish and emaciated when he arrived at Ihonatiria. Isaac Jogues nursed him until he himself felt indisposed; he had a fever and his head ached, he coughed and sweated. On September 17, Le Mercier, who acted as infirmarian, ordered Jogues to remain in his bunk beneath the shelf that stretched along the wall. That very same day, Mathurin, the workman, landed at the cove. All the way up from Quebec, he said, he had suffered from cramps and fever. Le Mercier judged Mathurin was having a relapse, and told him to stay under the blankets. There were now three patients, all showing different signs of the virus. On September 23 another workman, Dominique, burned with fever and was so weak he could not stand up. He too was put to bed.

De Brébeuf and Le Mercier, who nursed their four patients, felt helpless. They tried to remember what was done in France for such symptoms. They had no medicines, but thought that prunes and raisins, or broths of senna leaves and wild purslane, might be helpful as a purge. They had no food except corn mush seasoned with dried fish and an occasional egg. The workman, Petit-Pré, was searching for game, but thus far had not had a shot at the wild ducks and geese.

The bunks, a little bit raised from the floor, were dark and damp and uncomfortable, especially since the sick were sweating profusely and there was only a limited supply of linen and blankets. The cabin itself was like a deep-buried tunnel, with no ventilation for the acrid fire smoke except the slit along the ridge pole. Nothing was conducive to an adequate care for the four sick people.

When the savages heard that the French were sick, men, women and children surged into the cabin. De Brébeuf was exasperated for he knew that rest and quiet were essential for the patients. He tried to hush and silence the rabble that forced its way in, that shouted and pushed along the center passageway, that crowded about the bunks. Failing in this, he closed the doors on the villagers. They were suspicious, then felt insulted, and finally flared out in anger, since no one ever closed the doors to anyone, except to an enemy. When a person was sick, everybody visited him; the French must have some secrets about the sickness, they suspected. Since he could not exclude them, Echon begged them to move quietly and speak in low tones. They were resentful of this; when they were sick, the sorcerers and their friends screamed and chanted and danced about them. They grew more suspicious since silence was always connected with sorcery.

Père Jogues weakened and languished. For three or four days, he bled from the nose and his fever rose higher. The only remedy they could think of was a surgical bleeding. Since no one of them had ever bled a person, they feared that they might not be able to staunch the blood after the cutting of the vein. De Brébeuf volunteered to make the cut; Le Mercier was also willing to assume the responsibility. They consulted with Père Isaac, and he, knowing of their dread of killing him, said that he had seen a surgeon bleed a savage and thought he himself could cut the vein. The next morning, September 24, after he had received Holy Communion, he made the incision in his arm and the blood spurted out freely. They clotted the cut and laid him back on the blankets. Shortly, he fell asleep, as if in a swoon.

Dominique turned purple, and they recognized this as a symptom of a more virulent form of influenza. He had a raging fever and tossed restlessly when he was not as still as death in a coma. They bled him, but the bloodletting was not so successful with him as it had been with Jogues. While they hovered about him anxiously, Chastellain, who had been helping to nurse the four patients, felt light-headed and shaky. Since he, too, was running a fever, they put him in his bunk, as the fifth patient. That evening of September 25, they used the lancet on him.

The greatest need for the sick was some nourishing food. Petit-Pré scoured the swamps and the shorelines in his search for some bird or animal that could be eaten. During a full week he had brought back no game except a few ducks. In his extremity, Père Jean considered sacrificing their hen and rooster, but that would be of little help. He thought, too, of killing a dog. He had eaten dog meat at the Huron feasts, and though he and the French had an aversion to it, it would make a good broth. He remembered that a friendly savage had a plover tied in his cabin. He offered the man beads, then a hatchet, then a blanket for the bird; but the Huron said he loved his little plover so much that he would not part with it. De Brébeuf, counting no price too high in this crisis, obtained the bird in exchange for a deer skin.

Dominique was dying on Friday night. His body was purple, he breathed heavily in a coma, his pulse and heartbeats were faint. In the light of a flickering torch, Père de Brébeuf administered Extreme Unction to him. The four who were well, kneeling by his mat on the ground, and the four who were lingering between life and death in their bunks, recited prayers for the dying. De Brébeuf, Le Mercier and Pijart kept vigil through the dark hours, waiting for the final gasp.

Garnier, though engaged in the Spiritual Exercises of his annual retreat, had, however, been assisting the others in the care of the sick. He arose on Saturday morning with fever and a splitting head-ache. He celebrated Mass, then staggered back to his cot. He confessed to Père Jean that he had the fever for two or three days, but felt he could work it off, since there was more need for nurses than for patients. They put him to bed, the sixth to be stricken. There remained now only de Brébeuf and Le Mercier to tend the sick. Pijart spent most of the time in the cabins of the sick Hurons, while Petit-Pré was out hunting, night and day.

During the day, the open space of the cabin was a bedlam. Report had spread far and wide that the paleface French were sick, and the savages traveled miles to witness the strange spectacle. Never before had they seen the French ill and dying, never since the French first came to their land. They jostled about the cabin, they shouted and screamed, they ate from the kettles, they squatted in and above the bunks, they suspiciously watched every move of the Blackrobes. De Brébeuf was in despair since all of the six patients were dangerously sick.

On Sunday, the great sorcerer, Tonneraouanont the hunchback, followed by a howling mob came into the longhouse. He had been persuaded by friends, he said, to cure the Frenchmen. After boasting that no disease could ever touch him, he declared: "If you give me a present, I promise to put all the sick on their feet in three or four days." De Brébeuf asked him his price. "Ten glass beads," he stipulated, "and one extra bead for each sick one." De Brébeuf inquired how he proposed to cure them. He promised to give them some roots, to blow on them and chant, to consult his oqui, and to perform a special sweat. Echon, in tones loud enough for all in the jammed cabin to hear, told the sorcerer that his remedies were useless, that his sweats, chants, dances, games and such superstitions were absurd. He advised the sorcerer and all the savages to follow the practice of the French and to pray to the One-who-made-all, since only from God, and not from the demon, could health be given back to the sick and the dying.

The next day, two old chiefs called on Echon. They feared this would be a winter of disease. Already there were sick in almost every cabin, and many had died. They had no faith in the remedies of the sorcerers. They had heard that Echon wanted them to pray to his God, and asked him to summon a council, and to recite public prayers, as they phrased it, "to drive the contagion away from the Ouendats and send it elsewhere". They were gratified when he promised that, later on, he would do as they wished.

For the present, he was obligated to devote all his time and all his thought to the care of those whom God had entrusted to him as his sons. He thanked God that Père Le Mercier and himself had thus far been immune to the fever and been able to nurse the six patients through their crises. None had died, not even Dominique, yet all of them wavered in the throes of this baffling disease. Then, on October 1, Le Mercier, who had heroically sacrificed himself in tending to the needs of the others, collapsed with the influenza. He was bathed in sweat and shaken by chills, was insensible with lethargy and torn by aches through his whole body. De Brébeuf, now the only one on his feet except Père Pijart and Petit-Pré, bundled Le Mercier under the blankets. He opened a vein, but the blood would not flow. He feared that Père François, the last to be stricken, would be the first to be taken. Within three days, however, the crisis was passed, and Le Mercier began slowly to recuperate.

By the first week of October, all the seven invalids were recovering. Pijart, who had escaped the sickness, was able again to visit the cabins of the stricken savages. Petit-Pré, likewise untouched by the disease, was bringing in an abundance of duck, geese and other game. But all marveled at Jean de Brébeuf. During the two harrowing weeks, through the night as through the day, he had fed and eased, cleansed and soothed the seven patients in the infected longhouse, had hovered about them as would a father, had brought them Viaticum daily, yet had shown no weakness either of spirit or of body. Le Mercier testified: "We would all have given our lives for the preservation of that of Père Superior who had so perfect a knowledge of the language. It pleased the Divine Goodness to keep him always in sufficient strength to exercise his charity toward us day and night."

Now that his own household was recovering, de Brébeuf devoted himself to the savages. By the end of October the contagion was in almost every cabin in almost every village. He thought that, as in France, the change of season would stay the spread of the epidemic; but the sickness continued to plague the people through November, when the cold was intense. As the old men had warned, this was to be a winter of disease and death. De Brébeuf feared it, yet found it a challenge. He knew that the Hurons would become more and more frenzied and hysterical, that the sorcerers would be driving the people more insane with their superstitions and would be invoking the aid of the devil himself in their seances. But out of the material evil of the epidemic, he hoped to gain spiritual profit through charity to the living and salvation for those dying.

Since the workmen were using their muskets to good advantage, he had a supply of soups and meats to distribute morning and evening to the sick Hurons. Then, he portioned out his small supply of raisins and prunes, which, to the savages, seemed sovereign remedies, and

cooked a broth of senna leaves for use as a purge. Simon Baron, who
had come up from Quebec in October, knew how to use the lancet
and so brought relief to many by bleeding them. While performing
these acts of charity, Père Jean was also seeking to prepare the minds
of the sick for baptism before death. With some he succeeded in
winning consent, but with the majority he failed. The savages feared
that baptism would kill them, since they reasoned that practically all
whom the Blackrobes baptized died a short time later. They began
to bar their cabins against Echon. Those who were sick drew their
cloaks over their heads, while others growled roughly: "*Teouastato*, I
do not wish it."

The Arendiowane sorcerers, having failed to drive away the
demons of the pestilence, excused their failures by proclaiming that
the French were more powerful sorcerers than they themselves, and
that if they and their charms were disposed of, the country would be
healthy again. One of them learned from his demon that the disease
was blowing down the lake from the direction that the French had
come into the country. Aënons repeated that an Island Algonquin
revealed that Champlain, shortly before he died, threatened to go
into the Huron land and to ruin it. It was said that the Blackrobes put
the disease into the meat and broth they gave to the sick.

Toward the end of November, a few of the elders again asked
Echon to recite public prayers to drive away the disease, as he had
when he brought the rain. He answered that he would hold a great
feast to which he would invite all the men. On November 27, when
he announced that his feast would be of deer meat, he attracted a
large number of guests. In the Huron custom, as host he entertained
them by talk. He was bowed down by sorrow, he told them, because
of the contagion that was in their cabins and villages. To dry their
tears he offered them a present of four hundred porcelain beads, some
hatchets and a moose skin. The only way to avert this scourge, he
continued, was to believe in God, to pray to God and to keep the
Commandments of God. He asked them to promise to serve God
and, as a proof of their sincerity, to vow that, if God took away
this pestilence from them, they would erect next spring a special
house for God's service. Though they applauded his propositions,
they answered that, since this was a matter of importance, they must
debate it in council.

Some of the elders returned two days later with the answer that they accepted his propositions to believe in the French God and to build a house for Him next spring. De Brébeuf, doubting their sincerity, impressed on them the seriousness of a vow. If they failed to keep their promise, he warned them, God would be more angry with them. They answered that there was no hypocrisy in their hearts. Echon then bade them all kneel before a statue of Our Lord and repeat after him a vow to believe in God, to keep His Commandments, and to build a chapel. The next morning, Père Jean, holding in his hands the Blessed Sacrament, pronounced in the name of the priests a vow to say a Mass in honor of Our Lord, another in honor of the Blessed Virgin, and a third in honor of Saint Joseph, and in the name of the laymen a vow to offer special communions and prayers, in petition that the village of Ihonatiria and their residence be spared in the epidemic of influenza.

Two nights after the pledge of the elders, the people of Ihonatiria, under the instigation and leadership of the sorcerers, were in a delirium of frenzy. They donned their masks, they shook the earth with the pounding of their dance, they howled and shrieked through the night, in their efforts to scare away the demon of disease that was killing them. Once again, the emotions of the villagers boiled over in threats against the Blackrobes. Significantly they informed Echon about a certain man suspected of being a sorcerer, of secretly weaving charms to sicken and kill people. The man had answered: "If you think it is I who makes you die, take this hatchet and split open my head. I will not stir." A chief answered: "We shall not kill you now at your bidding. We shall kill you the first time we catch you in the act of causing people to die by poisons and charms." De Brébeuf understood the meaning of the story.

CHAPTER VII

Assault on the Donjons of Demons

One: 1636–1637

THE TIME HAD COME, Père de Brébeuf judged, to challenge the devil hiding beneath the mores of the Hurons. He chose as the first arena the village of Oënrio, about three miles from Ihonatiria. Chief Aënons and the elders, impressed by the promises Echon made at Ihonatiria to save the people from the plague, invited him to advise them what they must do in order to gain the protection of the One-who-made-all.

At the council held in Aënons' longhouse on December 5, 1636, Echon sat with them in silence about the fires until they invited him to speak. He grieved with them in their affliction and mourned with them in their bereavements. He declared that, to be spared, they and all the Ouendats must believe in the one and only Master-of-All, the God of himself and the French. Being all-powerful, this God created them and all the things in the world. Seeing-all, this God watched over them each minute of their lives. This God demanded that they adore Him and serve Him. This Great Spirit, Echon continued, gave Commandments to all men, French, Algonquin and Ouendat, and obligated all men to observe these Commandments. To those who lived according to these Commandments, the Master-of-All would give everlasting happiness after death. Those who violated these Commandments, the All-Powerful-One would condemn to fires that never stopped burning and to tortures that never ended. They listened in rapt attention.

Echon then broke into the subject of their superstitions. Their faith in dreams, he declared, was absurd and childish; their dependence on the Arendiowane was insane and a delusion; the remedies commanded by these evil witch doctors were nonsensical for the

174

most part and inhuman in other respects. In the vibrant council pitch, he advised that they put aside forever these superstitions and evil customs of their ancestors.

"Do you wish," he asked, "to serve this Great Spirit and save yourselves from the pestilence that afflicts you?" They answered that they so wished. Echon then issued his prohibitions: "First, you must give up your belief in the power of dreams. Secondly, when you marry, you must bind yourselves to one woman for life; you must not change wives, you must not go to other women. Thirdly, you must not indulge in vomiting feasts, since God forbids such gluttony. Fourthly, you must not hold the Andacwandet, because such mating feasts offend God. Fifthly, you must not eat human flesh, even though it be that of your enemies. Sixthly, you must not attend or conduct the Aoutaerohi, and thus appease the demon." He concluded by recommending to them, as he did to the people of Ihonatiria, the building in their village of a cabin dedicated to the honor of the Great Spirit.

After some time in thought, the old chief spoke: "My nephew, we have been greatly deceived. We thought the Great Spirit would be satisfied with a house. According to what I have heard, He asks a great deal more." Then spoke Aënons, the chief: "Echon, my brother, I must speak to you very frankly: I believe that your proposition is impossible. I cannot be a hypocrite. I express my thoughts honestly. I judge that what you propose will prove to be only a stumbling block. We have our own ways of doing things, you have yours and other nations have theirs. When you speak to us about obeying and acknowledging Him as our master, Who, you say, has made heaven and earth, you are talking of turning the country upside down. Your ancestors assembled in earlier times and held a council. They resolved to take as their God the one whom you honor, and they commanded all the ceremonies that you observe. We have learned differently from our ancestors."

Echon rejoined that his brother Aënons was mistaken. His ancestors did not make a choice; they were taught by nature itself about the One-who-gives-life. Men did not prescribe these ceremonies; God revealed these to men. He continued: "The French way of doing things, it is true, is different from the Huron way. There are as many different ways as there are peoples upon the earth. The manner of living, of dressing, of building houses is entirely different in France from what it is here. But as regards God, all peoples should have the same belief, for there is only one God for all peoples. The reality of God is so clear that it is only necessary to open the eyes to see it written in large characters upon the faces of all creatures." Concluding, he told them it was not enough to build a chapel. They must keep the Commandments and give up their superstitions.

The old chief, seeking peace, spoke in favor of Echon's propositions, but the others hung their heads in disapproval. They agreed to hold another council the next morning. Assembled on the morrow, the old chief said that he had spent the night sleepless, pondering on Echon's words. He himself thought them very reasonable, but he feared the young people would find them difficult. "However, all things well considered," he reasoned, "I conclude that it is better to take a little trouble and live, than to die miserably like those who have already been carried off by the disease." No one dared contradict him, so plausibly did he speak. They all bound themselves to believe in Echon's God, to keep His Commandments, to renounce their superstitions, and to build a beautiful chapel in the spring. De Brébeuf returned to Ihonatiria much consoled by their favorable state of mind. A few days later, as had happened in Ihonatiria, the younger people of Oënrio were chanting, dancing and holding the orgies commanded by their dreams and sorcerers.

The chiefs of Ossossané sent Echon a message that they wished to consult with him about driving away the curse. He was gladdened, for Ossossané was the next great step forward in his plans. It was the center of the Bear nation and the gateway to the other Huron nations. If he could win the chiefs of Ossossané, he could influence not only the Bears but those of the Cord and the Rock peoples. He waited over the Feast of the Immaculate Conception to renew the vows of 1636. On December 9, while a keen wind blew and the trails were covered with ice and snow, he, Chastellain and the faithful Baron covered the twelve miles to Ossossané. Many were languishing with the disease, many were being carried to the cemetery. De Brébeuf, when he could, baptized those he thought would die. Baron spent the days using his lancet, some days bleeding as many as fifty.

On December 11, the supreme chief of Ossossané convoked a council to hear how Echon proposed to drive away the curse. Several

hundred men representing all of the longhouses attended. Echon proclaimed, as he had at Oënrio, that they must believe in God, accept
His Commandments, and renounce their superstitions. The presiding
chief answered that, since their sorcerers had not cured them of their
mysterious disease, and since Echon promised help, they should agree
to accept his terms.

De Brébeuf, fearing their fickleness and hypocrisy, suggested that
they give good thought to what he had said, and discuss the matter
further. The following day, they continued to be of the same opinion: if Echon could cure them of their sickness, they would accept his
propositions. Their only debate was as to the manner of proclaiming
these resolutions to all the people of Ossossané. They judged it best
that Okhiarenta, whose stentorian voice made him one of the most
powerful sorcerers, should go through the village and announce the
decisions of the Supreme Council.

That day, Okhiarenta strode through Ossossané proclaiming: "The
people of Ossossané take God for their Lord and Master.... they
renounce all their errors ... do not believe in dreams ... make no
feasts for the demon Aoutaerohi ... do not meet in the Andacwandet
... no vomit feasts ... keep the same wife ... not eat human meat ...
build a cabin to God in the spring ... provided He stops the progress
of the disease." In his comments, the pious Le Mercier remarked:
"What a consolation it was to see God publicly glorified through the
mouth of a barbarian and one of the tools of Satan. Never had such a
thing ever happened among the Hurons."

On December 17, de Brébeuf, having baptized about fifty persons,
returned to Ihonatiria. Le Mercier and Garnier, whom he sent to
Ossossané, reported that a few days after the public proclamation the
hunchback sorcerer held a ceremonial sweat in the longhouse where
they were lodged. Twelve men crowded into a little tent with him;
he threw tobacco on the fire, singing his invocation to the devil: *Io
Sechongnac*. Other sorcerers were also plying their trades as usual in
the cabins of Ossossané.

During the winter months of early 1637, pairs of Blackrobes and
fur-coated lay aides traveled back and forth along the white trails to
all the villages of the Bear nation. For the most part, they were given
the same courtesies extended to any Huron, food and a mat for sleep.
When they sat about the fires, they talked of the things of God, of

heaven and hell, of French and Huron beliefs, of the Commandments and the practices condemned by Echon. They tried to win
the assent of the sick to accept baptism. Sometimes they succeeded,
oftentimes they were repulsed by the dying people or their relatives.

Canards against the Blackrobes, originating mostly in Ihonatiria,
were spreading through all the villages. One man avowed that the
porcelain collar Echon presented at the Feast of the Dead now caused
them to die. He reasoned that since Echon declared that he did not
offer the collar to the dead, but to the living, in order to show them
the way to heaven; therefore, Echon was killing them in order to
send them to heaven. In Ossossané, whither de Brébeuf went, the
hunchback sorcerer, among other accusations, declared that, when
the people were getting well, the Blackrobes killed them by giving
them poisoned meats.

On his return to Ihonatiria from Ossossané, de Brébeuf found
his people in some consternation. A chief, raging at the Blackrobes
during a feast, had blamed the disease on them. If a Blackrobe entered
his cabin, he threatened, he would split the head of the first Frenchman he met. A few days later, he and his brother burst into the
cabin, in a terrific rage, and tried to provoke a quarrel. "If we do
not kill you," he shouted, "we will put you in canoes and send you
back to Quebec." So current was the belief that someone would
kill the French that children gathered about the cabin one evening
while the Blackrobes were chanting. They interpreted the chant as
the death song, and waited for the braves to murder all the French
and to burn down the house.

The sorcerers were in the ascendancy, everywhere. At Onnentisati, one of them secreted himself in a partitioned corner of the cabin
and tasted nothing but tepid water for six days. He announced that
several demons confessed to him that they caused the disease. But
now they took pity on the country and asked to be driven away.
They prescribed the holding of an Aoutaerohi feast, since they feared
nothing more than that. Later, the demons revealed to the sorcerer
that all the people should hang masks and stuffed men before their
doorways, so that they, the demons, would be frightened away. An
old friend of Echon begged him to help save the people by following the orders of the demons of disease by hanging masks before his
cabin. When Echon refused and reprimanded him, he apologized:

"My nephew, we do not know what we are doing. There is nothing we would not do to preserve our lives."

Over in Ossossané, while de Brébeuf was staying there in mid-January, Tehorenhaegnon, the powerful sorcerer, was promising to drive away the disease. He had observed a fast for twelve days in a hut on the sand of the lake shore. The demons had appeared to him and given him a remedy. The same chiefs who had proclaimed de Brébeuf's proposal in mid-December were now, a month later, sending envoys to invite this witch of Andiatae. He himself would not enter Ossossané, he said, but he would cure the sick from afar, through his assistant. He ordered three feasts on three successive days.

De Brébeuf witnessed them, since he was lodged in the long-house where they were enacted. A crier from the top rafters pleaded: "Come now! Behold us here assembled! Listen, you demons whom Tehorenhaegnon invokes! Behold us about to make a feast and have a dance in your honor! Come, make the contagion cease! Leave this town! If you still have a desire to eat human flesh, go to the country of our enemies! We now join ourselves with you, to carry the sickness to them and to ruin them!" Though the feasts were held and the rites enacted, there remained as many sick as professed to be cured. Later there occurred so many deaths that the sorcerer and his assistants were discredited.

Despite these waves of hysteria, de Brébeuf and the other missioners sedulously visited the cabins and sought to pour the saving waters of baptism on those who were departing this life. As always, there were some who refused or whose relatives drove the Black-robes away. But always, here and there, they won souls for God. They ingratiated themselves by distributing a few raisins or prunes and, besides the bleedings performed by Baron or the other laymen, they found that some colored ointments they had brought for pustules were beneficial, according to the Hurons, for all their diseases.

The epidemic of influenza abated about the middle of February. With it passed away the fury and frenzy of the Hurons. They forgot both their witch doctors and their promises made to Echon at their councils. They thought of the spring to come, of their corn planting, of their nets for fishing, of their peltries for trading, of their canoes for water journeys. The missioners, too, had their surcease of strife and travel.

In the furor of his ceaseless labors for the Hurons, Jean de Brébeuf held close to God in a prayer that often lengthened out through the eerie night. Very frequently, God seemed to grant him illuminations and visions that consoled and strengthened him. Occasionally, he jotted down what opened before his spiritual eyes in these times of prayer. He relates: "In the year 1637, Our Lord showed me a superb palace richly built, in beauties inconceivable, and in so many and such surprising varieties, that I was quite ravished out of myself, and could not comprehend even my own feelings. As this palace was empty—there being no one in it—it was given me to understand that it was prepared for those who should dwell in poor cabins, and who had condemned themselves to these for the love of God. This greatly consoled me."

On Ash Wednesday, February 25, a neighbor named Tsiouendaentaha squatted before Echon's cabin fire. He was about fifty years old, very intelligent, and most influential in the councils. He informed Echon he had learned much in the instructions he had listened to. He wanted to know if he could be baptized without being in danger of death. Echon gave him assurance that it would be better if he were not sick. However, since baptism was a matter so important, he wished to give further lessons to him. De Brébeuf thought it strange that the chief should seek to be baptized even while the missioners were being threatened with death as sorcerers. It might be that this chief was the answer to his prayer that God raise up a Huron champion of the Faith.

All during Lent, de Brébeuf and Garnier gave the man daily instructions which he well comprehended. He took delight in joining the French in their public prayers, and often went to the chapel to pray in his own way. Fearing that Tsiouendaentaha, like so many Hurons, would believe with the mind only, de Brébeuf questioned him exactly. The chief swore that he did not believe in dreams and other superstitions, hence had no regrets about giving them up. As for the Commandments, only one bothered him, that about women; but this would cause him no trouble, since his day had passed. He was ready to make a public renunciation of all superstitions and evil feasts.

On Saturday, June 6, Tsiouendaentaha gave a feast for all the men of Ihonatiria. He announced that on the next morning he would be baptized as a Believer. He put no faith in dreams; therefore, let no one bother him about them. He judged that the sorcerers were frauds; therefore, he would not comply with their orders. He did not wish to be invited to superstitious feasts, ritual dances, and shameless orgies, because he would not attend. He declared that hereafter he was taking God as his Master and intended to comply with His Commandments. His renunciation and his profession were complete. He invited all to be present at his baptism the next morning.

The young priests erected an altar at the far end of the long living room. Over it they formed an arch of summer flowers and evergreen, of tinsel and ribbons. They put out their statues and hung their sacred pictures. Tsiouendaentaha arrived early on Sunday morning, as did crowds of men, women and children, who wondered if baptism would kill him outright. After the exorcisms, renunciations and promises of this solemn ceremony were completed, Père de Brébeuf poured the living waters of baptism on the head of Tsiouendaentaha and gave him the Christian name of the first Apostle, Peter. At the Mass which followed, Peter received his First Communion.

The fires of the cabin were lighted again, and the kettles were filled with the best of corn meal and fish. Echon sent word to all the villagers that he had prepared a great feast to which all were invited. After they had gobbled their food, the Hurons stood stupefied at the magnificence of the decorations. Nothing so beautiful had ever been seen in their country. They looked wide-eyed at the statues and wondered if they were alive; they asked innumerable questions about the pictures; about one, in particular, they gathered in fear. It was that of the Last Judgment, explained Le Mercier, in which "the damned were depicted—having their entrails torn out by serpents and dragons, and being tortured by devils." The day was memorable for Père Jean and his community. At last, God had raised up a Huron adult to the level of a Christian. Peter, they hoped, would prove to be the foundation stone of Christianity among the Hurons.[1]

Two: 1637

To carry on his battle against the evil forces, Jean de Brébeuf planned that spring a direct offensive. While maintaining the house at Ihonatiria, he would attempt to establish permanent mission centers in the more important towns. With five zealous helpers, all of whom could talk the language sufficiently well, and with the expectation of more recruits in September, he was ready to push into the heart of the Huron land.

His first problem, however, was Ihonatiria. Last year, the five villages under Aënons seemed ready to unite and build a single large town. This spring he called a council on March 29, and asked them two questions: First, did they intend to keep their cabins at Ihonatiria, or would they unite in a large village? Second, would they listen to his teaching about God, and follow the Commandments of God, according to the promises they had made? Their answers were evasive. As for the first, they had not made up their minds. In the second matter, some would and some would not. At this point, a dispute arose between Peter the Believer and those who were hostile. Echon released them from their vow to build a chapel, since they had not followed his other prescriptions and God had not saved them from the disease.

Considering all things, de Brébeuf was more resolved to move the mission center out of Ihonatiria. After all his efforts, the people of the region were not influenced to accept the Faith. Then, this far northeast corner of the peninsula was remote and sparsely populated, and had very little influence in the affairs of the Bear nation. Ossossané seemed the obvious place for his main residence. He had originally intended to settle there in 1634; the chiefs and people had shown themselves very friendly whenever he visited them; it was a strongly fortified village, and was surrounded by a large number of smaller villages; from it, the trails to the Cord and the Rock Hurons, and to the Petuns, were shorter and less arduous. There seemed far greater probabilities of winning souls to Christ at Ossossané than anywhere else in Huronia.

He proceeded cautiously, in the Huron manner, by talking indirectly and casually about what he was thinking. At length, he requested that he be permitted to speak at a council. In a general assembly, held on May 18, all the leading chiefs of Ossossané not only enthusiastically approved the petition of Echon to live in their village, but even voted to build him a longhouse. Since so many had died of the pestilence, since some were still sick, and since others were leaving for the trade, they excused themselves from building a house as large as they would wish. But next year, they promised, they would build a bigger cabin. They accepted Echon's wish that the house be outside, but very near, the palisades. They decided on the dimensions, about sixty feet long and eighteen feet wide. Immediately after the council, the appointed chiefs, all together, chose the site of the longhouse and notched the trees that were to be felled.[2]

Pijart, appointed to supervise the erection of the cabin, complained that the work proceeded slowly. De Brébeuf hurried to Ossossané, because the Ihonatiria villagers were spreading malicious reports that Ossossané had stopped work on the cabin. He was reassured when he saw that the sustaining poles were firmly planted, the interior lines of posts were in place, the arch of the roof was being tied securely. On June 8, the longhouse of Ossossané was completed. De Brébeuf blessed it and dedicated it to Notre Dame de la Conception.

On the next morning, Tuesday, a troop of nearly fifty women and men from Ossossané arrived at the cabin in Ihonatiria. They attached the carrying thongs to their foreheads, shouldered the bags, boxes and barrels, the bundles of blankets and clothes, the pots, kettles and household utensils, and then, at a signal from the chief, chanting a song, the fifty Hurons trotted along the twelve-mile trail over the headlands to the new cabin of the Blackrobes at Ossossané.

A domestic problem arose that spring. The Frenchmen living with the missioners were good men, and were kept good by the influence of the priests. Since they were not bound by vows of chastity, they found difficulty in safeguarding themselves against the sexual promiscuity of the Huron girls. Père Jean was keenly aware of their temptations, for he had lived through three years with Frenchmen who were more lewd than the savages. Marriage with native women was thought of as a solution. Champlain had promised this and de Brébeuf, knowing the circumstances, rather approved of it. In one of the councils near Ihonatiria he asked the chiefs their thought on the marriage of the French with Huron women; they thought it would bind the two nations together more closely. He proposed that the matter be brought before a general council; they saw no reason for this. He explained that these marriages must be permanent and that the women could not divorce themselves or mix with other men; they did not think this reasonable. The matter ended by their demanding valuable gifts which the woman would own. It was clear to de Brébeuf that such marriages, at this time, would be ruinous for the Frenchmen.

Though the crest of the epidemic passed about February, there were many afflicted with the influenza until June, and all feared lest it might flare up again during the summer, when it would be more deadly. The suspicions and threats against the Blackrobes as the cause of the pestilence still prevailed. It was said that the sugar, which the Hurons called "French Snow", was a deadly poison. Then, that a French woman was seen in the sky above the lake blowing the disease upon the land; she was, they suspected, the sister of Étienne Brûlé, taking revenge for his murder. Then, the little images in the French cabin sent out invisible darts into the throats, thus causing the sickness.

Père de Brébeuf, as Superior of the Huron Mission, finished on May 20 his five-page Latin letter to the General of the Society of Jesus, Pater Mutius Vitelleschi. He recorded that "a pestilence of unknown origin, eight months ago, spread through many villages and caused many to die." He stated that it attacked the French, so that "we saw seven confined to their beds at the same time, and near to death." He related that the savages blamed the French for causing the disease. He told of the new house at Ossossané and of his plans to station some priests at Teanaustayé. "The faith gathers its harvest," he wrote, "but in toil, vigils, sorrows and patience." About the other priests, he expressed his praise: "They are in every way extraordinary workers who combine in an unusual manner prayer and union with God, with a burning zeal for souls."

All through June, the villages teemed with the excitement of preparations for the summer journey down to the trade with the French. Père Pijart and the domestics started with Aënons about June 24. The main flotilla of about 150 canoes did not get away till the latter part of July. De Brébeuf and Pijart had been scouring the country trying to persuade the parents to entrust some goodly boys to the care of the Blackrobes at Quebec. Despite the persistent rumors that the Blackrobe Antwen and two of the Huron lads had died of the disease at Quebec, they secured promises that twelve boys of varying age would pass the winter at the Huron school. At the departure of the canoes, however, fewer than half this number traveled down with the traders.

With the warm weather, the virus again began to spread alarmingly. When disease and death again gripped Angwiens, Onnentisati and Ossossané, the Blackrobes were blamed. Cabins were barred to them, threats were made against them, more openly they were charged with being evil sorcerers. It was said that the picture of the demons and the tortures showed clearly the Blackrobes wished to kill the Hurons; that a dead body kept in the little box on the altar also caused the disease; that a certain animal being raised in the house brought sickness. As confirmation, some told of the English palefaces coming far up the St. Lawrence and saying certainly the Blackrobes wished to murder the Hurons by charms.

Ossossané remained undisturbed by these charges until late July, when the number of sick increased. Then Ossossané was convinced: as soon as the Blackrobes moved to their village they were afflicted with the scourge; the pictures in the French cabin infected them; French kettles, needles, awls, brought with them the disease; the weathervane above the French house informed the demons which cabin to enter; a witch lived in the clock that seemed so amusing; early in the morning and at evening, the Blackrobes chanted their sorceries; when they locked their doors at night, they were brewing new secret charms. All the women, and all but a few men, swore that these things were true, that they must be true because everybody was saying them. Some of the more violent demanded that the Blackrobes be driven out of Ossossané, and even out of the whole country. The elders spoke sadly, lamenting that some foolish young braves might do something that would cause sorrow.

During the last weeks of July, while de Brébeuf was making a periodic visit to the Rock nation, he heard along the way that the chiefs of Angwiens, in a secret council, gave permission to the young men to kill a Frenchman in order to drive away the plague. He managed to get a letter to Le Mercier warning him and the others not to go near this village. Then he learned with astonishment that, everywhere and by everyone, it was being said he himself had been murdered.

He hurried back from the Rock country to Ossossané. As he strode into the village, all the people of Ossossané gaped at him. When he entered the cabin, Le Mercier and the others seemed stunned. Then they burst into jubilation. He was alive! They told him that two Ossossané chiefs, a few days before, expressed their sorrow because

Echon had his head split. They even named the two murderers, members of the Rock nation. Hearing this, de Brébeuf went immediately to show himself to the supreme chief of the Bear nation. Great was his astonishment, for he had heard for certain that Echon was secretly done away with. Later, many who came to the cabin to see for themselves looked on him as one returned from the dead.

A general council of the Huron nations met at Ossossané on August 4. The public proclamation declared that its purpose was twofold: to consider war or peace with the Seneca Iroquois and to determine the cause of the pestilence. Delegates of the Rock, the Cord, One-White-House, and the other nations were present. Echon, as the chief of the French, was also invited. Through the first night they debated on the question of war. The next night, August 5, they inquired into the reason for the sickness and death. The presiding chief, blind and feeble, exhorted them: "Speak frankly. Let no one conceal the truth in his heart." The council chief then harangued. With superb rhetoric, he described the grief of all the people when they saw their relatives helpless with disease and falling into death. He concluded with an innuendo that the French knew something about this sickness.

Echon complained that he could not clearly hear what the orator had said; he asked to move up closer to the speaker. Le Mercier, who was with de Brébeuf, remarked: "We took our places next to those who had the most bloody weapons to produce against us." Several harangued the assembly, with sighs and lamentations, enumerating the list of their dead. Echon sensed that this was to boil up their emotions. Then arose a Rock chief, renowned as a warrior and famous as an orator.

"I shall tell you what I have learned about this disease within the past few days," he declared. "First, however, you must understand that I speak without passion and that I intend to tell only the plain truth. I neither hate nor love the French. I have never had anything to do with them. We see each other for the first time today. I do not intend to do them any wrong. I shall only report faithfully the speech of a man of our nation who recently returned from the trade at Quebec."

With adroit skill, he enumerated the charges against the Blackrobes, and testified that there were fifty other chiefs who would confirm his statements. Echon asked to be heard and, according to Le Mercier, "closed the mouth of this chief in a few words, with reasons for which he had no answer." Still another old chief, followed by still others, reiterated the charge that the Blackrobes caused the disease. When he could get leave, Echon cast back at them his answers. One affirmed that the demon causing the deaths was a piece of cloth hidden in Echon's cabin. He assured Echon that the lives of the French would be spared if he surrendered this cloth. Echon denied that he had such a cloth. Blandly, one old man advised: "My nephew, that is not the way. Only admit you have the cloth. Do not fear, no harm will come to you." "If you do not believe me," answered Echon, "send some of the council to our cabin. Let them search every part of it. Since we have different kinds of cloth, you may fear you are being deceived. Take all the cloth and throw it into the lake."

Someone remarked for all to hear: "Take heed! That is just the way guilty sorcerers talk." Echon turned on him: "How do you wish me to speak?" His accuser retorted: "Speak this way! Tell us honestly what makes us die!" Echon responded: "That is what I do not know, and what I cannot tell you. Often have I told you that we know nothing about this disease. I do not think that you can discover its origin. That is hidden from me and from you. But I am going to reveal to you some things that are infallibly true." Boldly, he broke out into a discourse about God, His Commandments, heaven and hell, and their superstitions. They listened impatiently, until the presiding chief interrupted him by saying: "My nephew, we seek only to discover the persons who cause the sickness."

About daybreak, they postponed further discussion until the Huron traders returned from Quebec. The sentiment of all, however, was expressed by an old man: "If they split your head for you, we will not say a word."

Three: 1637

In the midst of all this fury, when the devil seemed to be accepting his challenge, Jean de Brébeuf received what gave promise of being a gift from heaven. About a week after the council that portended death, a serious-looking brave named Chihwatenhwa came to the

Blackrobes' longhouse in Ossossané to talk with Echon. Sweating and agitated, he was infected with the sickness, he said, after he and all in his cabin had been spared through the winter. He related to Echon that he had listened to his speeches at the council for the Feast of the Dead and at other councils. He approved of and believed in all that Echon had declared. Now that he was caught by the plague, he asked Echon what remedies he should seek and how he should act.

De Brébeuf had long been interested in Chihwatenhwa. He was a man of about thirty-five and belonged to a notable family of Ossossané chiefs. He seemed to be utterly sincere and humble in his attitude. De Brébeuf advised him to put his faith in God and to promise to keep His Commandments. His answer was startling, for he said that he had believed for a long time and wanted to live like the Blackrobes. De Brébeuf warned him that he must not trust in his dreams nor invoke the sorcerers during his illness. Chihwatenhwa answered that he never put any credence in such things and never practiced these superstitions. De Brébeuf brought the man into the chapel and prayed aloud for him in Huron. Chihwatenhwa added his own made-up prayers, asking God to protect him in his sickness, promising to be faithful if he lived, hoping to be happy forever if he died.

The next day, de Brébeuf brought him some natural remedies and a blanket. Chihwatenhwa was very sick but clear in his mind. From him and his wife, Aonetta, de Brébeuf learned more astounding things; they were married only once: they had never consorted in the native way with any other men or women; they never attended the revolting sort of feasts; and beyond all else, they did not smoke tobacco. De Brébeuf instructed the man, his wife and all in the cabin more specifically on the beliefs necessary for baptism and the sort of life required afterwards. Chihwatenhwa already understood and accepted what Echon told him.

When Chihwatenhwa seemed to be near death on Sunday, August 16, Père Jean asked him if he did not wish to be baptized. He answered: "My brother, I have asked you a hundred times to baptize me. During my sickness, you have never come to me that I did not say to myself: 'Why do they not baptize me.'" De Brébeuf could ask for nothing more. He baptized Chihwatenhwa and gave him the name of Joseph. The priests at Ossossané offered a novena of Masses in honor of Saint Joseph for his recovery, for they were convinced that, if he lived, he would become a great Christian. On August 18, when he seemed to have passed the crisis, he announced: "Since God has restored me to health, I am resolved to be very faithful to Him all my life. I shall so act that the others will recognize it."

Some days later, Joseph Chihwatenhwa gave a feast of rejoicing to which he invited all his kinsfolk and friends. He spoke while they ate, as became the host. Publicly he renounced all superstitions and lewd practices, declared his belief in God, and promised to be faithful to the Commandments, which he explained to his guests. "All admired him," related Le Mercier, "and said among themselves that he had a great mind. They expressed astonishment that he was resolved to live as a Christian."

Through August, the hate of the Hurons simmered. The women and a great part of the men were surprised, as well as regretful, that the general council of the chiefs had not officially condemned the Blackrobes. The young men, it was currently rumored, intended to take the matter into their own hands. They had already split the skull of two witches, and many of them would like to do the same with the Blackrobes. However, they abided by the wish of the elders and would wait the return of the traders from the St. Lawrence. Likewise, de Brébeuf, anxiously yet hopefully, waited for the return of the five hundred and more Hurons. He felt sure that Governor de Montmagny and Duplessis-Bochart would settle their minds, quiet their suspicions, and warn them against any unfriendly acts.

In his spiritual memoirs, Jean de Brébeuf revealed an illumination which then opened to him: "On the 21st, it might be the 22nd or 23rd, of August during evening examen of conscience and the litany of the Blessed Virgin, by an actual or an imaginary vision, I seemed to see a vast throng of demons coming toward me in order to devour me or, at least, to bite me. But not one could harm me. Indeed, those who were in the forefront were like horses of extraordinary size; they had long curly hair like goats; I do not remember the forms of the others. But this I do know, that each devil was under a different aspect, and so terrible that I have never seen the like elsewhere. That apparition lasted, perhaps, for the space of a *Miserere*. I do not recall that I was frightened, but I placed my confidence in God, saying: 'Do to me whatever God allows you to do.

You will not pluck out a hair of my head without His assent and commands.'" In still another place, he wrote: "At other times I saw death bound, with hands behind, to a post near me, endeavoring to spring forward in a fury, but unable to burst the bonds with which I saw it was restrained, until it fell at my feet, without strength or vigor, powerless to hurt me."[3]

The plague continued, and there was danger every moment. Many who recovered, relapsed; many who were healthy were laid low. Women wailed in the cabins and about the scaffoldings in the cemetery. Medicine men danced and chanted about the sick, blew on them and beat their rattles, ordered feasts, games and sweats, and drove the sick and the well into frenzies of madness. In the blistering summer heat, de Brébeuf and his companions knew not what day some brave, in a fit of insanity, would fell them with a stroke of an ax or a club. They were careful to avoid irritating the savages by forcing their way into hostile cabins. The uncle of Louis Amantacha carried to Echon a message from Teanaustayé. Many of the chiefs who had spoken against him and the Blackrobes at the general council had been infected by the disease. They wished to know why they were stricken, and they asked him to cure them. In the question and the request, de Brébeuf saw, was an accusation and a threat. He gave his usual answer: "Renounce your superstitions and pray to the One-who-made-all."

Père Paul Ragueneau arrived on September 1, with a few Ossossané canoes. He was welcomed effusively, as Le Mercier recorded: "*Bon Dieu*, how sweet are these meetings." He was twenty-nine, a friend of Chastellain, Garnier and Jogues, was robust and poised in his strength. His vitality and his eagerness seemed to give new life to the community worn down by the sullen struggle with the Hurons. To de Brébeuf, he seemed the embodiment of all the qualities required for a missioner. He gave them the news of Quebec. He confirmed the rumors that the two Huron boys, Tsiko and Satouta, after baptism died last September; Père Daniel had succumbed to influenza but had recovered; the three other lads seemed satisfied till the summer, when they became homesick and tried to escape, but Daniel had hopes that they would remain with him another winter. The good report of these three lads, de Brébeuf calculated, would influence the mood of the returning Huron men.

About mid-September, Pijart reached Ihonatiria with a disheartening report. Aënons had died at Three Rivers, but was baptized. Most of the Hurons whom he met along the way or at Three Rivers were sick. The Montagnais along the St. Lawrence and all the Algonquin nations along the Ottawa suffered even more than the Hurons. Three of the Iroquois nations, the Mohawks, Onondagas and Oneidas, were on the warpath and five hundred of them threatened to attack Three Rivers. De Montmagny armed against them, but they disappeared. He said he had left before the main body of the Hurons had arrived for the trade.

Since Pijart informed him that no more missioners would be sent that year, de Brébeuf made his assignments. He would remain at Ossossané with Le Mercier, Garnier and Ragueneau. He placed Pijart in charge of Ihonatiria with Jogues and Chastellain as assistants. He cautioned all that they must act prudently and, for the present, restrain their too great zeal, since threats were still being hurled at them. An attempt had been made to strangle little Jean Amyot, and other acts of violence might be expected at any time.

The main flotilla of 150 canoes reached their landing coves in all parts of Huronia about the beginning of October. For de Brébeuf and the missioners the return of the five hundred men brought joy and peace. They had held council with the French, they reported, had been well treated, and were given fine gifts. They were surprised that the French at Three Rivers spoke in exactly the same way about the plague as did Echon and the other Blackrobes. Le Mercier reported: "They all were the most contented men in the world. We saw admirable results from the council held at Three Rivers. They no longer believe, they say, that we cause their death, since all they saw and heard down there removed from their minds these sinister suspicions. Affliction and despair so greatly troubled the minds of these barbarians that if, by evil chance, those who returned from Three Rivers had spoken of us in terms less favorable, we would have been a prey to their fury."

October brought no cessation to the epidemic, which now had lasted for a full year. The savages were in the greater despair in that they could find no cause for the disease. They knew that it must be caused by some unseen and unknown demon. Since their most powerful Arendiowane had failed to drive this demon away, they were mystified and confused. Formerly, they had had other waves of the plague, but never had they experienced one that lasted so long and killed so many. They believed with their whole souls that they could be cured and saved only by discovering and driving out the witches and their demons.

Those who returned from Three Rivers found empty places in their houses and listened to the tales of the women about the Blackrobes. They heard that, in the August council, the decree of death was practically passed against the Blackrobe sorcerers; everyone agreed that Echon and the others should have been killed at that time. The returned traders remembered the Algonquins saying that the French had most powerful demons on their side, that these demons protected the French but killed the Hurons and Algonquins, that the palefaces were killing all the people so that they alone might possess all the land.

De Brébeuf was fully aware of the smoldering hate and the increasing abhorrence of the Hurons toward the Blackrobes. In Ossossané, there had been an attempt to burn down the longhouse. In Ihonatiria, one of the relatives of the dead Aënons pointed an arrow at Pijart. Despite the lurking danger along the trail, de Brébeuf traveled over to Ihonatiria, for it seemed that the hostility was flaring out there more intensely.

In the late afternoon of October 26, Le Mercier came running into Ihonatiria. Breathlessly, he told de Brébeuf that that morning an old chief, wild-eyed, had burst into the Ossossané cabin. "My nephews," he cried out, "you are dead men. The Attigneenongnahac are coming to split your heads while the people of Ossossané are away fishing. I have just learned it from the chief." Le Mercier said he had a confirmation from the great chief who was much worried but could not forbid the Cord nation from carrying out its threat. The three priests at Ossossané had no fears, said Le Mercier. If the murderers came to the cabin, they were resolved to await death standing at the altar. The workmen had confessed and were prepared spiritually, but they had their muskets loaded and had made up their minds to shoot. If they died, it would be fighting.

De Brébeuf recognized the absolute seriousness of this crisis. The chiefs of the Cord nation had openly attacked him at the council, so that any of the Cord braves who wished to kill the French would have the approval of their chiefs. He decided to return immediately to Ossossané. He gave directions to Pijart and Jogues. If they heard that those at Ossossané were massacred, they should take refuge in the cabin of Peter Tsiouendaentaha, and commit to his care all the chapel equipment; they must not expose themselves heedlessly; if they could save themselves during this danger, they might be able to carry on their labors for the Hurons afterwards.

De Brébeuf and Le Mercier took the trail for Ossossané. The three young priests and workmen were alive, they found. But last night, one of their best Huron friends flung himself into their cabin and shouted: "Come quickly! Answer to the council! You are dead men!" Leaving Ragueneau to guard the cabin, Garnier and Chastellain followed after the Huron. They entered the council cabin, they told de Brébeuf, and noted that one of their most violent enemies was presiding and was in the midst of a raging harangue. Keeping the Huron stolidity and calmness, they sat among the savages. The orator enumerated venomously all the accusations made against Echon and the Blackrobes. He made much of a charge directly against de Brébeuf, namely, that Echon, when he came back to the Hurons, said he would remain only five years. Four summers had passed, said the speaker, and during this time the wicked Echon had caused the ruin in their nation. In another year he would complete his work of destruction. He demanded that Echon should be brought before the council. Garnier answered, very quickly, that Echon would like very much to meet them in council as soon as he returned to Ossossané.

De Brébeuf, the next day, sought out some of the leaders. Joseph and most friendly chiefs were off fishing. The others whom he visited remained silent. He suspected now that there had been a later council which doomed them as evil sorcerers and he knew the blow would fall on his head first. He prayed that the Hurons, satisfied with his death, would not kill the others. While he waited for the summons to the council, he gave his final directions. On the morrow, October 28, they were to begin a novena of Masses in honor of the Patron of the Hurons, Saint Joseph. If he were killed, the others should take refuge in some friendly cabin and put themselves under the protection of the master of the cabin. They were to keep packed the sacred vessels and chapel things and, as opportunity offered, bring these to the cabin of Peter at Ihonatiria. They were to guard most of all the Huron dictionary and grammar. He exhorted them to welcome death as fervently as they had welcomed their arrival among the Hurons.

On October 28, after the first Masses of the novena were celebrated, de Brébeuf walked out into the village. He learned that the general council would soon be held, that there was no hope for him, that even now anyone had the right to kill him. He was told that Garnier and Chastellain narrowly escaped at the council they attended. If they had shown any fear, if their voices wavered, they would have been judged guilty and then and there they would have been murdered. De Brébeuf noticed that Ossossané was crowded, and recognized many braves and chiefs from the Cord village of Teanaustayé.

Returned to the cabin, Père de Brébeuf drew out a few sheets of paper, sharpened the quill, and lit a candle. He addressed a letter to Père Paul Le Jeune, the Superior of the Mission of New France.

MON REVEREND PÈRE:

Pax Christi.

We are, perhaps, upon the point of shedding our blood and sacrificing our lives in the service of our Good Master, Jesus Christ. It seems that His Goodness is willing to accept this sacrifice from me, for the expiation of my great and innumerable sins, and to crown, from this hour forward, the past services and the great and ardent desires of all our priests who are here.

The thing that gives me the thought that this will not happen is, on the one side, the excess of past wickedness, which renders me utterly unworthy of so wonderful a favor; and on the other side, because I do not believe that His Goodness will permit His workmen to be put to death, since, through His grace, there are already some good souls who eagerly receive the seed of the Gospel, despite the evil speech and the persecution of all men against us. But yet, I fear that the Divine Justice, seeing the obstinacy of the majority of these barbarians in their follies, may very justly permit that they come and destroy the bodily life of those who, with all their hearts, desire and procure the life of the souls of these barbarians.

Be that as it may, I assure you that all our priests await the outcome of this matter with great calmness and serenity of soul. As for myself, I can say to your Reverence, with all sincerity, that I have not yet had the slightest dread of death for such a cause. But we are all grieved over this, that these poor barbarians, through their own malice, are closing the door to the Gospel and to Grace.

Whatever conclusion they reach, and whatever treatment they accord us, we will try, by the Grace of Our Lord, to endure it patiently for His service. It is a singular favor that His Goodness gives us, to allow us to endure something for love of Him. Now it is that we consider ourselves as belonging truly to the Society. May He be forever blessed for having chosen us, from among so many others better than we and destined for this country, to aid Him in bearing His cross.

In all things, may His Holy Will be done! If He wills that at this hour we die, oh! fortunate is the hour for us! If He wills to reserve us for other labors, may He be blessed! If you hear that God has crowned our insignificant labors, or rather our desires, bless Him. For it is for Him that we desire to live and to die; and it is He who gives us the grace to do so.

As for the rest, if any survive, I have given orders as to all they are to do. I have deemed it advisable that our priests and domestics should withdraw to the houses of those whom they regard as their best friends. I have charged them to carry to the cabin of Peter, our first Christian, all that belongs to the chapel; and above all, to be especially careful to put our dictionary and all that we have on the language in a place of safety.

As for myself, if God grants me the grace to go to Heaven, I will pray to God for our people and for the poor Hurons; and I will not forget your Reverence. Finally, we beg your Reverence and all our Pères not to forget us in your Holy Sacrifices and prayers, to the end that, in life and after death, God may grant us mercy. We are all, in life and in eternity,

Your Reverence's
Very humble and very affectionate
servants in Our Lord.
Jean de Brébeuf
François Joseph Le Mercier
Pierre Chastellain
Charles Garnier
Paul Ragueneau

In the residence of
la Conception, at
Ossossané, this
28th of October
I have left Pères Pierre Pijart and Isaac Jogues in the residence of St. Joseph, with the same sentiments.

That afternoon de Brébeuf sent criers through Ossossané announcing that he was holding his Atsataion, the Farewell Feast given by those who near death. The French cabin was crowded with people, the kettles were filled to overflowing. Echon, as host and as the man about to die, alone had the right to speak. While the savages ate, he told them of God and the happiness he expected to have in heaven when he died. At appropriate intervals, in the Huron rhythms, the other priests chanted their hymns. The savages gorged themselves, without speaking or interrupting Echon and the Blackrobes. When they finished their food, they uttered their grunt of thanks and silently quitted the cabin.

The doors of the longhouse were barred, and that night the priests and domestics prayed in the chapel. They waited for the word of doom or for the dawn. Père Jean, kneeling in the darkness, was strengthened by a vision, such as he had had in August. He was surrounded and threatened by hordes of enraged demons. "These spectres gave me no horror nor any impulse of fear," he related. "I said to them: 'Do upon me that which God permits you to do. Without His will, not a hair will fall from my head.'"

Four: 1637–1638

No word came from the secret council of the chiefs that night, and no braves disturbed the Blackrobes. After Mass on Thursday, de Brébeuf wandered about Ossossané, hailed everyone as usual and chatted with whom he might. Though he knew he might be struck down at any time, he showed no concern and no fear. Some of the savages watched him with surprise, as if wondering how he could still be alive, while others glared malevolently, as if wishing to kill him. The day passed without incident and without any further news from the council or the chiefs. The second day after his death feast, Friday, he observed his normal routine and sauntered as usual into the longhouses. Following his guidance, the other priests and workmen went about their duties as heretofore, appearing to be totally oblivious of the still smoldering hostility. On Saturday, Peter of Ihonatiria, who had come to guard the sacred vessels and Huron dictionary, left to tell the surprising turn of affairs to Pijart and Jogues.

When they finished their novena of Masses in honor of Saint Joseph, Le Mercier commented: "I do not know whether the devil stirred up these barbarians against us, but I can say this, we had not yet finished our novena before all these storms were quieted. So much quieted were they that the Hurons, talking the matter over among themselves, wondered about it, and with reason.... At all events, since the sixth of November when we finished our votive Masses in honor of Saint Joseph, we have enjoyed an incredible peace, at which we ourselves marvel from day to day, remembering in what a state our affairs were only a week ago."

About this time, Jean de Brébeuf felt within him the burning urge of offering himself to God for all sufferings in life and for a violent death in God's service. Thus far, he reflected, he had been preserved a thousand times from death; henceforth, he sought no protection, rather, he aspired to a martyr's death. He wrote down in Latin a vow that he would renew every day at the Communion time of Mass:

What shall I return to you, Jesus, my Lord, for all which You have given to me? Your chalice, I shall accept, and your name I shall invoke. I, therefore, vow, in the presence of Your Eternal Father, and of the Holy Spirit, in the sight of your most sacred Mother, and of her most chaste spouse, Joseph, before the angels, apostles and martyrs, and my blessed fathers Ignatius and Francis Xavier—I vow, I repeat, to You, my Lord Jesus, that if the grace of martyrdom is ever offered, in your infinite mercy, to me, your unworthy servant, I shall not fail this grace; and I vow in such manner for the rest of my life that it will never be permitted for me either to avoid the occasions that offer themselves of dying for You (unless I might judge that it is for your greater glory to do so), or not to accept most joyously the stroke of death inflicted on me. To You, therefore, my Lord Jesus, my blood, my body and my soul, now from this very day, I offer myself rejoicingly, so that I may die for You, if so You wish, for You who deigned to die for me. Grant that I may so live, that at length You may wish me thus to die. And so, my Lord, I shall accept your chalice and I shall call upon your name, Jesus, Jesus, Jesus.

November continued to be a month of peace. The influenza had abated, the sorcerers were more or less quiescent, those who had been fishing returned with their canoes loaded with fish. All the hate and fury against Echon and the Blackrobes was apparently forgotten; the missioners sauntered into the Huron longhouses, and the Hurons squatted in that of the Blackrobes. Joseph Chihwatenhwa, back from the fishing camp, tried even Echon's patience by his desire to be further instructed, to be taught new prayers, to be told Bible stories in order that he might teach these things to his relatives. De Brébeuf planned to hold public instructions for the men of Ossossané such as he had attempted at Ihonatiria. Joseph was so enthusiastic that he helped Echon write sermons that would strike the Huron mentality.

The first assembly, in the form of an eating feast, held on Our Lady's day, December 8, attracted about 150 guests. As host, Echon had the sole privilege of addressing and entertaining the assembly. He interspersed his talks with the chanting of the *Veni, Creator* and other hymns by the priests. Finally, he proposed that all should come to his cabin at regular intervals to consult with him about things that were important for their well-being in this life and for their happiness in the world to come. They all beat their approval by striking their bark spoons on their bark plates and making the cabin resound with their "*Haau, Haau, Haau.*" But too many feasts, revels and debauches so occupied their time that they failed to attend his public instructions.

As his next resource to attract hearers, de Brébeuf persuaded the ranking chief of Ossossané, a relative of Chihwatenhwa, to invite all the leaders to a great feast and council on January 9, 1638. He and Joseph entertained all the guests with explanations of belief and exhortations which were highly approved by all. On February 1, another influential councilor feasted his friends and declared to them that Echon would reveal to them something worthy of their attention. Le Mercier, who wrote the *Relation* that year, exclaimed: "It is my great regret that I cannot here reproduce the native simplicity of the language which P. de Brébeuf has mastered so perfectly. Without any doubt, I judge this discourse capable of conquering even the most obdurate heart."

After the feast, said Le Mercier, "many spoke in support of this proposition: they were obliged to believe the Blackrobes and believe in God." They resolved to send criers through the town proclaiming that Echon was raised to be a chief of council and that all must believe in God. According to the *Relation*: "Everyone talked of nothing else than the resolution passed by the chiefs and elders to believe in God. Some made feasts especially to announce that they and their families desired to become Believers."

De Brébeuf was more than ever convinced that the conversion of the Hurons could be effected, not through the women, or boys, or even the young men, but through the chiefs, especially the influential old ones, and through the matured heads of families. "If the master of a family is for God," Le Mercier remarked, "the remaining members will not offer us much resistance." During the early winter of 1638, therefore, de Brébeuf as Chief Echon started public religious services which were well attended by the older people. At these council services, he intoned a prayer slowly in the usual shrill council pitch. The priests sang other prayers to the tune of Huron chants. A topic for discussion was announced, and was cast in the form of catechism questions and answers. These pleased the Hurons tremendously. Joseph Chihwatenhwa was a leader, sometimes objecting, sometimes pretending ignorance, sometimes preaching.

While de Brébeuf rejoiced in these present blessings, he knew that the wave of fervor would ebb out. He could teach their minds, but he had not yet been able to curb their passions. Many who sought to be baptized, he held off, wishing to test them by the rule of the Commandments and by their absolute rejection of their superstitious practices. About Joseph Chihwatenhwa and his family, de Brébeuf had no doubts. He solemnly christened Aonetta, Joseph's wife, with the name of Mary, and conferred the Sacrament on some of their relatives. On the same morning, in the presence of a cabinful of wondering people, he united Joseph and Mary in the bonds of Christian wedlock, the first Catholic marriage ever performed between two Hurons.

Meanwhile, de Brébeuf had made up his mind to abandon Ihonatiria and to attempt the bold expansion of establishing a permanent center at Teanaustayé. The three priests at Ihonatiria were laboring zealously but fruitlessly. They derived consolation from a few Christians like Peter, who was not only steadfast but saintly, and from a few prospective converts like Atsan, one of the great war chiefs. The whole region where they had begun their apostolate was being depopulated, by so many deaths, by so many locating their cabins in other towns. On the contrary, Teanaustayé was even more populous than Ossossané and far more centrally located. It was the capital of the Cord nation, the progenitors with the Bears of the Ouendat confederacy. The people were vigorous and aggressive; the chiefs enjoyed even greater power than the Bears in council and war.

The Cords claimed priority over the French, since they were the first to pledge alliance and friendship with Champlain. They also held first right over Echon, since their men had brought him to the Huron land in 1634. For that reason, they had the warrant to kill him last October when they invaded Ossossané. Though they took advantage of the trade, they secretly disliked the French and, to the fullest extent, detested Echon and the Blackrobes. They held most tenaciously to their savage customs and practiced with greater intensity their diabolic rites and orgies. De Brébeuf, who had visited Teanaustayé regularly, was cognizant of the hostility of the Cord people, yet he knew that, if he gained influence among the Cords as he had among the Bears at Ossossané, he could more easily complete the conquest of all the Ouendats for God.

During April and May, while de Brébeuf was visiting the relatives of Louis Amantacha and some other families that were hospitable, he let it be known that the French would like to have a cabin in Teanaustayé. When the word had sufficiently got around, he talked to the old chief, Ondihorrea. Judging there might be some advantage in the French trade if the Blackrobes lived in his village, in the first half of June, he convoked a council to discuss the proposition of Echon, whom they now had to recognize as a Bear chief of council. The argument that it would create better trade relations with the French at Three Rivers if the French lived in Teanaustayé prevailed. The speakers made it clear, however, that they had little love for the Blackrobes and great suspicions of their sorcery. They added that it might be well to have them near, where they could be watched more closely. Though they refused to build a new longhouse for Echon and the Blackrobes, they were willing to give them an empty cabin which, as de Brébeuf discovered, was so small, so sordid, so ramshackle that none of the villagers would live in it.

For de Brébeuf, the permission was an unexpected victory. Since he had experience of the fickle Huron change of mind, he sought to take possession immediately. He summoned some of the workmen from Ossossané to come to Teanaustayé to repair the cabin, and ordered others to pack the belongings at Ihonatiria and to transport them by trail and canoe. He placed the new mission under the charge of Père Jogues and Chastellain. He dedicated the residence and the village to Saint Joseph, transferring the title from the deserted Ihonatiria settlement. They celebrated the first Mass in Teanaustayé on June 25, with astonishment, as one stated, "because this village had so greatly abominated us just a little while before".[4]

Antoine Daniel, gaunt, skinny, fever-eyed, stalked like a specter into Ossossané on July 9. They gaped in surprise at his coming, especially this early. In turn, he expressed surprise that any of them were alive. Ever since last autumn, he told de Brébeuf, it was reliably reported at Three Rivers and Quebec that all the French had been brutally massacred by the Hurons. Montmagny had intended sending a detachment of soldiers at the first breaking of the ice to protect them if they were still alive. Since the rumors came from the Algonquins, it was thought better to determine their truth. Two of Daniel's young men, Joseph Teouatiron and John Armand Andehoua, volunteered to go up to their homeland to investigate. Père Daniel joined them. After hardships and dangers incredible, they reached the Island Algonquins, where they met a Huron canoe on its way to Quebec. When they learned that the Blackrobes and the French still lived, Joseph Teouatiron returned with the Huron party to the St. Lawrence, while Père Daniel and Armand Andehoua struggled upward to Ossossané, fearing they would die from exhaustion along the way.

While the general assembly of the Huron confederacy was debating through the winter the question of a more vigorous prosecution of the war against the Seneca Iroquois, it was deciding also in favor of an act of peace and humanity. Envoys had come to Ossossané from the Wenrôhronons, a people of the Huron-Neutral-Iroquois stock. Their country lay to the west of the Neutrals, and they had formed part of the Neutral Federation until a few years back when the Neutrals withdrew their protection and left them a prey to the Iroquois. Driven from their land by the Iroquois, they were forced to move westward along the shores of the Lake of the Eries. Their envoys, piteously describing how they were being exterminated by the Iroquois and, during the past year, were being killed off by the pestilence, begged the Bear nation, their brothers, to save them from total extinction and to give them space and protection in the Ouendat country.[5]

The Bear chiefs gave their answer: they had pity on their brothers, the Wenrôhronons; they invited them to make their homes in the Huron land and thus form one people; they understood that about six hundred would come, most of these women and children, many of them sick with the disease; they feared that the Wenrôhronons would have troubles, since it was a long journey of more than two hundred miles, and since their enemies the Iroquois might molest them; they resolved to send large parties of their war chiefs and warriors to protect them, and bands of stocky women to help them carry their goods.

At the end of June, the Huron braves and the sturdy squaws took the trails southward and westward to the Wenrôhronon villages. About mid-August the vanguard of migrants began arriving in Huronia. By the end of August, the main body of Wenrôhronons, led by their chiefs and braves, followed by their women and children, stretched for miles along the shore and the forest trails leading to Ossossané. All the people from Ossossané, all from the villages about, hurried out to greet them on their arrival, to give them food, to offer them lodging, to care for their needs after their twenty days of travel.

The Huron chief in official council welcomed the Wenrôhronon chiefs and their people, and pledged undying union with them. The orators, related the chronicler, "exhorted their Huron people with so much earnestness and compassion to help these poor strangers, that I do not know what more could have been said by a Christian preacher, most zealous in works of charity and mercy." Thereafter, the newcomers were distributed through many villages, though the greater number were lodged at Ossossané. "Wherever they were received," one of the missioners related, "they were given the best places in the cabins, and had full liberty to use the chests of corn."

For Christian motives, de Brébeuf and the French also welcomed these poor strangers. They cured many sick with the influenza virus by bleedings and other remedies. They consoled them with gifts that pleased them and food that would nourish them. Since they could make themselves partly understood, the languages being dialects of the same tongue, they instructed them about God and the future life. Through the saving waters of baptism, great numbers of Wenrôhronons passed to heaven from their new homes among the Hurons.

CHAPTER VIII

Peace in the Haven of Sainte Marie

One: 1638

WHEN PÈRE JÉRÔME LALEMANT LANDED at the beach below Ossossané on Thursday, August 26, 1638, Jean de Brébeuf and the other priests were here, there and everywhere aiding in the corporal care and ministering to the spiritual concerns of the newly arrived Wenrôhronons. Upon their return in the evening to the La Conception longhouse, they gathered about Père Lalemant in a rousing welcome and asked him a thousand questions about Quebec and old France.

In a private conversation, Père Lalemant presented to Père de Brébeuf the documents whereby he was named to succeed him as the Superior of the Huron Mission. Jean de Brébeuf was overjoyed and tremendously relieved. Often he had begged that someone wiser and someone holier would be sent to replace him, someone to whom he could give his obedience and on whom he could rely. Spontaneously, he knelt before Père Lalemant as his new Superior and relinquished all authority over all the priests and workmen, over all the material things and the spiritual apostolate, and pledged his obedience to Père Lalemant and to the Superiors. Despite his usual placidity, he blurted out only one question: was he ordered to go down to Quebec or would he be permitted to remain among the Hurons? Lalemant gave him immediate assurance that he was to remain, and offered him a confirmatory letter from Père Le Jeune. Jean de Brébeuf thanked God for the favors he had received that night.

Not one of the other priests shared his joy. They revered Père Jean as a saint, and they had molded themselves according to his spirit. They were daily witnesses of his austerities and self-chastisement, of his prayer lengthened in the blackness of the cabin chapel through the hours of the night, of his trust in God in regard to all that happened, of his sinlessness and his striving for perfection, of his zeal for God and his sacrifice of himself. They loved him for his integrity and honesty, for his never-varying serenity and patience, for his kindliness, sympathy and care for them.

They did not know that, some time before, he had written the following item in his spiritual memoir: "While making a review of the state of my soul, I had the thought that God, in His goodness, has given me a gentleness, benignity, and charity with respect to everyone; an indifference to whatsoever may happen; a patience for suffering adversities; and the same Divine Goodness has willed that, through these talents which He has given me, I shall advance to perfection and shall lead others to eternal life. Consequently, I will henceforth make my examination thorough, to see whether, indeed, I make a good use of those talents for which I am responsible."

Some of them, perhaps, thought it was a tragedy that he should be removed as Superior. He was regarded by the nations as the great chief of the French, and it would be difficult to make them understand that another Blackrobe was greater. He knew the ordinary language as well as any Huron, and he spoke their council language as metaphorically as their best orators. He had absorbed the Huron customs and procedures, and understood their patterns of thought. He had won the respect of the strongest warriors by his own great height, strength and endurance, as well as by his wisdom, his courage, his determination. To the Ouendat nations he was the tongue of the French.

It may have been that some spoke of his removal as Superior, after only four years in that office, as some sort of condemnation of him or, at least, as humiliating him. He himself had no such thought, as one of his closest friends could testify, when he wrote, at a later date: "When any humiliation befell him, he blessed God for it, and felt from it an inward joy—saying to those from whom he could not conceal all the emotions of his heart that those were not humiliations for him, because in whatever low place he might be, he always saw himself higher than he wished; and that he had as much inclination for descending continually lower as has a stone, which never has a tendency to rise. Accordingly, he begged the Superiors to humiliate him; and the good thing is that when, in order to co-operate with the grace of God upon him, they did not spare him, they always found an even spirit, a contented heart, and a most serene countenance."

While their admiration swayed them to Père Jean, the missioners recognized in Jérôme Lalemant a man of eminence. He was the same age as de Brébeuf, but had become a Jesuit seven years earlier. Not only was he a brilliant student and professor, but he had proved himself to be a splendid executive at Clermont College in Paris and as Rector of the College of Blois. He had been longing to come to New France ever since 1625, when his older brother Charles, the pioneer Superior, with de Brébeuf and Massé, had been sent to Quebec. He had read all the *Relations* sent by Le Jeune and de Brébeuf, and had learned much from his brother.

Though an apt and receptive learner, Lalemant arrived with his own preconceived notions about the Huron Mission. One of his most enthusiastic ideas was that of forming a class of lay auxiliaries whom he called *donnés*. He had evolved the plan in France, he told de Brébeuf, after hearing of an experiment in the Province of Champagne. The French Provincial, Père Binet, had been favorably impressed by it, but referred him to Père Le Jeune, at Quebec, and Père de Brébeuf among the Hurons. These lay aides, he explained, would be men who sincerely desired to serve God in close union with the priests of the Society, but who did not wish to enter the Society nor to pronounce religious vows. On their side, they would bind themselves by a civil contract to employ themselves, without any pay or any remuneration, in serving and assisting the missioners in their apostolate for souls. They promised, in addition, to abjure all possessions, to obey the Jesuit Superior and to observe chastity. Over and above the civil contract, they would obligate themselves in conscience by some sort of private vow.[1]

The Huron Mission, on its side, would guarantee by civil contract to support the *donné* as if he were a member of the Society, supplying him with clothing, lodging, and other necessities, caring for him in sickness, and giving him life security. In addition, the Society would make him a participator in all its spiritual remembrances and suffrages. It expected the *donné* to lead a semireligious life and sacrificially to assist the missioners in erecting, maintaining and supporting their mission houses, in accompanying them and guarding them in their journeys, and in laboring for and instructing the savages.

The plan, de Brébeuf pondered, was not only feasible but highly advantageous. During his first stay with the savages, he had lived among Frenchmen who, for the most part, were immoral and vicious. The workmen he had employed or who acted as agents for the trading corporation during the past four years were mostly men of high principle, fine morality and veritable apostles. They were not bound, however, in any way to the Huron Mission. De Brébeuf believed that some of these faithful laborers would be willing not only to pledge themselves for life by a civil contract but would be happy to pronounce a religious vow binding themselves in conscience. He and Lalemant proceeded to draw up the terms governing the formation of this body of lay aides and officially to present them to the higher Superiors.

Another idea of Lalemant was that of conducting a complete census of all the Huron settlements and population. Though de Brébeuf knew quite well where the villages were located and about how many cabins and families they contained, Lalemant desired more accurate and scientific information. Still another plan brought by Lalemant from France was that of establishing a permanent and central French headquarters where the missioners would live and from which they could go off on journeys to the Huron settlement.

In all the many conferences on these and other matters of administration and stabilization, Lalemant protested that he deferred to the wider experience and good judgment of Père Jean. With his habitual spirit of obedience, de Brébeuf accepted Lalemant's plans and promised full co-operation. But it was with a leaping joy that he finished the series of conversations and was free to escape along the trail to join Jogues and Ragueneau at Teanaustayé. For in this new mission, he knew, the devil would rise during the coming winter and there would be more suffering, more cruel persecution and greater danger than at Ossossané.

The war frenzy pulsed among the Hurons that summer and autumn of 1638. In every village, fiercely painted warriors, armed with tomahawks, knives, javelins, clubs, bows and arrows, chanting their battle songs and slamming down their feet in the war dance, shouting their defiance of the enemy and their boasts of valor, shrilling their piercing war cry of *wiewiewiewie*, whirled out of the gates at a mad gallop along the trails toward the Iroquois.

They were more victorious than they had been for many years. One band brought back more than eighty prisoners, about a dozen of whom were allotted to the chiefs of Teanaustayé. De Brébeuf, Jogues and Ragueneau watched the raving braves of Teanaustayé "caress" and "welcome" these naked captives, and marveled at the courage and the fighting defiance of the Iroquois, whose fingers had already been torn or bitten off and whose bodies were already festering and blood-caked. Outside the village, they saw the Hurons form for the gauntlet with sticks and clubs and the Iroquois being hurled one by one into the lines where they were pounded and beaten. The Huron women and children, no less than the braves and old men, were mad with the blood lust and aroused with the prospect of the tortures.

De Brébeuf found his chance to talk to the Iroquois, while they were huddled outside waiting for the gauntlet, and later when they were given a rest. At first, the Iroquois were hostile to this inhuman-looking giant dressed in a black gown, but then they judged that he was friendly, especially when he talked to them in Huron, which they could partly understand. Echon sympathized with the chief and his men in the sufferings they had already endured and consoled them with words of courage for the tortures to which they would soon be subjected. Their pains would soon be over; but, he asked, what would happen after death when they passed to the world of the souls? He assured them that he could make them happy in the land of souls if they assented to what he advised. The chief and the other Iroquois were interested and, after he had instructed them, answered that they believed his words and wished to gain eternal joy in heaven.

During the night, in the large cabins, the Hurons shrieked their hate and vengeance, while the Iroquois howled their challenge and defiance. The Hurons burned them in all parts of the body with torches, heaped burning coals on them, seared them with white-hot hatchets. They tied them to the posts or shackled them on the earth where they agonized them with delicate, obscene cruelties. One by one, they exhibited them on platforms during the day, blistered them from head to foot with firebrands, jabbed awls into them and carved off slices of their flesh. Finally, having scalped them and crashed in their heads, they fed themselves courage by eating the roasted flesh of the Iroquois.

At first, the savages were too engrossed with their torturing to notice the Blackrobes. When they heard the Iroquois courageously chanting and boasting that they were going to heaven after they were killed, they became suspicious of Echon, and gathered that he was giving their victims strength to withstand them and to cry them down. Thereafter, they prevented the Blackrobes from talking to the prisoners. Before that time, however, the missioners contrived to baptize most of the Iroquois savages.

One of the first to listen to de Brébeuf and to be baptized Peter was the Oneida chief, Ononkwaia. He was held till the last, and since he was chief, for him would be reserved the most intense torments. On the platform in the field outside the village, they began his final burnings. Some Hurons on the platform shoved flaming torches into him, while others beneath pushed burning brands upward through the poles. Ononkwaia grabbed the torches and attacked the Hurons. While the platform spurted with the bursts of flying embers, Ononkwaia missed his footing and fell off the platform. They threw him on a fire. Covered with burning coals, brandishing fiery torches, he leaped up and rushed against the Huron braves. They scurried out of his way. He ran toward the stockade of the village to set it on fire, and had gone a hundred paces before he was felled with a club. They cut off his hands and feet, and twisted his body over a fire. His blood quenched it. They roasted him over another fire, and seven more fires. He still wriggled and struggled. They stuffed him into the flames beneath a blazing tree trunk. Rolling himself free, he crawled on knees and elbows toward them. They stood transfixed while this man, without hands or feet, burned to a cinder, advanced menacingly against them the length of ten paces. A Huron leaped on him, cut his throat and severed his head. They cupped his blood and drank it, and sliced pieces of his charred flesh to eat.

Never had the Hurons of Teanaustayé witnessed such astounding courage. It was a bad omen; the Iroquois would be victorious in the next battle. They speculated as to the reason for his valor. It was Echon. He had inspired the Iroquois with the courage to defy them by promising him happiness after death. They roused themselves and the whole village to new furies against the Blackrobes, and some even threatened to treat them like Iroquois enemies. De Brébeuf and his two priests also wondered. One recorded: "We have reason to believe that this brave spirit Peter is now enjoying the freedom of the children of God in Heaven, since even his enemies cried out loudly that there was something more than human in him, that, without doubt, baptism had given him such strength and such courage as surpassed everything they had ever witnessed."

Captives were being brought back until December, and always de Brébeuf seized his chances to talk to them. One, he secretly baptized, on December 1, with the name of Francis Xavier, whose feast was occurring two days later. That night before his final torture, the Hurons flattened his palms on the earth, thrust through them a length of white-hot iron, and raised and lowered the hands till holes were pierced through. The next day, de Brébeuf was startled when the pierced hand of Francis Xavier was hurled into the cabin. The savages wished to show their detestation of the Blackrobes by this mockery, and also to warn that this might be their fate. The priests took up the pierced, blackened hand with reverence and, since it was the hand of a baptized Christian, they buried it reverently in the earth of the cabin.[2]

During these autumn months of 1638, de Brébeuf, in his labor to plant Christianity in Teanaustayé, divided the village into three sections, one for himself, one for Jogues, one for Ragueneau. Daily, they would walk through their cabins, talking to the people and seeking out the sick. He experimented with a plan for holding a public assembly, about noon, one day each week. To announce it, one of the missioners went through the village ringing a bell and proclaiming that Echon was holding a council. To their surprise, crowds of bare-bodied men attended. Some few came with sincerity to learn while others, merely curious, sought to be entertained. The greater number were hostile, for they hoped to trap Echon in his words, to learn about his sorceries, to contradict him and close his mouth.

De Brébeuf followed the same procedure as at Ossossané, with prayers and chanting, and with a middle period for discussion. Here the battle of minds and of forces clashed. Echon calmly and fluently preached to the savages about God and the Commandments, heaven and hell, baptism and the moral code, and boldly condemned them for their foolish and malign superstitions. They interrupted him, delivered speeches filled with venom and threats, accused the Blackrobes of turning the minds of the people upside down with their new teaching, and threatened them with the fate of sorcerers. These denunciations were listened to more intently than were the instructions of Echon, and were repeated everywhere. During the recurrence of the influenza, the persecution was intensified. Women barred the cabins to them, men dangled their hatchets before the doors, old and young threw sticks, clubs and rubbish at them when they walked between the cabins. At night, some of the young braves created uproar by banging against the bark of the cabin and shouting like lunatics. When Echon complained to the chiefs, their only answer was that some of their people had no sense.

In addition to the public forums, de Brébeuf held council with a smaller number of chiefs and elders who showed some signs of friendliness. Most of these, he knew, would not seek baptism, but they would exert a mollifying influence in the councils of the nation. With these, he discussed and debated the reasons why the Blackrobes had come into the Huron country. It was not for women, nor for trade, nor for fishing and hunting, nor to get gifts, nor to wage war. It was to teach them truths that would benefit them in this life and in the next. These rather friendly elders suggested another reason, namely, that the Blackrobes found the Huron country a good place to concoct their sorceries. They sought out the sick, rather than the well; when they baptized a person, he died shortly afterwards; they first went to Ihonatiria, and it became a ruined and deserted region; whenever they journeyed to other villages disease and death spread everywhere. The old men, speaking in a puzzled rather than in an angry way, wished to learn more about this from the Blackrobes.

By November, de Brébeuf had attracted a more select group of about thirty, whom he thought might be future Christians. They were sincere and seemed to be spiritually seeking for the supernatural. They were, for the most part, allured by the promises of happiness in heaven. But they had doubts; some were afraid they might fall from such a great height; some older ones thought they might not be able to walk that far; others had objections about not being able to marry; still others were curious about what they would eat; and more than one wished to be assured he would have tobacco. Patiently, in the first faltering steps, Echon strove to lift them out of the mire of their material world. In the next steps, he sought to reveal to them the brightness of the world of revelation. He labored to break the chains of slavery which their fallen natures and the devil had forged on them, and hoped to free them through Christ. By God's grace, there was already a Peter of Ihonatiria and a Joseph of Ossossané. Would there be others like them in Teanaustayé?

Two: 1638–1639

One old chief named Aochiati had been an intent listener and a persistent questioner in these conferences. Because, as he often affirmed, he feared hell-fire and wanted heaven-joy, he asked for baptism and promised to keep the Commandments. De Brébeuf doubted his sincerity and his future fidelity. While Aochiati was wise and amiable, he was rooted in his superstitions, and held the great distinction of being master of the dance of the nudes. In early December, Aochiati begged more insistently for baptism. He was going to trade with the Neutrals, he argued, and might starve or freeze to death, or be killed by the Iroquois. Echon told him he must wait until he returned. Despondently, he set out on his journey, but two days later he was back because the trails were too deep in snow and the Iroquois were threatening.

Joseph Chihwatenhwa, who happened to be in Teanaustayé, held long conversations with Aochiati and frankly told the old man all that he must give up and all that he must begin to do if he became a Believer. Aochiati showed such proper dispositions that Joseph believed he would be faithful. Père Jean, having made his own tests, agreed with Joseph. When Aochiati understood that he would be baptized, he asked the same blessing for his two little granddaughters. The three baptisms were set for December 20. The night before, Aochiati held a feast at which he publicly renounced for all time any participation in any superstitions condemned by Echon, and particularly in the dance of the nudes, and promised he would keep the Commandments of the God of Echon. With full ceremony, he and the two children were christened and he was given the name of Matthias, for the reason, says the chronicler, that "he was the one to whom the lot had fallen to be the first Christian baptized in good health and with solemnity in this village of Teanaustayé."

With Chihwatenhwa's advice, probably, de Brébeuf baptized eleven more of his most promising catechumens on December 24. All of them renounced Satan and all his pomps; all of them pledged themselves with Matthias Aochiati to observe the Christian Commandments. The villagers of Teanaustayé awaited the result; they knew for certain that everybody baptized immediately grew sick and died. When this did not happen, they were astonished. On January 1, 1639, the fourteen new Christians attended Mass in the chapel of St. Joseph's longhouse, and declared the chronicler: "This is the day that we shall always observe and recognize as that of the birth of this new Church of Teanaustayé."

De Brébeuf had been visiting Scanonaenrat,[3] the home of the Tohontaenrats, the Nation of the One-White-House, a short five miles from Teanaustayé. This people had settled in Huronia about two generations before, and had brought rites and sorceries that were even more devilish than those of the Hurons, so that they were known as "the demons of the country". They had, accordingly, given worse treatment to Echon than had the other villages. During the autumn and early winter, Daniel, Garnier and Lalemant came down from Ossossané and fitted up a semipermanent residence, after securing approval from the twelve governing chiefs. The missioners tried to assemble the villagers for public instruction, but the meetings were riotous. Armand Andehoua, who had been trained by Daniel at Quebec, and Joseph Chihwatenhwa, from Ossossané, helped to explain the message of the Blackrobes. The villagers grew hostile to them, and harassed the few sincere people who listened to the Blackrobes.

A half-dozen men of intelligence and good will, however, defied their infidel persecutors, and laughed at the frenzy of the village. They silenced the orators by asserting: "You say we will die if we are baptized. We will show you that we are men of courage by being baptized. We do not fear death." Four of them knew enough and seemed staunch enough for baptism. One was the father of the family in whose cabin the missioners lived, two were ranking chiefs, and the fourth was the brother-in-law of Armand. They were christened on January 2 with all the ceremonies and solemnities. Lalemant dedicated the day as the birthday of the Church of St. Michel in Scanonaenrat. But he wrote: "Their wives and children were not baptized, the fear and terror still remaining too strong in this village.

Here as elsewhere, it was believed that baptism causes death, or renders those who receive it liable to a thousand evils and miseries."

Still a fourth village was added to de Brébeuf's plan of expansion. It lay some six miles from Teanaustayé in an easterly direction. Its people called it Taenhatentaron, but he dedicated it to St. Ignace. He and Jogues visited it when they could, and thought themselves fortunate in being able to administer some baptisms. The people seemed more friendly, like those of Ossossané, and he foresaw the possibilities of gathering there a group of catechumens.

At Ossossané, the number of Believers was growing. By Christmas, thirty persons, men, women and children, all in good health, had joined Joseph and the half-dozen of his family. Midnight Mass in the new chapel built of logs was magnificent beyond the belief of any Huron. Joseph Chihwatenhwa carried on a running discourse during the Mass, offering prayers and teaching lessons. Lalemant exclaimed: "He has not only intelligence, eloquence, integrity and reputation, but also the knowledge of our beliefs and a love for them in an eminent degree. We are beginning to regard him as an apostle rather than a barbarian of these countries."

Outside of the fifty Christians, the twenty thousand and more Hurons were immersed that winter in their ancestral beliefs and customs. An old man of Ossossané dreamed that only a three-day feast, each feast ending with the Andacwandet, could cure the ulcer in his shoulder. He specified that twelve couples should take part, with himself and a woman as the thirteenth. Special honor and the choicest food were given to those who were to perform at the end of the eating. While leaders at each end of the cabin chanted and beat the time, the rite was performed in the central passageway of the cabin. At the end, says Lalemant, "the old man thanked them for the health that had been restored him." He was not cured, however, and blamed the Blackrobes who had talked against the Andacwandet.

A sick woman required a dance of fifty persons lasting through three hours, in order to be cured. Another invalid learned from his demon and dream that he could be cured only by the Aoutaerohi, the fire dance, in which the masters handled burning coals and clasped heated stones in their mouths. Still another woman, so weak she had to be supported, walked through more than two hundred fires; she was not burned, but she was not cured. A sorcerer would proclaim that the only remedy for a sick person was the Ononharoia, the feast of the madmen, during which all the participants feigned insanity and destroyed all they could lay hands on.

These ceremonies and rites de Brébeuf and the missioners denounced and castigated. The only results were new flares of resentment, hatred and persecution. The newly baptized were blamed for causing the death of their relatives because they refused to join in the traditional forms of cure. Though de Brébeuf warned them against the abominations and deviltries, it was almost impossible for them to abstain from these practices that their ancestors and all their relatives believed in. Their constancy was always under attack, and the missioners felt helpless, except through prayer. "All our power lies at the end of our tongues," Lalemant remarked.

At Teanaustayé, an old chief, master of some diabolic rites, but friendly to the Blackrobes, was dying. After exhausting all the forms of ceremonial curatives, he sent for Echon and begged for baptism. Père Jean instructed him as best he could and, at the moment of death, baptized him. Immediately, the old man recovered his senses and his strength, and leaped up from his mat, cured. To all who visited him, he boasted that he was a Believer. A short time later, however, he again led the orgies. His example weakened the resolutions of many of those who seemed most sincere and stabilized. They continued to protest, on the one side, that they wished to be Believers; on the other side, they resumed their barbaric customs. Echon was forced to exclude them from the cabin and the religious services.

Some few were not corrupted. In his report, Lalemant stated: "In each of our three churches, there are found Christians, in whose practice there could be desired nothing purer or more complete, nor more tenderness of conscience." At a later date, he reported that from the summer of 1638 to that of 1639, the missioners had baptized nearly three hundred Hurons and Wenrôhronons, almost all of whom died. At Ossossané they counted about sixty professed Believers; at Teanaustayé, about thirty; and about six at Scanonaenrat. That there were so many faithful Christians was due in great part to Joseph Chihwatenhwa, and his wife, Marie Aonetta. He was forever among the neophytes teaching and inspiring them with courage. The arguments he used so amazed the priests by their aptness and brilliance that Lalemant attested there seemed to come from him "flashes of the spirit of

God". He added: "This good soul seems to us to be more and more filled with the Holy Spirit, and to have entered the paths of the saints. He has given many proofs, not only in the attacks against his chastity and religion, but in his exercise of charity and mercy."

During this spring lull, Père de Brébeuf addressed on May 13, 1639, his official report to the General of the Society of Jesus in Rome. He first acknowledged the receipt of a letter from his Paternity, dated at Rome, January 1, 1638. This was given to de Brébeuf by Lalemant, but was written prior to Lalemant's appointment as Superior. With the kindly optimism that permeated his whole character, Jean de Brébeuf alleged: "The number of the faithful increases more and more. This is due to the arrival of the Reverend Père Hierosme Lalemant, who is now Superior of this Mission, and in truth, the future apostle of the Hurons, as we hope, for he is endowed with so great a zeal that he omits nothing of what might further our perfection or the conversion of the heathen. So great is his love, and so gentle, that it conquers the hearts of us all, and his excellence is to us a great encouragement to perfection."

Though Père Lalemant admired the zeal and religious spirit of de Brébeuf and the other veteran missioners, he was imbued with the French fervor for a most rigid observance of religious discipline. He assigned a period in the morning and afternoon when the priests might visit the longhouses of the natives; he required that the missioners' cabins be closed at four in the afternoon, with no one going out after that hour; and, in order to preserve the quiet of the cloister, he excluded from the cabin all natives except those "by whom we hope to profit". In accordance with these notions, Père Lalemant planned a most important change, that of a permanent residence removed from all the Huron villages and standing alone. This house, according to Lalemant, would be centrally located and would be built in the French style of stone and timber. It would be the headquarters and the home of the missioners where religious discipline could flourish as in a French Jesuit residence. From it, missioners could make excursions to all the settlements where, perhaps, some sort of staying place could be maintained. About this central residence, farms and vegetable gardens could be laid out. In the years to come, Christian Hurons could be encouraged to form their own Christian village nearby. This residence, Lalemant believed, would

unite and solidify the missionary efforts and establish the indepen-
dence of the French in the Huron country.

While de Brébeuf appreciated the wisdom and the vision of such a
plan, he saw in it a reversal of all his program and of many of his fun-
damental principles in regard to the conversion of the heathens. He
had believed that separate houses should be established in each village, with missioners living in them all the time. He had such centers
at Ihonatiria, Ossossané and Teanaustayé, and hoped to found similar
houses in all the more important villages. He wished the missioners
to be a part of the village, to be near the sick as well as the sorcerers, to
make friends who would become Believers. He had labored to iden-
tify the French priests and laymen with the Ouendats, as if they were
one people. This new plan of Lalemant made the French an alien,
though allied, people.

De Brébeuf, however, offered no great objection to the Lalemant
project. In his humility and spirit of obedience, he probably accepted
it as a better method for the future, now that the pioneer days were
finished. They discovered what they considered an ideal place. It was
about ten miles directly east from Ossossané, roughly in the region
below Ihonatiria. Going from Ossossané there was a trail descending
from the headlands and leading to a small stream that flowed into a
marshy lake called Isaragui, about six miles in circumference. This
lake emptied into a river forty or fifty yards wide which, about a mile
beyond, opened on an extensive bay. Beyond this bay was the Lake
of the Hurons up and down which the French went and came back
from the St. Lawrence.[4]

This territory belonged to a small clan called the Ataronchronon,
the Nation-Beyond-the-Morass. Their villages were small and not
numerous, their people of no great importance in Ouendat affairs.
Lalemant and de Brébeuf had some trepidation about approaching
the chiefs of the villages, since these had never shown any desire
for friendship with the French. They asked to hold council and to
declare what was in their minds. The Ataronchronon chiefs, surpris-
ingly, were most cordial and affable; they welcomed the Blackrobes
as their brothers and declared they would accept their presents. Lalemant and de Brébeuf had expected debates to range through several councils and so brought no gifts with them. Lalemant sent word
to Ossossané that the gifts of porcelain collars and beads should be

sent immediately. When they came, another council was convened, the proper number of gifts were presented to the chiefs and were accepted. Cryptically, Lalemant observed: "If we had delayed two hours, I doubt that the affair would ever have been successful."

Three: 1639–1640

"We have given to this new house the name of Sainte Marie, or Notre Dame de La Conception," Père Lalemant wrote in his *Relation*. "The general and the special obligations that we owe to this great Princess of Heaven and Earth, make it our keenest disappointment that we are not able to show her sufficient gratitude. At the least, we henceforth claim this consolation, that, as often as people shall speak of the principal residence of this Mission of the Hurons and call it by the name of Sainte Marie, they will be rendering to her so many homages for what we are to her and of what we wish to be to her forever."

The lay workmen and some of the priests, with the help of some friendly Hurons, chopped down the trees of the dense forest and made a clearing near the point where the lake flowed into the little river. By the end of August, 1639, they had constructed a house that combined the Huron exterior of bark and the French interior of rooms. It was large enough to accommodate the twelve or fifteen French who would be occupying it, and sturdy enough to be a protection from the cold of the oncoming winter. They transported all their community belongings from La Conception at Ossossané, leaving in that cabin only what was needed for transient visitors. It was thought better, however, to retain the wretched little cabin at Teanaustayé, where de Brébeuf and one or two others would continue to live during the winter.

A canoe of copper-skinned savages slid into the sedgy shore near Sainte Marie in early September. They lifted a sick man out of the canoe. Lalemant was called to look at the man, whose face and entire body were covered with pustules. Recognizing the disease immediately as *la variole*, the smallpox, Lalemant in horror exclaimed: "Without being a prophet, we can rest assured that the smallpox will soon spread through all the Huron country." The Hurons, who said their comrade had become sick on the journey up from Three Rivers, laid the man on a stretcher of bark and carried him along the woody trail to their village of Ste. Anne, about three miles away. Within a few days the man died. Within a week, almost everybody in the cabin and in the village had contracted the smallpox. Visitors from nearby villages, coming to console the sick, went home with backaches and headaches, with chills and vomiting, in weakness and oftentimes in delirium. All the Ataronchronon cabins were soon full of the plague-stricken.

On September 10, a new young missioner, Père Pierre Joseph Marie Chaumonot, reached Ossossané. Two days later, after having been abandoned he knew not where, arrived another young Jesuit, Père Joseph Antoine Poncet. In addition to their other news, notably that three Ursuline and three Hospital nuns had come to Quebec, they told of the prevalence of *la variole* along the St. Lawrence and up the Ottawa. Toward the end of September Père Le Mercier, having journeyed from Quebec with Chihwatenhwa, reported that the Algonquins were abandoning their foul-smelling sick and fleeing to the forests and mountains, that corpses along the shores were being eaten by the dogs.

Some Hurons stopped at Sainte Marie, to bring word that the Frenchman, Robert Le Coq, had died. Others confirmed the story by saying that they had seen his body on the shore of the Great Lake, two days' distance. A French aide and four Huron paddlers were sent to search for Le Coq. When they returned to Sainte Marie with his slimy, pus-covered body, he was still alive and able to talk. Lalemant attested: "I do not believe that one could look on a human body more covered with miseries. Not one of us could ever have recognized him. He was in a state of sickness which caused as much horror as compassion to all those who had the courage to examine the ulcers with which he was covered." They absolved him and administered Extreme Unction. Though Le Coq was now content to die, he continued to live, his sores began to heal and soon he had recovered.

Thirteen priests and fourteen lay helpers were dwelling among the Hurons that October of 1639. With Sainte Marie firmly established, and with accommodations sufficient for all the French, Père Lalemant was now ready for the second stage of his plan, that of sending priests and lay aides on missionary expeditions through the country.

He, as Superior, Le Mercier, as his assistant, Pijart and Poncet were to remain at Sainte Marie. De Brébeuf and Chastellain occupied the cabin at Teanaustayé. Ragueneau would be in charge of Ossossané, and have as helpers Du Peron and Chaumonot. Daniel and Le Moyne were to open a new mission center among the Arendarhonons, the Rock nation, who occupied the eastern and southern part of Huronia. Garnier and Jogues were given the mission that all had longed for, that among the Khionontateronons, whom the French called the Petun nation.[5]

The smallpox was sown everywhere, and everywhere, too, the savages were in frenzied despair. They sat about their stricken ones picking and wiping their sores, and feeding them from the bark dishes and pots they used. They breathed the foul-smelling air in their closed, dark cabins. One after another, they fell sick, so that scarcely a cabin, scarcely a family did not have its pus-covered victims. De Brébeuf watched the dread plague creep into Teanaustayé. He knew that it must pass its course, that great numbers would die, that once again the sorcerers would be seeking intercourse with the devil and degrading the people to the level of hell. With anguish of soul, he foresaw that his Believers would be weakened and would desert. He feared that he could not gain access to baptize those nearing death.

A story spread as rapidly as the plague. It was told in horrified whispers everywhere, by everyone. It was examined by the chiefs and found to be true. According to the story the Frenchman Le Coq, before he died of smallpox on the shore of the lake, revealed that the Blackrobes so hated the Ouendats that they were secretly killing them, first by influenza and now by smallpox. Le Coq confessed that the Blackrobes also hated him and had given him the disease. Since he loved the Hurons, Le Coq was resolved to save them from the Blackrobes.

Le Coq, so ran the story, just before he died, revealed to his Huron comrades the cause of the diseases and the way to get rid of them. The Blackrobes were the criminals. They secreted the ancient serpent of disease in a hidden part of their cabin, Le Coq said, and they cherished a toad, marked with pits, that was really a demon in guise of a toad. They had even a more crafty demon imprisoned in an arquebus, Le Coq revealed; when they fired the arquebus and released the demon it went about sickening people. These were the last words of a dying man, and they must be believed. Le Coq advised them: kill the Blackrobes before they ruin the Ouendat nation. Then he died.

Despite the new wave of hate aroused by this story of Le Coq, de Brébeuf and Chastellain kept visiting the cabins of Teanaustayé. Though they realized that they, as well as the Hurons, were exposed to this contagion, nevertheless they went among those festering with sores from head to foot, they choked down the insupportable stench in order to win consent for baptism. When they advised the relatives to segregate the sick and to give them separate utensils and mats, no one listened to them. Rather, everyone showed hate and vengeance; Huron men threatened them if they were about to enter a cabin; women screamed in fright when they came near; children hid from their sight; for all believed that the Blackrobes planted in them the demon of disease and death. In the councils, the chiefs orated furiously against Echon and the Blackrobes. Le Coq had revealed all that they themselves had suspected. But how catch them in their sorceries? They resolved to watch more closely, and at the very moment they caught Echon and Arioo casting their evil spells they would split their heads.

A new story spread: Le Coq, the Frenchman, lived. So incredible was this, that the chiefs of Teanaustayé sent a committee to Sainte Marie to investigate. The deputies returned with the astounding news that they saw Le Coq alive and his sores cured, that he denied he had died, and declared that his so-called dying confession was a lie. They were puzzled by this new mystery. Why did the Blackrobes give him the disease and then cure him? Was this a ruse to deceive the Ouendat people? Was it possible that Le Coq consented to become sick, but with the understanding that he would not die? Apparently, the Blackrobes were greater demons than they had thus far shown themselves, since they could cure the disease as well as strike people dead with it. They remembered now that the Blackrobes did the same thing two years ago. Most of them were sick, for one reason or other, but none of them died. Echon was not sick; therefore, Echon was the one who could kill or cure, just as he wished.

Teanaustayé was a town of the insane and the despairing as the autumn turned into bleak winter. The nights were frightful with the screams and shrieks of the sorcerers and their fanatical followers, and the cabins were madhouses where feasts and dances and orgies raged from evening till dawn. The wild superstitious rites that Echon had known before were nothing in comparison to those enacted in this village and in the cabins near his own. He and Chastellain were aware that they lived only from minute to minute, that the secret council had passed sentence against them, that in the public councils the charges and threats were more outspoken and more insistent. They fully expected some excited brave would take courage and brain them, for they could see that the women were inciting the men to vengeance. De Brébeuf suspected that they refrained from killing him only because they feared that, after death, he would return and do them even greater harm.

For this same reason, the wiser chiefs argued against splitting the heads of Echon and Arioo. It would be much better to terrorize them in the way they frightened the demons, and thus drive them out of the village. Accordingly, they shouted deafeningly in their ears, grimaced horribly and gyrated menacingly about them, mocked and jeered and yelled invectives at them. Sometimes a mob tried to drive them out by hurling stones and missiles at them. Braver ones rushed at them as if about to knock them down with a club or a hatchet. On one occasion, when de Brébeuf was beaten with clubs and felled to the earth, he awaited the final blow on the head with such equanimity that he stopped his assailant. Bands broke into their cabin and destroyed their few furnishings, shook the rafters to topple the cabin down, and tore away the cross above the cabin door.

De Brébeuf and Chastellain always replaced the cross. They walked through the village with Huron stoicism, with the same air of defiance and courage that the Iroquois captives had brazened in their tortures. They did not betray anger, or impatience, or annoyance. They well realized that they were dead men if they showed fright, for that would be a sure sign of their guilt as sorcerers. By their manner and their words, they made it clear to all that they would not leave the village. Echon complained to the leading chiefs about the persecution, and assured them that he and the Blackrobes concealed no evil thoughts about the Hurons nor had they power to cause or cure the disease. The chiefs' only answer was that they could not restrain the youth.

Chastellain, whose courage equaled that of de Brébeuf, stole or broke his way into cabins where he had hope of baptizing some soul. Once, while he was pouring the water on the heads of two dying children, a young brave leaped up roaring blasphemies against the French God. Chastellain answered him fearlessly. That night, the man had a dream in which his demon told him he must have the head of a Frenchman. The next morning, he rushed through the village shouting that he must have a French head. Some chiefs, running to Echon and Arioo, begged them to remain in the cabin, while others caught and bound the madman. Everybody attested that such a great frenzy was never seen before. His friends and the chiefs reasoned with him, and persuaded him that, according to his dream, an Iroquois was as good as a French head. Since there was an Iroquois just captured, the madman was given the privilege of splitting his head, and thus obeying the demon of his dream.

During the early autumn, de Brébeuf and Chastellain were likewise seeking new baptisms at Scanonaenrat and Taenhatentaron. The former village had always been the most degraded in its superstitions and the most hostile to the Blackrobes. With the scourge of smallpox, the villagers became demented at the very sight of Echon and Arioo. Finally, the chiefs forbade Echon and other Blackrobes from entering since, they stated, their young men intended to murder them, and they did not wish to have such killings in their village. The same prohibition was proclaimed to de Brébeuf at Taenhatentaron.

Saddest of all things to de Brébeuf was the apostasy of those on whom he had built the church at Teanaustayé and Scanonaenrat last January. Aochiati, whom he had thought would be another Joseph or Peter, publicly renounced all his previous promises of being a Believer. Since he was not stricken with the disease, other former Christians followed his example and joined in the clamor against the God of the Blackrobes. Only a few remained faithful. One was an old woman of seventy, whom de Brébeuf had named Anne. She withstood the accusers and championed Echon. "It is true," de Brébeuf told Lalemant, "that this new church has not many such courageous hearts, but there are some who give us much consolation."

Four: 1640

The wave of smallpox waned in early February, 1640. Large numbers had died by it, and those who lived were nearly all pockmarked.

Though the delirium decreased with the disease and the persecution quieted, yet in the minds of all the people of Teanaustayé there lingered a sullen hate against the Blackrobes because they had bewitched and killed so many of their kinsfolk. In this lull, when there were few to save and little to suffer, de Brébeuf returned to Sainte Marie in order to spend the annual days of prayer in the Spiritual Exercises.

It was at this time, undoubtedly, that Père de Brébeuf's confessor, or perhaps his Superior, Père Lalemant, ordered him to write out in a spiritual memoir the graces God granted him through visions and inspirations. Many of these experiences in prayer he did not understand; yet, they seemed important to him and worthy of recording by virtue of obedience. On February 11, Saturday, probably the day of his arrival from Teanaustayé, he wrote:

> On the day before I began my Retreat, during the time of examen of conscience, and confession and the saying of my penance, there appeared two suns, shining with the utmost brilliance, in the midst of which was a cross. The arms of the cross seemed to be of the same height and width, but I did not see of what material the cross was made. On each of the ends there was visible a lily or the face of a cherubim. On that part which was uppermost, there appeared a likeness of Our Lord Jesus Christ, if I am not mistaken. I was in doubt afterwards if it were not a likeness of the Blessed Virgin. Then it was that I felt called interiorly to the cross and mortification.[6]

For more than a week, in the solitude of Sainte Marie, he spent hours every day in silence and recollection. According to the command given him, he noted some of his illuminations:

> On the following day, the twelfth of February, which was the first day of the Exercises, when I was trying to employ myself only in loving notions of God, and while I was rejecting from my mind all created things, and when I was disturbed by various distractions and bothered with annoyances, it seemed to me I heard inwardly: "Turn toward Jesus Christ crucified, and let Him be both the basis and source of your contemplation." Thereupon I felt myself drawn to Christ.
>
> On that same day, I seemed to see a most terrible face, just like the lion's face which is, I think, in the picture of Pater Joseph Anchieta, but larger by far, and increasing little by little. I thought it was a demon. However, I was not disturbed by any fear and I said: "Do

whatever God permits you to do." I believe I signed myself with the Sign of the Cross, and at once the figure vanished.

Contemplating the enormity of my sins and their countless number, I saw Our Lord Who, in infinite mercy, was holding out His loving arms to embrace me. He pardoned me the past and forgot my sins. He restored in my soul both His gifts and His graces. He called me to His love and said to me what formerly He said to Saint Paul: "This man is to me a vessel of election, to carry my name before the gentiles; I shall show him how great things he must suffer for my name's sake" (Acts 9:15). Hearing these words, I thanked Him for them, and offered myself for all things, and said to Him: "What dost Thou wish me to do? Do strongly unto me, according to thy heart; nothing in the future will separate me from thy love, not nakedness, not the sword, not death, etc."

On the 14th, during the time of meditation, it seemed to me I saw Christ, Our Lord, hanging on the cross and coming toward me, as if He would remove the burden from Himself and would place it on my shoulders. I willingly placed it on my own shoulders, but I do not know what happened.... That same day, toward evening, when I was preparing to meditate on Christ's perfections, and on the many different relations that were between Him and me, and between miserable me and Him, I thought how all other designations ought to be referred to His extraordinary love for us, as to a central point. All at once, I seemed to see a huge rose, or some rounded flower, extraordinary at one time for its size, at another for its variety, all the varieties of which were proceeding from the center. On the 18th, I seemed to see the Blessed Virgin, as if in a blue cloud, carrying the Child Jesus, while through different parts of the cloud there burst forth golden rays of remarkable beauty. I was expecting that the Blessed Virgin might present me to Christ, but she did not do so.

Refreshed in soul and relaxed in body, de Brébeuf returned to the grim diabolism of Teanaustayé. During this period he continued to commit to paper the consolations and the agitations of his soul. "During the days when I was at Teanaustayé," he stated simply but arrestingly, "I was often seized and lifted up to God by motions of love." He attested that on "February 26, while I was reciting the rosary in the evening, it suddenly seemed to me that I saw the tabernacle of Sainte Marie, on which are depicted seven angels, and I was drawn to prayer. Afterwards, I seemed to be in the room and the chapel, and to see the relics that are there, so that I was impelled to invoke all those saints." At the end of March, he recorded: "When after Mass I was interiorly recollecting myself so that I might hear Christ speaking within me, it seemed to me that I saw some hand or another anointing my heart and all my inmost parts with oil. From this vision, there came to my soul the utmost peace and tranquility."

During February and March, likewise, his prayer was disturbed by visions as grim and fearsome as the actual happenings among the savages of Teanaustayé. "On February 23, during the time of evening examen," he noted that he saw a "Spaniard wearing a crenated ruff and Spanish hat," but suspected that a devil lurked beneath that form. In another apparition, he specified that "on the 9th of March, when after examen I was reading a spiritual book by the hearth, I saw near the house of Sainte Marie a huge serpent coming, as it were, out of the river and gliding toward the house." This serpent, five or six cubits in length, was dragging off a Frenchman, but was seized and dashed to the ground by one of the priests. Later, he had an apparition of four massive dogs haunched behind the gable of Sainte Marie.

"On March 11, when I was beginning morning examen before the Blessed Sacrament," he related, there came before his eyes a pictured bust of some Jesuit, and as he gazed, horns like those of a crab grew out of this head. He attested: "This vision did not last long; but it affected me with the greatest fear and trembling, lest I should be that unhappy Jesuit in whom such a terrible change should take place." While in prayer before the altar at Teanaustayé, on March 21, he saw a winged face fly out from the summit but pause in mid-air, as if held back by a thong. "From that vision," he concluded, "I thought that I or someone else was marked as one who would strive to fly to heavenly contemplation, but was held back from reaching the goal by affection for earthly things."

At Teanaustayé, the persecution continued during April, as de Brébeuf declared in his spiritual notes: "On the 11th of April, when a quarrel arose at St. Joseph's residence, in which Pierre Boucher was wounded in the arm and Père Chaumonot and I were beaten, we were all suffering from injuries and were much afraid because we had been ordered to leave the village by Ondihorrea and other leaders of that village. Later, when I was giving thanks to God for all these things and, though disturbed in mind and being in distress, I was striving, nonetheless, to conform my will to the divine, I seemed to see the Blessed Virgin, in the manner that she is depicted in sorrow, with three swords in her wounded heart. I felt interiorly as if she were telling me that, although she was sorely afflicted, she, the Blessed Mother of God, was nevertheless always conformed to the divine will and ought to be an example to me in all my adversity."

During May, de Brébeuf confided to his little book further revelations of his soul. "On the 9th of May, when I was in the village of St. Joseph, I was, as it were, carried out of myself and to God by powerful acts of love, and I was transported to God, as if to embrace Him." But this union, he went on to say, was disturbed by the appearance of an old woman whom he supposed to be the devil in disguise. "On the 17th of the same month," he stated, "while I was praying to God during the day, I felt myself lifted up in spirit to consider a cross fashioned after that of Sainte Marie, in which some relics are enclosed, or like certain crosses which are made in the shape of a star. This vision lasted a long time, and all during it I had no thought but that God wished to send me some new crosses." On May 27, he put down: "On the feast of Pentecost in the year 1640, being at night prayer in the presence of the Blessed Sacrament, I saw myself in a moment invested in a great fire which burned everything which was there around me, without consuming aught. While these flames lasted, I felt myself inwardly on fire with the love of God, more ardently than I had ever been."

About this time, one of the sorcerers some miles distant from Teanaustayé prophesied that Echon was dead. When Pijart hurried down to the village, he found de Brébeuf desperately sick. They concluded that an attempt had been made to poison him. But, Lalemant observed, "if the devil and his ministers are devising our death, the prompt cure of Père de Brébeuf—he was not sick more than twenty-four hours—plainly shows us that there are spirits a thousand times more powerful who watch over our defense and preservation."

The residence at Teanaustayé was finally abandoned at the end of May, and the few belongings were transported to Sainte Marie. The villagers rejoiced, for they believed that at last they had driven out Echon and the Blackrobe sorcerers. De Brébeuf left with regret, but with the strongest of determinations to go back often in his missionary journeys. He still believed that Teanaustayé could be lifted up to Christ and that the small church could be resurrected in quieter years. He and Chastellain carried some consolation away with them. Despite all the obstructions and hostility, they had poured the waters of salvation on the heads of 260 savages, most of whom had died and were believed to be in heaven.

At Sainte Marie, the missioners, having gathered after their winter campaigns, told their experiences. Le Mercier was so near being burned to death that stories of his murder were reliably reported in other villages. At Ossossané, Ragueneau was badly beaten and saved by an inch from a blow of a tomahawk. At the new mission among the Arendarhonon or Rock nation, Daniel and Chaumonot had, at first, been cordially welcomed, but, said Daniel, "the devil crossed the affairs of God." Everything possible was done to drive him out, and he might have been killed except that Chihwatenhwa fortunately paid a visit to Cahiagué. Garnier and Jogues in the new mission among the Petuns suffered more than all during the winter. They, too, were rescued by the opportune coming of Joseph Chihwatenhwa. They had baptized many, but had converted not one in the three hundred longhouses they had entered. Joyously, Lalemant remarked in the *Relation*: "We are alive, thank God, all full of life and health."

The general council of all the Ouendat nations convened in a village near Sainte Marie during March at the time when de Brébeuf was having his visions of the devil. The chiefs and councilors passed a resolution that the Blackrobes be massacred, and one orator added: "The more promptly, the better it will be." One single nation, probably that of the Bear, opposed the resolution. "Kill the Blackrobes if you wish, take on yourselves the blame for it," their speakers declaimed. "Our nation shall prove its innocence to the French at Quebec." The conflicting deputies accepted a compromise and a delay offered by an old orator: "There are our own sorcerers living in our midst. First, kill these. Then, if the disease still lingers among us, we will have reason to kill the French and to prove whether or not their massacre will stop this evil plague."

CHAPTER IX

Vagabonds Barred by the Neutrals

One: 1640

A T THE VERY TIME THE HURONS harangued about killing the Blackrobes, Lalemant was writing: "Never for any warnings, threats or evil treatment which the devil may have contrived to stir up against us, have we forsaken any plan or let slip any opportunity of serving the Master Who employs us." Telling how easy it would be for the savages to murder them, he concluded: "We manifestly discern that it is God Who directs our affairs. No one can deny this who will open his eyes to the things we see daily."

Though their faith in God was not weakened nor their love of God less ardent, they were puzzled by Divine Providence. Lalemant attested: "The Hurons observed with some sort of reason that those who had been nearest to us, happened to be the most ruined by the disease. Whole villages of those who had first received us, now were utterly exterminated. It has happened very often and has been remarked a hundred times, that where we were most welcome, where we baptized more people, there it was, in fact, where they died the most. On the contrary, in the cabins to which we were denied entry, although they were sick to extremity, at the end of a few days, one would see every person happily cured." With de Brébeuf, he had to exclaim: "We shall know in Heaven the secret and ever adorable judgments of God therein."

The secret was intensified on August 2, with another test and a poignant sorrow. Joseph Chihwatenhwa was murdered. He had gone to the woods near Ossossané to find some cedar sticks for the canoe he was building. Some hours later they found him in a trampled little clearance, gashed by a javelin, his head split with two

228

strokes of tomahawks. When they brought him back to his cabin, Maria Aonetta was, at first, silent; then tranquilly, she spoke: "I have often heard him say: 'He Who is the Master of all, has so arranged it. What can we do about it?'" One of his little nieces, Theresa, kept repeating: "No, I will not cease to believe in God because of this! May God have pity on me! Even though they massacre all of us, and even though they kill me, I will never abandon You, my God!" Most of the people of the village, de Brébeuf and the missioners, believed that he was struck down because he was a Christian. But the elders of Ossossané, having examined all details, passed final judgment that his assailants were Iroquois.[1]

Joseph Chihwatenhwa could not have been surprised, for Père Le Mercier recalled what Joseph had said, six months before, to his brother Teondechoren: "My brother, they assure you that I am one of the causes of the ruin of the country, that I have been taught the secret by the French and am a master in spells. Others will tell you that a resolution to kill me is adopted, or even that they have already split my head. Listen peaceably to all these sayings without disturbing yourself. Lower your head and be silent, lest you speak rashly. Do not fear that the family will be marked by any disgrace. If God does the favor to our country to have it embrace the Faith, my memory will be honorable to all posterity. It will be said forever that I have been the first who preferred closing life to losing the liberty of living openly like a Christian."

The day after the murder, August 3, Lalemant wrote to Quebec: "It seems that the last canoes are waiting only to permit me to send you a piece of news that will surprise you as much as it has surprised me, and will cause you to include it in the number of the profound secrets and of the adorable dispensations of Divine Providence, which we cannot contemplate without astonishment." Lalemant added a note to his report: "Since the saints have more power when they are in Heaven than here below on earth, we are bound to believe that we have gained more than we lost at his death."

They buried Joseph Chihwatenhwa, the greatest of Huron confessors and, perhaps, the first martyr, on August 4, with all the solemnity of Mass and interment in consecrated ground. Echon, his father in Christ, his teacher and oldest friend, delivered the funeral oration. That evening, de Brébeuf divulged in his spiritual memoir the confirmation of what his thoughts had been: "On the 4th of August, upon my return from the burying of our departed Christian, during evening examen I had diverse visions. I remember nothing at all of the first one. The second seemed to me to be like a pavilion or dome which descended from heaven and placed itself on the grave of our Christian. And then it seemed to me that someone turned up this same pavilion by the two ends, and that it was drawn up on high, as if someone wished to raise it to heaven. Nevertheless, I did not see how it was lifted up, nor the persons who drew it up. This vision lasted a rather long time, and ended there. The feeling that I had then was that God wished to give me to understand the state of the soul of this good Christian."

On the day after the funeral, Teondechoren, an elder brother of Joseph, asked Echon to baptize him. De Brébeuf gaped at him in astonishment, for this man was one of the most active and expert masters in one of the most diabolic rites of the Hurons, the Aou-taerohi. He clasped burning torches and hot stones in his hand; with his teeth, he plucked white-hot coals from the fires; he plunged his bare arm to the bottom of burning kettles, all this without pain or injury to himself. As one expressed it: "Teondechoren was a mass of flesh that covered a soul as gross as his body."

De Brébeuf told him that he could not be baptized until he had been instructed and had given up his immoral life and superstitions. To this Teondechoren answered that not only did he think he knew enough, but that he was also willing to give up all his past practices. He said that he had learned from his brother, Chihwatenhwa, all that was necessary. De Brébeuf, after testing him, was surprised at his comprehensive knowledge. But he refused to baptize Teondechoren until absolutely certain of his sincerity. Yet, he could not but believe that the saintly Joseph Chihwatenhwa had already begun to perform miracles of grace.

About a week after Joseph's burial, Père Jean revealed that he saw, in vision, a high mountain up the sides of which were ranged women saints, though he was not sure but that some of the saints were men. "From the foot of the mountain up to its peak, the saints diminished until they were reduced to a single one, Our Lady, who was seated on the crest of the hill. Then, Joseph Chihwatenhwa came to me in mind, but I could not discover him on that hill. I thought that the excellence of the Blessed Virgin over all the saints was pointed out to me."

On August 31, he noted another apparition in which, first of all, he saw a woman's petticoat of ravishing beauty, then lifted up the eyes of the spirit to see a "high and venerable statue, covered with veil and crown, in the manner Our Lady is represented. But this vision did not last long and was not so clear." After that, near to where Our Lady appeared, "something like a huge sphere was opening", the inside of which contained many things of beauty and shone with radiant light, so that, he says, "I have never seen anything like it, nor even read of it. The feelings I then had were of admiration and love of God, but also fear of being deceived."

Through the summer, de Brébeuf continued to look after Teanaustayé. The violence of the past winter was largely forgotten, but bitter resentment still manifested itself and the people still watched him closely, speculating on what new machinations Echon and the Blackrobes were plotting. Acting as if he did not recall the ghastly horrors of the months past, he talked with the chiefs, if they would converse, and chatted about the fires with all who would receive him. He was seeking to give courage to the few who had remained faithful and to bring repentance to those who had relapsed into their savage ways.

Sainte Marie was rising and expanding. Great patches of the forests had been cleared, corn had been planted during the spring, timbers had been sawed and large stones had been gathered in piles, extensions had been made to accommodate the greater number of artisans and priests who would be arriving and bringing with them the tools and equipment for erecting a solid house and enclosing walls. But greatly were they disappointed in September when the canoes arrived with the news that the Jesuit building of Notre Dame de Recouvrance in Quebec, where all the Huron goods were stored, had burned to the ground and all was destroyed.

In pursuance of his plan to aggregate to the Society the class of helpers he designated *donnés*, Père Lalemant and Robert Le Coq signed a civil contract on December 23, 1639, following which Le Coq pronounced private religious vows. A few other workmen had asked to become *donnés*, but Lalemant thought it wiser not to receive them until he was authorized to do so by his higher Superiors. Not only did a favorable answer come that September, but five *donnés* arrived with contracts already signed in the name of the Huron Mission and with private vows pronounced. They were sturdy men and solidly religious. They asked for support and not for wages; they wanted to work for souls by assisting the priests; they were determined to live a semireligious life, in chastity and obedience. Charles Boivin was a master builder; Joseph Molere was a skilled nurse; and the other three, Guillaume Coûture, Christophe Regnault, and Jacques Levrier, were intelligent men for general purposes.

In the conferences which the missioners held during the summer and the early autumn, they assessed the results of their labors. In the course of the past winter, they calculated that they spoke to about 10,000 Hurons and Petuns, baptized about 1,000 persons, of whom 460 were under fourteen years of age, and though they had won about twenty adults in good health, they lost more through apostasy. In all the Huron land, there were not more than fifty who still professed to be Believers or who could be salvaged. Though these were heartbreaking statistics for Jean de Brébeuf, he was not dispirited. In his own good time, God would water these Huron roots.

Heart-rending, also, to de Brébeuf were the totals of the surveys the missioners had been conducting that summer and last. They calculated that there were about twenty-three villages and hamlets in the Huron territory. They counted seven hundred longhouses and two thousand fires, and estimated the Huron population as about twelve thousand. If these figures were correct, they were shocking. Four years ago, in 1636, de Brébeuf judged that there were twenty Huron villages and thirty thousand souls. Champlain in 1615, the Récollets and de Brébeuf in 1626, also estimated that the Hurons numbered about thirty thousand. The Iroquois wars, the influenza epidemic, the smallpox plague had decimated the Huron people.[2]

Since the Hurons were dying out, it seemed imperative to the missioners that they must extend their efforts to other nations. Seven of the thirteen priests were assigned to minister to the Hurons during the coming winter. Two would seek new peoples by joining the nomad Algonquins. Garnier and Pierre Pijart were appointed to return to the now permanent mission they had last year established among the Petun nation. The most important by far of all the decisions was that, at last, of sending missioners among the Neutrals. Jean de Brébeuf and Joseph Marie Chaumonot were chosen to plant this new mission dedicated to the Holy Angels.

For fourteen years, de Brébeuf had been visioning this apostolate among the Attiwandarons, or Neutrals. In 1626, the Récollet, de la Roche, after having spent some months with the Neutrals, came back convinced they were more important to the French than were the Hurons. They had more villages and more people, and they were hospitable, tractable and easy to deal with, until the Huron mischief-makers had turned their minds. They were hunters, de la Roche said, and could furnish more peltries than the Hurons if they traded directly with the French. Their country could be reached easily and quickly from the St. Lawrence by a level route along Lake Ontario, not like the arduous journey up the Ottawa. Since they maintained peace both with the Hurons and the Iroquois, de la Roche cherished the idea that, with a Neutral alliance, the Iroquois might conclude a peace with the French.

Through all the subsequent years, de Brébeuf gathered all possible information about the Neutrals from the French agents who occasionally traded with them, from the Hurons who made great profit by exchanging French goods for beaver skins, from the Neutrals who visited the Huron villages. Despite his persistent inquiries, his exact knowledge was scant. The Neutral country lay directly south, at an approximate distance of 120 miles, a journey of six days by land. The line of villages lay in a wide band, from Lake Ontario on the east to the western end of Lake Erie. But how many villages there were and how closely knit together in a confederation was not known. They were of the same blood as the Hurons and had the same traditional customs. Their language derived from the same roots, though the two dialects seemed quite as far apart as were French and Italian.

De Brébeuf and Lalemant regarded the project of settling among the Neutrals as the greatest pioneering advance yet attempted. The Neutral country was not confined to a small pocket like that of the Hurons, but extended to the nations of the west, so that their trails were the natural road into the heart of the continent. A permanent French settlement among the Neutrals would become the western outpost of New France. In his *Relation* that year, Père Lalemant stated: "He on whom the lot fell was Père Jean de Brébeuf. He it was who, in earlier years, had been chosen as the first to introduce us and to establish us in these [Huron] regions. God has given him, for this purpose, a remarkable blessing, namely, in the language. It seemed to us that this might be considered a forejudgment of what the Divine Providence wished of us in this matter, where it was a question of an entirely new introduction into a nation different in language, at least in many respects. Also, if it should please God to grant His blessing, there could be established a fixed and permanent dwelling, which should be the retreat of the missioners from round about that region, just in the same way that this residence is the retreat for the missioners of the regions in these parts in which we now are."

Jean de Brébeuf, on the morning of November 2, 1640, strapped his blanket and bag to his shoulders and hung about his waist his smaller pouches. Père Chaumonot, smaller by half a foot, bundled himself with as much as he could carry. Two Frenchmen in their mooseskin suits loaded their personal needs and merchandise in a hump on their backs. In the chapel of Sainte Marie they said their final prayers and begged God and His Holy Angels to bless them all the winter till they should return. That evening they found lodging in Teanaustayé. De Brébeuf had arranged to buy corn enough to last them till they reached the Neutrals, and also had the pledged word of two Hurons to act as guides and to be interpreters among the Neutrals. The men offered various excuses about not going, but de Brébeuf knew these were lies. He thought to persuade them, by argument and added presents. They grew more obdurate and gave their answer by silence.

Even before this, de Brébeuf suspected that the evil tongues of the Hurons were trying to prevent him from journeying down to the Neutral villages. They feared that Echon and the Frenchmen were intending to interfere with the Huron monopoly by persuading the Neutrals to trade at Three Rivers. Another concern was that the Blackrobes would further strain the unsteady relations developing between themselves and the Attiwandarons. A third interpretation was that Echon was using the visit to the Neutrals as a pretext for making an alliance with the Seneca Iroquois, just then their most bitter enemies.

This suspicion, de Brébeuf knew, was serious. Many Hurons were convinced that though he seemed friendly, he held in his heart a secret hate for the Hurons. He had shown this hate by bringing death and calamity on them by the successive plagues. Since he had not yet succeeded in killing them all, he was plotting to offer presents to the Senecas in order to persuade them to exterminate the Hurons by war. Some of the friendly Hurons warned Echon that this ugly rumor might cause his death, first as a sorcerer and then as a traitor. They indicated that something of the same sort had been said about the murdered Étienne Brûlé. They, themselves, held a different interpretation and had spoken of it publicly. They admitted that Echon was a great sorcerer, with power over disease and death. They remembered that when he spoke at the funeral of Chihwatenhwa, he had cried out in loud tones: "Sonontoerrhonon, it is finished for you. You are dead." Now, three moons later, he was carrying out his threat to destroy the Senecas by disease. They were persuading the people, they said, that this was the object of Echon's journey to the Neutrals.

De Brébeuf could now well understand why his Huron guides refused to join his party. They feared that other Hurons might follow and strike them down, together with Echon and the French, deep along the trail; that Iroquois, roving the forests in the south, might massacre or capture both themselves and the French; that the Neutrals, who had heard Echon brought disease and death, might slaughter them as accomplices for leading this witch into their country.

The dangers alleged by the Hurons were true. If he and his comrades were killed on this journey, the Hurons would prove their innocence to the French along the St. Lawrence, even though they committed the murder. There would be no witnesses. He realized that by going to the Neutrals he was putting himself beyond the pale of protection, both of the French and of the Hurons. Nevertheless, he was determined to proceed, under the protection of God.

Two: 1640–1641

Nowhere, in all of Teanaustayé, could de Brébeuf find anyone who would accept his presents, nor even listen to his pleadings. Since Chaumonot was not daunted and the two French donnés were not afraid, he resolved to start for the Neutrals, with or without Huron guides. On their way out of Teanaustayé, he chanced to meet a young brave whom he knew. On an impulse, he greeted him: "*Quio*

Ackwe! Come, let us go away together." The man looked startled; then thoughtful; then answered that he had not thought of going anywhere. Why, de Brébeuf did not know, but the young brave, without further ado, started with them along the trail to the south.

All day long they trudged along the narrow path that dipped down into the gulleys of rivulets, that climbed over ridges of hills, that always was closed in by huge, ancient trees and a roof of overhanging branches. The November air was cold when, at their camping place for the night, they put their kettle of ground corn over the sticks of their fire and, wrapping themselves in their blankets, soundly slept on their bed of pine needles and twigs. The second day and night, the third, the fourth they pressed on sturdily. On the fifth day, when the trails were better defined and more trampled, they knew that they would be reaching the first Neutral village on the morrow. In his usual way, that evening Père Jean withdrew somewhat from the party to pray. As he knelt in the silent forests, he stated: "I seemed to see the faces of many angels appearing before me." They were, he believed, the angels to whom his Mission of the Holy Angels was dedicated.

They marched into the first Neutral village the next day, and de Brébeuf gave to it the name of All Saints. Ignoring the crowds of villagers who flocked out to inspect them, they plodded with a steady pace and a stoical silence till they found a longhouse large enough to lodge them. Entering, they sat by a fire and waited till they were given bark bowls of corn mush. While they ate, the house rocked with the pushing and the clamor of the men, women, children and dogs who milled about them. After a polite silence, de Brébeuf greeted his host and gave his name as Echon. He could hear Echon repeated through the cabin; they had all heard of the giant Blackrobe who was a chief of the Bear nation and the greatest of all the French sorcerers. They crushed in to look at him more closely. He pronounced Chaumonot's name, Aronhiatiri, but they repeated it, he noted, as Oronhiaguehre. He was told that the name of the village was Kandoucho. When he informed them that he proposed to hold council with the great chief of the Attiwandarons, they advised him that Tsohahissen lived several days' journey beyond in the heart of the country.[3]

They remained at Kandoucho for a few days of rest and friendship. The language, de Brébeuf noted, was not unintelligible to him but had marked differences in pronunciation. He drew out as much information as he could about the trails and the towns. For their amusement, he and Chaumonot exemplified the trick of one writing what someone said, and the other, at a distance, speaking it. The two Frenchmen pleased them by trading beads and other trinkets. The villagers of Kandoucho, de Brébeuf judged, were agreeable but not too friendly. In their customs, they were not unlike the Hurons. The men did not bother much about breech clouts in the cabins, and the women observed only the essential decencies. Their distinctive mark seemed to be that of tattooing; faces, bodies, arms and legs were traced with black charcoal in bands, circles and grotesque designs.

While he was at Kandoucho, de Brébeuf noticed some Hurons idling about, and suspected they had no good purpose in his regard. When he and his comrades left, they were accompanied by some Neutral guides. They arrived at the second settlement and, to their surprise, were met by a crowd of yelling women and scowling men. A bad report had gone before them, de Brébeuf concluded with a great deal of concern. So clamorous was the outcry against Echon as the bearer of disease and death, that they could not force their way through the mob into the cabins. At a third village they again were greeted by similar shouts and threats.

De Brébeuf quieted the savages by stolidly ignoring them, the while the two Frenchmen opening their pack of beads and trinkets, diverted them by trading. As they progressed they were sometimes able to enter the village and force some cabin to give them food and lodging according to the immemorial laws of hospitality; but oftentimes, their bed was in some spot sheltered from the keen November winds. By now, de Brébeuf fully realized that Huron enemies were abroad, repeating the old Huron calumnies and lies and arousing in the Neutrals terror and loathing for himself and Chaumonot.

Arrived finally at the capital village, Echon sought out the leading councilors and chiefs. According to the habitual diplomatic code, he announced that he proposed to hold council with the great chief, Tsohahissen. With expressionless faces, they informed him that Tsohahissen was on the warpath and would not return until the spring. He declared that since he came on an urgent mission that could not wait until the spring, he would be pleased to hold council with the

chiefs who conducted public affairs. They could not refuse his proposition because their nation and his nation were not at war.

Being the visitor, Echon spoke first at the council fire. Two matters of great importance had brought him into the land of the Atti-
wandaron, he proclaimed. The first was that of revealing truths never
before heard in their country, about the One-who-made-all, about
what He commanded and forbade, of life after death in happiness or
in suffering. The second was that of learning their thoughts about
a special alliance of peace and trade between their people and the
French. To prove the desire of the French for this alliance, he offered
them a collar of two thousand porcelain beads. The presiding chief
affirmed that matters of such great importance needed to be discussed
in a special council.

The Neutral spokesman, at a consequent meeting, tactfully declined
to accept the porcelain collar and explained that no formal alliance
with the French could be concluded without the approval of Tsohahissen. Furthermore, the porcelain collar was rich, their treasury was
poor, and so they could not return a gift of equal value. To Echon's
request that he and his comrades might remain in the country until
the spring and might visit the villages, he responded that they had no
power to forbid them such freedom.

Since his proposition and present were not rejected outright, a thing
that might have happened if Tsohahissen were present, de Brébeuf
had gained what he sought, the opportunity to travel through the
country. But he understood that he journeyed at his own risk, since
he was not a guest of the governing chiefs. They retraced their steps
toward Kandoucho. Along the way, the French aides traded their
wares, while Echon announced to all that, by decision of the chiefs,
they were free to visit the villages till Tsohahissen returned. At Kandoucho, the two Frenchmen, having helped ease the introduction to
the Neutrals, returned to Sainte Marie.

De Brébeuf and Chaumonot were now alone, for whatever might
happen. Having made their first sally into the interior, they planned
systematically to journey around the boundary villages. They started
westward, along the northern area, toward the village of Khioetoa,
a hundred miles distant where a remnant of the Wenrôhronons still
lived. It was a cold December, the snow lay deep along the foot-size
trails, and the wind pinched their faces and fingers. Only by keen

perception could they follow the route. The people in the first few villages, evidently warned about them, eyed them with suspicion and malevolence. Though they observed the code of hospitality, they did so grudgingly.

In one town, however, they were greeted effusively by a Huron named Awenhokwi and his comrade. De Brébeuf knew him as one who disliked the Blackrobes; but now Awenhokwi appeared to be most friendly and offered to guide the Blackrobes to the villages toward the south. Echon politely refused. In his spiritual memoirs, de Brébeuf recorded: "On December 13, being at Andackhroeh, while making my examen of conscience, I saw as it were a skeleton which fled from me. Whether or not it went away from me, or approached me from another direction, I do not know. One thing I do know: when I saw it, it stood near me, and at once went away."

At Khioetoa, to which they gave the name of St. Michel, they were most cordially welcomed. Some of the Wenrôhronons who had migrated in 1639 to the Hurons and had later gone back, remembered with gratitude the kindness of Echon in their hunger and sickness. De Brébeuf was surprised that they had carried with them so great a remembrance of what he had taught them about God. During the few days he remained there, he instructed them further and baptized a few sick children and some lingering old people.

From friendly Khioetoa, they turned toward the south along the far western region of the Neutrals, through a fifty-mile stretch of snow-clad forests and frozen trails. In each of the villages, they encountered the same treatment, cabin doors barred against them if they were seen coming, curses and threats if they happened to enter a cabin unperceived. Their reputations as white devils and planners of evil were always in advance of them. Along the way, they often heard the remark: "This is what Awenhokwi, the Huron, says." They realized that their suspicions of him had been sound, that his invitation was to lure them into a secluded place where he could split their heads and blame the act on the Neutrals.

It was imperative for them, they decided, to return to the capital village and confront Awenhokwi. He had gone elsewhere, but the chiefs were debating in council the propositions he had proclaimed. These venomous and malicious calumnies de Brébeuf attempted to answer, but he found few to listen to him. Awenhokwi had, in the usual council manner, protested the love of the Ouendats for the Attiwandarons. Because this love was so great, he had traveled from his country to their country in order to warn them of an impending evil and to show them the means of preserving themselves from utter ruin. All too late had his people learned the cause of the disease and death that had fallen on them. He prophesied a similar calamity would oppress their people, and he urged them to protect themselves. Echon, he dramatically revealed, was the most evil demon that had ever entered his country. He killed so many children that all the mothers were bowed in grief. Echon, he declared, was visiting the Neutral nation to ruin it. He hung nine iron axes on the post, as proof of the truth of his words.

The axes, he implied, were given so that they could be used on the heads of Echon and Aronhiatiri. By killing these two invaders, the Attiwandarons would not only save themselves but would perform an act of friendship for the Ouendats. All his people clamored for the death of the Blackrobes, but some chiefs were fearful of war with the French. The Attiwandarons, having no French alliance and no French trade, were free to strike down Echon. Despite the French peace, even that winter his people were resolved to massacre all the French in his Ouendat land. The same justice should be given to the two Blackrobes who were bringing death and ruin to the Neutral people. Thus spoke Awenhokwi.

Chaumonot recalled,

One night, while they were deliberating about our lives in an assembly of the notables of the village, Père de Brébeuf had this vision while performing his examen of conscience. A furious-looking specter held in his hand three javelins with which he was menacing us. He hurled against us one of his shafts. A hand more powerful stopped the spear in its passage. The same happened with the second and third javelins. When our examen was finished, Père de Brébeuf warned me of the danger in which we were. Without being alarmed, we heard the confessions of one another and, having finished all our prayers, wrapped ourselves up for sleep. When the night was far advanced, our host returned from the council. He woke us up to inform us that at three different times we were on the point of being massacred. Young braves offered to deliver the stroke. But all three times, the elders had restrained them by their arguments. This recital explained to us what Père de Brébeuf had seen only as an enigma.

Having thus escaped, they continued their journeys to other villages of the south. Despite the hate and fear, the threats, curses and maledictions of the Neutrals, they spoke about God to as many as would listen and searched for souls to save by baptism. Chaumonot recorded,

> One bitterly cold night, when all the cabins were closed to us, we crouched outside a door. When a man lifted the bar to pass out, we leaped in. The people in the cabin almost swooned away with fear. After recovering from their terror, they sent messengers to the chief to tell him that we were in their cabin. Immediately the cabin filled with people. The elders threatened to throw us in the kettles. The young men shouted that they were tired of the blackish flesh of their enemies and would willingly eat our white meat. A warrior rushed in and drew back the bow of his arrow, pointed at us. I looked at him steadily, and prayed with confidence to Saint Michel. The furious enemy subsided. We talked to them and they listened. We assured them that our single reason for coming into their country was to teach them the truths we knew, in order to make them sanctified in time and happy in eternity.

The two vagabonds, passing on to other settlements, were barred entry because of what Oëntara, the Huron, had revealed about them. The sight of them seemed to dement everyone with horror. They well suspected that Oëntara was traveling before them and spawning the Huron lies. To their surprise, they were received with courtesy in one village. Oëntara was there, and the chiefs invited the Blackrobes to listen to the charges he made against them. In connection with this crisis, de Brébeuf revealed: "On January 16, 1641, when I was asleep, I thought I was with the blessed Père Coton, who told me that on the next day he was to plead his cause before the judges. Then I told him that I also would be tried within the next few days, but still, I had given no thought as to how I would defend myself. When I awoke, however, I thought the blessed Père would be my faithful advocate in pleading my cause."

At the council, Oëntara and Echon faced each other. Oëntara, ranting boldly yet persuasively, repeated with subtle viciousness the crimes of the Blackrobes. As reported by de Brébeuf, he told the Neutrals "that we had bred the malady in our cabin, that our writings were sorceries, that we had caused almost every one of the

Hurons to die under pretense of giving them presents, that we were planning to bring all the rest of the country to the grave." Because he loved the Attiwandarons, he begged them for their own sake to close every village and every cabin against the Blackrobes, and to show their spirit by inflicting on these two Blackrobes the punishment given to witches and evil sorcerers.

Echon, answering as boldly and as fluently, denied and refuted each of the charges made by Oëntara. He, also, assured his hearers that he loved the Attiwandarons and that, because of his affection, he had come into their country to open their eyes so that they could see the Spirit-who-made-all. He desired to teach them great truths which would give them peace of soul in this world, which would show them the trail to happiness in the future life, and which would warn them against the path leading to the pit of fire and torments. All he asked them to do was to open their ears and listen to him.

Following upon this encounter with Oëntara, while they were trudging through the snow from place to place in the southern borders, and were being treated like omens of evil, they were summoned to appear in the capital village of Tsohahissen. When they arrived, they were given mats and food in the cabin of a chief and were told that the council would debate about them that night. The one deputed to give this message said that, even in the absence of the great chief, the matter was so pressing that an immediate decision had to be reached. De Brébeuf knew that the council was only a formality, that the resolution was already passed. The Huron emissaries had so poisoned the minds of the Neutrals that he and Chaumonot would be denounced publicly as witches and, perhaps, publicly or privately murdered.

Late that night, after the council, a chief and his committee came to de Brébeuf's cabin. Divesting themselves of their robes, they haunched quite naked about the fire with the Blackrobes. The spokesman informed Echon that his collar of twelve hundred porcelain beads had been refused. From this de Brébeuf understood that the Neutrals rejected a peace treaty and an alliance with the French. He accepted the answer with a face as impassive as stone, in which not a muscle twitched. After the appropriate silence, he recalled that, at the first council, he had offered two propositions. What answer did they return to the important matter of believing in the One-who-made-all and the other truths he promised to reveal to them. After consulta-tion with his associates, the chief replied, according to de Brébeuf: "As for the Faith which had been preached to them, they accepted it since they found nothing but good in it. As for the gift offered to them, they refused it absolutely." The answer pleased de Brébeuf since, as he records, "we believed that we had gained the principal things to which we aspired, which was the liberty of preaching and publishing the gospel in the country."

He felt free to argue about the first proposition. He had been deputed by his people, he said, to offer a valuable collar to the public treasury. On his return, he would be asked the reason why it was refused. What could he tell the French? The chief answered that the treasury of his people was so very small and poor that a gift as valu-able as that of the French could not be given in return. Knowing that he was lying, de Brébeuf assured him that the French asked nothing in return, that they offered the porcelain collar as a testimony of their love for the Attiwandarons, and expected nothing else than the friendship of this nation.

De Brébeuf commented: "The chiefs persisted in their refusal. They were not able to bring forth any pretext that we did not imme-diately set aside. At last, the spokesman blurted: 'Quoi! do you not know what Awenhokwi said? And what he came here to do? More than that, do you not realize the danger in which you are, and the danger to which you expose the country?'" Echon started anew to refute the accusations of Awenhokwi, but the chiefs donned their robes and walked out of the cabin.

Three: 1641

By refusing to accept the collar of beads, the Neutral chiefs withdrew all protection and every responsibility. De Brébeuf and Chaumonot were now tramps, beggars and criminal sorcerers. Anyone could split their heads for any reason, without blame or penalty; rather, who-ever murdered them would be honored for doing a good deed for the public welfare. According to de Brébeuf: "We did not consider ourselves driven out of the country by the resolution of this coun-cil. However, we judged that, if we had trouble going through the villages in the past, for the future we would have more trouble than ever before."

After this January council, they admitted to one another that their apostolic hopes for this year had been ruined by the evil machinations of the Hurons. Next year, with the information they gathered about the country, the people and the language, they or other missioners would again campaign for Christ among the Neutrals. They were determined to finish their survey of the country. Accordingly, they struck out to the south and the east, the direction in which the Iroquois Senecas lived. In addition to the danger from the Hurons and Neutrals, they had now to fear being murdered or captured by the Iroquois. Along the way, de Brébeuf told Chaumonot of a vision "in which a great cross appeared to him, coming from the direction of the Iroquois nation". When Chaumonot asked him for further details of this apparition, he answered only: "This cross was so great that it could hold, not only one person, but all the Frenchmen who were in these countries."

Truly had they surmised that they would be treated worse than before. "No sooner did we come near a village," they recounted, "than the people screamed out from all sides: 'Here come the Agwa! Fasten your doors!' (Agwa was the name given to the most deadly Neutral witches.) Sometimes we were allowed to enter the cabins, but that was through fear we might resent a refusal and cast even a more evil spell on the cabin and the village." As they progressed, they said, "We felt as if we were like a ball with which the demons, in the midst of this barbarism, were playing, but with a command from the Divine Providence that nothing should be lacking to us."

Even though they found food and lodging, they were always looked upon with horror and terror. De Brébeuf stated: "It was said that when we went to the brook to wash our dishes, we poisoned the water. When we went into a cabin, the children were seized with a cough and a discharge of blood, and the women became sterile. There was no misfortune, present or to come, of which we were not considered the source. Many in whose cabins we lodged, did not sleep either day or night. They did not dare touch the food we left. They returned the presents we gave them. Poor old women considered themselves already doomed, and mourned over their grandchildren who would not grow to people the land."

In his spiritual notes, de Brébeuf related: "On February 7, it seemed as if two hands were clasped in agreement. I saw also, as it were, the center part of the globe. Then also, as I believe, on several days during evening prayers, I seemed to see many crosses which I fervently embraced. On the following night when in prayer, I was striving to conform myself to the Divine Will and I was saying: 'May thy Will be done, O Lord,' I heard, as it were, a voice saying to me: 'Take up and read.' When morning came I took in my hand that small golden book of the *Imitation of Christ* and happened upon the chapter on 'The Royal Way of the Holy Cross.' From this there followed in my soul a great peace and quiet in the things that chanced to happen."

They judged, about the second week in February, that they should return to the first village, Kandoucho. They were unable to do any spiritual good, and their presence was causing increasing bitterness that would be remembered and would hinder missionary work in the years to come. They were satisfied because they had succeeded in introducing themselves throughout the country, in giving to the savages an idea of God and the afterlife, and in collecting exact information about the location and the population of the Neutral villages.

The distance to Kandoucho, they calculated, would be about fifty miles northward, through dense forests deep with snow. On February 13, after fighting all day against a blinding snowstorm, they chanced upon a village toward evening. The moment they entered a cabin, the savages screeched out in panic and mobbed about them threateningly. A woman pushed her way through, spoke sharply to the frenzied people, and hospitably motioned the Blackrobes to sit at the fire. While she ladled out the sagamité and bade them eat, she quelled with loud and angry words those of her own cabin and the visitors who had rushed into it. That night the blizzard raged, so that the next morning snow was piled half the height of the cabins. They were forced to keep indoors, though they were eager to reach Kandoucho, where they intended to wait for the French aides from Sainte Marie.

The woman of the cabin showed by smiles, gestures and words that she desired them to stay. She gave them the best food and the best places to sleep. From her, they learned the name of the village, Teotondiaton; they christened it St. Guillaume. Her own people and the villagers so menaced and threatened Echon and Oronhiaguehre that, day and night, the cabin was in a perpetual turmoil. The woman defied the braves and chiefs when they ordered her to drive the Agwa out into the snow. They told her all the evil crimes the Blackrobes had committed among the Ouendats, and tried to terrify her with the calamities they would plot with their black magic in her cabin. But, said de Brébeuf, "so cleverly did she refute all the calumnies heaped upon us that we ourselves would not have been able to do so more pertinently." The chiefs begged her, out of pity for the people of the village, to send away these evil-minded Blackrobes who brought disease and death. She lightly answered that it was usual for people to die, that she herself would sometime die. They turned on her viciously, and accused her father of being a sorcerer, crying out: "It is no wonder that you should keep and care for these foreign witches, since you are the daughter of a witch."

Though the woman was free to keep the Blackrobes at her fire, she could not curb the freedom of others to annoy or harm them. During a feast of the insane, when the pretended madmen bellowed and pounded in and about the cabin through several nights, one seized a firebrand and tried to set Chaumonot's soutane on fire. But the woman so well scolded them and threatened them with revenge, that she protected the two priests from everything except snarling insults and menacing threats.

She was like a tender mother to them, and even prepared special pots of corn and fish, since it was Lent and they could not eat meat. She was as eager to teach them the Neutral language as they were to learn it. According to them: "She took the greatest possible pleasure in teaching us the language. She dictated the words, syllable by syllable, as a teacher would do to a little pupil. She even dictated to us several narratives. Following her example, her little children vied with one another to render us a thousand services, and were never tired of talking with us, whereas everywhere else the children ran away and hid." They even fought bloodily against other children in defense of the Blackrobes. In his *Relation*, Lalemant wrote: "The delay of the Pères in this place was, without doubt, an exceptional Providence of God. During the twenty-five days that they remained in this cabin, they were able to harmonize the dictionary and the syntax of the Huron language with that of the Neutrals, and to accomplish a work which a person, by himself, would require a residence of several years in the country to achieve."

Early in March, the woman's father returned and approved all she had done. Cordially and affably, he told de Brébeuf a great deal about the Neutral country, about the Iroquois, about the peoples of the west. He named some forty Neutral villages, with a population, they calculated, far in excess of twelve thousand souls. He said that the Neutrals had, until recently, four thousand warriors but that, during the past few years, the curse of influenza and smallpox as well as that of famine had killed thousands of the people. Checking their journey, de Brébeuf and Chaumonot could list eighteen settlements they had attempted to enter, and in ten of these they had been permitted to make longer stays. In these ten, they estimated there were about five hundred fires, and one thousand families.

Robert Le Coq and another Frenchman, Joseph Teondechoren and another Huron comrade, trudged out of the snow into Teotondiaton on March 10, 1641. All at Sainte Marie had been worried about the safety of the two missioners, for scarcely a week passed without a report that the Blackrobes had been struck down by the Neutrals, that they had been secretly murdered by some Hurons, that they had been caught by the Seneca Iroquois. The reunion of the four friends with the two Blackrobes was so effusive that the villagers gaped at the show of so much love. Le Coq fascinated all who saw him. Since his face and neck were pockmarked as much as were many of their own, they began to revise some of their notions at the realization that the French were not such great demons that they could ward off the pestilence.

Bidding farewell to Teotondiaton, de Brébeuf and Chaumonot expressed by words and presents their deep gratitude to the valiant Neutral woman who had championed and taught them so much. They regretted that they could not baptize her. Though she had listened with interest to their instructions, she showed little inclination to become a Believer and to keep the Commandments. Her father promised to visit them in the Huron land. The other villagers, by this time, had lost their demented fears and sought to be friendly. As the Blackrobes, with their four comrades, set forward on their way, they were followed with shouted invitations to return.

Though March had come, deep snow blanketed the forests. They labored along trails slippery with ice up to Kandoucho, the village of

their first arrival, and from there marched northward on their homeward journey to Sainte Marie. Before them were five or six days of
steady tramping on snowshoes, and four or five nights of sleeping
on the open earth. "The winds were very violent," related Chaumonot, "and the cold very piercing.... Nevertheless, we proceeded
joyously and with courage, despite the cold, the fatigues and countless falls on the ice."

De Brébeuf, while crossing a stream, slipped and crashed on the
ice. He lay stunned. When the others helped him to his feet, he
winced with pain in his left shoulder and he could not well lift his
arm. It was only shock, he assured them, that would pass away in a
short time. They examined his shoulder and concluded what he was
loath to believe, that he had fractured his collarbone. They strapped
his left arm to his body and offered to make a sled to drag him over
the slippery trails. He refused, asserting that he could still use his legs
and make his own way on his snow raquets. Only one concession
did he make, that of surrendering his shoulder pack, and this only
because his arm and shoulder seemed paralyzed and limp. To Chaumonot, he happened to reveal that the pain was most intense, but no
greater than the agony he had asked from God.

They had hoped to reach Sainte Marie by March 18, so that they
could celebrate Mass on the following day, the Feast of Saint Joseph.
But the weather had turned warm and, instead of travel over crusted
snow and hard ice, they had to struggle along muddy trails and cross
swollen streams. The last night caught them about half a day's journey from Sainte Marie. De Brébeuf and Chaumonot estimated that,
if they broke camp at the first light of Saint Joseph's Feast, they
could reach Sainte Marie before noon and so celebrate their Masses.
Abstaining from food and water, they started along the slippery forest paths in the gray, misty dawn. Sliding and slushing forward, they
watched with anxiety the light flooding the treetops, then the sun rising higher in the heavens. Breathlessly, they pushed on as fast as they
could, passed hurriedly by the villages of St. Louis and Ste. Anne, and
came to the last hills, down which they dropped into the level fields
before Sainte Marie.

It was nearing twelve when they hurried into the gate. They delayed
greetings and waved off welcomings. They confessed themselves and
washed while the other priests prepared the chapel. About noonday

Père de Brébeuf and Père Chaumonot stood at the altars with the missals opened at the Mass of Saint Joseph. Not since November 2, four and one-half months ago, had they experienced the supreme and ecstatic joy of receiving the Body and Blood of Jesus Christ.

During the days that followed, de Brébeuf and Chaumonot gave their oral and written reports about the winter, and their hopes for further evangelizing the Neutrals. They were convinced that their failure of the past year was due, in the greatest part, to the malice of the Hurons. They concluded that the Neutrals, of themselves, would have been naturally antagonistic during this first lengthy visit but would not have been so diabolically aroused if the Huron envoys had not disseminated their calumnies. They recommended that, next year, they or other missioners, despite the Hurons, must go down again to the Neutrals, seek a French alliance and preach everywhere the word of God.

With consuming interest, de Brébeuf listened to the recitals of the experience of his brethren during the months of his absence. There had been no disturbances in the villages about Sainte Marie, but no notable conversions. In Ossossané the group of Believers had increased and was so faithful that they could attest: "We have scarcely a single one among our Christians of whose sincerity we doubt." The marvel of all was the miraculous change in Teondechoren, from being a master of the fire feast to becoming an apostle as great as his brother Chihwatenhwa. In Teanaustayé and the southern villages, Daniel said he had enjoyed comparative quiet and had some success in forming, once more, the nucleus of a church. Garnier and Pijart were satisfied with their second campaign among the Petuns. Though their presents were rejected by the chiefs, the people seemed far less violent and menacing.

The peace and serenity derived from the absence of any epidemics. Since there was so little death, all the missioners combined counted only about a hundred baptisms. The total number of firm Believers in all of Huronia was about sixty. De Brébeuf agreed with Lalemant's statement in his *Relation* of May 19, 1641: "If the sufferings endured in so noble an enterprise are a measure of the hopes we should entertain for the conversion of these nations, we have reason to believe that, at last, we shall make good Christians of these poor unbelievers. Whatever resistance earth and hell may bring to the designs we have, we shall not, for that reason, lose a jot of our confidence."

Jean de Brébeuf humbly bowed his head in obedience. He accepted the decision of Père Lalemant and his consultors that he return to Quebec with the canoes leaving in May. Very kindly, Lalemant recounted that he had lived among the Hurons for seven successive years and a change would be good for him; moreover, he professed to be deeply worried about his fractured collarbone, which apparently was not knitting and was causing excruciating pain; there was need for him at Quebec, to confer with Père Vimont and Governor de Montmagny, and to offer them comprehensive reports on the affairs of the mission and the Hurons. Lalemant indicated that he might be held at Quebec for a year and succeed Ragueneau as the procurator of the Huron Mission.[4]

He agreed, though with a heartbreak, that his Superior was right. He had to admit to himself that he was incapacitated, with his left arm strapped to his body and with the shoulder bound so as to help the bones to knit. The pain was great, but he did not mind that nearly so much as the forced idleness. It would be better for Paul Ragueneau, strong and active, to replace him. He had hoped with full-blown soul to go down again to the Neutrals; however, Chaumonot was competent to carry on that apostolate. The other priests were now able to speak Huron fluently and were experienced enough to combat the infidels and increase the number of the faithful. Straightforwardly, he faced the fact that no longer was he essential, or even needed, for the evangelization of the Hurons.

With unmitigated grief all at Sainte Marie, priests, brothers, donnés, workmen, heard that Père Jean was being retired to Quebec. They knew they would miss his spirit breathing among them, for they loved him for his humility, for his unswerving patience, for his spontaneous charity, and admired him beyond all bounds for his saintliness, for his consuming zeal, for his indomitable courage. As he began the Huron Mission, so through the years he was the embodiment of the mission, not only for the French but for the Hurons. One of his friends was later to write:

Often the infidels conspired for his death. If any misfortune befell the country, it was the priests who were the cause of it, and Echon the chief of all. If pestilence prevailed, and contagious diseases depopulated certain villages, it was he who, by his spells, caused those demons of hell to come, with whom he was accused of having dealings. Famine appeared here only by his orders, and if the war were not favorable to them, it was Echon who had a secret understanding with their enemies; who surreptitiously received pensions from them for betraying the country; and who had come from France only to exterminate all the tribes with whom he should deal, under the pretext of coming to announce the Faith, and of procuring their welfare. In a word, the name of Echon has been, for the space of some years, held in such abhorrence that it was used for terrifying the children; and often sick people have been made to believe that his look was the demon who had bewitched them and who gave the deathblow. But his hour was not come; all those evil designs which they had against him served only to augment his confidence in God, and to cause that every day he walked like a victim devoted to death, which he awaited only with loving desire, but of which he dared not speed the moments.

Lalemant was sending from Sainte Marie two large canoes. These were manned by four *donnés*, Sondatsaa, an Ossossané chief who sought baptism, and five other Hurons. Four or five other canoes of Huron traders planned to join with the French. They judged it better to leave early, even though the Ottawa would be swollen and the cascades and rapids would be more hazardous, hoping thus to reach the St. Lawrence before any Iroquois war bands laid their traps along the waterways. Early on the morning of May 20, after the blessings and farewells, Jean de Brébeuf, with his arm strapped tight, eased his big body into the light canoe. With a pang in his heart sharper than that in his shoulder, he lifted his eyes to the crosses above Sainte Marie, let them fall on the gabled roofs, the bastions and palisades, and lowered them to gaze at the Huron Believers who had gathered about the moat, at the faithful *donnés* and workmen, at his black-gowned brothers, in full truth, his sons. He shook himself out of such sentimental sadness. He would be back among them in a year or two.

The canoe slid into the little river Sainte Marie, skimmed out among the waving water grass at its mouth, bounded across the choppy waves of the bay, and pointed to the rocky, evergreen archipelago near the mainland. He looked back fifteen years since he had first seen the forested headlands, clear above the water mist, where had been Ihonatiria and Toanché.

CHAPTER X

Iroquois Scourge on the St. Lawrence

One: 1641

AFTER FLOATING SAFELY out of the last rapids into the St. Lawrence, de Brébeuf and his comrades sneaked cautiously down the river lest they fall into an Iroquois ambush. They were in the lead, with four more Huron canoes following a half-day journey behind. At last, on June 20, with jubilation they discerned the low black mound of Three Rivers. As soon as they beached their two canoes, the French mobbed about them excitedly and, almost ignoring welcomes, kept shouting: "Any Iroquois?" "How did you escape?" "A miracle!" Later on, in the log cabin of the Jesuits, Ragueneau explained the excitement to de Brébeuf.

In February, the Iroquois carried off two Frenchmen, Marguerie and Godefroy, who were hunting near Three Rivers. Nothing more was heard of them until two weeks ago, June 5, when Iroquois canoes suddenly appeared before Three Rivers, and a lone man in a canoe paddled toward the settlement. He was Marguerie, sent as a messenger from the Iroquois, while they held Godefroy as a hostage. The Iroquois, he was instructed to announce, desired to hold councils of peace with the French. On his own, Marguerie informed de Champflour, the Commandant, that the Iroquois numbered five hundred warriors, thirty-six of whom had Dutch muskets, and warned against treachery.

De Champflour summoned Governor de Montmagny from Quebec the while he deputed Père Ragueneau and Sieur Nicolet to accompany Marguerie to the Iroquois camp. In the council, the Iroquois spoke lovingly of the French and their desire to trade with them. When Ragueneau asked if they also desired peace with the Algonquins and Hurons, they avoided direct answers. When he told them that they must await the arrival of Governor de Montmagny from Quebec, they replied that they were eager to hold further peace councils with the French. In this and succeeding parleys, the Iroquois were so friendly that they stroked the beards of Ragueneau and Nicolet with the remark: "Not only will your customs be our customs, but our chins will be clothed with hair as are your chins." They released both Marguerie and Godefroy.

Ten days ago, continued Ragueneau, with a barque and shallops carrying seventy men, de Montmagny held council with the Iroquois up along the south shore of the river. They in their canoes, he in a shallop armed with swivel guns, discussed the proposition of peace. They sought an immediate peace treaty with the French and a present of thirty French muskets. They gave assurance that they would negotiate in their own way for peace with the Hurons and Algonquins. The council concluded with polite words but suspicious thoughts, and both parties agreed to meet the following day. But the next morning, the Iroquois spread along the shore chanting and gesticulating in a war dance, drove their canoes out against the shallops and fired with their muskets on the French. De Montmagny pursued them on water and land, but in vain. The only result of the peace parley, concluded Ragueneau, would be a more intensified guerilla warfare.

De Brébeuf shared the astonishment of all at Three Rivers that his two canoes had passed safely through five hundred Iroquois braves. He was even more amazed a few days later when a Huron, who reached Three Rivers by land, reported that the four Huron canoes following Echon's two canoes were attacked near Rivière des Prairies a few hours after Echon had passed the spot. Three canoes surrendered; one escaped and sped back to warn the Hurons upriver.

De Brébeuf and his Hurons were eager to hurry down to Quebec. There he was greeted affectionately by the Superior, Père Vimont, by the veteran Massé, by his old comrade, de Noüe, and the younger missioners. The Jesuit residence on the Heights, near Fort St. Louis, was a ramshackle house that had been leased after Notre Dame de Recouvrance was destroyed by fire last year. There, also, he was welcomed by the already famed Governor de Montmagny, whom the natives called Onontio, Great Mountain. He judged that all the praise given to de Montmagny as a soldier, a charming diplomat, and a pious Catholic was true. He had an immediate instance of the Governor's graciousness. He had promised Sondatsaa, his canoeman from Ossossané, that he would baptize him at Quebec. De Montmagny, when he heard this, suggested that he be the god-father and the ceremony be performed in the Algonquin Christian settlement of Sillery. On June 26, in the presence of a great number of the French who had come to Sillery from Quebec, and of all the Algonquin Believers, with the greatest pomp Père de Brébeuf christened Sondatsaa, and de Montmagny took him as his god-child, giving him his own name of Charles. De Montmagny, as a baptismal gift, presented Charles with the greatest mark of affection and trust, a musket and munitions.[1]

Sillery fascinated de Brébeuf, for it was a village of Algonquin and Montagnais Christians, more wonderful than anything he had ever dreamed. The money to create it, he learned, was generously donated by Chevalier Noël de Sillery in 1637. It was established in 1639, and had now become the heart of the apostolate among many Algonquin peoples. The village was built on the shore of a rounded cove four miles up the St. Lawrence from Quebec. On one side of a ridge that speared down from the highlands to the rear, the Jesuits had built their residence and a church. On the other side of the ridge, the Hospital nuns had erected their convent and halls for the ailing natives. About the nuns and the priests, the Christian families located their tent-shaped cabins of bark and the more important leaders were given houses constructed in the French style.

With deep interest, de Brébeuf and his Hurons inspected l'Hôtel-Dieu of Sillery. La Duchesse d'Aiguillon, niece of Cardinal Richelieu, founded and supported this work of charity. Three Hospitalières of Dieppe came, in 1639, to build a hospital for the natives in Quebec. But when they learned of the Sillery settlement, they decided they could better fulfill their aspirations by establishing themselves in Sillery among the natives rather than in Quebec. On the day of their arrival, they began nursing the natives then stricken with the smallpox epidemic, and ever since had cared for the sick like loving mothers. Sondatsaa and the Hurons were dumbfounded at such charity on the part of the paleface women.

Still another foundation gave de Brébeuf the greatest joy and drew from the Hurons bursts of admiration. In 1639, three Ursuline nuns, under the leadership of Mère Marie de l'Incarnation, sailed to

Quebec for the purpose of opening a school for the daughters of the Algonquins. They were accompanied and supported in great part by Dame Marie Madeleine de la Peltrie, a widow who was dedicating her wealth and herself to the apostolate of the Ursulines. The nuns had attracted several Algonquin girls to their school and had won the love of all the natives. With exuberant joy, the Hurons and de Brébeuf greeted Theresa, the niece of Chihwatenhwa, who had been living for a year with the Ursulines.

While at Quebec, de Brébeuf was told definitely by Père Vimont that he would not return that year to the Hurons. Paul Ragueneau would take his place at Sainte Marie, and he would carry on Ragueneau's work as the Huron administrator on the St. Lawrence. Vimont was much concerned about de Brébeuf's injured shoulder and advised him to consult a surgeon as soon as possible. Despite the pain which still bothered him, and the limpness of his left arm, de Brébeuf was of the opinion that the fracture was healing; still, when he found time, he assured Vimont, he would consult a doctor.

After their few days in Quebec, Sondatsaa and the Hurons, accompanied by Echon, started their homeward journey. When they landed at Three Rivers, about July 4, they were told that the upper river was free of Iroquois. Père Ragueneau, the *donnés* and the Hurons, their canoes loaded with supplies, paddled off the next day, while de Brébeuf blessed them and suffered in his soul, inasmuch as he could not return with them. The following day they struggled back to Three Rivers after hearing from some Algonquins that the Iroquois were infesting all the waterways beyond the St. Lawrence. The Christian Algonquins of Sillery volunteered to convoy the Hurons through the dangerous places of ambush, and many unbelieving Algonquins agreed to join the war party. De Montmagny, in addition, offered to send some soldiers as an escort.

Just then, two envoys of the Abenaki people reached Three Rivers. Their purpose was to make reparation for the murder of a Montagnais by one of their nation. In anger, the pagan Montagnais decreed the death and torture of these two envoys, whereas the Christians and the French demanded custody of them. The dispute flared into violence. When the pagans refused to join the escort for Ragueneau and the Hurons, Commandant de Champflour thought it wiser not to permit the Sillery Christians and the French soldiers to undertake the hazard. Sondatsaa and his men fretted and, on July 14, decided to break away and to dare the journey when it was reported that the Iroquois had left the river. For the second time, de Brébeuf, praying they might escape the clutches of the enemy, watched the canoes grow small up the river.

A few days later, a Huron canoe arrived with the good news that the river was clear and that a large flotilla of traders were on their way. When de Brébeuf greeted the Hurons with joy, some responded gruffly, others were sullen and silent. The reason sickened him, for he knew what harm it would do to his brethren among the Hurons. A Huron, who was in one of the canoes of his party captured by the Iroquois, was led off a prisoner. He escaped and revealed what he heard from the Iroquois about Echon. The Blackrobes, he related, have an understanding with the Iroquois; while in the Neutral country, Echon held council with the Seneca Iroquois, and urged them to finish the Hurons by war, as he had tried to finish them by disease; the Senecas informed the Mohawks what Echon had urged; and so, while they were waiting to trap Hurons, the Mohawks recognized the Blackrobe, Echon, in a canoe; that night the Mohawks secretly visited Echon in his camp and were given presents by him to strengthen their arms against the Huron canoes that were following his.

However false this calumny, de Brébeuf knew that it would be believed by the Hurons. The penalty for such treachery being a cleft skull, de Brébeuf feared lest this punishment might be inflicted on some of the missioners in Huronia, instead of on him. Even if no one were killed, the rage and fury of the Hurons would again break out violently against the Blackrobes. With all his power, de Brébeuf himself denied the story to all the Hurons at Three Rivers; some believed him, others remained silent. His only hope was that Charles Sondatsaa, who had been in his canoe, would triumphantly refute it, if and when he safely reached the Huron country.

After bidding farewell to the Hurons, de Brébeuf went down to Quebec. He had more leisure to note how Quebec had grown under the government of Cardinal Richelieu and the generosity of the Company of One Hundred Associates. Substantial houses of stone lined the streets of the lower town along the river, residences covered a goodly area about Fort St. Louis atop the Rock, fields were cleared and cultivated. Quebec was a city like those of Normandy, and New France was become a colony worthy of the King.

New France grew greater that very summer. Paul de Chomedey Maisonneuve, forty colonists, and Mademoiselle Jeanne Mance came to establish a new settlement on the Isle de Montreal. They were financed by the wealthy and influential Société de Notre Dame de Montreal. The single purpose of the Société was that of attracting the savages to a mission center in order to teach them the Catholic Faith, to care for their sick in a hospital and to train their children in a school. It had no commercial aims, sought no profits from peltries, and searched only for spiritual successes. The project, forwarded through ten years by a series of coincidences that seemed miraculous, was now being realized, in 1641, under the leadership of Maisonneuve.

To de Brébeuf, the arrival of these colonists, inspired with a spirit of such high idealism, courage and spiritual aspirations, seemed truly the work of God. So felt Governor de Montmagny and all at Quebec. But the determination of Maisonneuve to proceed immediately to Montreal that late in August, and to winter there, seemed preposterous. In fact, settling at Montreal, 180 miles up from Quebec, with so few men, seemed a hazardous folly. The Iroquois so infested all of that region that they would exterminate the colonists before they could erect any defenses. After lengthy and heated argument about the whole project, Maisonneuve consented to pass the winter in Quebec. He, Jeanne Mance and a few others were put in possession of a residence on Pointe de Puiseaux, near Sillery; the rest of the company were housed further up the river at Sainte-Foy.

De Brébeuf was called into many conferences that summer and autumn by Governor de Montmagny. The paralyzing problem of New France was the mounting insolence of the Iroquois. De Montmagny wanted peace, but not a peace which left the Algonquins and Hurons at the mercy of the crafty, treacherous Iroquois who were ruining the colony. Three Rivers, despite its fortifications, was vulnerable; the trade in peltries was decreasing because the Algonquins and Hurons feared to fall into Iroquois traps along the water routes; and the Iroquois were becoming invincible through the muskets sold to them by the Dutch. If New France were to survive, Cardinal Richelieu must send military help. Soldiers must be stationed at Three Rivers, at the new colony of Montreal, and at a fort which must be built at the entrance of the river of the Iroquois. Furthermore, steps must be taken to prevent the Dutch from selling firearms to these savages. So imminent was the crisis that de Montmagny decided Père Le Jeune must go to France to present the facts to the Cardinal and the directors of the company.

Under the annual obligation of writing his report to his Paternity in Rome, Père Jean included in his letter his observations both on the Huron Mission and on affairs at Quebec. "In regard to those who live among the Hurons," he stated, "great peace and union flourishes. Religious discipline is not only observed as perfectly as in the large colleges, but the exact keeping of the rules increases day by day. All are zealous for virtue and self-denial, according to their power. I doubt that so much excellence was ever found anywhere among so few. Père Hierosme Lalemant, the Superior, gives the greatest satisfaction. The good order of the Mission is due, under God, to his wisdom."

He spoke of the *donnés* with praise, and asked that their form of civil contract be approved. The Huron Believers numbered about sixty, but they will increase little by little, he opinioned. He related that he and Père Chaumonot "spent five months in the Neutral country and assuredly we suffered much. We were listened to sufficiently well by a few but very badly by most. We were attacked by calumnies and insults. However, when we departed we were invited back by the better ones. Père Chaumonot, I hope in Christ, will accomplish notable work in this territory. He has already made progress in the Neutral language which is different from the Huron. He is a most exceptional man."

About conditions among his brethren at Quebec and Three Rivers, he was not so jubilant. "Because some are not apt at languages," he reported, "they lack almost any occupation; and because they are not contented, they become hindrances to the cause. They take the places of many young men who could both quickly learn the language and perform the work notably." He asked that the power of Père Vimont, as Superior, be so increased that he could send the drones back to France.

Two: 1641–1643

No assignment could have pleased Père Jean more than that given to him, the charge of the Mission of St. Joseph at Sillery. He would again be living among and ministering to the natives. His first thought was to study and perfect himself in the Algonquin language, and in this he had the help of Père de Quen, who had been laboring among the St. Lawrence peoples for six years. Thirty Christian families lived permanently at Sillery, but nomad Algonquins from far and near were always camping in the vicinity. The Christians governed themselves in native fashion under the leadership of two chiefs, Noël Nega-bamat and Jean Etinechkawat. While preserving their own traditions and customs, they had totally renounced and banned all Algonquin superstitions, feasts, revels and orgies that were in the slightest way objectionable, and they almost fanatically condemned the native code of promiscuity and changing mates. Though they mingled with the unbelievers, they refused to permit such to live at Sillery until they had been tested and baptized.

De Brébeuf learned for himself of their loyalty and piety. Every morning and evening they gathered in the little church of St. Michel, where Père de Quen said their prayers with them and gave them instructions. They themselves meted out punishment not only to those who were delinquent but to those who were not sufficiently zealous. They lived almost sinless lives and were forever preaching to the pagans about the value of believing and vehemently denounc-ing the traditional superstitions. Here was a miraculous transforma-tion of the savages he had known in 1625, de Brébeuf concluded after he had been at Sillery. The grace of God had broken the reign of Satan. If the Algonquins, who were of a lower race, could rise to such spiritual heights, why should not the Hurons, of a superior race, rise with them? More than ever he believed that the Hurons would eventually become a nation of Believers.

In November, some Hurons wished to winter at Three Rivers but were dissuaded by their comrades as well as by the French. Two of these, however, were brought to Sillery by some Christian Algonquins in December. De Brébeuf knew them, Atondo and Okhukwandoron, from Scanonaenrat, where he had been treated so viciously. He wel-comed them warmly and invited them to pass the winter at Sillery. Noël Negabamat, as chief, imposed on them the condition that they must follow the customs of the Believers and not indulge in the vices of the pagans. The two Hurons were well-behaved, and soon asked Echon to teach them prayers such as they heard the Algonquins recit-ing. They were completely fascinated by the Paleface Virgins who nursed and cared for the sick. At Quebec they were astounded at the stone houses, and in the church they noted how the French listened so attentively to the Blackrobes. After de Brébeuf introduced them to the Governor, they concluded Echon must be a chief of great importance, since Onontio heeded his words. They visited the Ursuline convent, and were awed when they gazed at these other Paleface Virgins who taught and lodged the niece of Chihwatenhwa and many Algonquin girls.

By February, Atondo and Okhukwandoron were listening to Echon in rapt attention. They asked insistently for baptism and they renounced all evil, for they wished to be like the Sillery Algonquins and the Huron Believers. Judging them to be sufficiently instructed and resolute in their pledges, Père Jean baptized them on March 30, 1642. Atondo, aged thirty-six, was christened Paul, with Sieur Paul Maisonneuve as his god-father. Okhukwandoron, twenty-five years old, sponsored by Jeanne Mance, was named John Baptist. On April 20, in the church of Quebec, kneeling alongside of Governor de Montmagny, the two Hurons, elegantly clothed in beaver robes, received their First Communions.

Through the winter de Brébeuf often talked with his neighbors, Maisonneuve and Jeanne Mance, about the mysterious way God led them to Montreal, and about the visions of the founder of the project, Jérôme de la Dauversière. Often he visited the Hôtel-Dieu, on the other side of the Sillery ridge, and every time he thanked God for sending these courageous and tireless Hospital nuns. In his frequent visits to Quebec, he paid his respects to the Ursuline nuns who were achieving marvels of grace, not only among the Algonquin women and girls but also among the men, and he enjoyed very much chatting with Theresa, the saintly little Huron girl.

Two of the Ursuline nuns attracted him. One was Mère Joseph, who wished to be the mother for all the Hurons and who studied their tongue with great devotion. The other was the Superior, Mère Marie de l'Incarnation. She saw in him, and he recognized in her, the mystic. God was working in both of them, and they were fully responding to the extraordinary graces God gave them. They could converse on that union with God which cannot be described in words. Both were granted the "gift" whereby they were one with God and habitually in His presence.[2]

Père Jean, at last, consulted with the surgeon, Monsieur Gendron, about his shoulder and arm, not because of the pain but because he found difficulty in using his left arm as vigorously as he wished, and because of Père Vimont's insistence. To Vimont, Surgeon Gendron gave the following report:

> I have not the slightest doubt that R. P. de Brébeuf suffered a great deal. The collarbone on the left side was broken about three finger lengths from the shoulder, and he had not had any treatment. He did not have any of the things that should have been necessary on this occasion to soothe, even to some slight extent, the afflicted part. Necessity constrained him to continue his daily round of duties, and this retarded in no slight way the reducing of the fracture. Then, too, in moving the arm, be it ever so slightly, one part of the bone necessarily slips and separates itself from the other, for the reason that the collarbone has no independent movement but follows the movement of the arm and shoulder, which pulls downward the part that is joined to it. From this condition resulted the continual pain which he always suffered in this part of his body, but most especially during the space of two years [sic] when he was entirely unable to help himself with his arm.

The two Hurons, Paul and John Baptist, were eager to get back to their homeland, and de Brébeuf approved, for he believed they would become apostles of Scanonaenrat. Noël Negabamat prepared a great farewell feast for them on May 6, and fervently exhorted them to have courage: "We are convinced that you will be firm and constant in your Faith. We hope that, through your efforts, all your village will enjoy the same blessing that you have found here, so that, finally, we may have but one heart and one mouth." After glowing thanks, Atondo concluded: "We will urge strongly all of our countrymen to be baptized. I have many relatives, many nephews and nieces. I offer them all to Jesus Christ. I hope they will be the first to give me their ear."

In the first week of May, Maisonneuve, Jeanne Mance and the Montreal colonists, trusting in God and their divine vocation, restrained by no fear of the Iroquois or the wilderness, happily sailed up the St. Lawrence to establish their colony at Ville-Marie. Later in the summer, de Montmagny would send his barks, heavily loaded with timber, his soldiers and workmen to build Fort Richelieu at the mouth of the Iroquois River. Through these two new outposts at the Iroquois gateway, all hoped that the French could curb the vehemence of the enemy.

In the late spring, de Brébeuf transported to Three Rivers the great amount of supplies needed at Sainte Marie for a full year by the forty Frenchmen living there. On his arrival, he heard with troubled soul that the Iroquois again intended to redden the summer with blood. An Algonquin, who had slipped away from them, reported that seven hundred, armed with Dutch muskets, planned a blockade of all the waterways from Three Rivers far up the Ottawa. Two Algonquin women who escaped gave information that already three hundred were concealed along the river.

With surprise, then, the watchers of Three Rivers spotted four large Huron canoes driving down the river on July 17. De Brébeuf hurried along the scarp of the hill to greet them. Père Jogues slipped nimbly out of the canoe in an instant. He nodded toward Père Raymbault, who was thinner almost than a skeleton, and whispered to de Brébeuf that Charles was dying of consumption. After a tender welcome to Charles Raymbault, de Brébeuf beamed happily on Coûture and the other two *donnés*, and on the Hurons, mostly all Believers, Charles Sondatsaa, Joseph Teondechoren, Stephen Totiri and, most surprising of all, the greatest war chief of Teanaustayé, Ahatsistari, who became a Christian and was named Eustace.

When the greetings and shoutings were over, Jogues poured forth the news of the mission. He and Raymbault had brought the greetings of the French to the Nipissing Feast of the Dead in the far north, where Lake Huron and Lake Superior join. Raymbault, after that, contracted the disease that would soon kill him. At Sainte Marie, the bastions and stone walls were rising, and the timbered residence and chapel were well under construction. The place was truly becoming the center of Christianity in which Believers fortified themselves with the Sacraments, prayer and instruction, to which the infidels were coming in ever-increasing numbers. Everywhere, at Ossossané, at Teanaustayé and Scanonaenrat, even at Cahiagué and the more distant settlements, the number of Believers was growing and their influence was becoming dominant.

De Brébeuf accompanied Jogues, Raymbault and the Hurons down to Quebec. Together they called on the Ursulines, and talked with little Theresa, who was sad because her uncle, Teondechoren, was taking her to her Huron home. They walked out to Sillery, to the Hospital nuns, where Jogues met René Goupil, a young *donné* who was skilled as a surgeon and was eager to go up to the Hurons. They joined in the festivities and reunion between the Believing Algonquins and the Believing Hurons at Sillery; they repaired to the chapel where they chanted their prayers in Algonquin and Huron; they deliberated in the councils, where the Christians exhorted one another to be faithful to God, to keep all the Commandments and to raise the war hatchet against all superstitions.

The party ascended to Three Rivers. The Hurons, having finished with the trading, and the French, having collected the supplies, were ready to brave the dangers of the homeward journey. Père Jogues, Coûture, Goupil and another Frenchman, the Huron Theresa, had places in the four canoes of the Christians, under the leadership of Eustace Ahatsistari. Eight other Huron canoes strengthened the flotilla and increased the number of voyagers to forty. From all that could be learned, there were no Iroquois enemies lurking along the river in parties strong enough to attack them. On August 1, after Mass at dawn, the Huron canoes shoved into the river, while Père Jean, with lifted hand, blessed them. He felt as if his heart were being carried away with them. He had begged Père Vimont to give him leave to return to his Huron people, but had been told obedience required him to pass a second year at Sillery.

At a later date, his confidant, Paul Ragueneau, related about him:

One day, while praying to Our Lord, he asked: "Lord, what dost Thou wish me to do?" He heard the answer which Jesus formerly gave to Saint Paul: "Go to Ananias and he will tell you what it is required of you to do." From that time, P. de Brébeuf was so confirmed in the resolutions which he had, of never seeking other guidance than obedience that, in truth, I may say this virtue was perfect in him. Seeing only God in the person of the Superior, he discovered his heart to him with a child's simplicity, showed an entire docility to the answers which were given him, and acquiesced without resistance in everything which was said to him, although contrary to his natural inclinations—not only in that which appeared to the eyes of men, but in the depth of his heart, where he knew that God sought the true obedience.

Some of the Hurons came paddling furiously back the next evening wailing the death chant. The vanguard canoes had been ambushed in the swamps above Lake St. Peter, they related. Ondessonk, the Frenchmen, and many Hurons were prisoners of the Iroquois. De Brébeuf gasped in horror. Later an escaped Huron described the battle in which the Hurons were overpowered and Ondessonk, the two Frenchmen, as well as all the Hurons of the first four canoes were killed or made prisoners. De Brébeuf felt his heart and head would burst, but again, and again, God's will be done. All the supplies he had prepared were plundered. The Christians, who would have been the apostles of their people, were dead, or reserved for death after torture; brave little Isaac Jogues, his brother, courageous Coûture, gentle Goupil, were the victims of the Iroquois savages.[3]

Though he accepted God's way and dispensation with humility, he could not but help wondering at the mysteries of Divine Providence. Just when the Hurons were believing, they were stricken down. As so often in the past, God seemed to chastise the Christians and to spare the pagans. Like Lalemant and Vimont, he could not understand how these things could be, yet he never doubted but that God would one day bring all things to His honor and service.

In September, 1642, de Brébeuf addressed his Paternity in Rome. He acknowledged the receipt of an answer to his last letter, in which he was told that the matter of the civil contract with the *donnés* had not yet been decided. In this connection, he noted that two of these *donnés* had been captured with Père Isaac Jogues, and that a third, who escaped, "did not hesitate afterwards to expose himself to danger, to return to our Jesuits to whose service he pledged his life for God. This is one of the reasons why we prefer men of this kind, since they gladly undergo all dangers with us, which are certainly frequent, and they do not act as mercenaries."

From the *Relation*, de Brébeuf stated, his Paternity will be able to see: first, how great is our peace and unity; second, how great is the fervor of the neophytes; third, how our Iroquois enemies attack us and the natives allied with us. He continued: "It is greatly to be feared that in a short time all our affairs and the religion of Canada will perish completely unless a speedy remedy be applied." He begged his Paternity to urge the Jesuits in France to seek help. Adopting the viewpoint of Le Jeune, de Montmagny and the other officials in Quebec, he condemned the Dutch for selling muskets to the Iroquois and advised that "they should be altogether driven out of these parts or be conquered in war like the Iroquois." He dated his letter October 1, 1642, just prior to the sailing of the fleet.[4]

He himself alleged that "he was being detained at Quebec because of the urgency of Huron affairs." The Superior, in his report, explained that a school for Hurons at Sillery would be one of the most effective ways of converting the Huron people. "It was for this reason," he attested, "that I again detained P. Jean de Brébeuf, who had wintered here last year and had not yet gone up again, in order to instruct and take charge of these Hurons."

Jean de Brébeuf was again stationed at Sillery for the winter of 1642. To his great satisfaction, two Hurons arrived in September. Armand Andeouarahen, who was Daniel's schoolboy five years before, had become a notable warrior. Having experienced in battle what he believed were two undeniable miracles, he had vowed thereafter to live with the Christian Algonquins. He brought with him a comrade, Saonaretsi, about twenty years old, who belonged to an influential and large family of Taenhatentaron, heretofore hostile to the Blackrobes. So well did Saonaretsi learn and so perfect was his conduct that Père Jean baptized him on December 24, 1642, giving him the name of Ignatius, the patron of his village. A third Huron, from Arenté, near Ossossané, who was wintering with the Algonquins, came seeking Echon in mid-January. He was boarded and fed by the charity of the Hospital nuns and, in the words of de Brébeuf, "he had very good wit and judgment, was mild-mannered and thoroughly obedient." A fourth and fifth Huron came to Sillery at the end of January, declaring their ardent desire to become Believers.

The conduct of the five young Hurons could not have been more exemplary, nor their eagerness to learn more intense. When they were invited to join the Algonquins in hunting, one replied: "I did not come from so far away to go hunting. I have come to know God and to learn to serve him. It is the knowledge of God that I hope to carry back with me to my country, not the skins of moose or other animals." Another replied: "The time for staying here is short. I have not the best of memories. If I had wished to hunt for meat, I would have stayed with the other Algonquins where the hunting is better."

On March 8, 1643, in the chapel of the hospital, Père de Brébeuf conferred, in baptism, the name of Peter on the Huron from Arenté.

He became the most fervent of all, praying early in the morning and late at night in the chapel of the nuns. The two Hurons, who came late in January, had so eagerly sought instruction that de Brébeuf christened them with the greatest solemnity in the parish church of Quebec on March 25. Present were Governor de Montmagny and his staff, the most important French colonists, the other three Hurons and the Algonquins of Sillery. They were named Joseph and René. A sixth Huron, who that winter was baptized at Montreal, found his way to Sillery.

More than once, Armand asked to remain at Sillery. He told Echon: "I have a strong desire to act rightly and to save myself from the fires which burn without ceasing. To attain what I desire, I would like to live with you always, and not return to the Hurons. The occasions for sin are frequent in our villages, the liberty in them is too great. Nevertheless, I shall do what I am told." De Brébeuf consulted Vimont. They thought that he might become a *donné*, or even a Jesuit lay brother. However, said Vimont, "to be a savage and to be a religious are things which seem most contradictory". They judged it best for Armand to be a lay apostle among the Hurons.

Père Vimont, who lived that winter at Sillery, wrote in his *Relation*: "Generally speaking, all the Hurons have greatly edified us. They were always the first at Mass and prayers; they were the last to leave, at evening and in the morning. The peace and amity in which they lived among themselves and with our French and Algonquins, showed very well what the power of the Faith and Divine Grace can do when it has gained possession of hearts, even of savages." After his happy experience with his six Hurons, de Brébeuf was more than ever convinced of the value of a school for young Huron men at Sillery where they learned the truth in quiet and practiced the Christian code without obstruction. All that was good in them grew, all that grew was firm and strong. Though he confidently believed these six would become the apostles of the year, he mused: "If some of them should happen to stumble, we need not be surprised."

He went up with them to Three Rivers in May. All winter, he heard, Iroquois were seen about Three Rivers, and had been in such numbers about Fort Richelieu and Montreal that these outposts were cloistered. According to Algonquin scouts, bands of them were prowling along the St. Lawrence and lurking along the portages of the lower Ottawa. To the utter surprise of all, early in June, 120

Hurons in more than twenty canoes floated proudly into Three Rivers. They had met no Iroquois, they said with regret. But, they told a tragic story of their homeland. Last autumn, the frontier village of Contarea was burned and the people massacred by the Senecas. Near Teanaustayé, forty men and women gathering vines for the fishing nets were surprised at night and butchered. In broad daylight, near Ossossané, women working in a field were killed. The land of the Hurons was a country of blood and dread.

The six Christians joined the other Hurons for the homeward journey. No Iroquois attacked them, though the Iroquois must have watched them pass, for new atrocities were shortly afterwards perpetrated. Five Frenchmen, working in a field two hundred paces from the stockade of Ville-Marie, were attacked by Iroquois; three were struck down and scalped, two were carried off as prisoners. Later, thirteen canoes and sixty Hurons were trapped in the Rivière des Prairies, back of Montreal; some were massacred, some held for torture, some led off as prisoners. As de Brébeuf learned later, with this band was lost Lalemant's *Huron Relation* and the letters of the missioners to their people in France. The Iroquois were making good their threats to scourge the Algonquins, Hurons and French with massacre and terror.

Last year, Père Le Jeune came back from France with hopeful tidings. He had exposed the peril of New France to a great number of persons of power and wealth, among them the Duchess d'Aiguillon, the foundress of the hospital at Sillery and Quebec, who in turn represented the dire state of New France to her uncle, Cardinal Richelieu. Last year, Richelieu sent to Quebec an increased number of soldiers and munitions. This coming summer of 1643, would Richelieu provide many more soldiers and much more equipment to protect the colony against the Iroquois enemy? Anxiously, hopefully, prayerfully, Governor de Montmagny, Père Vimont, Père de Brébeuf and all at Quebec, Three Rivers and Montreal awaited the fleet from France.

Three: 1643–1644

Though their bodies were shrunk and their faces were carved with deep creases, Père de Brébeuf recognized the two naked Hurons who came to the cabin of Three Rivers on June 12. With surprise and deep emotion he welcomed Joseph Teondechoren and Peter Saoek-bata, the two brothers of Chihwatenhwa. They had been captured last August with Isaac Jogues, and though they had been tortured, their lives were spared. This spring, they related, they and three other Huron prisoners were ordered to accompany a war party, to paddle the canoes, to carry the corn bags, to make the fires and to perform like menial tasks for their Iroquois masters. That afternoon, they escaped from this war party of forty Iroquois which was hiding about ten miles above Three Rivers.

Through the night, de Brébeuf was enthralled by their story of the capture of Jogues, Coûture, Goupil and the Believers, of how they had been tormented along the way, of how they had been burned and carved in the Iroquois villages, of Goupil's death, of the slavery of Ondessonk during the winter, of the tortures and heroic deaths of Eustace Ahatsistari and the other Hurons, of Theresa, who lived in sorrow, longing for the good mothers of Quebec. The Iroquois talked of peace, Joseph declared, but he warned that they were thinking of a treacherous peace with the French, in order to destroy completely all the Hurons in their own land and all the Algonquins along the St. Lawrence.

That month, and during July and August, Three Rivers was quiet but uneasy. The Iroquois were known to be about, hence the Hurons and Algonquins avoided the river. Governor de Montmagny arrived with four large shallops, armed with swivel guns, and a detachment of French soldiers and Algonquin scouts. Determined to break this Iroquois blockade, he sailed up as far as Montreal, crossed to Fort Richelieu, sent scouting parties to the usual places of ambush, but nowhere could he discover a single Iroquois. Yet he knew that hundreds of them were concealed along the shore, no doubt watching his every movement. Against this sort of guerrilla warfare, he felt impotent. The only method of combating the Iroquois would be that of sending down a powerful expedition to ravage their country and to destroy them at the source. But France would not send him the help he needed.

While he was at Three Rivers, a shallop arrived from Fort Riche-lieu, and the officer reported that, on August 15, several Iroquois canoes deployed before the Fort. A single canoe with a single savage was given leave to come ashore. He identified himself as a Mohawk deputed to talk about peace with the French, and presented a letter sent by Ondessonk to Onontio. They detained him, telling him that the matter must be referred to de Montmagny. He asked them to shoot a cannon once, as a signal to his comrades. They fired the cannon. Immediately, all the canoes spurted toward the shore; the French threatened to shoot; the canoes drove on; the French fired one volley; the Iroquois veered away and fled into the woods. The reason for it all, no one knew.

De Montmagny called de Brébeuf and Vimont to examine the letter. It was signed by Isaac Jogues and dated June 30. Père Jean deciphered it, for it was written partly in French, in Latin and in Huron. It began: "Here is the fourth letter I have written since I am with the Iroquois." Jogues then warned that there would be seven hundred Iroquois, carrying three hundred muskets, along the river all summer. He wrote: "The design of the Iroquois, as far as I can see, is to capture all the Hurons. When they have put to death the more important ones and a large part of the others, they propose to make of them one people and one land." About himself, he stated: "The Dutch have tried to ransom us, but in vain.... I am resolved to dwell here as long as it shall please Our Lord, and not to escape, even though an opportunity should present itself."

They sat awed. De Montmagny asked de Brébeuf to carry back to Fort Richelieu letters for Père Jogues and to examine the Mohawk held as a hostage. At Fort Richelieu, de Brébeuf recognized the Mohawk as a born Huron, adopted by the Iroquois. He found the man saturnine and silent. He offered presents to the Huron-Mohawk to carry back letters to Ondessonk. The man refused, finally alleging he did not dare to return, for the Mohawks would split his skull as a French spy and a traitor. More and more were the French disheartened by the failure of the peace efforts and the increasing tragedies of the Iroquois incursions.

For the third year, de Brébeuf was held along the St. Lawrence, while his heart was weary with longing to be back among his Hurons. Even though he were permitted to depart, he could find no means of going. His urgent problem was that of forwarding supplies to the Huron missioners, since those of last year were captured and no canoes could be expected this summer. His hope, though faint, was that some Huron young men might again appear somehow, and that he could school them in the Faith and the Christian life during the winter. He might be useful, too, if the Iroquois, as rumored, were intending to open new peace negotiations with the French.

Because of the necessities, he was to remain through the coming winter at Three Rivers, and be deprived, he felt, of the fervor of Sillery. As assistant he had a brilliant Italian, Père François Bressani, who yearned to labor among the Hurons. According to orders, Bressani was directed to attempt the journey up to Huronia at the very first, tolerably safe, opportunity. By stealth and by chance, some Hurons were reaching Three Rivers. Two canoes of Believers stole in, bearing with them letters from the missioners and a condensed version of the *Relation* of that year which had been lost. De Brébeuf confided to them the letters to the French at Sainte Marie, and loaded their canoes with baggage. With them went a French surgeon who had signed the contract and pronounced the vows of a *donné*. A few days later, the word came that all were massacred by the Iroquois.

On September 23, Père de Brébeuf finished his annual letter to his Paternity in Rome. He explained that the *Relation* and letters from the Hurons had been captured by the Iroquois; he narrated what he had learned about the captivity and torture of Père Jogues; he told of the Iroquois scourge. In conclusion, he stated: "From these things it is evident in what a wretched state Canadian affairs are placed. But, on the other hand, the more wretched these unhappy afflictions are, by so much are they richer in heavenly gifts. Vice does not rule here, but virtue and piety, not only among Ours, who show themselves men and true sons of the Society, but also among our Frenchmen and among the barbarians, and not only among those who have given their name to the Faith but among the rest who do not yet profess the Faith. For they scarcely ever practice their former superstitions and, if we now enjoyed peace, we might hope quickly to bring all to the Faith."

To Three Rivers came a Huron who had escaped from the Mohawk village where he was baptized by Jogues. Another Huron, who had been captured in June, snatched his freedom and made his way to Three Rivers. In November, amid the first ice and snow, arrived a canoe of four Hurons, down from their own country, for the explicit purpose of living with Echon and the Believers at Sillery.

Unexpectedly, de Brébeuf again found himself with six scholars and six mouths to feed.

With great earnestness, the Hurons listened to Echon's lessons and learned to pray. The two who were baptized helped the others with the lessons. Since all six were exemplary in their conduct, toward the end of December, de Brébeuf baptized the four catechumens and supplied the ceremonies on the other two. After their baptisms, they surpassed the French in their piety and devotion. During February and March, they visited Sillery and went off on hunting trips with the Algonquins. In no way did they revert to their superstitions or seek Algonquin women. On March 17, the Saturday before Holy Week, in the presence of the Commandant and the French, they received their First Communion.

With the coming of April, the ice bridge across the St. Lawrence began to crack and rumble down with the current. The six Hurons grew restless and wished to return to their families. They were profuse in their thanks to Echon and the French, and boldly promised that they would make their kinspeople also believe in the One-who-made-all and be baptized. De Brébeuf favored an early departure before the Iroquois would be along the river. He judged that here was an opportunity to send Père Bressani up to the Hurons. On Wednesday, April 27, the six Hurons, Bressani and a young Frenchman departed in the three canoes that had been given them. Though all felt courageous and confident, they seemed to have a presentiment. Before they left, the Hurons and French declared they were ready for life or death.

Two weeks later, about May 14, Henry Stontrats, one of Bressani's party, stumbled into Three Rivers. He was starving, gaunt and haggard, his fingers were but festering stumps, his body was scarred and scabbed. He told that he had escaped from the Iroquois several days' journey along the trail and had picked his way back. With a leaden heart, de Brébeuf listened to his story. Fifteen miles beyond Three Rivers, the three canoes were trapped and captured by two bands of Iroquois who immediately cracked open the skull of the Huron called Bertrand, boiled and ate him, the while they forced Bressani and the others to watch. At first, Bressani was neither stripped nor bound, though they talked about burning and eating him in their villages. Later on, when they met another war party, he was clubbed and knifed. Henry knew no more of his fate.

Again de Brébeuf offered an act of submission to the Divine Will, but marveled at the mysteries of Divine Providence. These six Hurons, whom he had so carefully prepared as apostles through the winter, were in the spring destroyed by the Iroquois. Père Bressani, who had given such great promise as a Huron missioner, was carried away as Jogues had been, and might have been tortured and killed. Dire, also, was the further news brought by Henry. Ten war parties were even then, in May, hidden along the Huron route, from the lower Ottawa about Montreal and down the St. Lawrence to Three Rivers itself. Late in the summer, other bands intended to come hunting men.

De Brébeuf was called to Quebec for conferences with Governor de Montmagny and Père Vimont. Certain facts were all too clear: the Iroquois fever of blood lust had risen with their victories; they were along the St. Lawrence in greater numbers and with more Dutch muskets than ever before; they were as baffling as they were murderous; the Hurons and Algonquins, with only bows and arrows and javelins, were an easy prey to them; the French could never find them, except when they were pounced upon; after a disastrous foray early in June, the Algonquins sought safety in the northern mountains, so that scarcely any remained along the river; the Hurons would not dare to journey to Three Rivers.

In the words of Vimont: "Where eight years ago one could see eighty or one hundred cabins, barely five or six can now be seen. A chief who then had eight hundred warriors under his command, now has not more than thirty or forty. Instead of fleets of three hundred or four hundred canoes, we see now but twenty or thirty. And the pitiful part of it is that these remnants of nations consist almost entirely of women, widows and girls who cannot all find lawful husbands and who, consequently, are in danger of much suffering, or of committing great sins."

Certain questions could be solved only with the arrival of the French fleet. Père Le Jeune had again spent the winter in France, pleading for help for Canada. Cardinal Richelieu and King Louis XIII were dead. Would the Regent, Queen Anne, and Cardinal Mazarin, and the directors of the company send soldiers to defend the country against the Iroquois? Would the fleet arrive late, as in the past few years? There would be very few peltries this summer, therefore diminished profits for the bankers next winter, and reduced supplies next summer. Then came the fleet, and with it a company of soldiers well equipped with arquebuses, munitions and armor. There was hope for Quebec, for Fort Richelieu, for Montreal, for Huron Sainte Marie.

Père Isaac Jogues, almost like an apparition, disembarked from the first ship that reached Quebec. Having finally escaped from the Iroquois last summer through the help of the Dutch, he had reached France on Christmas morning and won his heart's desire to return to New France. Almost his first question was whether he could get up to the Hurons again. Though they informed him of the state of affairs, he still hoped and asked to be sent to Sainte Marie.

With de Brébeuf, Jogues went up to Three Rivers in July. In broad, open day, to the amazement of all, twelve war canoes bearing sixty Huron chiefs and braves floated down the river. With them were Père Pijart and some *donnés*. They proclaimed that they had not come to trade, but were on the warpath. All along the route, they had searched for Iroquois, but nowhere could they find the enemy. After a time along the St. Lawrence, they declared they would again hunt Iroquois.

Here, thought de Brébeuf, was his chance. Pijart could remain at Three Rivers, and he could go to the Hurons under a safe escort. He hurried down to consult Vimont, at Quebec. Père Vimont assented to his pleadings, and assigned Père de Brébeuf once more to the Huron Mission. In doing so, he confided to him certain documents and secret information that Père Jèrôme Lalemant was appointed Superior of the Mission of New France and was to return to Quebec at the earliest moment, that Père Paul Ragueneau was the successor of Père Lalemant as Superior of the Huron Mission.

De Brébeuf bade his hurried farewells to Quebec, to his Jesuit brethren, to the Ursulines and Mère Marie, to the Hospital nuns, who had been forced by the authorities to abandon their hospital at Sillery, because Sillery had become a deserted village through fear of the Iroquois. He was off to the Hurons, after three years of waiting. With him went two young missioners who would be stationed at Sainte Marie and labor among the Algonquins, Père Noël Chabanel and Père Léonard Garreau.

At Three Rivers, he learned that the Hurons and some Algonquins had gone searching for Iroquois. On July 26, fifteen canoes gently floated down, the paddlers chanting their song of victory. Three

Iroquois stood up in the canoes, waving their arms and bodies in defiance. After landing, they were led to the Algonquin camp, where two of the Iroquois were given to the Hurons and one to the Algonquins. When Commandant Champflour heard that the Algonquins were torturing their prisoner, he sent orders that they must delay the torture and execution till Governor de Montmagny arrived. De Montmagny in a general council demanded that the Algonquins surrender their Iroquois to his custody, since he intended to open further peace negotiations with the Iroquois. They returned the answer of thirty-two straws, the number of gifts they demanded.

He requested the Hurons also to hand over their two prisoners. The sixty Huron warriors were silent. He offered them presents, but they were not moved. Finally one of the chiefs spoke: "I am a man of war, not of trade. I came to fight, not to barter. My fame does not consist in bringing back presents but in bringing back prisoners. I cannot touch your axes and your kettles. Take our prisoners, if you are so anxious to have them. I have enough courage to find others. But if the enemy kill me, it will be said in my country that, because Onontio took our prisoners, we exposed ourselves to death to capture others."

In a milder tone, Charles, a Christian Huron, addressed de Montmagny: "Be not angry, Onontio. It is not through perverseness that we act thus. It is because we fear to lose both honor and life. You see here only young men; in our country, the elders govern our affairs. If we returned to our country with presents, we would be called grasping traders, not warriors. We have given our word to our chiefs that, if we captured prisoners, we would deliver them into their hands. You prove by your words that peace is desirable. We are of the same opinion. Take note, we have done no harm to our captives. We treat them friendly, because we hope to have them as friends." De Montmagny was so impressed that he was satisfied to let the Hurons use their prisoners for peace negotiations in their own way. The two Iroquois, having been brought before the council and told of the resolutions, were eloquent in their gratitude.

De Montmagny had previously ordered a score of soldiers who had arrived that summer from France to act as escort to the Huron war party. Père de Brébeuf appreciated the fact that he and the Hurons would have protection along the route, but he had some doubts about the wisdom of having the soldiers all winter at Sainte Marie. He had heard they mutinied on the ships, and at Three Rivers he had evidence that they were a tough, boisterous crowd of young adventurers. By fighting with the men and consorting with the women, they could ruin the Huron Mission. However, he discovered enough good in them to accept them.

Under a blistering sun in the first week of August, the flotilla of some twenty canoes got under way. All the baggage and tools so badly needed during the past two years were stowed away. The sixty Hurons were still inspired with the lust of warfare, the twenty-two French soldiers were fretting for new adventures, the two young priests, Chabanel and Garreau, were pulsing with expectancy.

De Brébeuf enjoyed a peace, amidst the turmoil, that was complete and overwhelming. For the third time—and he was sure it was the last time—he went to his Hurons. He knew that he was being guided by God to his final destiny, and he prayed again that God would accept the vow he had made eleven years before and had repeated each day at the altar. In a profound repose, he felt the canoe slug beneath his knees, heard the guns of the Fort boom their thunderous farewells, and saw Three Rivers itself recede into the forests.

CHAPTER XI

Faith Comes to the Doomed Hurons

One: 1644–1645

AFTER THIRTY DAYS OF JOURNEYING, on September 7, 1644, the canoe slid through the water weeds at the mouth of the river of Sainte Marie. In guttural resonance, the Hurons chanted their song of arrival the while they clapped their bark paddles on the bark canoe. Jean de Brébeuf eagerly watched the trees along the narrow river pass by him. He saw a man look down from the bank, then another shouting in French, and heard the calls repeated beyond. He was abreast of Sainte Marie and, in a flicker, was surrounded by his black-robed brothers, the *donnés* and the workmen.[1]

They greeted him tumultuously with shouts, laughter and hugs, and led him into the timbered chapel where they all vibrantly recited the *Te Deum* in thanksgiving to God for his safe arrival. They sat him down in the common room and all together peppered him with questions. Yes, he answered, the journey had been easy. No, he had not seen any Iroquois. Two new missioners were coming, Noël Chabanel and Léonard Garreau; twenty-two French soldiers would be arriving any moment; Père Isaac Jogues was back in Quebec. After he had answered their thousand questions, he had a thousand to ask them.

Later, he held a quiet conversation with Père Lalemant, transmitted to him the private messages sent by Père Vimont, and handed him the special packet containing the documents whereby he was appointed to succeed Vimont as Superior of the Mission of New France and whereby Paul Ragueneau was named as the new Superior of the Huron Mission. Though ordered to go down to Quebec as soon as notified, it was clearly impossible for Père Lalemant to leave before next spring.

All rejoiced at the appointment of Père Paul Ragueneau. He was much like de Brébeuf and, in fact, had modeled himself after Père Jean. He was deeply religious, zealous and generous, with a warmth of charity and understanding. He had keen intelligence and trustworthy judgment. His happy, even exuberant disposition made him a favorite with all the priests and French. He understood the Hurons, likewise, and was well liked by them. Aondechate, as they called him, had almost as much influence over them as Echon.

Charles Garnier expressed not only his own attitude but that of the others in his annual letter as consultor, dated last April 8, when he wrote: "For Superior, we have a man distinguished in virtue, most prudent and kind, considerate toward his subjects. However, he is somewhat lacking in this, that he does not sufficiently find his way into their hearts. There is nothing, however, that would urge that he be removed. But when he is to be changed, no one seems to be equally worthy of appointment to his office than P. Paul Ragueneau, since he is endowed with extraordinary gifts of virtue, talent, prudence and learning. In many respects, he excels him whom we now have for Superior, P. Jérôme Lalemant."

Fifty-eight Frenchmen would be living that winter at Sainte Marie. Fourteen of these were priests, of whom ten labored among the Hurons and four among the Algonquins; two were Jesuit lay brothers; eleven were *donnés* who had signed the civil contract and pronounced private religious vows; nine were workmen and growing youths; twenty-two were the soldiers who had just arrived. There no longer existed the problem in housing and feeding this great number of French.

De Brébeuf marveled at the great progress that had been made in the building of Sainte Marie during his three years' absence. It had become a veritable fortress that combined French architecture with the Huron style of stockade. The walls had been extended toward the river bank so that the enclosure was a square of about 180 feet. The east wall of solid masonry was broken by a turreted gate and terminated on the north and south by jutting bastions. Half of the north wall was also of stone and was guarded by another bastion in process of construction. Beyond this, the wall was solidly built of planks and clay. The west and the south walls were of planks and palisades about twelve feet in height. A small cannon was mounted over the eastern doorway, and the bastions extended out from the corners to permit cross fire along the curtains. The only vulnerable side was the south, along which ran the moat from the river. To defend Sainte Marie against a thousand Iroquois armed with muskets would require very few fighting men.

Within the compound were five buildings of varying size and shape. Along the east wall were workshops and storage rooms. Opposite the eastern gate was the residence of the missioners, a gabled house of two stories surmounted by great crosses and two stone chimneys some thirty feet high. The ground floor was divided into a community room, dining room and kitchen. It had a wooden flooring and two large fireplaces, and was furnished with substantial tables and chairs. The upper story was partitioned into ten or twelve living rooms. Far different was this French residence from the Huron cabins in which de Brébeuf and the early missioners dwelt.

Adjoining the residence toward the north was the chapel, about forty feet long and twenty feet wide. It was substantially built of posts and planks, and within was finely finished with a wooden floor, a raftered ceiling and a large fireplace. The altar was based on flat stones nicely fitted together. On the walls were an abundance of pictures and statues, and in the sacristy were fine vestments and altar decorations. All that the community had not made, they had carried the nine hundred miles from Quebec.

Extending from the chapel and the middle bastion along the north stockade was a house some sixty feet long in which the visiting Believers could be housed and fed. A smaller structure ran parallel to the west wall. The largest building was on the south side, stretching from the residence of the priests to the western stockade, with three wings in the rear. In this were lodged the *donnés*, workmen and soldiers. There was a good well within the enclosure, deep pits had been dug for storing roots, vegetables and other eatables, and a forge was set up for the making of nails and other iron artifacts. Chickens cackled and pigs grunted in the courtyards.

Sainte Marie had taken on the aspect of Quebec or of old France, here in the far western wilderness of the Huron land. Well might Père Jean praise loudly the vision of Jérôme Lalemant, who had visioned and directed the growth of Sainte Marie, the incredible toil of the *donné*, Boivin, and his fellow laborers in constructing it with a limited amount of tools brought up from Quebec, with stones carried a number of miles, with immense trees hewed down and sawed into planks and posts. Sainte Marie, it must have seemed to him, would last forever, and forever be the mission center of the Hurons and the Algonquins, and perhaps of the unknown native nations of the west, the south and the north.

Outside of the French enclosure, Père Jean noted with joy the other structures built in the Huron fashion. Here was a bark-covered chapel in which services could be held on Sundays for the ever-increasing number of Christians. There was another longhouse in which the sick Hurons could be kept and nursed as in a hospital. Beyond was a cabin in which transient Hurons, not yet baptized, were received and fed but not lodged. Above on the hillside was the cemetery in which, already, the Believers buried their relatives with Catholic rites. The meadowland to the east was bristling with cornstalks which this September would yield a plenteous harvest. Patches of vegetable gardens were under cultivation, and grapevines were strung up in long lines. Not only was there stability at Sainte Marie but there was an abundance of produce that could be used for the support of the natives. There was needed now only the longhouses of the Believers in a nearby village that would be totally Christian. There could rise another Sillery, a settlement greater than Sillery, from which vice and superstition would be banished, in which religion and piety would reign supreme.

Through all the country the news spread that the giant Echon had come back to Sainte Marie. The Christians flocked over from Ossossané and up from Teanaustayé, from Scanonaenrat and Taenhatentaron, and from the villages farther away. Echon welcomed them with a warmth of affection, for they were the children he had borne in God. One from Ossossané told him: "Have courage. The number of Believers increases, that of the pagans decreases. When we are a little stronger, of a sudden all will join us and our whole village will be Christian." They were proud of their Faith and zealous in propagating it. The church of the Hurons, Père Jean believed, was now so firmly established on the rock of Christ that no work of the devil could ever again shatter it.

Though no plagues or disease frenzied them as in the past, famine desolated the Huron people and all the neighboring nations. That spring, the squaws had scarcely enough seed corn to plant their fields; this autumn the harvests were so scant that many had nothing to eat but wild pumpkins, acorns and roots. For fear of the Iroquois they could not go to their fishing haunts or travel abroad for hunting. Terror was in their hearts when they contemplated the hunger they must suffer in the winter to come.

Even greater was their dread of the Iroquois. Most of those who journeyed to the trade with the French during the past few years were killed or captured by the eastern Iroquois. The war parties that bravely poured out of the villages were massacred or carried off as prisoners by the western Iroquois. Grown bolder with their victories and confident with their Dutch muskets, the enemies were everywhere in the Huron country. That past year, they had captured the village of Contarea and butchered or led off all who were in it. No one felt safe along any of the trails, nor anywhere in the forests, and not even near the villages. In despair, the Ouendats called themselves a ruined people.

Père Lalemant made his appointments to the missions for the coming year. De Brébeuf was stationed at Sainte Marie, but was given charge of the five neighboring villages of the Ataronchronons, Ste. Anne, St. Louis, St. Denis, St. Jean and St. Xavier. Ragueneau preferred to live among the Christians of Ossossané. Garnier held his post in Teanaustayé, and with him was Ménard for work among the Algonquins to the south. Chaumonot and Du Peron were appointed to Scanonaenrat and St. Ignace of Taenhatentaron. Daniel, with Le Moyne, was assigned to the frontier village of Cahiagué. In the more distant villages, they had their own cabins and chapels, thus reverting to de Brébeuf's original plan. Sainte Marie, they had found, was a place to come back to, a home and a haven, but the battle had to be fought in the Huron villages.[2]

Through the snow and cold of the winter, Père Jean faithfully traveled the trails from Sainte Marie to the villages committed to his care, and oftentimes visited the more distant towns. His supremest delight was in the piety and fidelity of the Believers, since he perceived the spirit of God quickening in their savage souls. However, the pagans were still defiant and, though they no longer dared to play their evil tricks upon him, they nursed their own grievances and suspicions that Echon and the Blackrobes had destroyed the Ouendats.

In turn, he grieved over their blindness and hardness. In his spiritual notes, he exclaimed: "O my God, why are You not known? Why is this barbarous country not all converted to You? Why is not sin abolished from it? Why are You not loved? Yes, my God, if all the torments which the captives can endure here in the cruelty of the tortures were to fall on me, I offer myself thereto with all my heart, and I alone will suffer them."

A quavering truce with the Senecas appeared to have been in force from the winter through to the spring and early summer. There had been fewer Iroquois raids than in the preceding years, and a stronger hope that an eventual peace might be effected. However, the elders and chiefs were not so sanguine as were the people who interpreted their feelings as facts. Oftentimes, to arouse the villagers from their mistaken confidence and lethargy, the chiefs would send out false rumors of Iroquois threats and would proclaim to the young men that they must remain at home to defend the country. Many of the warriors, however, turned traders in the spring and prepared to take advantage of the escort of French soldiers to Three Rivers.

Père Lalemant, as Superior of the Mission of New France, was now able to follow orders to go down to Quebec. In his final conferences to the missioners, as judged by his annual report, he seems to have forgotten his usual reticence and rigidity by lauding all his fellow laborerers among the Hurons and all that they had accomplished. To the joy of everyone at Sainte Marie, the twenty-two soldiers, who had been a nuisance and a heavy expense, departed with their stocks of peltries. About sixty canoes of Hurons from all parts of the country assembled at the meeting place up the lake. The flotilla got under way about the first week of August.[3]

That summer, Sainte Marie again settled into a haven of peace and a retreat for prayer. It was a hive of activity, however, for the brothers, *donnés* and workmen were sedulously completing the stone walls and bastions and buildings. No one knew when the Iroquois would be threatening in greater numbers and wilder ferocity; hence, Sainte Marie must be completely fortified. There was bustling activity, too, on Saturdays and Sundays when the Believers assembled for prayers, instruction and Mass, and always some excitement through the week when itinerants would come for food under the pretext of seeking to be taught.

Père Jean entered upon his annual Spiritual Exercises in mid-
August. He inscribed the following in his book of remembrances:

During the Exercises of the year 1645, August 18. Every day from
now on, at the time of communion, with the consent of the Superior,
I will vow that I will do whatever I shall know to be for the greater
glory of God and for His greater service.

The conditions of this vow are twofold: (1) I, myself, when the
matter appears properly, clearly and without doubt, will judge a thing
to be for the greater glory of God; (2) If there appear some doubt, I
shall consult the Superior or Spiritual Father.

As to the declaration of this vow, note the following: (1) I vow that
whatever is of precept, so that it would be a mortal sin according to
the precept, may be also a sacrilege, by force of the vow; however,
should it be a venial sin according to precept, let it remain a venial sin
according to the vow. (2) In a matter that is only of counsel and not
of precept, yet very important, and which might work exceedingly to
the glory of God, I shall be held to accomplish this matter under the
penalty of mortal sin; but in a matter not too important, I shall not be
held, except under venial sin. (3) So that I may be held under venial
sin by force of my vow in a matter not notably important, it must be
clearly and certainly evident to me, and with no doubt, that that matter may be to the greater glory of God, whether I myself judge it to be
so from the divine law, from the "election" in the Spiritual Exercises,
from the dictates of reason, from the grace of God, or whether the
Superior or Spiritual Father judge the matter to be such.

More and more, Père Jean seems to have revealed the motions
of his spirit to Père Ragueneau, his Superior. Later, Ragueneau was
to write:

He derived his spirit of confidence in God from prayer, in which he
was often much uplifted. A single word would give him a theme for
whole hours—not to his intellect, of whose inaction he was wont to
complain—but to his heart, which relished the eternal truths of the
Faith, and which remained attached to them with serenity, with love
and with joy. Notwithstanding this facility of converse with God,
he prepared himself for prayer as punctiliously as a novice would do
in his early stages.

At one time I find in his writing that, while he was in prayer,
God detached him from all his senses and united him to Himself;

again, that he was enraptured in God, and fervently embraced Him; at other times, he says that his whole heart was transported to God by bursts of love which were ecstatic. But above all, this love was tender with respct to the sacred person of Jesus Christ, and of Jesus Christ suffering.

Often he felt this love as a fire which, having inflamed itself in his heart, kept increasing from day to day, and consuming in him the impurity of nature, in order to cause the spirit of grace and the adorable spirit of Jesus Christ to rule in him.

In September Père François Bressani, to the utter surprise of de Brébeuf, Ragueneau and all at Sainte Marie, stepped out of the canoe. Nothing had been heard from him or about him since his capture by the Iroquois in April of last year. He recounted how he had been tortured, then ransomed by the Dutch and sent by them to France last autumn. This summer he had again landed at Quebec, and here he now was, once more, in the Huron country. He brought current news that made them all thank God. A peace treaty was being concluded with the Mohawk Iroquois. At a council at Three Rivers, the terms of a truce and a final peace were ratified. John Baptist Atironta, the Huron spokesman, proclaimed: "It is done; we are brothers. The resolution has been taken; now the Iroquois, the Hurons, the Algonquins and the French are cousins. From now on, we are one people."

With fascination, de Brébeuf gazed at the scars on Bressani's neck and face, arms and legs, at the hands from which some fingers had been amputated and others chewed into stubs. He venerated Bressani as he would a martyr and prayed that he, too, might be chosen to suffer likewise, perhaps to a bloody death.

The Hurons flocked to Sainte Marie to see the returned Blackrobe. Deeply impressed, one of them exclaimed: "It must be true that God should be loved and obeyed. A thousand deaths and a thousand tortures more frightful than death could not stop him from coming back to announce the word of God." Another remarked: "If there were not a paradise, could there be found men who would walk through the fires and the flames of the Iroquois in order to draw us from hell and lead us to heaven?" Reasoned another: "I can no longer be tempted. Those fingers which have been cut off are the answer to all my doubts. That man is well convinced of what he comes to teach us. He has suffered horrible cruelties, yet he exposes himself to them a second time." Ragueneau concluded: "His mutilated hands have made him a better preacher than we, and have served more than all our tongues to give a better conception than ever of the truths of our Faith to our Huron Christians."[4]

Two: 1645–1647

Jean de Brébeuf, with a young *donné*, paddled away from Sainte Marie in early November. Having heard that some Christian Hurons, through fear of the Iroquois, had taken refuge with the Nipissings at their village of Tangouaen, he wished to visit and strengthen them. For four days, the two drove their canoe up Lake Huron to the French River and Lake Nipissing, and for two days more they traveled by land to the north. It was an exhausting journey both by water and forest trail. At Tangouaen, de Brébeuf's "consolation much surpassed his hardships", related the chronicler. "He found in the midst of those profound forests and those vast solitudes a whole family of Christians who adored God in those woods, who lived there in innocence, and who received him and his comrade as guests who had been sent from heaven."

De Brébeuf had brought chalice and vestments for Mass, so that the Huron family was overjoyed "when they saw their cabin was become the house of God. All devoutly performed the duties of Christians, received the Sacraments and esteemed as sacred all the moments of so blessed a visit.... Their discourses were of nothing but heaven.... They propose their doubts to Echon, they torment him with love both by day and by night. They importune him piously and, though he was fatigued from a journey of six days, they will hardly allow him two or three hours of repose. 'Echon,' they say to him, 'you have come here for our sake! We are famished! You must satisfy us and feast our souls! Your sayings give us life! God speaks through you, and He tells us in our hearts what issues from your lips.' "

After some days he left them, for he and his Frenchman feared that the ice and snow would impede their journey and that they might perish from hunger and cold. Difficult and hazardous as the journey to the north had been, the travel back to Sainte Marie was far more dangerous and laborious. The country down from Tangouaen was cut by small rivers and lakes, the trail led over steep hills and deep gorges. Lake Nipissing was becoming icebound, the French River and its rapids were treacherous, and the Great Lake was rough and coated with ice. Happily, through God's Providence, as they attested, they finally were safe at Sainte Marie.

During the winter that followed, Père Jean again walked daily the five or six miles to the villages under his care. He garnered some souls through his patience and disposed many more to incline toward the Faith. Ossossané was becoming more Christian and the Believers were extraordinarily zealous and saintly, but the reports from elsewhere that winter were far from encouraging. A kind of dysentery that attacked both the missioners and the Hurons was prevalent. With this new disease arose new clamors against the Blackrobes. At Teanaustayé, the persecution not only of Garnier but of all his Believers was intensified. During a mad feast of Ononharoia, one of the pretending insane was about to crash in his head when a Christian parried the blow. The cross they had erected in the cemetery was profaned, and the chapel, according to rumors, would be burned down. Similar stories came from other villages. The country once again was in an uproar.

New lies, many of them based on the teachings of the Blackrobes, were whispered about and believed. It was learned from a distant nation that souls do not go to hell, but pass from one body to another stronger body and from one country to a far happier country. It was said that a Huron had met a man of prodigious size in the forest. This man, who was god, said that all souls are happy, and that there were no fires and tortures down in the center of the earth. It was related that a woman buried in the Christian cemetery had come back to warn the Hurons against the danger of being baptized and going to the French heaven. After her death, she said, she went to the French heaven and there she was beaten with blows and tortured with fire. She declared that the Blackrobes hated the Hurons so much that they wished them to go to the French heaven in order to torture them in the next life as in this. After she escaped, she went to the place where those who are not baptized gather, and found it was a happy place of feasting and dancing.

In addition to such fabrications, more subtle than those of former years, the pagans sought to break down the resistance of the Believers by more direct action. Leading Christians were said to be sorcerers and it was an open secret that anyone who struck down such sorcerers would be helping to save the country. A Christian girl who had been an important performer in one of the lewdest and most secret cults was warned that, if she did not perform in the dance, she would be killed in such a manner that all would blame her death on the Iroquois. The chiefs and elders incited the women to entice and allure the Christian men to have relations with them.

While the devil was still powerful among the Hurons, de Brébeuf could testify that God was also shedding His grace on them. The Christian men repulsed the pagan women, fearing to lose faith with sin. The Christian girl mocked those who threatened her: "Now, with more truth than ever, I shall think that I am dead to the world and that I must live for God alone." The chief who was in danger because he was reputed to be a sorcerer, flung back the challenge: "If you desire to make me lose either my life or my Faith, massacre me as soon as possible. I shall lower my head to the man who chooses to kill me because I am a Christian. We Christians do not grow pale at death. Our Faith is proof against what you consider most frightful."

Alarms swept through the country again. The Iroquois were on the warpath. A band of them lurking about a village on the lake shore to the south dragged off a great number of women going to work in their fields so quickly that their canoes were out of sight before the Huron men could pursue them. At Teanaustayé, the Hurons kept vigil all night, since Iroquois were known to be in the vicinity. In the early morning, two of the guards in a watchtower high up in the palisades were found scalped and their heads crushed. There was no defense against the Iroquois, whether they came in large bands or in small.

While the Senecas and other western Iroquois brandished the war hatchets, the Mohawk Iroquois were again confirming the peace pacts that summer of 1646. Negotiations had progressed so far that Père Isaac Jogues and Jean Bourdon went down to the Mohawk country in May and concluded all the final negotiations for a firm peace in which Mohawks, French, Hurons and Algonquins pledged their sincerity with presents. None of the other four Iroquois nations joined with the Mohawks; hence, the Hurons still dreaded the onslaughts of the Onondagas, the Oneidas, the Cayugas, and most especially, the neighboring Senecas.

In October, according to information brought to Sainte Marie, Père Jogues and a young *donné*, Jean La Lande, trusting so strongly in the peace pacts, journeyed down to the Mohawk villages in order to establish the first mission among the Iroquois. De Brébeuf and the other missioners rejoiced exceedingly. But up to the Huron country came rumors that the Mohawks had treacherously repudiated their solemn peace treaty and again were lifting the crimson tomahawk against the French, the Hurons and the Algonquins. Later in the winter, de Brébeuf and his brethren learned that Père Isaac Jogues and Jean La Lande were tomahawked upon their arrival at the Mohawk village of Ossernenon. Their sorrow for these martyrs was lesser than their grief over the treachery of the Mohawks. Not one of them had a doubt about the eternal reward being enjoyed by these two intrepid apostles, for their zeal for souls and their love of God had brought them to their deaths. De Brébeuf remembered how Isaac revered René Goupil as a martyr. In turn, he could think of Isaac and La Lande only as martyrs. He envied them for they had been granted the gift that he himself was begging from God.

In January, 1647, a Huron war party brought in prisoners belonging to the Onondaga nation. The Christian Hurons secured the reprieve of the chief, Annenraes, and sent him back to his country as an envoy asking for peace. In July, he returned with an official embassy and announced that he was the tongue of the Onondagas. In a council held at Taenhatentaron, the Hurons concluded their peace with the Onondagas and deputed John Baptist Atironta and four other chiefs to carry word of their decision to the Iroquois. Atironta returned in October, bearing the good news that not only the Onondagas, but also the Cayugas and Oneidas were ready to bury the hatchet with the Hurons. Not so the western nation of Senecas, nor the eastern nation of Mohawks, who were fiercely determined to annihilate the Ouendat people.

While these happy negotiations with the three central Iroquois nations were under way, the Hurons were seeking the help of the Susquehannas, a people of their own blood living far to the south. Charles Ondaaiondiont and four pagan chiefs left in April. They returned in October with the gladdening message: "We have learned that you have enemies. You have only to say to us: 'Lift the tomahawk.' We assure you that your enemies will make peace with you or we will make war on them." Charles reported that the Susquehannas had sent ambassadors to the three Iroquois nations, the Onondagas, Oneidas and Cayugas, urging them to be friends with the Hurons. To the hostile Senecas and Mohawks they had forwarded messages threatening war if they did not join in the peace negotiations with the Hurons.

During the winter, de Brébeuf began again to plod his way through the snows and ice to the villages that were his care. He had gathered his Believers into a firmly bound nucleus and he was not much obstructed by the unbelievers. His greatest consolation, however, was at Sainte Marie. More and more of the Christians made their pilgrimages there to talk to Echon and the other Blackrobes. They were strong in their Faith, vibrant in their denunciation of the sins and superstitions of their past lives, and zealous apostles spreading the Gospel among the pagans. The church of the Hurons, de Brébeuf could think, was firmly established. After all the toils and the pains in the planting, the harvest of souls was being gathered in jubilation.

The scourge of the Iroquois, however, fell heavily on the land. All the hopes of peace with the three central nations were dissipated, for they were once more united with the Senecas and the Mohawks in war against the Ouendats. Near Ossossané, to the west, Iroquois warriors slaughtered some Christian families at a fishing camp. At Teanaustayé, an alarm was shrilled that the Iroquois were gathering in great numbers for an attack on the village. While the women and children quaked with fear, and as many as could escaped, the chiefs and braves manned the stockades. Père Daniel gathered the Christians in his chapel and pronounced the absolution over them. He conferred baptism hurriedly on the catechumens and even on the pagans who screamed that they "feared hell more than death". The scare passed when, some hours later, it was discovered that the alarm was false.

No Huron canoes dared to leave the country for the summer trade, since the Mohawks were known to be hidden along the lower Ottawa and the St. Lawrence, while the western Iroquois nations were said to be planning new incursions against the Huron country. The missioners were cut off from communicating with the French except by a far northern route along mountain trails to the headwaters of the Metaberoutin River that flowed down to Three Rivers.

They could expect no French supplies, and no new laborers, so badly needed now with the increase of converts.

Sainte Marie, being in the north, was not subjected to the Iroquois threats like the villages to the south and east. Nevertheless, Ragueneau urged the brothers, *donnés* and workmen to hurry the construction of the remaining bastions and walls of the Fort. Before long, it might be that Sainte Marie would become the last refuge of the Hurons. As it was, Sainte Marie, through its plenteous harvests in its well-cultivated farm, was helping to save the Hurons from starvation. Ragueneau wrote: "During the past year, we have given shelter to more than three thousand people. Within a fortnight, we have had with us as many as six or seven hundred Christians. As a rule, we gave three meals a day to each one. An even larger number came unendingly to pass the day with us."

Three: 1647–1648

In the autumn conference of 1647, the missioners considered the feasibility of extending their labors to the nations beyond the Hurons. They had begun the conversion of the Petuns, they were having success with the northern Algonquins, and they hoped to return to the Neutrals. Now they were exploring the possibilities of reaching nations far to the west and south, of going down among the Huron-speaking Susquehannas, of whom Charles had told them, of sending missioners to the Nation of the Eries, who were of the Huron race and dwelt beyond the Lake of Erie, of penetrating to the north, where Lake Huron and Lake Superior meet, and evangelizing nations of that region. Not merely were they visioning this mission expansion, but were waiting for the day they could begin it.

They somewhat revised, in these conferences, their conclusions about Huron customs and superstitions. Ragueneau recorded: "I am not afraid to admit that we have been too severe in these matters and that God has strengthened the courage of our Christians beyond that of ordinary virtue. They have deprived themselves not only of harmless amusements, because we injected scruples in their minds, but also of the greatest pleasures in their lives. We did not permit them to enjoy these since there appeared to be something irreligious that made us fear they were sinful. It is easy to call that irreligious which is only stupid, to see diabolical intervention in something that is merely human."

They considered the state of Christianity among the Hurons. Though, as yet, the majority were pagans, the Christians were increasing rapidly. Within the past year thirteen hundred men, women and children, healthy or sick, had been baptized. All of these were well instructed and rigorously tested. Many of the Christians were chiefs and elders who could use their influence against the pagan feasts and orgies, and also could beat down the malicious persecutions. Ragueneau wrote confidently that the Huron church "was filled with the spirit of God, that its Faith was as strong and its simplicity as holy, in the majority of those who belonged to it, as if they had been born in a society totally composed of faithful Believers".

In the assignments for the winter of 1647, Ragueneau, Le Mercier and Chastellain would remain at Sainte Marie, as would Chabanel who evangelized the Algonquins. Jean de Brébeuf would make his headquarters at Sainte Marie, where he would meet the visiting Christians, but would also travel the rounds of the villages of the area. Chaumonot was in charge of La Conception at Ossossané, Daniel held the care of the frontier villages of Cahiagué to the east, and Teanaustayé to the south, and Garnier, with Garreau, would spend the winter in the Mission of the Apostles among the Petuns.

Danger lurked everywhere that winter, for the missioners and the Hurons alike. The Senecas in large and small parties were along the trails, in the forests and on the lakes. Though the Huron warriors bravely went out to battle them, more went down in defeat than came back victorious. The eastern frontier village of Cahiagué belonging to the Rock nation had to be abandoned in January, 1648, and its people lodged in other villages till they could again build their own cabins and a stronger stockade. Some Christians belonging to a hunting party of men and women from Taenhaten-taron were brutally butchered by Senecas, and some few days afterwards another party from the same village was attacked by more than a hundred Mohawks.

The terror of the Iroquois brought dissension among the Hurons. The infidel chiefs blamed the Iroquois war on the Blackrobes. Once again, clamoring for their death or expulsion, they enumerated the

woes that had ruined their once strong nation since the Blackrobes
first came: disease, famine and war. Fifteen years ago, they said,
their wise men had predicted that this desolation would come. It
would have been well, if the advice of those chiefs had been followed and the heads of the Blackrobes had been smashed. Though
the Christian chiefs ranged themselves against the pagans, they
could not restrain them.

Jacques Douart, a twenty-two-year-old *donné*, was struck down
near Sainte Marie on the evening of April 28. The Christian chiefs
gathered hurriedly and assured Ragueneau and de Brébeuf: "Our
brothers, this murder clearly shows there is a conspiracy against you.
We are here, ready to die in the defence of our Fathers." The Christians, learning that six pagan chiefs were resolved to wipe out the
French, demanded that the whole nation meet in council and offer
reparation for the murder of Douart. The pagan chiefs expressed no
concern over the murder; rather, they declared they would not be
unhappy if all the French were killed. They expressed the opinion,
furthermore, that it would be well if all the Huron Believers were
expelled from the land, for they even as much as the Blackrobes
brought ruin and death. The Christian orators turned the charge
against the pagans, and accused them of being spies in the pay of
the Iroquois. After three nights of acrimonious debate, the majority voted that the French must be appeased and reparations must be
given for the murder.

They summoned Aondecheté and Echon. The great chief addressed
Ragueneau: "My brother, I speak in the name of all eight Ouendat
nations here assembled. We are now but a handful of people; you
alone support this country. We are here to weep for your loss and
ours. This country is now but a dried skeleton, without flesh, without veins, without sinews, without arteries. We are like dry bones
tied together with threads. That wretched murderer thought he was
aiming at the head of a young Frenchman. But he struck his own
country and inflicted on it a deathly wound. My brother, have pity
on this country."

Coached by a Christian, Ragueneau handed the great chief a bun-
dle of fifty sticks, meaning the number of presents demanded. On
May 10, four chiefs, two Christian and two pagan, accompanied by
hundreds of Hurons crowded into the enclosure of Sainte Marie.

With solemn ceremony they hung up the presents in reparation for the killing of Douart, and attached to each one a metaphorical significance. Ragueneau responded by gifts and appropriate words. Through these interchanges, and through the debates and voting that preceded them, the Christian chiefs gained a clear ascendancy over Ouendat affairs, and the Catholic Faith was officially recognized as the religion of the Huron people.

As consultor of the Huron Mission, Père Jean was under the duty of sending his annual letter to Rome. He addressed it to Reverendissimum Patrem Vicentium Caraffa, who had succeeded Mutius Vitelleschi as General, and dated it, "From the House of Sainte Marie, among the Hurons in New France, June 2, 1648." Speaking of the French, he stated: "In one aspect, the condition of our affairs appears to be most excellent, because at home the utmost peace, union and tranquillity flourish among Ours and those of our household, and all apply themselves most diligently to piety, virtue and perfection." Later, he remarked: "Though nothing whatever was brought to us from France in the past year, nevertheless up to this time, we have abundance and superabundance." This material prosperity, he added, tended to strengthen the condition of spiritual affairs since they could give more charity to the natives.

In regard to the Hurons, he averred: "Christianity makes very satisfactory progress, the Christians increasing more and more not only in number but also in virtue. Moreover, so many opportunities for promulgating the Gospel have opened up far and wide that the Faith would make great progress in a short time if the extreme dearth of laborers did not hinder our desires, efforts and opportunities. For this reason, we urgently request that Père Provincial send many laborers to cultivate this vineyard which, as never before, seems even now to be growing white for the harvest."

Two obstacles impeded their progress and threatened to ruin their work. The first, he described

as common to us and all the Hurons, namely, the enemy whom we call by the name of Iroquois. On the one hand, they close the roads and obstruct trade; on the other, they devastate this region by frequent massacres and, briefly, they fill every place with fear. The other hindrance is the hatred against us of certain infidel Hurons, which grew to such a point that a few days ago they killed one of our domestics.

They were ready to offer the same treatment to us, if opportunity had occurred. However, God has turned these latter difficulties into good, and abundant satisfaction has been made by all Hurons for the homicide. The Faith, far from receiving any detriment from this, has rather benefited thereby, so true it is that all things work together for the good of those who love God. We trust that it will be the same for all remaining obstacles. For, if God be for us, who is against us?

"One thing there is which gives me special anxiety," he continued. "In truth he who now governs, R. P. Paul Ragueneau, is most excellent. He has not his counterpart here, and I know not whether he will have one in the future. He has governed most prudently, most gently and most vigorously. Such is the condition of affairs and circumstances that I regard him as the one and only man who can govern it now with merit. If necessity should compel the choice of another Superior, it seems to me that he should be selected from those who are here, and not from others who have no experience whatever in these regions."

Despite the fact that the Iroquois had been creating terror by their raids all winter, the Hurons planned to go down to Three Rivers for the trade. Last summer they remained home to defend their country, but this summer, it may be, they judged that the fractured peace negotiations with the Iroquois were being mended, or that enough warriors remained to repel the invaders. They needed French goods, especially war implements. Accordingly, about 250 Hurons from many parts of the land got under way in more than fifty canoes about the middle of June. With them went some French domestics and Père Bressani.

Only by necessity had Sainte Marie been built up into a fort. Yet it remained what it had been intended to be, a house of peace and religious residence where the Jesuits with their *donnés* and domestics could live as devoutly and as rigorously as in old France. Ragueneau wrote of it: "I may truly say that this is a house of God and gate of Heaven. That is the feeling of all who live in it, who find in it a paradise on earth, a house in which dwells peace, and the joy of the Holy Spirit, charity and zeal for the salvation of souls."

During June, Père Daniel came up from Teanaustayé for his annual Spiritual Exercises at Sainte Marie. He and de Brébeuf renewed their memories, for they were the two oldest of all the missioners and had mastered the language and won the affection of the natives better than all the others. Daniel spent the eight days of the Spiritual Exercises in silence and prayer, purged his soul of all that had offended God, and strengthened himself, for the year to come, against temptations and persecutions. On July 2, despite the urging of all to remain for a few days of rest at Sainte Marie, he struck out along the trail for his Mission of St. Joseph at Teanaustayé.

Four: 1648

A frenzied runner carried the ghastly news to Sainte Marie on Saturday night, July 4. Teanaustayé was in flames! Antwen was murdered! Later that night, others brought details of the massacre, how more than six hundred Iroquois crept on the village at dawn, how they beat down the defenders and slaughtered the people, how they set fire to the cabins, how another band destroyed the nearby hamlet of Ekhiondatsaan, how the Iroquois had escaped before any war band of Hurons could gather to pursue them.

Père Jean slipped silently into the blackness of the chapel. Two mornings ago, when he was calling his farewells, he had an intimation that Antoine Daniel was leaving Sainte Marie for the last time. His first comrade was the first to die among the Hurons. For fourteen years, they had labored and suffered and prayed together. Though Antoine was fiery and courageous, though his zeal knew no bounds, he was meek and humble and generous. He had an excuse for everyone except himself; though gentle with the French and the Hurons, he was rigid in his own regard; he never complained, no matter how arduous and laborious were the duties assigned him; he was so eager to obey that he obeyed spontaneously; he was loved and revered by all as a saint. He was killed, as he had wished and as everybody expected, for he had begged always to be assigned to the most hostile Huron village and along the frontiers most exposed to the Iroquois. In the still chapel, Jean de Brébeuf prayed to Antoine rather than for him, and begged God to grant him the same token of love.

During the next few days, Echon talked to some who had fled at the first alarm, some who had fought till the end, some who were captured but later escaped. He traveled the trail he had known so well, over the ridges and valleys to the Teanaustayé that had been so obdurate. He remembered the broad plateau of many acres, the precipitous gorges that fell down into the valley, the triple palisade of poles, bristling with interwining branches, the hundreds of long-houses crowded within the stockade. There came back to his mind the braves threatening to crash his skull, the women screaming in fury at his approach, the council orators dooming him, the feasts and orgies that made horrid the night. Truly the devil had seemed to rule in Teanaustayé before its people began to turn to Christ.

He emerged from the forest to a scene of silent desolation. The palisades were stumps of charred poles, the cabins heaps of gray ashes and tortured posts. Bodies of men, women and children sprawled distorted in the open spaces, skulls smashed, blood-caked, scorched black by the flames. De Brébeuf picked his way to the missioners' longhouse and chapel. Not even a charred ember of it remained. It was a long blanket of filmy ashes. He searched among the soft ashes, hoping that he might find some part of Père Antoine's body, or some relic that he might revere. He found nothing, not even what might be Antoine's ashes.

From the survivors and the interpretation of experienced chiefs, de Brébeuf pieced together the story. Père Daniel reached Teanaustayé on the evening of July 2, and spent the following day ministering to his Christians. The village was comparatively deserted, for many of the men had gone down to Three Rivers for the trade and many of the braves were in war parties along the southern borders. Not more than fifteen hundred people were at home, most of them women and children. Rumors, as always, warned that the Iroquois were in the country, but the scouts, stationed at strategic points, had discovered no traces of the enemy. Nevertheless, the Iroquois, iden-tified as Senecas, were hiding themselves some fifteen miles off in the hills across the valley. While Teanaustayé slumbered peacefully that Friday night, the Senecas raced rapidly and silently through the trees of the valley and, before dawn, they lay concealed about Teanaustayé.

Very early on Saturday morning, Père Daniel celebrated Mass for his Christians. He laid aside his red chasuble and, before chanting the prayers, spoke a few words to his faithful Christians about the joys of paradise and the happiness of those who die in the state of grace. "The Iroquois! The Hotinonsionni!" He followed his people out of the chapel. Shrill above the shrieks of terror were the blood-curdling war whoops of the Iroquois. Hundreds of women and children fled toward the gates that led into the ravine at the back of the village. The chiefs and braves, seizing tomahawks, javelins, bows and arrows, hurled themselves into the conflict at the gates, or clambered up to the scaffoldings of the palisades. Tremolo war yells of the Hurons answered the shrill battle cry of the Iroquois.

Daniel, still clothed in white alb and red stole, hurried to the gate where the battle raged. With arm upraised he shouted the words of absolution toward his Believers, and paused over those who knelt for baptism, while musket balls whizzed through the palisades and arrows showered down from above. He ran through the cabins, where some were sick and others aged, ministering to them the Sacraments. He was caught up in a frantic mob trying to escape through the holes in the stockade. He dashed back to the chapel, while still there was time. Many of his Believers crowded in and about it. With a sweep of his hand, he pronounced general absolution over them and, above the din of the battle screams and the yells of the terror-crazed, urged them all to escape through the openings along the crest of the hill.

"Flee, my children, and bear with you your Faith even till your last breath." They begged him to go with them. "No, no," he called back, "I must await death here, as long as there is here any soul that can be sent to Heaven." They pleaded with him; the Iroquois were breaking through; he must hurry. "No, I shall die here to save you. I do not care any longer for life." As they were turning away from him, he cried out in parting: "We shall see one another again in Heaven." Some remained with him, old men and women who could not follow the young. Tenderly, he encouraged them: "My brothers, my sisters, today we shall be in Paradise. Believe this, and hope that God may love you forever."

From the ferocious yells of victory, he judged that the Iroquois had forced the gates and broken through the stockade. From the shrieks of those shrinking from the deathblow, he knew the enemy was raging through the streets and cabins. Blood-stained, wounded Hurons retreating past him, he urged to crawl through the breaches and scatter down the ravine to save themselves. Darting here and there in the open area about his chapel, absolving and baptizing the terrorized Hurons who were fleeing confusedly past him, Antoine

Daniel heard the horrible Iroquois *wiiiiii* grow louder and louder. He stood at the door of his chapel. He saw a band of Iroquois burst from behind the cabins, their faces and bodies striped with the crimson war paint, their upraised tomahawks dripping with blood, their mouths open as they screeched their ear-splitting war whoops. He watched them as they smashed the heads of those they were overtaking. He must halt them and save the escaping Hurons. From the chapel door, slowly, with crucifix uplifted, he strode against them.

The Iroquois stumbled in their onward rush and drew back before this portent. Who was this bearded being clothed in a white robe and a red sash over his shoulders? Who was this demon that, all alone, came toward them, without fear, as if threatening them with the thing in his raised hand, shouting at them words they could not understand. They slunk back in awe, muttering to one another in whispers, their eyes fixed on this strange apparition. Was he a devil that would strike them dead where they stood? He showed no fear of them, no, not any.

"The Blackrobe!" one of them cried out. "The Blackrobe sorcerer!" One lodged a musket ball in his heart, while others let fly their arrows in his face and neck. They stood still, awed even yet by this frightening spectacle. They regretted that they had killed him this way; it would have been better to take him prisoner and torture him in their village. It was too late. They crashed in his temples, tore off his robes and clothes, sliced his scalp lock, and slivered off pieces of his flesh to eat, bloody as it was, so that they might inherit his courage.

Exultantly, they chanted and danced about his naked body, shrieking like demons, then pushed into the chapel slaughtering some who had taken refuge there. They were in a hurry to get on with the massacre. About the posts of the chapel they built fires, and to the resinous bark they applied torches. In a few minutes, the fire was crawling up the walls and the roof, the smoke was whirling up in sheets. Taking him by the wrists and the ankles, they heaved the bleeding body of Antoine Daniel into his chapel, now become his pyre.

Some Christians, who had remained with Antwen, found hiding places from which they watched him die and the chapel burst into flame. The enemy discovered them, smashed the heads of the old and drove the sturdier toward the gate. Herds of other Huron prisoners were jostled through the alleys and out to the trampled, body-littered space beyond the stockade. Still feverish with the blood lust, the savage conquerors pushed through the shivering drove of Hurons, striking down those who looked weak or sick. Other Iroquois, meanwhile, were piling up the bundles of furs and robes, kettles, iron goods, beads and other loot. Still others raced through the cabins and along the stockades, hurling firebrands and lighting fires. Hurriedly, for fear of pursuit, the Iroquois packed the booty on the backs of the prisoners and, badgering them into a long file, drove them at a quick trot along the trail to the south.

Standing amidst the scorched corpses and dry ashes of Teanaustayé, Jean de Brébeuf mourned and prayed for those who were dead and for those who were carried off as prisoners. Four or five hundred had been massacred, nearly seven hundred, mostly women and children, were in the savage hands of the Senecas. Many of those who escaped were enabled to do so by the bravery of Antoine Daniel, who halted the Iroquois.

Père Jean, looking down upon the plot where Antoine's ashes mingled with those of his church, could not, except with difficulty, mourn or pray for his friend. Through his mind ran the thought that the Huron land and people now had a powerful intercessor before the Throne of God. Though Antoine was the first of the comrades to be martyred in the Huron Mission, three others from the Iroquois Mission welcomed him in heaven, Goupil and La Lande and Père Isaac. In the quietude of ruined Teanaustayé, Père Jean repeated his vow of martyrdom and begged God that he, like Antoine Daniel, be found worthy.[5]

CHAPTER XII

The Journey to Heaven or Quebec

One: 1648–1649

EIGHTEEN PRIESTS WERE NOW STATIONED at Sainte Marie. Jean de Brébeuf was proud of them all, and thanked God for sending such mighty apostles to evangelize these western natives. He felt old among his comrades, for he had passed his fifty-fifth birthday. His beard and hair were grizzly gray, and his legs could no longer carry him on the long journeys he would like to undertake. He reflected, however, that God had been especially good to him through the twenty-two years since first he came to the Hurons. He had never once been seriously ill, and had suffered little from aches and pains. The only time he was really incapacitated was when he fractured his collarbone seven years ago. As a result of that, he thought with some irritation, he was forced to live at Sillery and Three Rivers, where he grew corpulent. Despite all of his efforts, he could not reduce his weight. It was an affliction to him, but not enough to keep him from laboring as in the years past, and with as much vitality as the younger missioners.

In the autumn, before scattering for their various villages, the priests gathered for their usual conferences. They reviewed the events of the past year, the gains for God they had achieved, the opportunities they had failed to seize, and consulted as to their plans and strategies for the ensuing winter. While they were thus seated together, Père Chaumonot startled them by a gasp. His eyes shone wide in wonderment, as he exclaimed: "Père Antoine." They all stared at the wall on which Chaumonot's eyes fastened, but they could not see Antoine Daniel. It was the second time, Chaumonot revealed, that their martyred friend had appeared and spoken to him. "We felt his presence," wrote Ragueneau, "strengthening us with his courage, filling us with his light and the spirit of God that invested him."

The violent death of Daniel and the ever-recurrent and increasing danger from the Iroquois undoubtedly affected the spiritual life of Jean de Brébeuf and the other missioners. They felt certain that many of them, or all of them, would fall victim to these enemies. Some of the thoughts, prayers and divine illuminations that passed in the soul of Père Jean were inscribed by him in the book of his spiritual memoirs, and were later disclosed by Père Ragueneau, who wrote: "Our Lord often appeared to him, sometimes in a state of glory, but usually bearing His Cross or being, indeed, attached to it. These visions implanted in his heart such ardent desires to suffer much for His name that—although he had greatly suffered difficulties, fatigues, persecutions, griefs on a thousand occasions—all his sufferings were naught to him. He complained of his misfortune, believing that he had never suffered anything and that God did not find him worthy of having him bear the least share of His Cross."

Ragueneau revealed further that "Our Lady also appeared to him often. She usually left in his soul desires for suffering, but with feelings so serene and with such submission to the will of God that, afterwards, his spirit remained for the space of several days in deep peace and in a lofty realization of the greatness of God." He quoted de Brébeuf as writing: "I have been afraid lest I be of the number of the reprobate, seeing that God has hitherto treated me with such mildness. But I shall hope that God will choose to show me mercy when His goodness shall furnish me opportunities of suffering something for His love." To which Ragueneau added: "And yet, we may say that his life was but one continuation of crosses and sufferings." On another page, Ragueneau found the little item: "Toward evening, being in prayer before the Most Blessed Sacrament, I saw in spirit spots of blood upon my clothes and upon the blood of all our priests, without any exception. This left me with feelings of admiration."

In addition to the charge of St. Louis, Ste. Anne, and the other four small villages near Sainte Marie, for the coming year de Brébeuf was given the care of the Mission of St. Ignace. He welcomed this assignment, because the former obdurate and fanatically superstitious villagers of Taenhatentaron had taken on Christ and were become docile and friendly. During the coming winter, he hoped to add more converts to the already strong body of the Believers. Another reason for his interest was that the people of Taenhatentaron were building a new village. For more than a year, he had been consulting with the chiefs and elders about the situation and the fortification of a veritable Huron citadel. Even before Teanaustayé was destroyed, the chiefs had decided to move their village more to the center of the land in order to gain greater protection against the Iroquois raids.[1]

They chose a place about six miles from Sainte Marie. In their opinion, as well as in that of Echon, the site was unassailable by the nature of its formation. It was a tongue of level land, some six acres in extent, stretching out from the ridge of hills and shaped like a blunted arrowhead. The entry to this field was a strip of ground about one hundred yards wide. On both sides of the spur of land were ravines, gradually descending twenty to forty feet and meeting at a depth of fifty feet at the far end where a little stream curved by. The sides of these ravines were so precipitous and tangled with vines, that no Iroquois enemy could possibly scale these walls of the hill and reach the top level space without being discovered and massacred. The only place where an assault could be launched was the hundred-yard band that connected the village site with the ridge.

The chiefs and elders of St. Ignace planned fortifications of this impregnable site that would be invincible. They listened to Echon and adopted many of his suggestions about extending bastions and towers beyond the lines of the stockade, about zigzagging the walls of the triple palisades, about building a massive and complicated gateway, bastioned and double-storied, on the only vulnerable approach of level ground.

Since they desired to have a council cabin in which all the federated Ouendat nations might assemble, and since Echon felt the need of a chapel in which all the growing numbers of the faithful might gather, the chiefs and Echon plotted out a house such as never before had been built in Huronia. It was sixty feet wide, three times the width of any Huron longhouse. Three rows of sturdy posts ran the length of it and on these were fastened the beams that held up the flattened roof. All the Hurons were in admiration and wonderment of this massive council house, and all agreed that the new village was so invulnerable that never could the Iroquois capture and destroy it.

De Brébeuf's interest in the building of the new village bound the chiefs and people more closely to him. No longer was he subjected to their wild rages and their threats of splitting his skull, no longer was he feared as an evil sorcerer. Rather, he was listened to by the wisest as well as the most hostile. This same upsurge of the Faith was evident in the other villages throughout the country. Ossossané had become so dominantly Christian that the nation of the Bear was now generally called the nation of the Believers. Writing of this winter, Bressani declared: "The Faith had already taken possession of almost all the country. Public profession was made of it everywhere. The chiefs themselves were its protectors and its sons. The superstitious rites which were formerly a daily occurrence, began to lose credit. Persecution against us had already ceased. Curses against the Faith had been turned into blessings. I could almost say that the people were ripe for heaven."

About January, Père Gabriel Lalemant was appointed to help Père Jean in the care of his villages. Gabriel had reached Huronia only the preceding September. He was the nephew of Charles, who had come to Quebec as a pioneer Jesuit missioner in 1625, and also of Jérôme, the former Huron Superior. Unlike his rugged uncles, he was a small man who appeared to be almost emaciated, and at thirty-eight was rather old to undertake the fatiguing labors of the life of a missioner. During his four months at Ossossané under the tutelage of Chaumonot, he had made incredible progress in the Huron language and had manifested the qualities that proved he would become a great apostle, if only he were not so frail. But he protested that he was not sick, nor sickly, and that he could perform the work of those who looked stronger than he.

In their winter trappings, de Brébeuf and Lalemant were an amusing contrast. The former was gigantically tall, the latter less than medium height; the one was heavy and rotund, the other skinny and flat. They were one, however, in spirit and zeal. De Brébeuf was happy with such an apt helper; Lalemant was overjoyed in the intimacy with the great apostle about whom he had read and heard so much. Lalemant confided to Jean that his daily prayer since he became a Jesuit in 1630 was to come to New France and, if possible, work among the Hurons. He had begged the grace of shedding his blood for Christ, as Christ shed His for mankind. He had received one of the favors; he hoped for the other. To Lalemant, de Brébeuf confessed that he, himself, had offered himself to God, soul and body, and that he had begged God to treat him as He had treated Antoine Daniel.

In their routine schedule, they started off on Monday to make the rounds of their half-dozen villages and, by Saturday, were back at Sainte Marie to instruct and minister to their own villagers and the many others who came for Sunday Mass. During January and February, Père Jean thanked God for what seemed to be an extraordinary increase in the fervor of his neophytes and in the number that asked to be instructed. These months, he told Lalemant, had always been the most diabolic in the superstitious feasts and debauches. In these tours, de Brébeuf kept urging the villagers of St. Ignace to hurry the completion of their new stockades and to move from Taenhatentaron to the new longhouses they were building. But he had to battle against their lethargy and had to listen to their promises that, come the spring, they would surely finish their village.

In his visit to the new St. Ignace, during the second week of March, he found it largely deserted. Many of the twenty and more cabins were unoccupied. A great number of the chiefs and braves were off hunting the Iroquois who were reported along the southern and eastern frontiers, and many were away trading with the neighboring nations. All told, there were only four or five hundred people, mostly women, children and the decrepit, in St. Ignace. De Brébeuf and Lalemant trudged back along the snow-covered ridges the three miles to St. Louis. Its rickety palisades and moss-covered cabins made it look small and weak in comparison to the new St. Ignace.

They spent a day or two at St. Louis, instructing and fortifying the Believers, debating with and trying to persuade the stubborn pagans to accept the new doctrines. On Friday, they walked the three easy miles down the hills to be at Sainte Marie for Saturday and Sunday. Stephen Annaotaha, one of the renowned war chiefs from St. Louis, as well as one of the foremost Believers, came to Sainte Marie for the Sunday Mass. He asked Echon to listen to the recital of all the sins of his past life and to forgive them in the sight of God, alleging that he had a presentiment of some danger threatening him. When Echon pronounced the absolution over him, he expressed great joy since now, no matter what happened, he was sure of going to heaven.

On Monday morning, March 15, Jean de Brébeuf and Gabriel Lalemant strode out from Sainte Marie for their usual calls at their missions. They spent the day at St. Louis, finding much to occupy them among the four or five hundred villagers. That night they lodged in their own little cabin and Tuesday morning said their Masses a little after dawn. They intended to proceed to St. Ignace later in the day. About six in the morning, while they were finishing their prayers, they were startled by a piercing shriek, followed by shrill screams. They rushed out of the cabin and pushed among the villagers to the gate. Three men, naked and breathless, danced hysterically while they wailed their warning: "The Iroquois!" "They are in the new village!" "We alone escaped!" "The Hotinonsionni are at your door!"

Aghast, in trembling terror, the villagers screamed the cry: "The Enemy! The Iroquois!" De Brébeuf gasped in horror; the Iroquois were slaughtering his people at St. Ignace; they were racing through the trees to St. Louis and would massacre his children. More quietly, he thought that this might be his time. He was deafened by the frenzied shouts of the men and the despairing howls of the women and children. Clear above the clamor, he heard the stentorian commands of Stephen Annaotaha, to guard the gate and to man the scaffolding of the palisades. He looked down at the mad rush of his people circling about in bewildered turmoil.

De Brébeuf and Lalemant, with an interior peace, rushed through the alleyways and the longhouses of St. Louis. They quieted the quivering children who quaked and squalled where they stood, tried to calm the wild-eyed women as they bustled about screeching, and encouraged the old men and women who were hobbling about in frantic impotence. Over the Believers they made the sign of absolution, and on the heads of others they poured the waters of baptism. They helped the squaws pack their corn and clothes, urging them all to flee the village, save themselves in the depths of the forests, and pray to God.

The village emptied quickly. De Brébeuf and Lalemant, hastening the people outside the gates, watched the knots stumbling hysterically down the hillside and the trotting lines disappear in the curve of the trails. Jean looked downward on Gabriel and suggested that he hurry back to Sainte Marie. There was grave danger, he said, and there was no need for both of them to expose themselves. He himself would remain with the braves who were defending the village, but it would be better for Gabriel to follow after and help those who were escaping. Lalemant looked up pleadingly at de Brébeuf. His eyes said he would be obedient, but he begged to be allowed to remain. De Brébeuf, remembering Lalemant's prayer, visioned the will of God being effected.

Together, they turned back into the village, which, by now, was terrifyingly still. Less than a hundred bare-skinned chiefs and braves, streaked with their crimson war paint, waited tensely about the gates and up on the scaffolding of the stockade, listening for the signal from their scouts that the Iroquois were sighted. Stephen Annaotaha, racing about directing the defense, rushed to Echon and Atironta. "My brothers, save yourselves," he called to them. "Go now, while there is time." Echon told him that their place was here where there was danger, to care for those who were fighting.

They searched through the cabins for any poor people who could not escape. At the warning tremolo of the returning scouts, they dashed to where their warriors were concentrated. The men atop the stockade shrieked their defiance while the Iroquois streamed out of the forests, shrilling their blood-curdling *wiiiiii*. The attack burst against the main gateway and the palisades on both sides of it. Showers of arrows whistled back and forth, the Iroquois muskets cracked, the yells and screams, within and without the walls, ascended in fury. De Brébeuf here, Lalemant there, coursed along the stockade wherever the fighting was most furious. While arrows fell down on them from the sky, they shouted up their encouragement to the Hurons. When one tumbled down wounded, they bent over him to absolve or baptize him. They raised their voices in prayer and exhorted the Believers to beg God's help.

Gradually, there came a lull in the fighting as the Iroquois withdrew from the stockade and took cover in the woods. While the Hurons waited for the second assault, one of the infidel Hurons urged Annaotaha and his men to slip out the rear gates to save themselves by flight through the ravine. Stephen flared at him in anger: "What do you mean? Do you ask us to save our lives and abandon the Blackrobes? They were not afraid to sacrifice their lives for us. Their love for us will cause their death. We might escape, but there is no time left for them to flee across the snow. Let us die with them. Let us go in company with them to heaven."

The Iroquois, with menacing whoops, burst out anew from the forest and threw themselves against the gate and the walls. The defenders ranged themselves behind the posts and on the hanging runway, picking off the assailants with arrows and stones. Screams of warning and shouts of triumph rose in the rear of the village. The Iroquois had crept through the ravine, had hacked holes in the bark and intertwining branches at the base of the palisades, had scrambled through the breaches in so many places and in such numbers that they soon surrounded Annaotaha and his braves. He and his sixty survivors lowered their weapons in the gesture of surrender. With them, stood Atironta and Echon.

The Iroquois seized and shackled the prisoners, dragged and pushed them out of the gates, and herded them in the trampled spaces beyond the village. Other Iroquois bounded through the cabins, splitting the heads of all they found, gathering the furs and other booty, and hurling torches against and into the bark cabins. Hurriedly they reassembled about the prisoners, dancing and catapulting themselves in frenzy, yelling and shrieking like maniacs, swinging their tomahawks in menacing gestures. They beat the two Blackrobes and the Hurons into a long file, ordered them to sing, and started them off at a romping trot along the trail. Jean de Brébeuf looked back at the leaping, red flames and the dark smoke billowing up from St. Louis, then forward along the pathway that he had so often traveled to St. Ignace.

Two: 1649

When they reached the clearance before St. Ignace, the Iroquois stripped de Brébeuf and Lalemant as naked as themselves. Howling and shrieking like demons, brandishing clubs and sticks, they fought for a place in the two parallel columns that were stretching from the woods to the gate. Meanwhile, Echon shouting above the clamor to the Hurons huddled about him, exhorted them to have courage and place their trust in God. The Christians bellowed back to him their words of faith and loyalty, and joined their voices in the prayers which he intoned. The wriggling files of the gauntlet were formed. One by one, the Hurons, de Brébeuf, Lalemant, each in turn, was shoved into the mouth of the two lines of screeching Iroquois. As each victim bolted or struggled through, he was beaten and slugged about the body and legs until, stunned and breathless, he hurled himself out at the far end. The Iroquois laughed raucously and boasted how they had caressed their prisoners.

Aching from head to foot, de Brébeuf lay huddled among the prisoners. He thanked God for the favor that was being done him, for the answer to his prayers, but felt his heart dead with grief when he thought of his Christian Hurons and the ruin that would follow. All along the three-mile race from St. Louis, he prayed God to save the others. St. Ignace captured, St. Louis burned, other towns in jeopardy, the Huron people was doomed. He had foreseen this, but now he was witnessing the full vehemence of the catastrophe. Sainte Marie would be attacked and perhaps all in it would be slaughtered. The Mission of the Hurons would be completely blotted out. The triumph of the fiendish, impious Iroquois agonized his soul more than their cruelty could afflict his body.

As soon as he could find opportunity, he consulted with Stephen Annaotaha. They judged that there must be upwards of a thousand Iroquois crowding about St. Ignace. From what they could distinguish in the Iroquois talk and boasts, they concluded that last night several war parties had secretly converged from the east and south. Their discoverers sneaking about found the gates wide open and the palisades unguarded. They crept into the village and about the cabins before the sleeping people awakened. Having slain some, to whet their lust for blood, and imprisoned others, about six hundred of them raced over the hills to deliver the surprise attack on St. Louis. Among the triumphant Iroquois, Annaotaha pointed out to Echon some war-masked warriors who were Hurons by birth but had deserted their people and been adopted by the Senecas. De Brébeuf recognized some of them as those who had most pitilessly persecuted him and the other missioners.

Père Jean and Père Gabriel united themselves in prayer, as they haunched among their Hurons. They gazed at each other in certainty that they would soon be parted, first by tortures, then by death. There was no need for one to console the other, nor to arouse courage in the other, nor to lament, since each of them had revealed to the other his hopes of dying violently in the service of God. De Brébeuf, however, advised Lalemant that he might be spared, at least in the beginning, or might be carried down to the Iroquois country as a prisoner; in such case, he instructed Lalemant to make efforts to escape, as had Isaac Jogues and François Bressani. They listened to each other in confession and raised the hand over each other in absolution.

They shivered, in their nakedness, from the cold and winds of this bleak March day. About noon, they and the sixty Hurons were driven with blows and taunts into the huge cabin that de Brébeuf had designed and hoped would one day be his Huron church. Through the darkness, he saw, over toward the eastern wall, many fires burning about the half-dozen torture posts. He and his comrades were piled together while hundreds of Iroquois, grotesquely smeared with red paint and caked blood, whirled and gyrated in the serpentine files of the torture dance, and howled their ferocious chants and screaming boasts of how they would caress their victims. Echon and some Hurons, chosen for the first tormentings, were kicked to their feet and commanded also to dance and sing their death chant.

The ravenous rabble circled about the giant, white Echon, who towered above them. They stalked him as they would a moose, as he ran at their commands up and down the cabin, chanting his Huron prayers and hymns. They leaped on him, broke the bones of his hands, tore out with their teeth his fingernails, munched his fingers in their mouth. They dragged him to one of the posts. He stumbled on his knees before it, embraced it with his bleeding hands, and kissed it before they reeled him to his feet, threw back his arms and fastened his wrists to it.

He knew the code, what they expected of him, what he might expect from them. On their part, they must burn him and slash him and otherwise torment him till they made him weep, till they forced him to plead for mercy, till they beat down his courage, till they won their complete victory by smashing him. On his part, he must show no fear of them, must give no sign that he was suffering, must not let slip a sigh or a cry. With strength drawn from God, he resolved to go beyond their savage code. His defiance would not be that of the savages who yelled back hate at their cruel enemies, but that of the priest begging God to convert them from their savagery and to forgive them for their satanic cruelties.

Tied to that post, he was enraptured by God. The Iroquois whirled in circles about him, screeching their threats; but he did not hear them. They piled burning sticks about his feet, ran flaming torches up, down and between his legs, thrust firebrands around his neck and under his armpits; but he did not move, nor flinch, nor utter any cry. Puzzled, the tormentors pushed the torches closer until the skin frizzled, and slashed his flesh till the blood spurted out; but he remained as insensate as a huge white rock. They were astounded that any man could be so still, so silent. Jean de Brébeuf, visioning the God whom he loved, was truly oblivious of the pains of his body and the fury of the torturers.

Coming to consciousness after some moments, he opened his eyes, felt the pain of the burns and the wounds, looked down on the fires and the ferocious faces. He turned his head toward Lalemant and Annaotaha and the other Hurons, toward the other posts where some of the Hurons were being tortured. Shrugging himself up on his toes, he declaimed above the deafening uproar: "My sons, my brothers, let us lift up our eyes to Heaven in our afflictions. Let us remember that God is the witness of our sufferings, that very soon He will be our exceedingly great reward. Let us die in our Faith. Let us hope from Him the fulfillment of His promises to us. I have more pity for you than I have for myself. Bear up with courage under the few remaining torments. The sufferings will end with our lives. The grandeur which follows them will never have an end."

The Huron captives shouted to him their answers of courage and faith. One voice louder than the others reached his ears: "Echon, our spirits will be in Heaven while our bodies are suffering here on earth. Pray to God for us, that He may show us mercy. We will call upon Him, even unto death." While de Brébeuf continued to pray in a commanding voice, to exhort the Hurons being tortured at the nearby posts, to console Père Gabriel and the shackled prisoners, his tormentors stabbed him with javelin heads and sliced him with knives. Unmoved by their tormentings, he thundered at the top of his voice, "*Jésus taiteur!* Jesus, have mercy on us!" His plea rang out like a battle cry and was answered by the Huron Believers, "*Jésus taiteur!*"

Angered to insanity by his defiance, the Iroquois thrust torches against his face and into his mouth. He spat out the burning splinters, shook off the embers, and preached at his tormentors, especially at the renegade Hurons who were now revenging themselves on him. He exhorted them to believe in the God whom they had rejected. They screamed back their hate of him and the Blackrobes, they cursed him and his French for killing their relatives and ruining their nation by his sorceries, they ridiculed his speeches about baptism and heaven and hell. To show their hate, they burned and slashed him the more.

A chief drove away the yelping braves. Echon strengthened himself for the next torment, as he watched them twist a rope of green withes into a collarband and fasten to it six red-hot hatchet heads. They lifted the collarband and the glowing hatchets about his head, and slung them on his shoulders, so that three irons ate into his back if he bent forward, and three melted his chest if he leaned backward, and all six hatchets sizzled his flesh if he stood upright. While he writhed and twisted to swing off from him the burning irons, the Iroquois torturers screamed with delight, shouted their taunts of derision at the mighty Echon, and threw their bodies into the wild contortions of their blood dance. Undaunted, de Brébeuf heaved out his prayer for them, and his petition for himself, "*Jésus taiteur!*" until the cords burned and the luminous hatchets fell at his feet.

The Iroquois were frantic because they could find no weakness in Echon, could draw from him no shriek of agony. A torture chief and his men fastened a wide belt of resinous bark about his thighs and waist. While they bound him, they tormented him with their obscene mockery. Awaiting the flame, he turned toward Lalemant and the Believers exhorting them to keep their Faith, to pray as they suffered, to endure all so as to win the victory. The chief set fire to the bark belt, the copper flames licked up about his body and head, and the tarry black smoke enveloped him. Though a living torch, he gasped and choked out his words that, though this fire is great, it is feeble compared to the fires of hell, though this flame consumes the body for a time, the fires of hell will consume the soul forever.

When the Iroquois gazed at the flames quivering out about his blackened body and shoulders and face, and when they heard him still shouting out what they judged to be words of hate and defiance, their blood boiled with more hellish ferocity. They were being thwarted and defeated by this Echon, the Blackrobe sorcerer, since they could not burn out his courage nor could they devise torments that would break his spirit. The leader of the Huron renegades, who loathed and abominated him more than the Iroquois, offered a more devilish diversion. Over the raging fires, the former Hurons hung iron kettles filled with water.

The Huron-Iroquois spokesman quieted the tumult about Echon, and addressed him in amiable tones that made more horrible the derision and blasphemous mockery. "My brother, Echon," he declared, "you were our good friend in the days gone by. You have often said in the councils that you wished to help and save the Ouendat people. Now we wish to help you, since we have such great pity on you in your afflictions. We shall soothe your burns with water." De Brébeuf, standing shackled to the torture post, answered the spokesman as mildly as he had often answered his enemies in the Huron councils and pleaded with him to remember the One-who-governed-all. "Echon," the former Huron spoke sweetly, "you see plainly that we treat you as a friend. You have often told us that we must be baptized in order that we may have eternal happiness after we die. In turn, we wish to be the cause of your happiness in heaven. Thank us, then, for the good turn we do you. We believe what you have told us, that the more you suffer here, the more God will reward you hereafter."

They carried forward the steaming pots of boiling water and, while emptying them over his head, they shouted: "Echon, we baptize you so that you may be happy in heaven. You know that you cannot be saved by your God without a proper baptism." Shaking off the scalding, blistering water, he exclaimed that he pitied them more than he pitied himself, that he was willing to suffer all that they did to him, if God would accept his pains for their salvation. Loudly, he uttered his prayer for them, that God might have mercy on them, that God might forgive them since they knew not what they did, that God might lead them all to Him through baptism. "*Jésus taiteur!*" he cried out, and heard the re-echoing answer from the Huron Believers, "*Jésus taiteur!*"

They were more than ever enraged at him. He had no fear of them, he did not wince or scream, he treated them like dogs or squaws in pitying them. More than that, he was giving courage to the little Blackrobe Atironta, and to all the Huron prisoners who, by now, were crying out vociferously their defiances and bellowing their prayers. No longer could the Iroquois endure being shamed by his talk. One of them snatched his nose and slashed it off. Despite the blood spurting out, Echon endeavored to talk. Another sliced off his upper lip, then his lower lip, pulled out his tongue and hacked a piece off it. A third plunging a fiery brand against the bleeding flesh, forced it into his mouth. Echon cast his head toward the Hurons, as if to speak to them; he looked at the Iroquois before him; he lifted his seared face to God, forcing up from his throat and chest a hoarse, guttural roar, "*Jésus taiteur!*"

Even the most brutal of them rested for a time, awe-stricken and defeated by this demon whom they could not conquer. The huge body of Echon sagged to the fires about his feet, silent at last, for his jaws were tight-locked. But his eyes were open and, they thought, were still looking at them in pity for them and in defiance. One of them closed his eyes forever by gouging them out with a flaming stick. They had not conquered his spirit, but they had broken and burned his body so that he could no longer fight against them.

They feared that he might die before they had finished with him. They must offer him in sacrifice in the sight of their sun god, Areskoui, and so they dragged his body out of the murky cabin into the clear sunlight of the midafternoon. He lived, though he could no longer speak nor see nor stand. The Iroquois fought about his body, each one seeking to gash out a piece of his flesh to roast and eat, for it was the good meat of a brave man and would give them courage against their enemies.

They threw him up on the torture platform for the last rites in honor of Areskoui. The chief who claimed him as his prisoner, slid his sharp knife under the skin of the skull and yanked free the scalp as his trophy. As a token of victory, another chief hacked off the charred and blistered feet. While the mob howled and danced about the platform, he who claimed the final privilege felt about the ribs of Echon, then with his full strength thrust in his long hunting knife and cleaved a hole into which he pushed his hand. Tugging and cutting, he drew out the hand, with the heart of Echon clutched within his blood-drenched fingers. He licked the blood away, stuck the heart on a spit, roasted it and ate it with gusto.

Others chiefs and braves sprawled up on the scaffolding and cupped the still spurting blood into their hands to drink. Others, less fortunate, smeared their hands and licked the blood. Never had they tortured a Huron or an Algonquin who feared them less, never had they had a victim who aroused in them such raving frenzies. Well it would be for them, after their sport in butchering Echon, to devour him. But there were others waiting to be tortured. A chief raised his tomahawk over the head of Echon, and slashed it down, slitting the jaw in two. Since others had to be killed that afternoon before Areskoui hid, they threw the corpse of Echon on a long fire. As it roasted, the fat oozed out and extinguished the flames.

The sinless soul of Jean de Brébeuf entered its eternal happiness with God about four in the afternoon, on Tuesday, March 16, nine days before his fifty-ninth birthday. He began to endure his final tortures about midday. At the third hour in the afternoon, he reached the climax of his human endurance when he was silenced by his tormentors. In that swoon of his fourth hour, he commended himself to God, breathed his prayer of thanksgiving that he had been judged worthy, and united himself to God before God finally took him to Himself.

Gabriel Lalemant, already beaten and bruised, blistered and burned, in the preludes of the tortures, awaited his turn in the fetid longhouse. During the four hours of this day of doom, agonizingly yet exultantly, he had watched Père Jean throw off the cruelties of his persecutors, had listened to his exhortations, and responded with all his heart to the prayers being offered. When the savages dragged Jean's body out of the cabin, he had risen from his shackles, raised his hand and lifted his voice in the final Sign of the Cross and the words of the ultimate absolution. He listened to the maniacal screams and howls of the Iroquois outside the longhouse. When they lessened, he offered the prayers for the dying and commended the soul of Père Jean to God. Somehow, the spirit of Jean de Brébeuf seemed to pulse in his soul.

The Iroquois were pushing back through the doors and the gloom of the wide, post-lined longhouse. With deafening, guttural shouts, they boiled their corn mush over the flickering fires. While they gorged themselves, they thrust pots to Lalemant and the Hurons, bidding them to eat plenty and to be strong for the sport of the night. Père Gabriel felt strangely calm, even happy. God seemed to be near him, to be within him. Though he knew what awaited him, very soon, he had no fear of the ordeal, for it would pass as it had passed for Jean. If his soul could endure the anguish of his body, he would gain his reward with God. Having strengthened himself, he bethought himself of his people, of brave Stephen and his warriors of St. Louis, of those captured earlier at St. Ignace. He exhorted them to keep the Faith Echon had taught them, and they encouraged him to die as courageously as Echon.

About nightfall, as he could see from the slits in the roof, Lalemant sensed the movement about him, some stirring up the fires, others replanting the torture posts, chiefs shouting out to their men to treat the prisoners well. He was suddenly startled when sneaking, snarling braves pounced on him, pulled him to his feet, commanded him to chant and dance, and hustled him to a post. Like Père Jean he fell on his knees before it, embraced it, kissed it as if it were the cross of Christ. They mauled and pounded him with clubs and sticks, scratched his blisters and flesh with their fingernails, splintered his hands and crunched his fingers in their teeth before they bound him loosely to the pillar. They stood off and taunted Atironta. He was short as a squaw, skinny as a dog, too weak to bring back with them to their cabins. They boasted and threatened they would make him weep, they would draw yells of pain out of him, they would revenge themselves on him for the way Echon had defied them.

Little Atironta, like the giant Echon, faced them bravely, with no tremor of fear. He shouted over to the Huron Believers to have courage, to pray with him, to endure what God had ordered. "*Jésus taiteur!*" he cried out above the shrieks of the Iroquois, and heard the resounding "*Jésus taiteur!*" from the tethered Believers. The chiefs and warriors had expected no such defiance from this scraggly white dwarf. They raged about him viciously, determined to break his spirit, and with his, the spirit of the other Hurons being tortured with him. About his feet and legs they piled the burning sticks to make him dance, while they laughed gleefully as he tried to kick the fire away. Up and down his legs and body and arms they sizzled his skin with their burning torches.

At intervals, the chiefs drove off the braves, for the council had decreed that Atironta should not be killed that night, but must be preserved as a morning sacrifice to Areskoui. But after periods of rest, the paint-streaked, blood-coated executioners stirred him to his feet to test him further. They closed his arms over red-hot axes fastened in his armpits, and tightened his legs on glowing tomahawks. Though he shivered with the agony of it, he locked his jaws so that no screech and no sigh would be uttered. When the paroxysm of pain had passed, he hurled out his voice in prayer to God, and exhortation to his Huron Believers, and begged for mercy on his tormentors. When he opened his lips, they thrust burning coals into his mouth. When he swooned away, they let him rest for a while, watching for the first signs of consciousness so that they could begin again their lingering torments.

They roused him and fed him with gruel so that he might have strength to endure the more. They fastened the belt of bark about his waist, and chortled with glee as he swirled about enveloped by flames and smoke. Freed from the fires, blackened and roasted though he was, he appeared as if he felt nothing of the burning of his face and shoulders, but defiantly uttered his words of petition to God for himself and his comrades. The Iroquois, angered because they could not subdue this Atironta, were aroused to greater passion by his challenge.

The renegade Hurons swarmed about him with their cauldrons of steaming water. Remembering Père Jean, he denounced them in French and in the Huron he had learned, for their blasphemy and their treachery, for their blindness and obduracy, and he begged them to join with the other Huron Believers in adoring the God-of-All. While they poured the scalding water over his head, they protested in mockery that they were baptizing him so that he would be happy in the life after death.

They desisted, at the command of the chiefs, and let him recover, lest he die during the night. They looked down at his wizened little body, now burned almost to a crust, and felt themselves shamed and indignant that they had not been able to twist the spirit out of him and to crumble his courage. By his words and by his endurance, he was a bad omen for them, he was a demon who had no fear of them, he inspired the captive Ouendats with courage. Late in the night, or early in the morning, after a spell of resting, they roused him, out of his weakness or out of his silent union with God. Once more, to all who would listen, he raised his voice in prayer and exhortation. To shut him up, they forced fiery faggots into his open mouth, they pried open his jaws and sliced off his tongue, closing his jaws on burning embers. His eyes, challenging them as had his tongue, they carved out and filled the sockets with glowing coals.

Fearing that he might die before the sun god arose, and being exhausted with the blood fever of the morning battle, the afternoon of sport with Echon, and the wild struggle to beat down Atironta through the night, they tried to untie the leather thongs that bound him to the post. The straps were knotted, so they chopped off his hands, and to staunch the blood pressed white-hot axes to the stumps of his wrists. Letting him lay where his mangled body fell to the ground, the last of the Iroquois wrapped their robes about them and found a place to sleep among their snoring comrades.

The Iroquois were up with the sun, tingling with expectancy for another day of carnage and massacre. The chiefs, having held council together, instructed the warriors of their bands as to the plans for the day. Parties of them shook the earth with their war dances, and shrieked to the heavens their chants and their boasts, before they hurtled out of the stockades. Those who remained to guard the prisoners of St. Louis and St. Ignace had the privilege of finishing Atironta and the Hurons who had also been tortured through the night.

They dragged the bodies out of the cabin and into the morning sunlight. The heart of Atironta still beat, but faintly. That was good, for they would offer him up as a victim that Areskoui could look down upon. He had proved himself as brave as Echon, and to gain such courage for themselves, they carved off slivers of his flesh and supped his blood. They sliced off his scalp before one of them used his heart as a target for a musket ball. They dug out his heart, to eat, before they crashed a tomahawk into his skull below the left ear, with such force that the bone was split asunder and the soft brains welled out. They threw his corpse in the pile of the Huron dead.

Gabriel Lalemant began his martyrdom about six in the evening, two hours after Jean de Brébeuf escaped from the Iroquois and St. Ignace to God. All through the lengthening horror of the night, he had prayed and suffered. After fifteen hours, about nine o'clock on Wednesday morning, March 17, 1649, he was given the final stroke of victory. From that moment, the saintly soul of Gabriel Lalemant, freed from his puny, charred and tattered body, lying among the Huron corpses, lived in the splendor of God with his comrade, Jean de Brébeuf.[2]

Three: 1649

About nine o'clock on Tuesday morning, March 16, someone at Sainte Marie noticed a spiral of smoke rising out of the forest toward the east. He summoned Père Ragueneau, who looked with some wonderment at it, then climbed for a better view to the top of the bastion. The smoke spread into a wider column, massed and heavy, billowing up into clouds, with flames spurting up in flashes like colored lightning. Ragueneau knew this was no forest fire. He and his people calculated the distance; the village of St. Louis was afire. He thought of Père Jean and Père Gabriel. Were they caught in the fire, or had they already left for St. Ignace?

Ragueneau ordered some *donnés* to hurry the three miles over to St. Louis. Scarcely were they out of the gate of Sainte Marie before they spied men racing down the path through the fields, shouting about the Iroquois and keening the death whine. They had escaped from St. Ignace, they told, when the Iroquois captured the village early in the morning; they had warned St. Louis and other villages that the Iroquois in great numbers were on the way to destroy them; they had seen Echon and Atironta at St. Louis.

Not long after, slow-moving, heavy-burdened women, with their children and their aged, stumbled from the woods and came wailing toward Sainte Marie. They told the further story of how they fled, carrying with them all they could, of how Annaotaha and eighty warriors remained in St. Louis to defend the town against the Iroquois, of how Echon and Atironta urged them to escape but remained with the fighting men. Ragueneau watched the sickening smoke sprawling over the sky above St. Louis. Père Jean, Père Gabriel, were they trapped in that fire, or worse, were they captured by the Iroquois?

Men straggled in, one with a deep gash in his head, another with his hand cut off, still another with an arrow imbedded in his eye. They had fought, they said, against hundreds of Iroquois who assailed the stockade of St. Louis. For a time, they beat off the enemy, but when the Iroquois breached the walls and surrounded the defenders, they had devised their escape. Before they left they had seen Echon and Atironta in the midst of the fighting Hurons. Ragueneau's blood stopped. Père Jean and Père Gabriel were probably by now the prisoners of the Iroquois.

Since the Iroquois might come swarming over the snow to Sainte Marie, Chastillon, Desfosses and the other six soldiers, together with the *donnés* and the workmen, mounted guard and organized the defense. They counted forty Frenchmen who could handle muskets. They primed the little cannon atop the main gate, took position in the bastions, and stationed themselves along the wooded palisades to the west and the south, while the Huron men scouted along the trails and the rim of hills. Forty Frenchmen and a few dozen Hurons could defend Sainte Marie and all who were crowded in its court-yard against an Iroquois assault. But they would be almost powerless, they felt, to protect the Huron women and children who could find no room in the courtyard and who hid in the outposts and in the countryside. If the Iroquois came, these would be massacred in all the environs of Sainte Marie.

The smoke that had been hanging over St. Louis floated away with the March winds. Sainte Marie waited and watched for the stealthy approach of the Iroquois; but all who came were famished, terror-stricken Huron refugees. Toward sunset, some of the sharp-eyed watchers discerned blurred, dark figures stealing behind the shelter of trees, and identified them as Iroquois uncoverers. The attack of the Iroquois might be delivered in the dusk, or during the raw March night, or at dawn with the rising of the sun. Hurons watched in the woods, sentinels made their rounds about the Fort, the French dozed with their muskets in their hands. Père Ragueneau, with the priests and brothers, kept vigil with God in the chapel. They prayed for Jean and Gabriel, not knowing that one was dead and the other was enduring excruciating torments that very night.

The sentinels gave the alarm in the hour before dawn. Men were coming from the west, along the banks of Lake Isaragui. These soon identified themselves as chiefs and braves from Ossossané and the Bear villages, who had traveled the snow-covered trails to Sainte Marie. Three hundred were coming, they reported, and later in the day war chiefs would be leading hundreds more. As silently as they had come, so silently they melted away, toward the hills leading up to St. Louis. A few hours later, those at Sainte Marie were startled by war whoops screeching out from the hills to the east, discerned among the trees braves fighting in hand-to-hand conflict, stared aghast as some retreated and some pursued down to the plains, watched bands of others, presumably Hurons, gather from all sides, saw them strug-gle up the hills and disappear in the forests, the while the war cries faded into silence.

That night, Ragueneau heard from a few survivors of the tragedy of that day. The Ossossané vanguard discovered the Iroquois halfway to St. Louis. Both sides attacked, but the Iroquois being superior in number drove the Hurons back until the main Huron body joined the fray. Then the Hurons forced the Iroquois to retreat, tree by tree, hill by hill, up to St. Louis. Some of the Iroquois made a stand in the stockades that still remained, but the Hurons surrounded and captured them. In turn the Hurons were besieged by about seven hundred Iroquois who were on their way to attack Sainte Marie. The battle raged through the entire day, and at nightfall only thirty Hurons were still alive, all of them wounded.

Great was the sorrow of Ragueneau, since most of the brave warriors who had come from Ossossané to defend Sainte Marie and battle the Iroquois were Christians. Great, likewise, was his fear for the safety of all at Sainte Marie. The refugees told him that the Iroquois numbered about twelve hundred and that they planned to surround Sainte Marie that night or on the morrow. He and his people begged their patron Saint Joseph for protection for themselves and for the Hurons gathered about them and in the villages. Each vowed to say a Mass in honor of Saint Joseph every month for the coming year.

They celebrated the first Masses of their vow the next morning, March 18, the eve of the Feast of Saint Joseph. That day, Sainte Marie and all the country about was ominously silent. Only an occasional Huron, escaped from the Iroquois, darted out of the woods or across the fields. Only starving women and children crept out of their hiding places to beg the Blackrobes piteously for food. Through the long hours of the day, the French and the Hurons kept watch and vigil, not knowing when or from where the Iroquois, like phantoms, would pounce on them. They prayed and stood guard through the night, and waited the dawn with tense nerves and haggard faces.

Then came Stephen Annaotaha, the brave chief of St. Louis, and a few comrades. He announced to them that the Iroquois had fled, in the greatest disorder, and even in panic. They had gone about like madmen slaughtering the prisoners, and had driven before them hundreds of captives. In the confusion of the Iroquois flight, Stephen said that he managed to slip away to freedom. With stony, glazed eyes he related to them the story of Echon and Atironta, how they remained with the fighting men at St. Louis, how they were tortured at St.

Ignace, and how they had died. Ragueneau and the French listened
mutely to Stephen. It was the will of God that Jean and Gabriel were
chosen, and that all at Sainte Marie, on the Feast of Saint Joseph,
were saved.

On the following day, Saturday, March 20, Père Ragueneau
sent Père Jacques Bonin, Regnault, Malherb and other *donnés* to St.
Ignace, to recover the bodies of Lalemant and de Brébeuf. Stephen
guided them, first to St. Louis, where the corpses of hundreds of
war-painted Hurons and Iroquois were strewn about the stockades;
and then along the muddy trail to St. Ignace, where all was gruesome
silence and death. Stephen pointed out the blackened body of Jean
de Brébeuf lying among the gray embers. They searched for Gabriel
Lalemant and finally identified his body, a short distance away, piled
among the corpses of the tortured Hurons. Tenderly and with sobs,
Père Bonnin and the *donnés* lifted the sacred remains on stretchers of
bark and carried them back the six miles to Sainte Marie.

They laid them side by side on the floor of the living room, just
as they were. All the priests, brothers, *donnés* and workmen looked
at the bodies with awe and examined them with care. Père Bonin
testified that he knelt near the body of Gabriel, his dearest friend,
for the space of two hours, and kissed the wounds as he would the
relics of a saint. Père Ragueneau exclaimed: "They are the relics
of the love of God which alone triumphs in the death of martyrs."
He wrote his thoughts at a later date: "I would gladly call them, if
I were allowed, by the glorious name of Martyrs, not only because
they voluntarily exposed themselves to death for the love of God
and the salvation of their neighbor ... but much more because
hatred for the Faith and contempt for the name of God have been
among the most powerful incentives influencing the minds of the
barbarians to practice as many cruelties as ever the rage of tyrants
inflicted upon the Martyrs, who have triumphed over life and death
at the very height of their tortures."

Christophe Regnault, the *donné* who helped carry back their bodies from St. Ignace, testified:

> They were brought to our cabin, and laid uncovered upon the bark
> of trees. I examined them there at leisure for more than two hours to
> see if what the savages had told us of their martyrdom and death were

true. I examined first the body of Père de Brébeuf which was pitiful to see, as well as that of Père Lalemant. Père de Brébeuf had his
legs, thighs and arms stripped of flesh to the very bone. I saw and
touched a large number of great blisters, which he had on several
places on his body, from the boiling water which these barbarians had
poured over him in mockery of Holy Baptism. I saw and touched the
wounds from a belt of bark, full of pitch and resin, which roasted his
whole body. I saw and touched the marks of burns from the collars of
hatchets placed on his shoulders and stomach. I saw and touched his
two lips, which they had cut off because he constantly spoke of God
while they made him suffer. I saw and touched all parts of his body,
which had received more than two hundred blows from cudgels. I
saw and touched the top of his scalped head. I saw and touched the
opening which these barbarians had made to tear out his heart. In fine,
I saw and touched all the wounds of his body, as the savages had told
and declared to us.

The bodies of Jean and Gabriel, cleansed and clothed in priestly
vestments, were laid in rough-hewn boxes. All through the night, side
by side, they lay before the Blessed Sacrament. Ragueneau related:
"We buried these precious relics on Sunday, the 21st of March, with
so much consolation and such tender feelings of devotion in all who
were present at the obsequies, that I know none who did not desire,
rather than fear, a similar death, and who did not regard himself as
blessed to live in a place where, perhaps a few days from then, God
would accord him the grace of shedding on a similar occasion both
his blood and his life. Not one of us could force himself to pray to
God for them, as if they had any need of prayer. On the contrary,
our spirits were carried up toward Heaven where, we had no doubt,
their souls were. Be this as it may, I pray to God that He fulfill in us
His will, even to death, as He has done toward them."

Père Ragueneau, in the afternoon, went through their papers.
Among the notes of Gabriel Lalemant, he found a document that
was written in France four or five years before. It was a complete
oblation of himself to God, asking for extraordinary sufferings, and
concluding: "Rise, then, my soul! Let us lose ourselves blessedly,
in order to give this satisfaction to the Sacred Heart of Jesus Christ.
He deserves it, and you are not able to excuse yourself, unless you
wish to live and die ungrateful to His love." In another paper,

written also before coming to Canada, Gabriel pledged and consecrated himself to Our Lord, for the purpose of receiving from
God a violent death, either in exposing himself among the plague-
stricken of old France, or in seeking to save the savages of New
France. He added a clause, in which he begged to be allowed to die
for God's glory in the flower of his age.

Among the few things left by Jean de Brébeuf was his book of
spiritual notes. Ragueneau knew what was in it, for Jean had revealed
to him that, some years back, Superiors ordered him to record his
visions and his spiritual thoughts. He had, also, as Superior, been told
by Jean of the vows and pledges he had made to serve God more perfectly, of the burning desires to live with Christ and suffer more for
Him. With brimming eyes, he read the vow of 1638: "I vow, I repeat
to you my Lord Jesus, that, if the grace of martyrdom is ever merci-
fully offered by You to me, your unfaithful servant, I shall not fail to
accept this grace. Grant that I may so live, that You may wish me at
length to die for You. Thus, my Lord, I shall accept your chalice, and
I shall call upon your name, Jesus, Jesus, Jesus."

Père Ragueneau read on until he came to the short paragraph:
"Two days in succession, I have felt in me a great desire for martyrdom, and for enduring all the torments which the Martyrs have
suffered." He laid aside the little book, and recalled a conversation he
had with Père Jean. "If you were captured by the Iroquois," he had
asked, "would you not feel a very great repugnance if they stripped
you naked?" "No," answered Jean, "that would be the will of God.
I would not think of myself but of God." He remembered that he
had then asked: "But, would you not have a horror of the fire?" To
this, Jean replied: "Oh, yes. I would fear it if I regarded only my own
weakness. The sting of a fly is capable of making me impatient. But I
trust that God will always help me. Aided by His grace, I do not fear
the terrible torments of fire any more than I fear the prick of a pin."

Four: 1649–1650

"Père Jean de Brébeuf had been chosen by God to be the first apostle
of the Hurons, the first of our Society who set foot there," wrote
Père Ragueneau in his obituary. "Not having found there a single

savage who invoked the name of God, he labored there so success-fully for the salvation of those poor barbarians that before his death he had the consolation of seeing nearly seven thousand baptized, and the Cross of Jesus Christ planted everywhere with glory, and adored in a country which, from the birth of the world had never been Christian." Wrote Père Bressani: "It appeared that God had determined to put an end to the Mission of the Hurons at the same time that he put an end to the life of him who had begun it. This was Père Jean de Brébeuf. At his death, began the irreparable ruin of the Huron nation."

Fifteen Huron villages were abandoned within a week or two after de Brébeuf's death. Those to which he ministered were evacuated at the time of the attack on St. Louis and St. Ignace. The great Ossossané, after the brave attempt of its three hundred warriors, was deserted by the time he was buried. The Bear nation, almost as a whole, men, women and children, fled in great disorder and fear to the land of the Petuns. Hundreds more from the other nations sought refuge among the Neutrals to the south or, in deadly fear of the Iroquois, migrated to the western nation of the Eries. While many families found haven in the nearby islands, greater numbers escaped to safer security among the Algonquins far up the lake. Scanonaenrat alone made peace with, and was adopted by, the Seneca Iroquois.

The once mighty confederacy of the Ouendat peoples was oblit-erated. The remnants of the race were scattered among alien peoples, their homeland was forsaken forever, their villages were silent, their cabins were in ashes. No Hurons walked in their own land when the trees turned green that spring. None, except the hundreds who camped about Sainte Marie. Père Ragueneau and the missioners were as desolate in soul as was the Huron country. They conferred, during April, on two problems: how to preserve the Faith among the dis-persed Christians, and what should be done about Sainte Marie. As for the former, the missioners determined to search out their Huron Believers during the summer, wherever these might gather. As for the latter, one thing was certain: they must abandon Sainte Marie as quickly as possible. Else, they would also be massacred by the Iroquois who still ravaged the rest of Huronia.

Being resolved not to forsake the Huron, Petun and Algonquin missions around Lake Huron, they determined to build a new Sainte

Marie. But where? They concluded that it would be wisest to establish themselves on the island called Ekaentoton, to which they had
given the name of Sainte Marie. It lay 180 miles northward, out of
the reach of the Iroquois. It offered easy passage to the route to Quebec, and was a gateway to Lake Superior and the nations of the west.
Already, great numbers of the Hurons were building a village there.

They changed their minds when twelve Huron elders held council with them at Sainte Marie. The spokesman announced that the
Ouendat people, rising again to life, and once more becoming a
united nation, had all agreed to build an impregnable village on the
nearby island of Ahoendoe, called by the missioners the Island of
St. Joseph. This village would attract the dispersed Ouendats who,
within a few years, would return to their former villages on the
mainland. The twelve chiefs begged the Blackrobes not to desert
them in their need, but to unite with them and to save their people
and their nation.

Ragueneau recorded: "We could not doubt that God had chosen to speak to us by their lips. Although at their coming we had
decided upon another plan, we all found ourselves changed before
their departure. With an unanimous consent, we believed that it was
necessary to follow God in the direction whither He chose to call
us—for the remaining future—whatever peril there may be in it for
us, in whatever depth of darkness we may continue." Thus, they
elected to erect a new Sainte Marie on the Island of St. Joseph, separated from the Huron land only by a channel.[3]

They lost no time, since the Iroquois might burst upon them
any moment. Boivin and the carpenters began building a barge
some twenty feet long, and down near the mouth of the little river
they were assembling tree trunks into a raft forty or fifty feet long.
Within the house, the priests, brothers, donnés and workmen were
packing the corn meal, the dried vegetables, the smoked fish and
meat, all the food that would be needed for more than fifty men
during the course of a full year. Feverishly, they bundled and packaged their clothes and other goods they required for the winter to
come. With special care, they wrapped up the sacred vessels, the
vestments and chapel goods, their writings, their paper and their
books. They could carry off with them only as much as the barge
and the raft would hold; all the rest, they must destroy.

Most precious of all their possessions were the bones of the martyred Jean and Gabriel. Scarcely a month after the bodies were buried, they were disinterred. Molere and Regnault, overcoming their nauseating horror, dismembered the bodies and boiled them in strong lye water until the bones were loosed from the flesh. The flesh and the water, they buried once more. The skulls and the bones they scraped and cleansed, and stretched them out on a plank to dry in the sun and, finally, hardened them in a slightly heated oven. Père Ragueneau wrapped in finest silk the skulls and the bones of Jean and Gabriel, and encased them in two firmly locked, iron-bound chests.

Three months had nearly passed since de Brébeuf and Lalemant had died. Ragueneau and the French were finished their packing and were steeled in their resolution to destroy Sainte Marie. On Monday, June 14, after being assured that no Iroquois were hidden in the region, they piled all they needed and all they prized on the barge and the long, narrow raft. Père Ragueneau made his final inspection, then shouted out to the *donnés* and workmen his order. About five o'clock in the evening, they built fires around and within the chapel, in the rooms of the community residence, applied torches to the sheds within the enclosure, kindled the woodwork within the bastions, and set ablaze the palisades and the longhouses outside the palisades.

They raced to the barge, which they shoved down the little river, and to the raft anchored at its mouth. They paddled furiously into the clear waters of the bay, and while the June sun was sinking in front of them, they looked back at the clouds of smoke forming a roof over the woodlands, at the bronze pillars of fire leaping high into the heavens. They heard the crackling and the roaring of the mighty conflagration, and smelled the acrid odor of the burning wood. All that had been Sainte Marie was now smoke and fire, and soon would be ashes.

Later, Ragueneau wrote: "We have left our dwelling place, rather I might call it our delight.... Nay, more, we even applied the torch to the work of our own hands, lest the sacred house should furnish shelter to our impious enemy. In a single day, and almost in a moment, we saw consumed our work of nearly ten years.... Desolated now is our home, desolated are our Penates. In the land of our exile, we were forced to seek a new place of exile." Elsewhere, he recorded: "On each of us lay the necessity of bidding farewell to that old home of Sainte Marie.... We were obliged to abandon the place which I might call our second fatherland, our home of innocent delights. It had been the cradle of this Christian Church; it was the temple of God; it was the home where dwelt the servants of Jesus Christ.... Fear that our enemies, only too impious, might profane this holy place, and might use it to their advantage, we ourselves set fire to it. We watched it burn, in less than an hour, our work of nine or ten years."

With superhuman strength, they paddled and guided the clumsy barge and the long, narrow raft some twenty miles around the Huron headlands to the cove of Ahoendoe. After a prayer of thanksgiving and an act of dedication, they immediately began the building of the second Sainte Marie. By November, they had erected a fort of solid masonry, about one hundred feet square and fourteen feet high with each corner flanked by a bastion. Within the enclosure they extended another wall and roofed over the living quarters. The fifty Frenchmen were secure against the winter and the Iroquois.

As early as June, some three hundred Huron families assembled on Ahoendoe. The larger number of these were widows, with their children and old people. As best they could, they threw together their longhouses and made clearances for their cornfields. Their only food was acorns, boiled in lye, roots and what fish they could catch. During the summer, other bands struggled into the new settlement, so that, by the autumn, the population of the new village had reached nearly a thousand. These had been living in hunger since March, and Chaumonot remarked: "Seeing the Hurons, you might conclude that they were dug-up corpses."

Ragueneau was almost as desperate as the Hurons. He had only a limited supply of corn, scarcely enough to keep alive the French, while the Hurons had no food whatsoever. Almost by a miracle, some of the Algonquin missioners brought six hundred bushels of acorns and canoe loads of fish, which they had bought from the northern Algonquins. Ragueneau knew that this would merely postpone the death, rather than save the lives of his thousand Hurons. With worried mind, he watched the snows cover the island during November, and the lake freeze over during December, and with terror-stricken soul he witnessed the people, famished and despairing, succumb to the influenza and pneumonia. They were imprisoned on the island, for the Iroquois still haunted the mainland.

In November, some Hurons, returning from the Petun country, brought the terrifying news that the Iroquois had raised the hatchet against the Petuns and boasted that, before the winter was advanced, they would burn their villages. Ragueneau was in consternation since four of the priests were living that winter among the Petuns, Charles Garnier and Noël Chabanel in the frontier village of Etarita, Adrien Grélon and Léonard Garreau some twelve miles back in the hill country. Immediately, he wrote his orders to Garnier, directed him and the other three to return to St. Joseph's Island immediately, unless some paramount reason detained them.

Garnier and Chabanel received the command at Etarita in the beginning of December. Sadly and silently, they looked at each other. There was danger from the Iroquois, they agreed, but was not that a reason to remain among their Christians? Garnier had the hard duty of ordering Chabanel to return, since only one of them was needed. He explained about himself in a letter sent to Ragueneau: "I have no fears about my health. What I should fear more would be that of deserting my flock in their misery of hunger and amidst the terrors of war, since they have need of me more than ever. I would fail to use the opportunity which God gives me of losing myself for Him, and so render myself unworthy of His favors.... At all times, I am ready to leave everything and die in the spirit of obedience. Otherwise, I shall never come down from the cross on which His goodness has placed me."

Under the double command of obedience, Noël Chabanel bade his farewell to Charles Garnier after Sunday Mass, December 5. "I go where obedience calls me," he said. "Whether or not I shall obtain from my Superior the favor of returning to the Mission, I do not know. But God must be served till death." He was accompanied by and under the protection of some Christian Hurons who thought it wiser to escape to Ahoendoe rather than to await an Iroquois attack on Etarita. That same Sunday, Petun war bands whirled out of the village to search for some three hundred Iroquois who were reported to be gathering for the purpose of attacking Etarita. The chiefs planned to surprise the enemy and to disperse them. They made sure, however, to leave warriors enough to defend the triple palisades and the six hundred families against any Iroquois attack.

Père Garnier had won over a large number of the Petuns to the teachings of Christ, after having endured for ten years their threats and their hate. He had gained the affection of the great number of Hurons who had poured into Etarita after the exodus from Ossossané. The labors of caring for and teaching the increasing number of Christians was wearing him down; though, as he protested to Ragueneau, he had no fears about his health. He would spend almost the whole of the day wandering from cabin to cabin, tending the sick and instructing those who would listen to him.

On Tuesday, December 7, while he was making his usual rounds, about three o'clock in the afternoon, he heard a shriek, then a terrified bedlam of screams: "The Iroquois! The Iroquois!" Garnier hurled himself out into the open. He saw the war-painted Iroquois already streaming through the gates of the village and slashing down the men, women and children in their onward rush. The Petun braves were desperately forming into bands to halt the invading enemy, but it was too late, and they as well as the squaws were being massacred. There was no safety for anyone except in flight.

With his black robe flapping about him, Garnier ran to his chapel there to await death. To the Christians who were cowering near, he called out: "My brothers, we are dead men! Pray to God, and take flight! Escape any way you can! Go quickly! Keep your Faith as long as you live! May death find you thinking of God!" He pronounced the absolution over them. "Ouracha, save yourself! Escape with us!" they pleaded with him. He waved his refusal and turned to other groups scurrying past him.

The Iroquois, swinging their tomahawks and howling like fiends, were closely following in pursuit. He felt the sting of a musket ball in his breast, another in his stomach before he fell unconscious. When his senses returned, he found himself stripped naked and the blood flowing from his wounds. He breathed his final act of contrition. Lifting his head, he saw a man writhing in agony a short distance away. Thinking to help the man, perhaps to baptize him with the melted snow, he gained his feet, but stumbled to the earth after a few steps. Gathering himself together, trying to stem the blood, he walked and crawled another few yards toward the dying man. At that moment, according to a woman who had concealed herself nearby, an Iroquois rushed on him, scalped him, and slashed him with a hatchet on each of his temples, deep into the brain.

Some few, who escaped, reached Ekarenniondi, where Grélon and Garreau were living. At dawn, they started down the twelve miles to

Etarita. The fires still smoldered, the air was heavy with the odor of burned bark and bloody bodies. The two young missioners searched among the ashes and the carnage for the remains of Père Charles. At last, with the help of some returned Petuns, they found him. Not a speck of his white flesh showed. He was completely caked with blood and ashes, and the frozen mud in which he lay. They washed his body and clothed it with garments taken off themselves. They dug a shallow grave near where his chapel had been and there recited the funeral prayers as they lowered him. Later, they would rescue his bones, which they revered as the relics of a true martyr.

Not until December 12 did Père Ragueneau learn of the fate of Charles Garnier and the massacre of Etarita from the Hurons who had set out with Noël Chabanel. Along the way, they were forced into the woods through the fear of the Iroquois. Chabanel could not keep up with them in their flight, and urged them to save themselves. They had tried to help him, but he sent them away, telling them: "It makes no difference if I die. This life is not important. The Iroquois cannot rob me of the blessedness of Paradise." Since they could not save him with themselves, they had left him, and knew no more about him.

A week later, Ragueneau learned that an apostate Huron said he had met Chabanel crossing a stream near the shore of the lake, and had assisted him on his way. Suspicion so fastened on this renegade that Ragueneau concluded finally: "It seems to us most probable that Père Chabanel was murdered by that Huron, once a Christian but since an apostate.... A trustworthy Christian told us that he had heard the man, from his own lips, boasting that he was the murderer, and that he had rid the world of the carrion of a Frenchman, that he had brained him at his own feet, and had thrown his body into the river."

Père Chabanel died on December 8, the day dedicated to the Immaculate Conception. Shortly before he had left for the Petuns, he had told his confessor, Père Chastellain: "I do not know what is going on within me, or what God wills to do with me. In one respect I am entirely changed. Naturally, I am very timorous. Now that I am going on a most dangerous mission, and death does not seem to be far away, I no longer feel any fear. This state of mind does not come from myself." In bidding his last farewell, Chabanel said: "May it be for good and all, this time, that I give myself to

God. May I belong to Him." A priest who heard the remark, said to Ragueneau: "Truly, I have just been deeply moved. That good priest has just now spoken to me with the look and the voice of one who immolates himself. I know not what God wills, but I see that He is fashioning a great saint."

Charles Garnier, too, they all regarded as a saint. Ragueneau recalled about him: "He often said to us that he would be pleased to fall into the hands of the Iroquois and be their captive. If they burned him alive, he would at least have a chance to instruct them as long as they prolonged his torments. If they spared his life that would be a precious means of obtaining their conversion."[4]

The new year of 1650 increased the hopelessness of the French and the Hurons imprisoned by the Iroquois on the Island of St. Joseph. In God alone, could they trust; from Him alone, could they hope for help. Under the guidance of the priests, the Hurons gathered morning and evening for prayers, instructions and spiritual talks. Practically all of them were now baptized Christians. Their piety and their sinlessness seemed almost like a miracle of God, and their thought was perpetually of the happiness of heaven that awaited them after death.

They lived in perpetual fear, since the Iroquois were known to be prowling about the shores of the mainland, and could easily cross the narrow channel on the solid ice. The Hurons were always on the alert, and of the French, Ragueneau wrote: "Our sleep was but half-sleep. Whatever the cold, whatever the snow, whatever winds might blow, sentinels kept watch all night long, exposed to every severity of weather in the never-ending rounds. The others who, during this time, were taking their period of sleep, were always under arms, as if awaiting the signal for battle."

The fiercest enemy was famine, since fear of the Iroquois kept those who could hunt from bringing in meat. The stock of acorns was completely eaten, and no more were to be found under the snows on the island. The corn brought by the missioners was rapidly diminishing and would scarcely last till the spring. The Hurons, pleading for food, died for lack of it. Ragueneau wrote: "Scarcely a one who is alive, does not live by our aid. Hardly a one who has died, but has acknowledged that he owed more to our charity than to any other human being."

In their extremity of hunger, they searched for the dung of men and beast, and dug up the carrion of dogs, foxes and other animals. Day by day, the missioners ministered to the people, with food if they had any, with encouragement always. They could do little for the wasted, shriveled bodies that dwindled into death. They were horrified at the sights they saw, yet consoled by the words they heard. A woman who held close her three dying babies, in almost her last breath exclaimed: "You who are the Lord of our lives! We shall die, since You will it. But how good it is to die Christians. I firmly believe that we, companions in death, shall all rise again together."

So many were the dead, that the Hurons could not bury their own. The French searched for the corpses in the cabins, and interred them as best they could in the frozen earth. Sometimes, the Hurons hid their dead so that they themselves might live. "Not once, but many times," related Ragueneau, "they have used as food those who were most precious to them, brothers given to brothers, children to their mothers, parents to their own children." Again, he stated: "They even devoured one another, but this in secret, and with horror. Necessity had no longer law. Famished teeth ceased to discern the nature of what they ate. Mothers fed upon their children, children no longer recognized in a corpse him whom, while he lived, they had called their father."

The bloom of spring brought no surcease to the cold gloom of the winter. The sick died and those who were well became sick. A band seeking to cross the ice in March, in search of food, drowned in sight of the Fort; others who reached the mainland, were massacred by Iroquois; in April, other parties who felt secure in hidden fishing haunts were butchered. Through a chance survivor who found his way back, Ragueneau learned that two large Iroquois war parties were coming that summer to Huronia, one to level the villages, the other to attack the new Sainte Marie on Ahoendoe Island.

Two old chiefs consulted with Ragueneau, and after a long discourse concluded: "Aondecheté, you alone can give us life, if you strike a daring blow. Prevent this dispersion of the people. Gather them together in a place you may choose. Cast your eyes toward Quebec. Transport thither the remnants of this ruined nation. Do not wait till famine and war have violently killed the last one of us. Bear us in your hands and in your heart."

Père Ragueneau's soul wept in the anguish of this last crisis. Gathering the priests into conference, he related that "fifteen, twenty times we discussed this matter." Would they move to the northern island of Ekaentoten, and there establish the third Sainte Marie? Would they be cowards if they returned to the St. Lawrence, and thus abandon the far west missions among the Hurons, Petuns and Algonquins? They prayed piteously for guidance, until at last, Père Ragueneau wrote his decision: "It seemed to us more and more clear that God spoke to us by the lips of these Huron chiefs. We ourselves saw what they said was true. The entire Huron country was a land of horror and massacre. Everywhere we cast our eyes, we saw convincing proof that famine, on the one hand, and war, on the other, were completing the extermination of the few Christians who remained. If we were able to guard them to the shelter of the French fort at Montreal, Three Rivers or Quebec, that would be their place of refuge."

The Huron council, however, was divided. While the old chiefs argued in favor of escape to the St. Lawrence and protection for the remnant of the Hurons under the French, Stephen Annaotaha and many of the fighting men were determined to live and, if need be, die in their own land. There was no conflict, however, between those who elected to leave and those who chose to remain. Père Ragueneau and the French were quite unanimous in their resolution. They prepared feverishly, once more packing up their valuables, their chapel goods, their relics, their books. Père Garreau had brought back with him the bones of Charles Garnier from the Petun grave. These were also wrapped in their chapel silk and deposited in a little chest, like those containing the sacred remains of Gabriel Lalemant and Jean de Brébeuf.⁵

All through May, the French and Hurons were building their canoes for the thousand-mile journey down to Quebec. Fifty, sixty or even more canoes would be needed to transport the three hundred Hurons and the half-hundred French. Always, they were feeling the pangs of hunger in their empty bellies, and always they were haunted by the fear of Iroquois swarming across from the mainland. By June, all was ready. Stephen Annaotaha and his men, who had been scouting the shores, reported that no Iroquois bands were in the vicinity. On June 10, at nightfall, in dread silence, the Hurons, mostly widows, children and old folk, and the French Blackrobes, *donnés* and workmen took their places in their canoes.

In the dusk of that mellow June evening, the flotilla of sixty and more canoes crept stealthily out of the arc of the cove of the second Sainte Marie, paddled through the creased, lapping waters of the lake toward the islands along the mainland, and were enveloped in the darkness of the night and the black anguish of their souls. In his canoe, Père Ragueneau carried the chest containing the bones of Jean de Brébeuf. It was only twenty-four years ago that Père Jean had come to the Hurons. It was only sixteen years ago since he had won his first Huron Christians. But during those sixteen years, by the Providence of God, which none could understand and none could question, the Huron people and nations were brought to God and to death at the same time. Truly, the Huron Mission died with the death of him who had begun it.

"It was not without tears that we quitted the country that owned our hearts and held our hopes," recorded Ragueneau, "which had already been reddened by the glorious blood of our brethren, which promised us a like happiness, and road to heaven and the gate of paradise. *Mais quoy!* One must forget self, and relinquish God's interests for God's sake."[6]

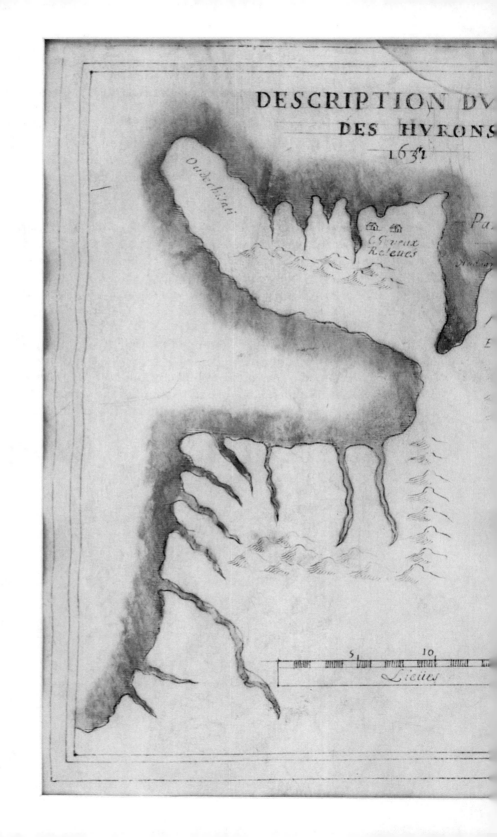

DESCRIPTION DV

DES HVRONS

1632

Oudchiati

C. Joseux
Releues

Pa.

5   10

Lieües

IS

I. Gahsandoe

I. Ondiontanen

Etondotrata

S. Cecile
Taenteaton

grand   S. Charle
Huron   Teanu
        S. Magdelaine   Khionchiara
Haskama   S. Louis Ataratiri   S. Elizabeth
                        S. Marie   S. Jean
        Karouinondi   Kouta   Ipranio S. Joachim
                              S. Denis S. Ignace ou
Elia Sei-   S. Xavier   Chantie   Aretsi   Contarea ou S.
ondia   Jean Baptiste
        S. Michel   S. Joseph Andien
Nation   Ela Van.   Ataas-
du Petun   Conception   Carisati   Annontari

                      LAC   Haskaeri Tannen
                                                 rahi
                OVENTARENK

                    Sainte
                        Ondiara
                          tOnhonai

                                        PARTIE
20
                                    DV LAC ONTARIO

ACKNOWLEDGMENTS

Whenever Jean de Brébeuf and his confreres were confronted by an inextricable situation or sought an impossible favor, they prayed to the Patron of the Hurons, Saint Joseph, and to Notre Dame, under the title of the Immaculate Conception. In like manner, whenever in the composition of this book I became entangled in hopeless predicaments, I turned to Saint Joseph and Our Lady, who always, somehow, rescued me and aided me to continue till the last page. To them my most fervent thanks, and to them the honor and glory.

In a very special way I am indebted to Vincent L. Keelan, S.J., who as the Reverend Provincial of the Maryland Province of the Society of Jesus, granted me an extended leave of absence and encouraged me in countless ways. I am likewise grateful to his successor as Provincial, David Nugent, S.J., who has not only enabled me but urged me to complete the work. My most sincere thanks are due to Lawrence C. Gorman, S.J., President of Georgetown University, and to the members of his community, for their hospitality during my residence at the University as well as for the use of the Georgetown University library. To my own community of Loyola College, I can never be sufficiently grateful for its understanding and its forbearance. Thomas J. Lally, S.J., Director of the Martyrs' Shrine at historic Sainte Marie, near Midland, Ontario, has granted me such gracious hospitality and co-operation that I cannot find adequate words to express my appreciation. With affectionate respect, I express my thanks to Père Victor Gravel, S.J., who assisted me most faithfully in the research concerning the Quebec area. Likewise, I owe gratitude to Père Paul Desjardins, S.J., who so generously helped me in studying the precious documents preserved in the Archives of the College of Saint Marie, Montreal. A special word of appreciation must be added for the charity of the Philadelphia Sisters of Mercy, and for the invaluable services rendered by Mrs. S. Valden Coulter and Mrs. William F. Hormes, and for the generous co-operation of my assistant, Rev.

Paul J. Gibbons, S.J. Many more, whose names are too numerous to list but whom I remember vividly for their help and inspiration, I thank heartily and frequently commend to Saint Jean de Brébeuf and the North American Martyrs.

NOTES AND REFERENCES

CHAPTER I

1. Until the discovery of the *Catalogus Provinciae Franciae*, which definitely fixes the date and place of birth, earlier writers stated that Jean was born in Bayeux, either in 1592 or 1593. Baptismal records in what is now the St. Lô area either were not kept at the period of his birth or were not preserved. (Rochemonteix: 1–329, note.)

2. Following the assault on Omaha Beach, June 6, 1944, the objective of the United States First Army was St. Lô. The city and the surrounding country were reduced almost to rubble by the American attacks and the German counterattacks.

3. After he restored the Society of Jesus, Henry IV gave authority by royal decree, dated February 28, 1604, for the establishment of a college and a novitiate in Rouen. The novitiate was situated in la paroisse [the parish of] Saint-Vivien, near l'Hôtel de Ville. After the French Revolution, the buildings were used as a prison.

4. The date of his entry into the Society of Jesus is now definitely settled by the *Catalogus* as November 8, 1617. Père Paul Ragueneau apparently erred in stating that he entered on October 5. (*Relations*: 34–195.)

5. The small book of Spiritual Exercises was written by Ignatius of Loyola in the cave of Manresa, Spain, in 1522, and was revised till 1548, when it was approved by Paul III. It guided and governed all the subsequent spiritual life of Jean de Brébeuf.

6. The College was founded in 1593 by Cardinal de Bourbon, Archbishop of Rouen. When the Jesuits were banished by Henry IV in 1595, the College was continued for a few years but finally closed. After he recalled the Jesuits, King Henry not only authorized them to reopen the College in 1604, but contributed and forced others to contribute to its foundation. Part of the original structure still remains under the name of le Lycée Corneille.

7. In a manuscript written in his own hand and found after his death, he recorded: "*Anno dominj 1621 Lexoniis subdiaconatum accepj mense septembrj eodem autem anno diaconatum accepj Baiociae decembrj anno vero 1622 sacerdotio insignitus Pontisarae initio quadragesimae et die Virginis Annuntiatae primum sacrificium deo obtulj Rothomagj.*" (*Quebec Archives, 1924–1925*, p. 71. Melançon Mimeographed Corrected Text, 147, 191.)

8. The Récollets belonged to the Order of Friars Minor founded by Saint Francis of Assisi about 1208. Like the Discalced and the Reformati, the Récollets sought for a stricter observance of the Rule according to the ideal of Saint Francis. They established the first Province in France in 1606. At the invitation of Champlain they established a mission in New France in 1615, and were the pioneer apostles at Quebec and among the Hurons.

CHAPTER II

1. The natives inhabiting the eastern half of Canada and the northeastern territory of the United States belonged to two distinct racial stocks, usually referred to as the Algonquin and the Huron-Iroquois. The Algonquins were divided into what might be called nations or peoples or tribes, each of these a unit, each occupying a certain area, but all observing the same traditional customs and all speaking dialects of the same root language. They were scattered through the New England States, along the Atlantic coast, up the St. Lawrence and Ottawa Rivers, westward beyond the Great Lakes, and northward to the Arctics. The nation having its homeland along the St. Lawrence from Tadoussac to Quebec was called Montagnais by the French. The Huron-Iroquois stock was likewise divided into many nations occupying defined regions, but all having a marked affinity in regard to customs, language and physical appearance. Thus, the Susquehannas had their villages in Pennsylvania, the Iroquois in New York, the Hurons on Georgian Bay, the Neutrals in southern Ontario, etc.

2. In terms of modern Quebec, the Récollet convent was situated on the bank of the little St. Charles River where the Hôpital Général is now located.

3. Echon, according to the most likely explanation, is the Huron attempt to pronounce Jean. It is alleged that the same word meant a certain tree valued for its medicinal purposes. In the original documents it is sometimes spelled Eschon and Hechon. The preferable pronunciation is the guttural Ekon. It may be noted that the Huron pronounced Antoine as Anwennen or Antwen, Pierre as Arioo, Charles as Ouracha, etc.

4. Lalemant wrote to Champlain, under date of July 28, 1625: "One of our priests went to the trading place with the intention of going to the Hurons or the Iroquois, together with the Récollet Père who just came from France, as they should think best after consulting with Père Nicholas who was to be at the trading place to confer with them. But word came that Père Nicholas was drowned at the last rapids; for this reason they returned, knowing no one there, nor the language, nor the country. We are therefore awaiting your arrival, to determine what it will be well to do."

5. The site of Notre Dame des Anges was at the turn of the first loop of the St. Charles River. The approximate spot is marked by the Monument Cartier-Brébeuf, at the termination of Avenue Jacques-Cartier.

6. Père Charles Lalemant in his letter to Pater Mutius Vitelleschi, General of the Society of Jesus, dated August 1, 1626, made only a short reference to de Brébeuf's wintering with the Montagnais: "Père Jean Brébeuf [sic], a pious and prudent man, and of robust constitution, passed the bitter time of winter with the barbarians, whence he derived a considerable knowledge of their foreign tongue." He was equally brief in the statement in his long letter to his brother, Jérôme: "And so this good fortune fell to the lote of Père Brébeuf [sic]. He left on the 20th of October and returned on the 27th of March, all the time being distant from us 20 to 25 leagues." The reader is referred to the vivacious narrative by Père Paul Le Jeune in regard to his wintering among the Montagnais in 1633–1634. (*Relations*: 7–209.)

CHAPTER III

1. On August 1, 1626, Père Lalemant at Quebec was writing Pater Vitelleschi in Rome: "To those that have fixed settlements, we

shall in a short time send one of our number, or rather two: Père
Jean de Brébeuf and Père Anne de Noüe. If their mission is successful, a most promising field for the Gospel will be opened.
They must be taken there by the savages, for they cannot use
any other boatmen." Writing to his brother, Jérôme, he stated:
"Your reverence will, perhaps, be astonished that I have sent
Père de Brébeuf, who already has some knowledge of the language of this nation; but the talents that God has given him influence me; the fruits which are expected from those nations are very
different from those we hoped for here." (*Relations*: 4–181, 221.)

2. In the Archives du Collége Sainte-Marie, Montreal, there is preserved a most interesting manuscript entitled *Voyage de Montreal à
Michilimakina*, by Joseph Derouen. It was written before the death
of Père Pierre Pothier in 1781. Derouen listed in great detail the
distances, the cascades, the portages, etc., along the Ottawa River,
thus furnishing exact information in regard to the canoe journey
made by Jean de Brébeuf in 1626.

3. The Huron country corresponds to what is now known as Simcoe
County, Ontario. The villages where the French first dwelt were
located along the northern headlands of Tiny Township. Remains
of Huron villages have been found by [Andrew F.] Hunter and
others, but the identification of these by name is, thus far, rather
conjectural. The landing cove of Toanché might be Thunder Bay
on the west or Penetanguishene Bay on the east. Several other
smaller inlets and beaches, such as Saw Log Bay, were probably used as Huron ports. Making deductions from the findings
and calculations of the great archaeologist Andrew F. Hunter,
Arthur E. Jones, S.J., and later researchers, the following locations
are tentatively offered: Toanché: in the vicinity of Lake Farlain.
Quieunonascaran: concession XVIII, about lot 23. Quieuindohan: concession VII or VIII, above the beach of Nottawasaga Bay.

In this and following attempts to determine the sites of villages
and areas, one is guided by the *Tabula Novae Franciae, anno 1660*,
inserted in *Historiae Canadensis seu Novae Franciae Libri Decem*, by
P. Franciscus Creuxius, published in Paris, 1664. The map of Du
Creux comprises the vast stretch of territory from Newfoundland
to Lake Superior and from Chesapeake Bay to Hudson Bay and
the northern shores of Labrador. Most important for the present
study is the small insert map entitled *Pars Chorographia Regionis*

Huronum, hodie desertae. The distances, the shorelines, the locations are not correct according to our modern topography, but they represent the amazing amount of knowledge of the New World possessed three hundred years ago. The more comprehensive features of the large map were drawn from contemporary French, Dutch and English maps. The portions showing New France and the interior of the country were undoubtedly based on the reports and the drawings prepared by the Jesuit missioners in Canada. The insert of Huronia, certainly, was a reproduction of a sketch drawn by de Brébeuf, Jérôme Lalemant, Ragueneau, Le Mercier and other Huron missioners. The identifications in the Neutral country, to be mentioned later, could have been made only by de Brébeuf and Chaumonot. Though dated 1660 and published in 1664, the Du Creux map of Huronia was copied from a map drawn between 1642 and 1648.

4. The quotations in this chapter are taken from de Brébeuf's *Relations* of 1634–1636. (*Relations*: Vols. 8 and 10.)

5. This catechism was an excerpt from *De Modo Catechizandi*, by the famed Spanish theologian Jacobus Ledesma, S.J., who died in 1575.

6. Champlain, in his autobiography, testifies: "Père de Brébeuf, obeying instructions sent to him by Père Massé, Superior, came back from the country of the Hurons leaving them in great grief over his departure. He assured them that, by the grace of God, he would come to them again, and bring whatever was necessary for teaching them to know God and to serve Him; and so he took his departure. This *bon* Père had, in fact, a remarkable gift for languages, and would learn and master them in two or three years more thoroughly than others could do in twenty." (Champlain Society Edition: 6–46.)

Some twenty years later, Père Paul Ragueneau would write: "He was sent to New France in 1625 by Père Pierre Coton. For his first apprenticeship, he spent the winter roving in the woods with the Montagnais people nearest Quebec, in which life he had much to suffer. In the summer of the following year, 1626, he came up here to the Hurons. He mastered the difficulties of these barbarous languages with a success so remarkable that he seemed to have been born only for these countries. He adapted his own nature and temperament to the customs of these peoples—becoming all things to all men in order to win them to Christ—with such ability that he ravished their hearts and was singularly loved by them." (*Relations*: 34–59.)

CHAPTER IV

1. Champlain's personalized and discursive account of the surrender of Quebec will be found in *The Works of Samuel de Champlain* (Champlain Society Edition: Vol. 6.)

2. After the death of Jean de Brébeuf, the then Superior, Père Paul Ragueneau, was at liberty to read the spiritual notes which de Brébeuf had recorded. Related Ragueneau: "He had been commanded to write these extraordinary things which occurred within his soul, at least, those which he could most easily remember; for they were too frequent and care for the salvation of his neighbor hardly gave him any leisure to write from time to time." (*Relations*: 34–136.) The command of his Superior or Spiritual Father may be calculated as occurring about 1640. De Brébeuf tried to recall former experiences which had a bearing on his spiritual life as well as to keep a record of the visions and illuminations which strangely opened out before him. Ragueneau used this spiritual notebook for his obituary of de Brébeuf in the *Relation* of 1649. His excerpts from it are attested in his own handwriting in the Manuscript of 1652, preserved in the Archives du Collège Sainte-Marie, Montreal. Quotations from this document will be used in later chapters of this biography.

3. Three Algonquin nations claimed authority over the Ottawa River. The Petite nation had cabins near the Chaudiere Falls above Ottawa. The Island Algonquins had their principal habitat on the Allumette Islands, near the present Pembroke. The Nipissings dwelt in the vicinity of Lake Nipissing. These Algonquins were nomads during the winter, but returned to their cabins in these fixed fishing regions during the summer.

CHAPTER V

1. In his report to Père Provincial, Le Jeune wrote in August, 1634: "We have lived in great peace, thank God, among ourselves, with our workmen and with the French. I have been greatly pleased

with all our priests. Père Brébeuf [sic] is a man chosen by God for these lands. I appointed him in my place for six months, minus nine days, while I passed the winter with the savages. Everything went on peacefully during that time." (*Relations*: 6–37.)

2. The place of desertion was either the beach near Pine (Pinery) Point or the cove at the entrance to Penetanguishene Bay, between the Square and Triangle Redoubts.

3. The northeastern portion of Tiny Township remains lumberland, and identification of Huron village sites is almost impossible. Hunter has reported on some findings in the cleared portions, and Jones, by his triangulation method, has reached theoretical conclusions. The determination, therefore, of the sites of the hamlets in this area is extremely conjectural. Jones places Ihonatiria on concession XX–XXI, lot 6, near Todd, or Methodist, Point. J. Paquin, S.J., locates it six miles to the east, at Pinery Point. The present writer believes that it was about midway between these two points. Oenrio is spotted by Jones on concession XVII, lot 5; it was more probably in concession XIX, near Macey Lake. The village de Brébeuf first stumbled into, Teandeouiata, should be in concession XIX, lot 1.

CHAPTER VI

1. Ossossané occupied a commanding position on a ridge above precipitous gulleys in the vicinity of Point Varwood and Dault's Bay on Nottawasaga Bay. Within the distance of a mile, remains of five villages have been found. Though these have been explored, they have not been uncovered scientifically. The people of the capital village of the Bear nation established themselves on three different sites during the missionary period, 1625–1650. The village of Quieuindohan was abandoned in 1634–1635 and was replaced by Ossossané, which the French called La Rochelle because the land formation resembled the bastioned port of old France. Reliable evidence leads to the conclusion that Ossossané of 1635 was located on concession VII, lot 16, that a new Ossossané was built about 1640 on what is now concession XII, lot 18.

2. A description of the Algonquin Feast of the Dead, attended by Père Jogues, was written by Jérôme Lalemant in the *Relations* of

1642–1643. He stated: "This solemnity among the nomad tribes up here is accompanied by rites of some importance, differing much from those of our Hurons." (*Relations*: 13–209.) The interested reader is referred to *Saint among Savages*, p. 149. [New York and London: Harper and Brothers, 1935.]

3. The exact location of the ossuary of 1636, that described by de Brébeuf, has been determined beyond reasonable doubt by Kenneth E. Kidd, Assistant Keeper of Ethnological Collections, Royal Ontario Museum, Toronto, Canada. This burial pit is in Tiny Township, concession VII, lot 14 N½. It was investigated by Mr. Kidd during the summers of 1947 and 1948. Remains of two copper kettles and some French artifacts were found. The number of skeletons was high. Post molds were uncovered, and the distances from the village of Ossossané were found to correspond with de Brébeuf's statements. The final report of Mr. Kidd is being prepared. It is alleged that some fifty years ago [approximately the year 1900], A. F. Hunter discovered traces of 140 ossuaries in Simcoe County. Practically all of these were emptied of the skulls and bones, and were filled with stones when the first settlers cleared the land more than a century ago. It is related that these pioneers were wont to carry on this desecration in a festive mood.

4. The complete text of de Brébeuf's book on the Hurons will be found in *Relations*: Vol. 10.

5. The school for Huron boys was at the original Jesuit residence, Notre Dame des Anges. Père Le Jeune, in his *Relation* of 1637, stated: "I wrote to Père de Brébeuf to send us some little Hurons. The Pères immediately set about finding some; from a great number of children they chose twelve very fine lads." Later he remarked: "The expenses that are incurred in clothing and feeding these boys are greater than one would imagine. They come as naked as worms, they return well clothed; they must be provided with a house, good furniture, mattresses and blankets, quantities of cloth and linen, a great deal of food, and persons to instruct and wait on them.... This is not all, for presents must be made to their parents and friends." (*Relations*: 12–39 to 115.)

6. Probably the first Iroquois baptized was the Mohawk being tortured by the Island Algonquins during Père Daniel's passage to Quebec in August.

CHAPTER VII

1. A year later when Le Jeune met Peter at Quebec, he commented: "I must frankly confess that never did I expect to see in a savage what I think I have seen and experienced in this one. He possesses a certain modest simplicity which emanates from the spirit within; it seems to me that I felt it when he approached me. I have now studied the other savages to see if I could observe the same dove-like simplicity in them that I saw in this one; I have not found it. Ten persons such as he would set on fire all the villages of the Hurons." (*Relations*: 12–261.)

2. The Ossossané cabin, according to Lalemant, writing in June, 1639, was "about a musket shot from the village". (*Relations*: 17–179.) In the same volume, page 39, he told of the Believers having "to traverse the considerable distance which lies between their village and our dwelling". Père Garnier in his letter to his father, June, 1638, wrote: "You must know that we are here living in a fortress, which has not its like in France. We are encircled by a wall quite different from that of the Bastille. Yesterday, they completed one of its towers.... Our ramparts consist of a wall of posts, ten or twelve feet high and half a foot thick. Our tower is made up of thirty odd posts, planted at one angle of the ramparts so as to command two of the sides of the enclosure, and another will be built to defend the other side. Our Hurons are in admiration over *our* [italics inserted] fortifications and imagine that those in France are modelled on the same pattern." (*Quebec Archives, 1929–1930*, p. 14.) Father Jones, in *Old Huronia*, p. 306, assumed that Garnier referred to the stockade of Ossossané. It is more than likely that he referred to the wall about the missioners' longhouse and chapel.

3. In evaluating these visions, one must recall the statement made by Père Paul Ragueneau in his obituary of Jean de Brébeuf: "Finally, he never guided himself by these visions, although God often had given him to understand things afar off, and even gave him great illuminations as to the secret place of conscience and in the depth of the heart. But he guided himself solely by the principles of the Faith through the operations of obedience and the light of reason." (*Relations*: 34–177.)

4. Teanaustayé, or St. Joseph II, was sanctified by the martyrdom of Saint Antoine Daniel. Jones, in *Old Huronia*, p. 22, argued boldly and confidently that the village was situated on the Flanagan farm, Medonte Township, concession IV, lot 7, overlooking Coldwater Valley. His conclusion was accepted and a monument was erected there. In 1947, Wilfrid Jury, Archaeological Curator, University of Western Ontario, and James McGivern, S.J., under the sponsorship of Thomas J. Lally, S.J., excavated this field. They concluded that this was the site of a small, pre-French village. Mr. Jury contended, with Hunter and others, that Teanaustayé was built on concession IV, lot 12, known as the Fitzgerald or Burnfield farm. It is on the same ridge as the Flanagan farm but juts out toward the valley of the Sturgeon River. It covers an area of about fifteen acres, and has yielded an abundance of French artifacts. Excavations to determine the lines of stockades, cabins, etc., are being undertaken.

Le Mercier recorded that, after they resolved to abandon Ihonatiria, "we were not long in deciding to what place it would be wise to go, the village of Teanaustayé being the most important in the whole country and, consequently, being once won to God would give a strong impulse to the conversion of all the rest. But what a prospect for commencing this project, to say nothing of success therein. For that village, just a little time before, was one of the principal shops in which were forged the blackest calumnies and the most pernicious plots against us, to such an extent that the chiefs had publicly exhorted the young men to come and massacre us at this village of Ossossané." (*Relations*: 17–59.)

5. The Wenrôhronons occupied the area roughly bounded by Lake Huron, Lake Erie and Lake St. Clair. At their dispersal under the impact of famine, disease and the Iroquois, some clans moved westward. Those adopted by the Ouendat federation retained their identity and formed one of the eight Huron nations mentioned in 1648.

CHAPTER VIII

1. Rochemonteix in *Les Jésuites et la Nouvelle-France* (I–388) discusses the contracts of the *donnés* or Oblates. The first contracts of 1638

and 1639, involving a private religious vow, were not acceptable to Pater Mutius Vitelleschi, General of the Society of Jesus. Correspondence between Pater Vitelleschi and Jérôme Lalemant continued, and under date of January 25, 1643, his Paternity not only forbade Lalemant to accept any more *donnés* but ordered him gently to get rid of those under contract. Lalemant offered a compromise, April 2, 1643, whereby the *donnés* would not offer vows, would not wear a religious costume and would not in any way be held as members of the Society of Jesus. They would be bound merely by the civil contract. This solution was fully accepted by the General. The Formula of Contract between the *donné* and the Superior of the Huron Mission will be found in Rochemonteix, p. 482.

2. From August till December, 1638, Le Mercier records the baptisms of about thirty Iroquois before their death by torture.

3. Scanonaenrat, or St. Michel, was three to five miles northwest of Teanaustayé. In terms of today, it was near Orr Lake, Medonte Township, concession III, lot 17. The village of Taenhatentaron, or St. Ignace I, is placed by Jones on concession VIII, lot 22, four to six miles from Teanaustayé. Since different "league" lengths have been used by the writers of the *Relations*, especially in regard to Teanaustayé, the computations in modern terms are rendered difficult.

4. Sainte Marie can be positively identified by the remains of the Fort, the oldest stone building in the Province of Ontario and, indeed, west to the Pacific Ocean. In modern terms it is on the little Wye River, near Mud Lake and less than a mile from Midland Bay. It is about three miles from Midland, Ontario, and about ninety miles north of Toronto. The old stone walls and timber houses of 1639–1649 are being restored by Thomas J. Lally, S.J., director of the Martyrs' Shrine. On the hill above the Fort, a pilgrimage church dedicated to the North American Martyrs was erected in 1926, the year after their beatification. As indicated in the text, the building of Sainte Marie was extended through ten years, beginning in 1639. During the summers from 1940 till 1943, the Royal Ontario Museum, Toronto, collaborated with Father Lally in excavating Fort Sainte Marie. The work was under the expert direction of Kenneth E. Kidd, Assistant Keeper of

Ethnological Collections. His findings are contained in his *Report on Sainte Marie* issued by the University of Toronto Press, 1949. Interim reports were carried in *Martyrs' Shrine Message*, in the October issues for 1941, 1942, 1943 and later. In 1948, Wilfrid Jury, Archaeological Curator, University of Western Ontario, discovered post molds of stockades, cabins, etc., in the field between the Fort and the river. He, Father McGivern and others explored this area. When thoroughly evaluated, these new finds will compel a reversal of many previous conclusions in regard to the extent of Sainte Marie and the structures devoted to Huron use.

5. The Petun country lay west of Huronia and roughly embraced what are now known as Grey and Bruce counties, Ontario. Travel between the Petuns and Hurons was most frequent. Champlain, de la Roche, de Brébeuf had visited their villages. The experiences of Jogues and Garnier are narrated in *Saint among Savages*, pp. 129–40.

6. Since the visions of de Brébeuf were frequent during this year, the reader is referred to chap. 4, note 2, and to chap. 7, note 3.

CHAPTER IX

1. The missioners did not assert, yet seemed to believe, that Chihwatenhwa was murdered by the Hurons out of hatred for the Faith. The present writer regards him as the first Huron martyr. A long prayer in Huron composed by Joseph may be found in *Relations*: 21–251.

2. In a letter addressed to Cardinal Richelieu, March 28, 1640, Jérôme Lalemant reinforced his argument petitioning help against the Iroquois by stating: "This will be readily granted, when one considers that in less than ten years they [Hurons] have become reduced from thirty thousand souls to ten thousand." (*Relations*: 17–223.) In 1645, he speaks of "ten to twenty thousand souls".

3. The Neutral country extended from Toronto and the Niagara River westward to Windsor and the St. Clair River, and northward about sixty miles above Lake Erie. The distance from Sainte Marie is given as "five or six days'" journey. Chaumonot, writing to R. P. Philippe Nappi, August 3, 1640, explained that "we made six days' route, continually in the woods. The paths in these

forests are very difficult, being very little worn, filled with brush-
wood and branches, cut up with swamps, brooks and rivers, without other bridges than a few trees broken off by age or the wind.
The winter is the best season for traveling, because the snow renders the paths more even." Since other indications are not more
exact than this, one attempts warily to determine the sites of the
Neutral villages visited by de Brébeuf. He gives the Neutral names
of five villages. On the Du Creux map, nine villages are spotted, some with saints' names, some with Neutral names. Remains
of a great number of villages have been found in the Neutral
area by Harvey, Hunter, Coyne, and others, in the earlier days,
and have been investigated by Jury and others in recent years.
The identification of these sites as those visited by de Brébeuf are
mostly conjectural. In terms of today, but not with certainty, the
writer traces the de Brébeuf tour as beginning about Brampton,
striking toward London, returning to Brampton, advancing west
past Guelph toward the St. Clair River, turning south toward
Chatham, starting east with a visit or two to the capital village in
the London area, reaching Brantford, and stopping at Teotong-
niaton, or St. Williams, halfway along the line back to Brampton.
De Brébeuf makes no mention of visiting Niagara Falls, but its
existence was known since Champlain's time and it was correctly
placed and titled as "Ongiara Catarractes" on the Du Creux map.

4. Père Lalemant undoubtedly instructed de Brébeuf to forward certain financial propositions. In his *Relation* of 1641–1642 and in his
letters to France, he was asking for money for specific purposes.
One of these was an appeal to support Christian Huron families
and thus procure the stabilization of marriage. Another project
was that of building and supporting a Christian village near Sainte
Marie. He was seeking benefactors, also, who would provide a
perpetual endowment for the support of two priests in each of the
seven mission centers.

CHAPTER X

1. The baptisms of the Algonquins and Hurons were carefully
recorded in the Baptismal Registers. The names of the natives
were given in printed letters. The Baptismal Register of Three

Rivers dates from February 18, 1635, when an Algonquin woman
was baptized. The Sillery Register was begun in 1639. The Quebec Register, up to 1640, was lost when the Jesuit residence
burned to the ground. The Register dating from 1640 still exists.
These original volumes are preserved in the Ecclesiastical Archives
of Quebec and Three Rivers. That the Huron missioners kept
accurate account of the numbers baptized is clear from the *Relations*. It is more than probable that they also recorded the names
in Baptismal Registers. Nevertheless, no reference is made in their
writings to such Registers.

2. This was revealed by Mère Marie. It would seem that Père de
Brébeuf ministered to the Ursulines regularly. Mère Marie wrote:
"We observed in this period (1639–1645) a small rule-book which
we had drawn up under the direction of R. Père Vimont, and
with the counsels of Pères de Bréboeuf [sic], Le Jeune and de
Quen, who showed great charity in assisting us in this and in all
other matters which concerned our establishment and our spiritual advancement." (*Marie de l'Incarnation*: II–405.) Likewise, he
acted as a spiritual guide to the Hospital nuns at Sillery. Under
date of 1641, the chronicler recorded: "Père Paul Ragueneau,
who had passed the winter at Sillery, ascended to the Huron Mission and Père Jean de Bréboeuf [sic] descended from it. Both
of these held our house in the greatest affection and have co-
operated in continuing the help given by Père Vimont ... and
who have aided and assisted us with all sort of charity." In the year
1649, the chronicler again wrote of "Père de Bréboeuf [sic] whom
we have known very well and who regarded us with the greatest
affection." She related that he asked all the Communities to take
a vow of offering Communion once a month for the conversion
of the Hurons. (*Les Annales de l'Hôtel-Dieu de Quebec*, 1939 ed.,
pp. 34 and 72.)

3. For the subsequent history of Père Jogues, the reader is referred to
Saint among Savages.

4. The French along the St. Lawrence and in the Huron country
not only bitterly condemned the Dutch of New Amsterdam for
selling muskets and munitions to the Iroquois but suspected that
the Dutch were leagued with the Iroquois for the purpose of
destroying the French colony. Jérôme Lalemant, in his letter to

Richelieu, March 28, 1640, referred to the English and Flemish "who line the seacoasts on our side" as hostile nations. Diplomatically, he suggested that they be curbed, as the Huguenots were in France. Le Jeune, when sent to France in 1641 "for the public and common good", was evidently instructed by de Montmagny to "drive away or punish" the Dutch who help the Iroquois. Père Charles Lalemant, the Procurator of the New France Mission, writing from Paris in 1642 to Père Etienne Charlet in Rome, presented Le Jeune's arguments for an attack on New Amsterdam, but "deemed this enterprise very hazardous" and offered six reasons why it should not be undertaken.

CHAPTER XI

1. Of de Brébeuf's arrival, Lalemant wrote: "A single band [of Hurons], which had passed through these dangers [from the Iroquois], reached here safely and brought to us Père Jean de Brébeuf, whose absence during three years has been very much felt by us, and Pères Leonard Garreau and Noël Chabanel, who had newly come to our assistance."

2. The site of the village of St. Louis is identified as being on concession VI, lot 11, Tay Township, above the Hogg River. A cairn dedicated to de Brébeuf and Lalemant was erected in 1923. The locations of the other villages in Tay Township are given by Jones as Ste. Anne, concession III, lot 9; St. Denis, concession V, lot 3; St. Jean, concession X, lot 6; St. Xavier, concession II, lot 93. The circuit of these villages would be about ten miles.

3. In his *Relation* of 1646, Père Lalemant attested: "In these beginnings of the conversion of these peoples, it must be admitted that, after God, all is due to the labors of our priests, of which Our Lord has deigned that I should be a witness. I have seen the fervor of their zeal, their indomitable courage, their patience in enduring all things, their activity in performing all duties, their humility in a life truly hidden in a world unknown; moreover, they are persons for the most part who are not lacking in qualities that would have made them commendable in France. When I observe that they embrace the cross with pleasure, sufferings with joy, and scorn with love; that each day they carry their souls in their hands, since

they are continually exposed to a thousand dangers of death, and that the majority of them are, perhaps, destined to die in the midst of the fires and flames of a cruel enemy who ravages these countries from day to day; when I see that these dangers animate their courage rather than depress it in the slightest, the thought comes to my mind frequently that God willed that so strong, so persevering, so vigorous a virtue should supply the absence of miracles which it seems that His Divine Providence does not choose to employ in these later ages to further the conversion of these pagan lands." (*Relations*: 28–99.)

4. In his *Breve Relatione*, published in Italy, 1653, Bressani included several letters written by himself describing his experiences with the Iroquois. (*Relations*: 39–55.)

5. Describing the death of Père Daniel to Pater Caraffa, Ragueneau stated: "He burned with a zeal for God more intense than any flames that consumed his body.... He was indeed a remarkable man and truly a worthy son of the Society, humble, obedient, united with God, of never-failing patience, with indomitable courage in adversity." (*Relations*: 33–265, 34–87.)

CHAPTER XII

1. The question of the location of St. Ignace II was forever answered by the discoveries made in 1946 by Wilfrid Jury. This most sacred site, now owned by the Martyrs' Shrine, is on concession IX, lot 6, on the east bank of the Sturgeon River. The first explorations were made by W.J. Wintemberg in 1937. Under the sponsorship of the Martyrs' Shrine and the University of Western Ontario, Mr. Jury completed accurate and comprehensive excavations in 1946. The report of his amazing finds, written in collaboration with W. Sherwood Fox, is still in manuscript but will soon be published. [William Sherwood Fox and Wilfrid Jury, *Saint Ignace: Canadian Altar of Martyrdom* (Toronto: McClelland & Stewart, 1949).] Preliminary reports have been carried in the *Martyrs' Shrine Message*, 1946–1947.

2. The basic contemporary source on the martyrdoms of Jean de Brébeuf and Gabriel Lalemant is that written by Père Ragueneau in his *Relation* of 1648–1649. (*Relations*: 34–123.) Though

accurate in fact, his narrative is confusing in that he described both tortures as if occurring simultaneously. The testimony of Christopher Regnaut confirmed the Ragueneau report. (*Relations*: 34–24.) Bressani, in his *Breve Relatione*, condensed the Ragueneau description, but added some further details. (*Relations*: 39–245.) Creuxius supplied additional but somewhat conflicting information drawn from a letter, now lost, written by Père Jacques Bonin, who supervised the transfer of the bodies to Sainte Marie. (*Historiae Canadensis*, etc., pp. 542–45.) Mère Marie de l'Incarnation stated that "Our Lord revealed to Père de Brébeuf the time of his Martyrdom three days before it occurred", and that he manifested an extraordinary gaiety which was noted by the other priests. Suspecting the cause of his joy, they had the surgeon draw from him some of his blood, so that they would have a relic should he be completely burned as happened in the case of Antoine Daniel. She also reported a vision in which he saw the tortures he must endure; but, strangely, in these tortures his hands were in no way fractured or mutilated.

Mère Marie boldly concluded: "Truly, it is for God and in hatred of the Faith that these apostolic men have suffered such horrible torments." In another letter she affirmed: "The Iroquois have martyred R. P. de Brébeuf." She also referred "to our holy Martyrs, the R. P. de Brébeuf, Daniel, Jogues and Lalemant". (*Marie de l'Incarnation*: 4–223, 228, 255, 268, etc.) The chronicler of the Hospital nuns shared the same belief: "They suffered with a courage and a constancy comparable to that which one finds in the most illustrious Martyrs. We have regarded them as such, especially the R. P. de Brébeuf." (*Les Annales*, p. 72.) More cautiously Père Ragueneau spoke: "If it were permitted to me, I would gladly call them by this glorious name [of Martyrs]." (*Relations*: 34–139.) All the French with Ragueneau in the Huron country, all the French with Jérôme Lalemant along the St. Lawrence, venerated them as martyrs and cherished their relics as those of saints. The cult was carried to France. The Archbishop of Rouen, who claimed ecclesiastical jurisdiction over New France, ordered that testimony be gathered with a view to instituting an Inquiry which might lead to canonization. Paul Ragueneau drew up a report, in 1651, that was duly presented to the Archbishop. A copy of this was returned to

Ragueneau, and was authenticated by him and Père Joseph Poncet
with oaths and signatures, dated 1652. The original document may
be seen in the Archives du Collège Sainte-Marie, Montreal. For
known and unknown reasons, the Cause of their official canonization was not prosecuted until after 1884, when the American and
Canadian bishops presented their petitions for the Introduction of
the Cause. After most exhaustive inquiries and processes, through
a period of more than twenty years, Pope Pius XI issued a Decree
of Beatification of the eight North American Martyrs on June 21,
1925, and on June 29, 1930, solemnly proclaimed the canonization
of Saint Jean de Brébeuf, Saint Isaac Jogues, Saint Antoine Daniel,
Saint Gabriel Lalemant, Saint Charles Garnier, Saint Noël Chabanel, Saint René Goupil and Saint Jean Lalande. Their feast is
observed on September 26.

3. The Island of Ahoendoe or St. Joseph is today identified as Christian Island. Remains of the stone walls of the Fort built in 1649 are
still visible. The site is on the northern sweep of a wide bay which
indents the southeastern coastline. The island is an Indian reser-
vation, and a Catholic mission is maintained on it. Ekaentoton, or
the Island of Sainte Marie, is the present-day Manitoulin Island.
Its southern shore is less than a hundred miles in a direct line
from Huronia. The missioners, in calculating it as sixty leagues,
counted a canoe journey along the indentations of the eastern
coast of Georgian Bay.

   The writer may be permitted to express a personal opinion.
Père Paul Ragueneau seems to have been guilty of a series of
blundering decisions both in settling on Christian Island and in
returning to Quebec. The second Sainte Marie could have been
built on Manitoulin Island, far from the reach of the Iroquois.
That mission could have been the center for the Hurons and
Algonquins, and from it, missioners could have penetrated to
Lake Superior and the west.

4. The obituary narratives of the deaths and virtues of Charles Garnier
and Noël Chabanel were incorporated in Ragueneau's *Relation* of
1649–1650. (*Relations*: 35–107, 147.) Père Garnier, in the last letter he wrote to his brother, Père Henri, under date of August 12,
1649, from St. Joseph's Island, expressed his desire to be martyred:
"If my conscience did not convict me of my infidelity to my good

Master, I would be able to hope for some favor like that which He has bestowed on our Blessed Martyrs, with whom I have had the good fortune to talk often, being in the same circumstances and dangers that they experienced; but His justice causes me to fear that I shall remain always unworthy of this crown [of martyrdom]. Nevertheless, I hope that His goodness will grant me the grace some day to love Him with all my heart; and that will be enough for me; when He shall have granted this, it makes little difference what sort of death I shall die." (*Quebec Archives, 1929–1930,* p. 41.) Mère Marie attested that "he was in continual colloquy and familiar conversation with God." Père Chabanel, unable to learn the Huron language though otherwise endowed with a brilliant mind, found life with the savages unbearable. "The sight of them, their talk and all that concerned them, he found burdensome," Ragueneau stated. "Residence in the Mission did such violence to his entire nature that he encountered therein extraordinary hardships, without any consolation." Nevertheless, in 1647, he bound himself to endure all: "I, Noël Chabanel, being in the presence of the Most Holy Sacrament of your Body and your Precious Blood, which is the tabernacle of God among men, make a vow of perpetual stability in this Mission of the Hurons, understanding all things as the Superiors of the Society expound them, and as they choose to dispose of me." In a letter written to his brother, Père Pierre, just before he left for the Petun Mission, he lamented: "Your Reverence has been very near to possessing a brother a Martyr. Alas, in the mind of God, a virtue of another stamp than mine is needed to merit the honor of martyrdom. Père Gabriel Lalemant, one of the three whom our *Relation* mentions as having suffered for Jesus Christ, had taken my place in the village of St. Louis a month before his death." (*Relations:* 35–155, 161.)

5. The subsequent history of the relics of de Brébeuf, Lalemant and Garnier is interesting but lengthy. The skulls and larger bones of de Brébeuf and Lalemant and, at least, a few larger bones of Garnier were brought to Quebec in 1650. Fragments of the bones were sent to France, and the skull of Lalemant was given to his sister, a Carmelite of Sens. The skull of de Brébeuf and the other bones were preserved in Quebec. The nephews of de Brébeuf, before 1700, sent a silver bust mounted on ebony as a reliquary

for the skull. After the suppression of the Society of Jesus, the last living Jesuit, Père Cazot, before his death in 1800, confided these precious remains to the Hospital nuns of the Hôtel-Dieu of Quebec. There they remained until 1925. In that year of the beatification, the relics were divided between the Society of Jesus and the nuns. The skull of Saint Jean de Brébeuf was dissected from front to back by Dr. Charles Vezina. The right half remained in the possession of the nuns and the left half was given to the Jesuits. The bones of Saint Jean and Saint Gabriel, having been subjected to lye, are white and dusty-looking. Those of Saint Charles are dark and hard. The skull of Saint Gabriel together with the other relics were destroyed, apparently, during the French Revolution. Some of these, however, were rescued by a young man who later became Père Donche, and are, at present, in Brussels.

6. The migration of the Hurons to the St. Lawrence is told by Ragueneau in his *Relation* of 1650. (*Relation*: 35–197.) The flotilla of canoes advanced in fear and stealth up Lake Huron, through to Lake Nipissing and down the Ottawa. The Iroquois had already devastated the route, and signs of massacres were frequent. All the Algonquins had deserted the region which had become a solitude. Halfway down to the St. Lawrence, Ragueneau and his refugees met Bressani and a party of forty Frenchmen and twenty Hurons ascending to Huronia. The latter joined the caravan which finally reached Quebec on July 28, having traversed some nine hundred miles in fifty days. The Hospital nuns, the Ursulines and some families supported about a hundred of the Hurons, but Ragueneau and the Jesuits had to feed and care for about two hundred who camped near Quebec. Other bands of Hurons continued to reach Quebec during the autumn and winter. In March, 1651, the Jesuits settled the Hurons on a property they held on the Isle of Orleans. A new village arose, surrounded by a strong stockade, and Sainte Marie III seemed firmly established. Meanwhile, the Iroquois had extended their conquests against the Petuns in 1649–1650, and had declared bloody war on the Neutrals in 1651, destroying or exiling these peoples. As a result, many more Hurons fled from their asylum in these countries and sought refuge on the Isle of Orleans. But the Iroquois pursued the Huron remnants even to the environs of Quebec, to such an extent that the village

of Sainte Marie on the Isle of Orleans was abandoned in 1667, those of the Bear and Rock nations joining with the Mohawks and Onondagas, those of the Cord nation, to the number of about five hundred, remaining at Quebec. These finally erected their village at what is now known as l'Ancienne Lorette, and in the beginning of the eighteenth century moved to la Jeune Lorette on the River St. Charles. Though they preserve their identity, the Hurons have ceased to exist as a race, those about Quebec having intermarried with the French and those who migrated west having been absorbed by other Indian peoples. As the nation, so the language is lost forever, the last Huron speaker having died some seventy-five years ago. But through all their adversities, they who went to live with the Iroquois as well as they who dwelt near the French, believed and practiced the Catholic Faith that was announced to them by Saint Jean de Brébeuf.

BIBLIOGRAPHY

I. The facts of this biography have been gathered from the manuscripts or books of those who wrote in the seventeenth century. Greatest dependence has been placed upon the following:

Alegambe, Philippe, S.J. *Mortes Illustres*, etc. Brussels, 1655.

Autobiographie du P. Pierre Chaumont de la Compagnie de Jésus et son Complement. Edited by Felix Martin, S.J. Paris: Oudin, 1885.

Bressani, F.J., S.J. *Relation Abrégée de Quelques Missions des Pères de la Compagnie de Jésus.*Traduit [Translated] and edited par [by] Felix Martin, S.J. Montreal: Lovell, 1852.

Carayon, Auguste, S.J. *Première Mission des Jésuites au Canada, Lettres et Documents Inédits.* Paris: L'Ecureux, 1864.

Creuxius, Franciscus, S.J. *Historiae Canadensis Libri Decem.* Paris: Cramoisy, 1664.

The Jesuit Relations and Allied Documents. Edited by Reuben Gold Thwaites. 71 vols. Cleveland: The Burrows Company, 1896–1901.

Le Clercq, Christian, Récollet. *First Establishment of the Faith in New France.* Translated with notes by John Gilmary Shea. New York: Shea, 1881.

Les Annales de l'Hôtel-Dieu de Québec, 1636–1716. Composées par [composed by] les RR. Meres Jeanne-Françoise Juchereau et Marie Andrée Duplessis. Éditées par [Edited by] Dom Albert Jamet. Quebec: l'Hôtel-Dieu, 1939.

Lescarbot, Marc. *The History of New France.* Translated by W.L. Grant. Toronto: The Champlain Society.

Marie de l'Incarnation: Écrits Spirituels et Historiques: publiés par [published by] Dom Claude Martin; réédités par [republished by] Dom Albert Jamet. 4 vols. Quebec: Action Sociale, 1929–1939.

Ragueneau, Paul, S.J. *Mémoires Touchant la Mort et les Vertues des Pères Isaac Jogues, Jean de Brébeuf*, etc. 1652. Manuscript in Archives du Collége Sainte-Marie, Montreal. Published in *Rapport de l'Archiviste de la Province de Québec, 1924–1925.* Corrected copy in mimeographed book by Arthur Melançon, S.J., 1936.

Richadeau, L'Abbé. *Lettres de la Révérende Mère Marie de l'Incarnation.* 2 vols. Tournai: Casterman, 1876.

Sagard-Théodat, Gabriel, Récollet. *Histoire du Canada et Voyages.* 4 vols. Paris: Sonnius, 1636.

————. *Le Grand Voyage du Pays des Hurons.* Paris: Tross, 1865.

Sagard's Long Journey to the Country of the Hurons. Edited by George M. Wrong. Toronto: The Champlain Society, 1939.

Tanner, Mathias, S.J. *Vita et mors eorum,* etc. Prague, 1675.

Travels and Sufferings of Father John de Brébeuf among the Hurons of Canada as Described by Himself. Translated from the French and Latin by Theodore Besterman. London: Golden Cockerel Press, 1938.

Works of Samuel de Champlain. 7 vols. Edited by H. P. Biggar; translated by H. H. Langton and W. F. Ganong. Toronto: The Champlain Society, 1922–1936.

II. Supplementary material and interpretations have been collected from later writers. Among those whose works were found most helpful are the following:

Casgrain, Abbé H. R. *Histoire de l'Hôtel-Dieu de Quebec.* Quebec: Brousseau, 1878.

Charlevoix, F. X. de, S.J. *History and General Description of New France.* Translated by John Gilmary Shea. 6 vols. New York: Shea, 1866.

Dionne, Narcisse E. *Samuel Champlain: Histoire de sa Vie et de ses Voyages.* 2 vols. Quebec: Cote, 1891.

Faillon, Abbé. *Histoire de la Colonie Française en Canada.* 3 vols. Montreal, 1865.

Ferland, J. B. A. *Cours d'Histoire du Canada.* Quebec: Cote, 1861.

Fouqueray, Henri, S.J. *Histoire de la Compagnie de Jésus en France.* 5 vols. Paris: Bureaux des Etudes, 1922–1939.

Jenness, Diamond. *The Indians of Canada.* Toronto: National Museum of Canada, 1934.

Jones, Arthur E., S.J. *Old Huronia.* Toronto: Bureau of Archives, 1909.

Martin, Felix, S.J. *Hurons et Iroquois: le P. Jean de Brébeuf.* Paris: Tequi, 1898.

Melançon, Arthur, S.J. *Liste des Missionaires Jésuites.* Montreal: Collège Sainte-Marie, 1929.

Parkman, Francis. *The Jesuits in North America in the Seventeenth Century.* Boston: Little, Brown & Co., 1867.

————. *Pioneers of France in the New World.* Boston: Little, Brown & Co., 1865.

Pouliot, Léon, S.J. *Étude sur les Relations des Jésuites de la Nouvelle-France.* Montreal: 1940.

Rochemonteix, Camille de, S.J. *Les Jésuites et la Nouvelle-France au XVII siecle d'après beaucoup de documents inédits.* Paris: Letouzey, 1895.

Roy, Pierre-Georges. *La Ville de Quebec sous le Regime Français.* 2 vols. Quebec: Redempti Paradis, 1930.

Sulte, Benjamin. *Histoire des Canadiens-Français.* Montreal: Wilson, 1882.

III. The following have also been helpful:

Archaeological Reports. Province of Ontario, Toronto.
Rapport de l'Archiviste de la Province de Quebec. Quebec: Proulx.

INDEX